J 239   £3500

KLOS

process on Return

GW00585201

)

This book is due for return on or before the last date shown below.

24/8/89

Don Gresswell Ltd., London, N.21 Cat. No. 1207   DG 02242/71

HEAD OF THE CIVIL SERVICE

HEAD OF THE CIVIL SERVICE

A STUDY OF SIR WARREN FISHER

EUNAN O'HALPIN

ROUTLEDGE
London and New York

First published 1989
by Routledge
11 New Fetter Lane, London EC4 4EE
29 West 35th Street, New York, NY 10001

© 1989 Eunan O'Halpin

Page-set and laser printed directly from the publisher's w-p disks
by NWL Editorial Services, Langport, Somerset.

Printed and bound in Great Britain by
Biddles Ltd, Guildford and King's Lynn

All rights reserved. No part of this book may be reprinted or
reproduced or utilized in any form or by any electronic, mechani-
cal, or other means, now known or hereafter invented, including
photocopying and recording, or in any information storage or
retrieval system, without permission in writing from the publishers.

British Library Cataloging in Publication Data

O'Halpin, Eunan
Head of the Civil Service: a study of Sir Warren Fisher.
1. Great Britain. Civil Service. Fisher, Sir Warren, 1879–1948
I. Title
354.41006′092′4

ISBN 0-415-03114-1

Library of Congress Cataloging in Publication Data

O'Halpin, Eunan.
    Head of the Civil Service: a study of Sir Warren Fisher/
    Eunan O'Halpin.
    Bibliography: p.
    Includes index.
    ISBN 0-415-03114-1
    1. Civil service—Great Britain—Reform   — History.
2. Civil service—Great Britain—History.   3. Fisher, Warren, Sir,
1879–   1948.   4. Government executives—Great Britain—Biography.
I. Title.
JN428.042 1989
354.41006′092′4—do 19
[B]

FOR ROSEMARY

Contents

Plates

Preface

Despite his central position in the British administrative system between the wars, Sir Warren Fisher has generally received little attention from historians. However, in 1965 Professor D.C. Watt published an important essay which drew attention to Fisher's influence on the course of British rearmament.[1] A decade later, Professor Max Beloff discussed Fisher in somewhat more general terms in an essay on 'the Whitehall factor.'[2] In 1979 Dr George Peden dealt authoritatively with the role played by the Treasury and by Fisher in rearmament in his book on *British Rearmament and the Treasury*.[3] This was significant not only for its subject but also because it was the first detailed examination of any aspect of Fisher's career.

The broader question of how he came to play such a part in matters regarded as outside traditional Treasury preserves has not been thoroughly explored. Little has been published on his career except in relation to defence and foreign policy.[4] It might be thought that the changes in the civil service which took place after the First World War, and which set the pattern of central government organization in Britain to the present day, would have received attention, at least from specialists, but these developments have remained largely unexamined.[5] A lengthy study of the Lloyd George Coalition published in 1979, for example, made only two references to Fisher and the Treasury — one of them incorrect — and none at all to the phenomenon of civil service reorganization which was encouraged and supported by the Coalition leadership.[6] Yet this was certainly one of the most important and enduring products of the thinking about post-war reconstruction on which the same historian has written so extensively.[7] Nor has anyone adequately explained the title of 'Head of the Civil Service' under which Fisher operated although it has frequently been criticized, especially by retired diplomats and their champions: Sir Lewis Namier concluded his summing up of the BBC's 'Munich Survey' in 1948 with an indirect reference to Fisher's efforts to bring the Foreign Office into the domestic civil service fold.[8]

This book is an attempt to remedy matters by giving an account of Fisher's career from first to last. It is a study of the man, not of the office which he held. For a combination of political, institutional, and personal reasons Fisher was a powerful official in a very wide range of areas, from the Treasury's traditional bailiwick of public finance to defence policy, and even to Anglo-Irish relations. To the extent that evidence of them survives, the various strands of his work are explored.

While this book is not directly concerned with British government after 1939, Fisher's career raises issues about Whitehall which are still topical. This is because he had a profound influence on the development of the higher civil service in the first half of the century. He was a generalist and proud of it. This approach to administration, exemplifying a belief that general administrative competence and all-round judgement rather than particular specialist expertise are the necessary qualities for the most senior ranks in Whitehall, came under fire in the 1960s. The high point was the tendentious first chapter of the 1968 Fulton report on the civil service.[9] There, most changes in the civil service that had taken place since the Northcote Trevelyan report of 1854, including much of Fisher's work, were ignored and the rest were condemned. The Fulton report was hailed at the time as presaging an administrative revolution which would sweep away the mid-Victorian cobwebs enveloping Whitehall. In practice Whitehall has continued to develop, as it did under Fisher, by adaptation; it is the Fulton report which gathers dust. Nevertheless, the Fulton critique of generalist administration has proved surprisingly resilient. Indeed, a recent study of Sir Edward Bridges commented that the anti-generalists have 'been eloquent and persuasive', and that the 'quantity and quality of replies and exposition in favour of generalist administration has been overwhelmed by the critics.'[10] The explanation for this is, surely, a simple one. Why should civil servants waste energy attacking a set of simplistic propositions that can safely be ignored?

This book is based on official records, on private collections of papers, and on interviews and correspondence with people who knew of Fisher and his work. He left no diaries and few papers. He took an interest in particular questions more or less at random. Many relevant official records, including some of those on civil service appointments, are still closed to research. Above all, much of his business was done by word of mouth.

Consequently it has often not been easy to judge what part he played in individual events or in particular policy areas. Nevertheless, a considerable amount of new material has been found, including an unfinished book and other papers held by his granddaughter, which throws light on his activities and on his ideas, even in the well-trodden field of defence policy. Interviews with his surviving son have also provided much background information which had not previously been available: this is important, as the one thing upon which all who knew him are agreed, friend and foe alike, is that he was a most unusual man.

Notes

1. Watt, *Personalities and Policies*, pp. 100–16. Hamilton, 'Sir Warren Fisher', published in 1951, deals concisely and admirably with many aspects of Fisher's career. It is essentially a lengthy obituary.
2. Beloff, 'The Whitehall factor', pp. 209–31.
3. Peden, *British Rearmament*.
4. In his *Statesmen in Disguise*, pp. 51–5, Dr G.K. Fry outlined some of the controversies surrounding Fisher's career.
5. Chapman and Greenaway, *Dynamics of Administrative Reform*, pp. 72–114, cover important ground. So too do the essays on the growth of government during the First World War in Burk (ed.) *War and the State*.
6. Morgan, *Consensus and Disunity*, pp. 52, 94.
7. See the biography of Dr Christopher Addison by Morgan and Morgan, *Portrait of a Progressive*.
8. Namier, 'Munich survey', p. 836.
9. *The Civil Service, Vol I, Report of the Committee 1966–1968* [the Fulton report].
10. Chapman, *Ethics in the British Civil Service*, pp. 34, 36.

Acknowledgements

This book is based principally on collections of documents and records in archives, libraries, and in private hands in Britain. These are fully listed in the bibliography, which contains only works and collections cited in the end notes. Portions of Chapter 3 were originally published in *The Historical Journal* in 1981, and I am grateful to the editors for permission to include an amended version here.

In my research for the book and for the earlier Ph.D. dissertation upon which it is largely based I received a great deal of help. Dr Henry Pelling was an accessible and helpful supervisor. Sir John Winnifrith, Sir Edward Playfair, Sir Thomas and Lady Padmore, and Sir James Dunnett both granted me interviews and gave me their comments on earlier drafts. Lord Sherfield, the late Lord Trend, the late Sir George Dunnett, the late Lord Armstrong of Sanderstead, the late Sir Robert Fraser, the late Sir Folliott Sandford, Mr K.B. Paice, Mr C.J. Carey, and Mr Raymond Nottage all gave me their time to talk about Fisher and Whitehall before the war. Sir Warren Fisher's son Mr Robin Warren Fisher has gone to considerable trouble to furnish details of his father's career and to track down photographs for inclusion in the book. Fisher's granddaughter Mrs Annette Pollock allowed me to consult her grandfather's papers, including the typescript of parts of a book that he was working on, at extremely short notice and at an inconvenient time. Mr Ralph Selby, Mr R.H. Bullock, and Miss Jane O'Malley told me of their father's views on Fisher, and Mr Selby gave me access to his fathers' papers.

I also owe thanks to the following people who provided information and opinions in response to queries from me. I list them in order of the contents of my correspondence file: Mr H. Montgomery Hyde, the late Lord Geoffrey-Lloyd, Lord Gladwyn, the late Lord Noel-Baker, Mr A.J. Sylvester, Mr Roger Custance of Winchester College, the late Sir Denis Proctor, the late Captain Stephen Roskill, Mr F.R. Wylie late of the Dragon School, the late Sir Anthony Rumbold, Mr A.D. Beresford of the Royal College of Music, Sir Harold Kent, Sir Alexander Johnston, the late Sir John Martin, Sir Bruce Fraser, the late Professor E.H. Carr, the late Lord Garner, Mr

Peregrine Worsthorne, Lord Inchyra, Lord Caccia, the late Lady Norman, Mr Harold Epstein of the Winston Churchill Foundation of the United States, Lord Allen of Abbeydale, Sir Richard Powell, Sir Clifford Jarrett, the late Sir John Laing, Sir John Peck, Professor David Marquand, Sir Norman Costar, Sir Charles Cunningham, Sir David Pitblado, the late Mr Peter Humphreys-Davis, the late Sir Martin Flett, Sir Neil Pritchard, Lady Lorna Howard, Sir Colin Crowe, Lord Houghton, Professor Peter Self, Sir William Murrie, Mr Frank Krinks of the Civil Service Sports Council, Professor M.R.D. Foot, and Mr Robert Brown of British Petroleum.

I am grateful to the following persons and institutions for permission to cite and to reproduce extracts from collections of papers: the Bodleian Library (the Addison, Dawson, H.A.L. Fisher, Milner, Monckton, Sankey and Zimmern papers), the Master, Fellows and Scholars of Churchill College in the University of Cambridge (the Hankey, Swinton, Hore-Belisha, Cadogan, Knatchbull-Hugessen, Halifax, and Phipps papers), the Syndics of Cambridge University Library (the Baldwin, Hardinge, and Templewood papers), the India Office Library and Records and Lord Scarsdale (the Curzon papers), the India Office Library and Records (the Blackett papers), the Director and Board of the National Library of Ireland (the O'Malley papers), the Master and Fellows of Trinity College Cambridge (the Pethick-Lawrence papers), the late Baroness Vansittart (the Vansittart papers), Mr Ralph Selby CMG (the Selby papers), the late Sir Anthony Rumbold (the Rumbold papers), the Trustees of the Liddell Hart Centre for Military Archives (the Liddell Hart, Milne and Pownall papers), the Royal Institute of International Affairs (RIIA archives), Lady White (the Thomas Jones papers), Vice Admiral Sir Ian Hogg (the Gwynne papers), the Rt Hon Julian Amery MP (the Amery diaries), Lady Forres (the Woolton papers), the BBC (BBC archives), the House of Lords Record Office (the Samuel papers), the British Library (the Hamilton papers), the trustees of the Inverchapel papers, Viscount Trenchard (the Trenchard papers), *The Times* (the Dawson and Barrington-Ward papers), the National Library of Scotland (the Haldane and Elibank papers), the Wiltshire Record Office (the Long papers), the University of Birmingham (the Chamberlain papers), the British Library of Political and Economic Science (the Braithwaite, Greaves, Collier and Passfield papers), Mr A.J.P. Taylor and the Beaverbrook Trust (the Bonar Law and Lloyd George papers), Mr Robin Warren Fisher and Mrs Annette Pollock (the Warren Fisher papers and photographs), and the Controller of Her Majesty's Stationery Office (official records and papers). I apologize if I have inadvertently infringed anyone's copyright.

Professor J.M. Lee, Dr T.J. Barrington, the late Professor Desmond Williams, Professor Patrick Lynch, and my friends Michael O'Kelly and Conor Barrington read and commented on earlier drafts. Professor Lee also suggested additional lines of enquiry, and he put me in touch with Mr Robin Warren Fisher. Professor Ronan Fanning introduced me to Fisher by showing me the 1920 report on Dublin Castle. Dr Christopher Andrew encouraged me to do research on Fisher's career. Dr Stephen Stacey, Richard Roberts, Dr George Peden, and Dr Keith Jeffery helped with information on where to find material. The late Colonel Dan Bryan spotted a letter written by Fisher on sale in Co. Kilkenny, and he gave it to me. Fergal Tobin gave me advice on publication. I am grateful to them all for their assistance.

The research for this book was financed largely by a Travelling Studentship from the National University of Ireland, and by a Robert Gardiner Memorial Scholarship at Cambridge. Churchill College Cambridge helped me with travel expenses while I was a research student from 1979 to 1981, and since 1982 NIHE Dublin has provided money for additional research. Finally, the Trustees of the T.P. MacDonnell Fund for Historical Scholarship at University College Dublin have given a generous subsidy towards the costs of publication.

This book has come into existence through the good offices of Sir Douglas Wass, whom Sir Edward Playfair enlisted in the hunt for a publisher. I am indebted to them both for their efforts, and to Elizabeth Fidlon and to Alan Jarvis for editorial advice, and to my indexer, Helen Litton.

I found the time to prepare the book for publication because I got a lot of assistance at work. Ms Mary Mason and Ms Anne-Marie Winnick retyped the original text. David O'Callaghan and David Kearney prepared the illustrations from rather faded originals. Dr Danny O'Hare, the president of N.I.H.E. Dublin, suggested I drop most of my duties to concentrate on the book. My colleagues in the Dublin Business School did most of my jobs for me. Tony Foley and Kathy Monks took the heaviest burdens. My biggest debt, however, is to my newly-enlarged family, to whom I have for months been little more than a grumpy stranger.

May 1988

I regret to record that after this book went to press, Robin Warren Fisher died suddenly on 23 October 1988. He went to great trouble to provide information on his father's background and career despite the unhappy memories which this revived for him. I am very sorry that he did not live to see this study appear.

Eunan O'Halpin, January 1989

1

A poor start overcome: 1879–1919

I

Sir Warren Fisher was offered the post of Permanent Secretary to the Treasury and Head of the Civil Service in August 1919, with effect from the following October. He was not yet 40 years of age, and his promotion was the culmination of a career already quite exceptional. He remained at the Treasury for twenty years: he took over before the treaties ending the First World War were signed, and technically he retired only after the Second World War had begun. It was a long innings, and one which produced a good deal of controversy. To an extent this was the inevitable consequence of interdepartmental wrangling, but his volatile personality undoubtedly gave an edge to many disputes.

Warren Fisher was born in Croydon on 22 September 1879, the only son of Henry Warren and Caroline Fisher. On his father's side Fisher came from a long line of Cumberland gentry which over the generations had produced a good number of officers, merchants, and clergymen. Henry Warren Fisher was a 'gentleman' of 'independent income', who spent a leisured existence in wandering where he chose.[1] His wife Caroline was the widow of a colonel of the Second Royal Dragoon Guards, by whom she had one daughter. After her marriage to Henry Warren Fisher she had another daughter, Frances, and a son, Norman Fenwick Warren Fisher. During Fisher's childhood the family lived in Croydon and in Oxford. In later years they moved to London.

Fisher told his own children and his friends that his family life had been unhappy. Although he was very close to his mother, he spoke of his father with loathing.[2] Henry Warren Fisher was a highly Victorian figure, conventional, moralistic and stern — he is said to have dismissed a housemaid for wearing a rose in her hat on her day off. He also beat both his daughter and his son, on one occasion so severely that the family nanny threatened to complain to the authorities.[3]

Fisher certainly fell out with his father, although what little direct evidence there is gives the impression of a less dramatic family life than he afterwards described. At both preparatory and public school he was remembered as a contented and outgoing pupil. In letters which he wrote to his Winchester and Oxford friend A.E. Zimmern, there are passing allusions to his family which do not suggest great strife. In 1902, while staying in London to attend a crammer's in preparation for the civil service examinations, he wrote, 'I am sure I could work much better at Oxford [where his family lived] if I had to choose between spending a year here or at home.' London 'is a most unpleasant place of residence though the governor has got me some very nice digs, very clean, & cooking good.' Later that summer 'my people and I went to Dover ... I had a very pleasant time.' He could not go to Zimmern's 'happy & hospitable home' as his parents had 'asked an uncle whom I think I ought to wait & see, as he can very rarely come & has been asked specially for my sister & me.'[4]

Such scraps suggest that family life was not always so difficult as Fisher later maintained. For whatever reason, however, he became a man of great emotional intensity. He always had difficulty in keeping personal relationships on an even keel, and his life was marred by violent rifts with those close to him. Once a split occurred, he would have nothing further to do with the person involved. Judged by these standards, his differences with his father appear rather mild: in his last years Henry Warren Fisher was an occasional if somewhat unwelcome caller to his son's home, and his photograph was dutifully placed upon the mantelpiece before each visit. Warren Fisher inherited his gold watch engraved with the Fisher arms, though he promptly gave it away to the fiancé of a family servant.[5]

Fisher became in most respects the antithesis of his father: he was a Liberal not a Conservative, a hard worker rather than a drone, and a believer in the innate superiority of women to men. He also became a determinedly unconventional man, who on occasion took a servant rather than his wife to social events, who eschewed formality, and who as Head of the Civil Service insisted that the private lives of officials were their own concern. Less happily, his difficult upbringing — as recounted to friends and to his sons — left him emotionally scarred, and it may explain the lack of balance apparent throughout his life in his personal relationships.

In 1890 Fisher became a day boy at the Dragon School in Oxford, where his family then lived. Although he was probably sent there because it had strong links with Winchester, the school was itself a celebrated institution: its headmaster, 'The Skipper', was an unconventional and progressive man who forsook traditional methods of teaching and of discipline, and who made a lasting impression on his pupils. According to Fisher, he 'taught us to be independent and human, and allowed us each to develop on his own individual lines' and 'gave us the idea of being natural.' The 'great thing is that this school does not turn out a mass production, but individual entities; the public school turns out the mass production.... This place spells side, team, everything but self ...'. In this congenial setting Fisher did well without ever excelling: he won prizes for classics, mathematics, French and drawing, was 'perhaps too boisterous, but played with plenty of action and confidence' as Orlando in *As You Like It*, was a forward in the school rugby team and in the cricket XI of 1892 he 'sometimes hit hard and made a score'.[6] He was a 'hardworking' rather than a brilliant pupil, who was remembered less for academic achievement than for his distinctive appearance and manner: 'as a young boy' he 'was often to be seen, elegantly slender in figure and attractive in features, walking ... with his father and grown-up step-sister, with a dog in attendance.'[7]

In 1892 Fisher tried to become a naval cadet, but was rejected on medical grounds because he had a bad back.[8] Instead he went to Winchester, being placed tenth on the 1892 College Electoral Roll and winning a scholarship. The scholarship examination coincided with a parliamentary election in Oxford. Fisher's obituary in the Dragon School magazine records that 'the Skipper, then an ardent politician, had a slight contretemps' with Henry Warren Fisher, 'who refused to "pair" with him in voting during his absence at Winchester in charge of the Dragon candidates'. The headmaster had to return to Oxford to cast his vote for the Liberal candidate, an episode

which suggests that Henry Warren Fisher was indeed a somewhat difficult man.[9]

Winchester was the most academic and intellectual of the
major public schools, and Fisher as a scholarship holder was a
member of College, itself an elite within the school. While he
recalled that 'it is rather a job when you first get to these places.
You ... suddenly find yourself a nobody — a healthy experience,
but an unpleasant one', his time there seems to have been
happy enough.[10] A contemporary has left an account of the
school in the 1890s: the food 'was execrable, badly cooked and
inconceivably monotonous' and the boys 'cold, dirty, and a little
savage'. But 'we had a tremendous zest for life and enjoyed it;
above all we were not soft and we were not prigs'. Although
only the classics and history were taught with any seriousness,
exceptionally for a public school there was no stigma attached
to hard work provided that boys participated fully in the life of
the college.[11] This Fisher did. Academically he was good but
not outstanding, and the same was true of his other activities:
he ran and rowed for his house, and achieved modest distinction as a member for three years of 'College Fifteen', although
on one occasion it was reported that 'Fisher was outclassed and
was not fast enough' for the peculiar brand of football played
in the school.[12] As 'Prefect of Chapel' in his final year he stood
almost at the top of the boys' hierarchy, but, judging by the
school magazine, he does not seem to have made as distinct an
impression upon college life as contemporaries such as
Raymond Asquith and A.E. Zimmern. It was only a few months
before he left that he made an 'effective maiden speech' to the
school debating society in support of the motion that 'the
condition and management of Public Houses' were 'a grave
scandal'. He 'made a good point out of the Portsmouth slums,
and maintained that gambling resulted from tied houses. He
quoted instances of corruption of magistrates, and stated that
the system of inspection was inadequate' — an observation
which indicated at least a rudimentary interest in administration. Though he was 'fluent and sensible, and spoke with some
conviction', he 'might have spoken louder'.[13]

Fisher went up to Oxford in 1898 as a Scholar of Hertford.
There he took 'a first in Mods., and, somewhat surprisingly, a
second in Greats', although he himself expected nothing more:
he told Zimmern that, after 'quite a short viva [voce] ... I trust
[I will get] a safe Second.'[14] He acquired a reputation as a

bookworm because he wanted to sit as many subjects as possible in the combined examination for the home and the Indian civil service.[15] In 1902 he had 'a futile shot at the I[ndian] C[ivil] S[ervice]', but no details of his performance have been found.[16] Fisher's interest in a career as a government official is explained partly by his education, and partly by his own beliefs. Winchester had a strong tradition of producing men for public service, though not for politics. In addition Fisher was a Liberal and he believed that the state had a positive duty to promote the common good. Finally, he was intensely patriotic and, having been found unfit for the navy, an official career was an alternative way of serving his country.

Apart from his ambition to become a public servant, very little is known about his time at Oxford. However, his correspondence with Zimmern casts some light on his student years. It covers holidays, family visits, and personal news: 'I have shaved off my budding moustache, to make it grow. Consequently my beauty is spoiled (this between ourselves).'[17] In it is evidence of traits which later distinguished him: his strong sense of personal honour, his sense of humour, and his mawkish way with his friends. He addressed Zimmern as 'My dear Chim[panzee]', signed himself 'with love' and 'your affect[ionate] friend the Badger', and wrote of other acquaintances such as 'Frowsie Brown' and 'the Mite (my holiday name for Ley)'.[18] Ominously, his letters to Zimmern also deal at some length with obscure disputes between him and friends at Hertford. A typical extract runs:

> Thanks very much for your letter & also Andy's enclosed ... Ley has also written: he was good enough to waste two or three pages in telling me what I was aiming at, when I said he was at present incapable of command ... For Ley to charge me with such a mean intention is singularly graceless [?]; my relations towards him have fully justified such an estimate. However you will be, I think, perfectly right in upholding his opinion (this is not sarcasm): only I must not be told of it, as my temper cannot stand that sort of thing. I am going to Thomson next Friday, & am thankful to say: I will be particularly kind & carry out Ley's advice, which ... may seem to you strong-minded: to me (I am in a very irritable mood) it seems uncalled for jingoism. I have had the pleasure of mildly expostulating: I

am sorry to hurt your feelings, but I am not going to have
[?] anything of the sort ... thrown at my head. I will write
again shortly (if indeed you will care to hear from me after
speaking in this way about Ley), but I really feel so annoyed by his letter that I had better stop for the present.[19]

Whatever the matters at issue in this and other rows with his
undergraduate friends, the letters testify to one of Fisher's
enduring characteristics, his propensity to fall out with those
closest to him.

In July 1902 Fisher went up to London to study for civil
service examinations at a crammers. He was not impressed:

> The cramming is simply loathsome — I would not go on
> with it for a year even to save my life. And besides, though
> it is good for putting on a few marks[?] in the 5 weeks I
> am sure I could work much better at Oxford if I had to
> choose between spending a year here or at home. The
> general tone of the place, the type of man it turns out &
> life in London are most depressing: the lecturers ... are the
> most outrageous bounders, vulgar & coarse as you can
> imagine. And the way in which they treat English history
> is simply disgusting. You know I'm not a literary type but
> I do consider that English & modern history should be
> treated with a spirit worthy of it.
>
> Most of the lectures I don't go to. It makes one's hair
> stand on end to think of what will happen if ever these
> precious 'crammed' men have to face an Indian Mutiny.[20]

After some weeks he returned to Oxford. In 1903 he sat the
Civil Service Commission examinations again. He was placed
sixteenth in the general competition for posts in the home civil
service, the Indian civil service and the colonial service, with a
total of 2,878 marks out of a possible 6,600 in the papers he
took. His highest mark, 319 out of 400, was in Logic and
Mental Philosophy. Perhaps appropriately for a future head of
the Treasury, his lowest, 50 out of 500, was in Political Economy
and Economic History. He was fifteenth in the list of those
opting for the home civil service. Amongst those ahead of him
were three men who later served under him at the Treasury,
E.W. Hoyer Millar, G.C. Upcott and the economist R.G. Hawtrey. Others also ahead of him included Arthur Dixon, Edward

Harding and Findlater Stewart, all of whom were to rise to high rank in Whitehall.[21] Fisher's performance was sufficient to secure him a position in a Whitehall department. In October 1903 he became a clerk in the Upper Division of the Secretaries' Office of the Board of Inland Revenue. In the words of his obituary in *The Wykehamist*, 'this was not so unlucky a chance as it seemed.'[22]

II

Before considering his civil service career, it is important to form some picture of what Fisher was like in his private life. At school and at university he showed himself to be diligent and clever without being brilliant. As a boy he threw himself indiscriminately into every sort of school activity, and he remained a believer in the importance of sport and organized recreation as cohering forces in any institution. However, once he left Winchester he did not really practise what he preached: although he occasionally played golf, and shared the rights of a shoot in Wales with a friend, he was no sportsman, and once told a subordinate that his favourite form of exercise was to spend thirty-six hours reading in bed.[23] Throughout his life he read a good deal of history, and from the 1920s on a lot of thrillers also. He loved music, being determinedly populist and nationalistic in his taste: he listened to the records of Harry Lauder and George Formby, and despised the 'amateur English intellectual' who 'in matters musical was so snooty about Sullivan, the descendant here in the tradition of Mozart', writing to the conductor Sir Adrian Boult in the 1940s that 'there is & always has been music' in England's 'being. But since the days of Purcell, these people have been told by the foreigner that this is not so.'[24] He disliked travelling abroad, perhaps because his father had enjoyed it, and was benignly chauvinistic in his attitude to other countries. An exception was Ireland, which he visited as a young man and for whose people he always had a soft spot, admiring 'the delicious, though sometimes formidable, unexpectedness of that most attractive race.'[25] In food and drink he had no special tastes, though he had a great affection for beer drinkers as the embodiment of Britishness. In London his first club was the Union, but by 1916 he had joined Brooks's, to which he belonged until his death (although he was elected to the Athenaeum in 1937, he seldom used it).

From all of this it might appear that he was an entirely conventional figure, distinguished only by his ability as a civil servant from the mass of suburban mankind. Such was not the case. In appearance, in manner, in his extraordinary handwriting, in his friendships and his enmities, his family affairs and his religious beliefs, he was exceptional, sometimes to the point of oddity. Much of this will emerge from the account of his official career, but some matters are best dealt with here. Fisher was a handsome man who took care over his appearance. He did not run to fat as he aged. He struck most people as very polite and courteous without being at all formal — indeed his desire to put people at their ease and to avoid stuffiness sometimes created its own embarrassments for junior Treasury officials. One friend wrote that

> physically he was slight, thin and finely drawn. He wore his clothes with an air, so that he looked always as if he had just come from the tailors.
>
> ... But while he was always spruce and tidy, he conveyed the impression that his clothes and his body alike were not really part of him but merely appendages to his spirit. It was that of which you were immediately conscious.[26]

Unusually for a civil servant he mixed a good deal in London society, although he was emphatically egalitarian in his friendships. Many of these were intense and unstable: he tended to think the world of people for a time, to seek their company and to fawn over them, and then as suddenly to become disenchanted and drop them. The novelist Ann Bridge, who had every reason to be grateful for his interest in her and in her husband Owen O'Malley, wrote in 1928 of 'Warren spreading love and peace over one like treacle'.[27] He was described by a colleague as 'an idealist' who 'is inclined to exaggerate his friends', and he seemed completely uncritical of those he admired and would do anything for them. *The Wykehamist* said of him that, 'having once given his friendship', he 'found it hard to believe that this gift was mistaken'.[28] His personal letters to colleagues, friends, and even ministers are bespattered with cloying though sincere endearments: he wrote to Neville Chamberlain 'with fond love', and addressed Chatfield, the bluff First Sea Lord, as 'Ernle Dear'.[29] What to an ordinary person would be the grossest affectation was to him perfectly natural. It sometimes made him sound like a schoolgirl with a crush; that seems to have been roughly how he felt. The corollary of this was that when an object of adoration fell from grace, he completely lost interest. By and large, his colleagues contrived to stay on good terms with him by adroit footwork, never getting too close for comfort, but his personal relationships were marred by his unreal expectations of other people: he had bitter and rather pointless rows with people such as Chatfield and Lady Ernest Cunard which ended long friendships, he sacked his housekeeper in 1936 after indulging her for years, he separated from his wife in 1921, and he fell out with one of his sons.[30]

There were few people to whom he was constantly close, but a little is known about two: Lady Florence Ebury and Colonel Sir Robert Johnson. The former, an American heiress described as 'the great love of his life', 'a very tall curious rather ugly looking woman', died suddenly in 1927.[31] A Christian Scientist, she had a profound influence upon his religious outlook — Fisher belonged to no particular church, but he had a streak of spirituality in him which borrowed from various forms of Christianity. Johnson, for whom he had fagged at Winchester, was undoubtedly a beneficiary of Fisher's loyalty to his friends. When Fisher was at the National Health Insurance Commission in 1912 he tried to have Johnson appointed to a key post, and shortly after becoming Permanent Secretary in 1919 he brought him into the Treasury as establishment officer. Johnson was not a success there and he acquired an indifferent reputation, yet thanks to Fisher he was made Deputy Master and Comptroller of the Royal Mint in 1922. This final appointment was vindicated by results: Johnson proved an excellent salesman and he made a great success of the position, although he came to a rakish end in 1938 in circumstances which Fisher was unable to keep out of the newspapers.[32]

Fisher's domestic life was not happy. In April 1906 he married 'Maysie', Mary Anne Thomas, the daughter of a retired army officer. She was Irish on her mother's side, and she was a Roman Catholic. He was then 26 years old, and his bride 24. Some months before the wedding he wrote to Zimmern in somewhat melodramatic vein about his financial affairs:

I'm just back after 5 weeks Gastric Catarrh, just short of
typhoid. I've thought it wise in case of an accident to make
an informal little document, leaving my few belongings to
Maysie; & I'm going to ask you & Jim to be executors. I
hope you will. In capital I've got about five hundred & ten
pounds ... consisting at present of £100 Chinese Bond,
£100 in Oxford Tramways, £250 Liverpool Corporation
Stock, £62 Canadian 4/- Government Stock. I've also a
little furniture with my people at Chesters [the family
home in Oxford], books etc. & a few things at my digs: also
balance at Bank. It's just as well to have things ready,
though I'm not in hopes of a premature decease![33]

The wedding took place in a Roman Catholic church in London. Like her husband, Mary Anne Fisher was highly strung.
Although one of a large family, she was apparently a spoilt and
rather foolish woman. Her son recalls her as hopelessly impractical and indecisive, incapable of managing a household or
of creating a tranquil home. She irritated and antagonized
those around her, including the servants whose side her husband always took. Despite the birth of two sons, Norman in
1907 and Robin in 1914, the marriage deteriorated, and it
ended amid great unhappiness and bitterness with a formal
separation in 1921.

Fisher then took a flat in Marylebone, employing his sons'
former nanny Bunny as a housekeeper. Thereafter the Fishers
had little to do with one another, and there was no attempt at
reconciliation. Although Fisher provided Maysie with a
reasonably generous income to support herself, she had constant money troubles.[34] It is said that she refused him a divorce
due to her religion, although she had ceased to be a practising
Roman Catholic.[35] Much of the responsibility for the break-up
lay with Fisher, who seems at first to have indulged his wife and
then to have grown bored with her, but she was undoubtedly a
rather tiresome woman. Her lack of common sense was illustrated in an extraordinary interview which she gave to a
Morning Post journalist in 1926, which appeared on the same
day as a parliamentary attack was made on the position of Head
of the Civil Service which Fisher held. 'Lying in a small room,
her body swathed in electrically heated blankets', she preached
the virtues of fasting as a cure. She declared that 'I dance every
night and walk at least two miles every morning', that 'most

10

people eat too much nowadays', and that she 'never felt so well in ... [her] life' after 27 days without food. She 'added that since her treatment her brain had been working with greater clearness.'[36] Her remarks were made in all innocence — she remained a devotee of 'the cure' — but they were an acute embarrassment to her husband. She made an equally unfortunate appearance in the press in 1953, when she gave evidence in the prosecution of a couple, as it happened named Lawless, who had defrauded her of almost all her personal property under the guise of placing bets and of making investments for her. Her husband had excluded her from his will, and she was not entitled to any state pension after his death in 1948.[37] She died almost penniless in 1970.

The end of the Fishers' marriage left their two children without a proper home. The elder boy, Norman, already had a definite career mapped out for him which took him away from home: like his father before him, he wanted to join the navy. After graduating as a cadet in 1928 he spent his entire working life in it. He had an adventurous career, twice escaping with his life in submarine disasters while serving as a torpedo officer. In 1929, he was thrown into the sea when his boat *L12* collided with another submarine off Wales, resulting in twenty-four deaths. Two years later, he escaped from the *Poseidon* when it sank off the coast of China. Eighteen of the crew were lost. During the war he was mentioned in dispatches and was awarded the OBE, and he retired as senior captain in the reserve fleet in 1960. Perhaps because he was away so much, he remained on good terms with his father. He died in 1981. The younger son Robin, who was brought up by his mother, was not so fortunate: he was only 7 when his parents separated, and his upbringing was marred by the conflict between them. After army service in World War II he went into publishing and became a director of Eyre & Spottiswoode. He afterwards worked for the British Council. Fisher's relations with his younger son followed the same tempestuous course that characterized many of his friendships. In 1944, following an argument with Robin, Fisher refused to see him again.

For most of his time at the Treasury, Fisher lived apart from his family and saw little of them. Inevitably for a personable man who was separated from his wife, and who constantly sought feminine company, his relations with women were the subject of some gossip. However his son Robin, who lived with

him from 1934 to 1939, believes that the various women in
Fisher's life in the 1920s and 1930s were friends and friends
alone. Most of his friendships with women do seem to have
been characterized by affection and sentimentality rather than
passion. Ann Bridge, the novelist of whom he saw a great deal
in the late 1920s, wrote emphatically that he never 'made a
pass at me ... at any point.'[38] Whether he did or not would be
irrelevant to a study of his career, were it not that he had
something of a reputation in the civil service as a ladies' man.
There is no doubt that he liked women, whereas the rather
contradictory suggestion also made — based largely on his
habit of addressing men as 'love' and 'darling', and aired only
by people who never met him — that he was homosexual, is
far-fetched. A subordinate who worked with him in the
Treasury for almost twenty years remarked that Fisher
resembled 'a woman' in his likes and dislikes, but was emphatically masculine in his personal relationships.[39] Everyone else
who knew Fisher personally took much the same view.

It is not surprising that Fisher's turbulent private life should
have been the subject of gossip, given his idiosyncrasies, his
many enemies, and his open friendships with various women,
including his sons' nanny. In succeeding chapters readers will
find sufficient material on which to make an assessment of
Fisher. Of his personal affairs, however, very little is known.

III

Fisher's first years as a civil servant were uneventful. Whitehall
was by all accounts a rather sleepy place, and the Inland
Revenue was not a prestigious department. It received little
ministerial attention, and played no part in policy formation.
However, it was a useful training ground for an administrator
for a number of reasons. As a tax assessment and collection
agency it had a large clerical staff and a network of offices
throughout Britain, unlike a major policy department such as
the Treasury. Secondly, and again unlike the Treasury, it was in
direct touch with the general public. Finally, the Liberal government elected at the end of 1905 was committed to extensive
social reforms, and to a broadening of the taxation system to
finance it. This involved the Inland Revenue in a great deal of
new work.

There is no doubt that Fisher benefited from his time at the centre of this large department. It was there that he learned the importance of the proper management and treatment of staff, and of efficient organization. However, for his first 'two or three years' he was:

> bored stiff with heading and tailing printed half-margin drafts on Excise problems, such as the amount of strange ingredients to be allowed into the composition of beer and the methods of rendering methylated spirit unpalatable as a beverage, particularly to the good people of Glasgow, who had a queer fancy for it. Included in this valuable training was the despatch of stereotyped letters, imposing fines on people who seemed indifferent to the existence of Stamp Duties, especially miscreants who unknowingly failed to put a postage stamp on receipts for £2 and upwards.
>
> Acquaintance with the Income Tax was strictly limited to the barest ABC, such as the completion of drafts (usually printed) about exemptions and abatements....
>
> Being perhaps a little unruly by temperament, I was thrilled by the advent at the end of 1905 of a Government with a policy which seemed to herald an era of change in place of the stagnation hitherto prevailing; in this respect (as in most others) I found myself not in sympathy with my seniors whose forty years of calm repose at Somerset House had only been twice disturbed, on each occasion by a Liberal Government...

Despite the change of regime, life went on much as before in the Inland Revenue. After four years at Somerset House Fisher had evidently had enough, as he took the unusual and perilous step of applying for a transfer to the Treasury. The danger in this was that he would antagonize his department by seeking to leave and give an impression of self-importance without persuading the Treasury of his virtues. His effrontery has become part of Whitehall legend; what is not widely known is that he had the temerity to repeat the request eight months later.[40] The Treasury was not impressed by his applications, but his persistence in making them may have helped to bring his name to the attention of his superiors in the Inland Revenue. Preparations were under way for the 1909 'People's

Budget', and Fisher caught the eye of the chairman of the Inland Revenue, Sir Robert Chalmers. Chalmers made him his private secretary, afterwards telling a royal commission that 'the one I appointed, I appointed with great care, because I knew that I was going to be in for a very stiff time in 1909.'[41] From then on Fisher was never out of the sight of those who mattered in Whitehall.

Luck plays a part in all careers. Not only did Fisher become a private secretary at a critical and exciting time in the Inland Revenue as planning for the 1909 budget and for the machinery necessary to collect the new taxes began, but he also came to the notice of the Chancellor of the Exchequer, David Lloyd George. Lloyd George was an inspiration to officials: devious, energetic, persistent and successful, he demanded and received the utmost effort and loyalty from his civil servants. His ruthlessness in dealing with those whom he judged to have failed him only added to his magnetism. The one certain reward for those who worked for him was excitement. Fisher worshipped him from first to last as the greatest politician of the century, a reformer with the practical capacity to bring about major change. When Lloyd George died in 1945 Fisher wrote to *The Times*:

> May an Englishman, who from the age of twenty-eight served under Lloyd George, knew him, and loved him, remind our English that to this Welshman we owe alike the awakening out of its callousness of our social conscience to the shocking conditions in our country of ill-health, slums, unemployment, sweated labour, and youngsters' treatment, and also the development of public interest in science, agricultural, medical and industrial?[42]

As private secretary Fisher was fortunate in his master. Chalmers was a brilliant civil servant and a very strong character, a Treasury man sent to Somerset House in order to shake it up and prepare it for its expanded role. As chairman he was respected for his ability and disliked for his ruthlessness. He 'never by any chance had an official file on his desk; he sat there very wisely to give his decision on problems which were of sufficient magnitude to be brought to him.'[43] He encouraged Fisher to use his initiative and to take decisions on his behalf — Fisher said he 'treated me as if I was a much younger brother and allowed me a first-rate seat in the stalls' — and he promoted him with a speed so unprecedented that he was specifically questioned in 1912 by the MacDonnell commission on the civil service as to how the salary of 'Mr Fisher' had jumped within four years 'from £200 to something like £800 to £1,000 a year.' Chalmers replied that 'he has earned every penny of that advancement', and that from being his private secretary Fisher

> was promoted in due course merely to an ordinary committee clerkship, and as a committee clerk I selected him for the work of organising and carrying through the super tax, a new branch. He has done it extraordinarily well; and I recommended him, because of his practical successes in the new work, to be made a special commissioner.[44]

The importance for Fisher's career of these four years from 1908 to 1912 lay not only in the opportunity they afforded him to display his exceptional ability and his absolute fearlessness in accepting responsibility; they also gave him in a short space of time an unusual range of experience. As private secretary to Chalmers he was privy to the management of the Inland Revenue's external relations with other departments, particularly the Treasury, and Chalmers also taught him the virtues of delegation and decisiveness in administration; as a committee clerk he devised and put into operation a new administrative structure to collect a new tax; and as a special commissioner, he was in charge of a part of the internal appeals procedure against administrative decisions unique to the Inland Revenue, and consequently was exposed to the impact of bureaucratic processes upon the general public. Finally, because it was formally subordinate to the Treasury the Inland Revenue suffered particularly at its hands. Somerset House was treated as a dumping ground for Treasury cast-offs, and the department greatly resented the Treasury's high-handedness towards it. There is no doubt that this is where Fisher's intense dislike of the Treasury's traditional attitude towards the rest of Whitehall came from.

Fisher's first promotion came in 1909, when he became a committee clerk. In retirement he recalled how he 'was told off to be Clerk to the Special Commissioners of Income Tax', responsible for assessment and appeals for the new super-tax, levied at the rate of '6d per sovereign above the first five thousand'. He was asked to 'start up the mechanics' for collecting it. This was the first time any citizen had been asked to disclose 'the whole of his private mysteries', and it naturally required sensitive administration. A few months after beginning this work in an office in the middle of Covent Garden, Fisher had 'an unexpected visit' from the Chancellor, Lloyd George, who was worried by 'censorious backchat' from the opposition about the new tax. It 'was imperative that he should see a typical completed Super-Tax return form (How this would help I still don't see ...). Sweating with funk', Fisher refused to show him any return without the written permission of the person who had made it. Once Lloyd George was satisfied that he could not see completed returns on demand, 'he patted me on the back and said, "Well done, young man"', and went off to assure the Commons that the secrets of the rich were safe.[45]

In 1911 Fisher was promoted again, to be a Special Commissioner of Income Tax, dealing with appeals against super-tax assessments. He was working at his Covent Garden office one Saturday in May 1912 'when I received telephonic orders from L[loyd] G[eorge] to join his latest venture', the National Health Insurance Commission, 'first thing on Monday morning ... I asked in what capacity I was to present myself, only to receive the brisk succinct answer that that was entirely my own affair.' The passing of the National Health Insurance Act of 1911 had been a great victory for the Liberals, and especially for Lloyd George, but even after its acceptance by Parliament its future was uncertain. The head of the English commission, Sir Robert Morant, was like Fisher a Wykehamist, and said to 'have no use for a man who had not been to Winchester and New College.' He had been the moving spirit behind the measure, but he was at odds with the Treasury and he detested the scheme as embodied in the act.[46]

The act covered millions of working people, and its implementation entailed an unprecedented administrative exercise which had to be completed by 1 April 1913, the day on which the scheme was due to come into operation. The Treasury, of which Chalmers was now Permanent Secretary, doubted whether this was possible. In a desperate attempt to ensure that everything would be ready in time, a group of promising young civil servants from various departments were attached to the commission. Amongst these were a number who made names for themselves at the work and subsequently rose to eminence in Whitehall or Westminster, such as Alexander Maxwell, Claud Schuster, Maurice Gwyer, Ernest Gowers, Arthur Salter and above all John Anderson.[47] But it was Fisher who occupied the pivotal position.

His tasks were twofold: to organize the work of the commission so that the scheme could be brought into operation on time, and to bridge the gap between Morant and the Treasury. Fisher admired Morant and was his subordinate, but he was also very close to his former chief Chalmers, now Morant's antagonist at the Treasury. He succeeded in all that he did, revelling in the need for speed, for cutting corners, for taking decisions and for diplomacy in keeping both Morant and the Treasury happy. His impact was immediate: he arrived to find that the commissioners 'had not been fully informed of LG's latest essay in recruitment.' The 'situation inside was chaotic, while outside the vehemence of the dislike for the Act had in no way abated'. The commissioners asked the Chancellor to put back by three months the date on which the act would become operative. Lloyd George 'thereupon sent for me; and I could only reply that, while I'd been a mere couple of weeks on the job and therefore knew little or nothing, any such postponement ... could only spell its permanent shelving. He said this was also his view, and refused' to sanction it.[48]

Fisher recalled that his job 'was principally that of a shop-walker and did not include higher thought or technicalities': he was there to set up a machine that would work. One colleague, R.W. Harris, wrote that 'it was not his job to know anything about the content of the Insurance Act, and it was not wise to approach him on the subject unless one was prepared to listen to a few of those ... forceful expressions of which he was always a gifted exponent.'[49] Another, W.J. Braithwaite, who had done the groundwork on which the act was based, told his wife a few months later that 'the office is doing everything on its own and Fisher's responsibility ... Morant retired to his tent ... Fisher was getting everything done without consulting him.' At the end of the year Braithwaite's diary records that Fisher 'has got things done, and introduced an organisation where there was nothing ...'. '[He] changed the whole place and the greatest credit is due to him, as he stood between the machine and worry, and had the confidence of the workers.'[50] C.F.G. Masterman, who as a junior Treasury minister had helped Lloyd

George in the political battle for the act, remarked that 'we never got going properly until Warren Fisher came in'.[51] In tackling the task Fisher 'spared neither himself nor others and he was quite pitiless in discarding failures or weaklings.' At the same time it was a team effort, not without its lighter side: on one occasion the austere Morant returned unexpectedly to his office to find Fisher, Harris and another colleague engaged in a competition to see who could make a complete circuit of the room without touching the floor.[52] Fisher had 'a triumphant success' in organising the commission and the insurance scheme ran smoothly from the appointed day.[53] He himself had no doubts about who the real hero of the act was: 'this conception of L[loyd] G[eorge]'s (including the provision for unemployment) became living reality, bringing hope to countless millions ... to him our gratitude is wholly due.'[54]

The 1911 National Health Insurance Act was the first major piece of social legislation of the century, and the first great step towards a British welfare state. The process by which it was brought into operation was similarly significant for the civil service. It brought together into a common enterprise officials from various parts of Whitehall who would otherwise never have worked as colleagues, gave them a far wider view of their service than was possible from within their own rigidly isolated departments, and showed what collective action by the civil service could achieve. Their success in getting the act to work was doubly satisfying for those like Fisher who believed that the state had a part to play in social improvement.

Once the act came into operation in 1913, Fisher returned to Somerset House with yet another promotion, becoming a Commissioner of Inland Revenue. His work on the insurance commission had made his name throughout Whitehall — he is said to have refused a knighthood — and he was widely regarded as the most promising official of his generation. In the same year Chalmers, who had supervised his rise through the ranks since 1908, fell out with Lloyd George and left the Treasury to become governor of Ceylon. But the departure of his mentor proved no hindrance to Fisher: in 1914 he received further advancement, becoming Deputy Chairman of the Inland Revenue.[55] While biographers tend to claim too much for their subjects, it does appear that it was Fisher rather than his nominal superior who provided the driving force at Somerset House. On Sunday 2 August 1914, according to his memoirs, he was in his club when he 'received in rapid sequence' telephone messages from the permanent heads of the Treasury and of the Board of Trade asking him to go and talk to them.

> The Secretary to the Treasury commenced ... by a hint of the possibility of a war. (This was intended as a clue, I imagine, for he knew that a mere East-ender like me could not have the information of Whitehall). He amplified this by saying that, amongst other war-like precautions, it had been decided to convert the August Bank Holiday ... into four, i.e. spanning the Monday to the Thursday, both inclusive. To all of which ... I listened with rapt attention, even though slightly bewildered ...
>
> But light came ... a few weeks back the Government had decided (we at Somerset House knew nothing about this) that ... the Treasury, whose business it would be ... should take all necessary steps for replacing the good old sovereigns and half-sovereigns ... by counterfeits consisting of paper. Thus enjoined, the Treasury, so I gathered, had done precisely nothing; this didn't greatly surprise me.

Fisher was told that 'by next Friday morning there have to be in every Bank and branch throughout the United Kingdom ... so many millions of paper pounds and ten shilling notes, and we, the Treasury, can't manage it ... Would the Inland Revenue undertake this?' Fisher found that 'no design, or water-marked paper, or experienced agency or anything else had been thought of', but he committed the Inland Revenue 'and by Friday the 7th August, all the Banks had the notes, made out of postage-stamp paper ....'

After his interview at the Treasury, Fisher went on to the Board of Trade, where the Permanent Secretary, 'not without some symptoms of excitement, told me ... that sundry instructions had been given by the Government ... some time ago' about shipping war insurance. His department 'had no clear idea of what they should do about the scheme.' On the specious grounds that insurance policies bore 'embossed stamps indicative of an Inland Revenue charge', the Board of Trade man claimed 'it's surely up to you to do the donkey-work ... and at all events get the scheme started. This struck me as a "non-sequitur".' Nevertheless Fisher committed the Inland Revenue again, after asking whether 'the Board of Trade had taken offices in the City where policy-seekers could conveniently repair, and had made the necessary staffing and other arrangements ... Of course not, was the rejoinder ... had we done any of these things, you and I would not be talking together.' The scheme was in working order just three days later.[56]

These two episodes, as recounted by Fisher, demonstrate again what he had shown in the National Health Insurance Commission, his extraordinary ability to establish good administrative machinery. They also indicate that his talent was recognized well beyond Somerset House. As Deputy Chairman of the Inland Revenue throughout the hectic wartime years he supervised the vast extension in direct taxation which the war entailed. His reputation grew further with officials and with ministers, especially Reginald McKenna, Bonar Law and Stanley Baldwin at the Treasury. In 1916 he received his first honour, a CB. Further promotion was clearly only a matter of time.

Fisher's achievements during the war were twofold. He reorganized the Inland Revenue to cope with the rush of new work. This was a notable success in itself, but one similar to what was done by other able officials in other departments. What set his performance apart was that, while making the necessary adjustment to wartime conditions, and at a time when most departments were too hard pressed to maintain any personnel policy at all, he managed also to make widespread changes in the career structure of the Inland Revenue's staff to rationalize their grading system and improve their prospects of advancement. Significantly, he also abolished departmental grades for administrative staff, arguing that the higher civil service was a unitary organism, not one where staff were inextricably bound to a single department for their entire careers: 'My proposals have proceeded throughout on the hypothesis of a unified Class 1 throughout the Civil Service and of absolute equality of treatment as between department and department.'[57] This theme was central to his later work as Head of the Civil Service.

Fisher's wartime performance made him the obvious candidate for the headship of the Board of Inland Revenue when it fell vacant in July 1918. He was then 38 years old. His reaction to his appointment was one of relief rather than of joy.

He wrote to the Chancellor, Law, in characteristically over-blown terms:

> The great kindness of your language in telling me of the promotion you have given me adds much to the meaning to me of the promotion. And one of its chief meanings is that you have spared me the humiliation of being passed over.
>
> You have always been so kind & trustful to me personally that in my feeling there is something more than just the official to his Minister. I cannot thank you as I would, but believe me I am deeply grateful.[58]

Fisher was Chairman at Somerset House for only fifteen months, but he left a lasting mark on the department. He is credited with the introduction of important changes in its internal organization, in its dealings with the public and in its treatment of its staff. Two problems arise in discussing his performance: first, very little material has been found; and second, it is difficult to distinguish his individual contribution to the department's development from changes which were anyway bound to happen. Nevertheless, the general lines of his activities emerge fairly clearly.

Evidence of his impact can be found in the comments of Inland Revenue officials. One of his successors wrote that Fisher 'was responsible for the organisation ... which existed when I went there [in 1958] and I always defended it vigorously.' It ensured 'that those at the top of the [Inland] Revenue did not have to deal with a mass of detail'. The same writer also attributed to Fisher the phenomenon that 'the whole organisation was permeated' with the 'view of thrusting down responsibility in case work'. It was 'a black mark against an inspector of taxes ... if he referred up to his superiors too many questions.'[59] Lord Houghton, who as secretary of the Inland Revenue Staff Association met Fisher during the 1920s, believed that he 'certainly ... pushed the Inland Revenue into the forefront of civil service professionalism. They rode on the back of wartime taxation into that position'. He also 'did a lot to boost the pride (and prejudice) of the Inspectorate with the introduction of the (short-lived) university nomination for recruitment.'[60] Fisher gave a further lift to the inspectors' *ésprit de corps* by arranging for them to be called H[is] M[ajesty's]

Inspectors of Taxes. At the same time, whereas the inspectorate had previously 'felt it natural to regard all taxpayers as enemies to be done down', Fisher 'drummed into them that it was certainly their duty to see that all taxes were collected; but that they owed it to the taxpayer to be constantly helpful and to draw his attention to any right or claim' that he might have overlooked, a principle reiterated for successive generations of entrants to Somerset House[61].

Fisher's achievements as Deputy Chairman and Chairman of the Inland Revenue stemmed partly from his ability as an organizer and his willingness to work hard. His success in transforming the spirit of the department was equally significant. This was done partly through the introduction of progressive personnel policies, as will be discussed below. What was also important was his standing with his staff. He acquired a reputation for taking on the Treasury, against which he had 'a great prejudice' for 'its tutelary attitude towards the Inland Revenue.'[62] He also stood up for his department in public. While serving on the Royal Commission on Income Tax in 1919 he caused a considerable stir by rounding on another member of the commission whom he believed to have made 'a very serious allegation' about evidence presented by an official of the Inland Revenue.[63] This willingness to defend his department and subordinates undoubtedly contributed to his success at Somerset House — long after he left he was still 'held in some awe and respect in the Inland Revenue'. It was also to do so at the Treasury.[64]

Perhaps the most illuminating evidence of his impact on the Inland Revenue is provided in a song composed in his honour, apparently for an Inland Revenue function held some time after he had left for the Treasury. It merits extensive quotation:

> With our guest we must in future from all flippancy abstain
> And a deferential atttitude endeavour to maintain
> We shall never have another chance to pull his leg again
> So we may as well this evening do it well, do it well,
> Yes, we may as well this evening do it well.

> When Sir Warren was our chief and there was something to be got
> Which Sir Warren thought was needful and the Treasury

thought was not,
Why, Sir Warren took his coat off, and let them have it hot,
And he generally came out rather well, rather well,
Yes, he generally came out rather well.

So when a man was needed to remove the Treasury moss,
The Chancellor was never for a moment at a loss.
Said he: 'The man to boss them is the man they couldn't boss'
And I think that he selected very well, very well,
Yes, I think he chose his man extremely well.

And so we lost our chairman, but we keep him still in sight,
Olympus seems more homely now with him upon the
height,
And whene'er he comes to dine with us as he has done
tonight
We'll always try and do him fairly well, fairly well,
Yes we'll always try and do him fairly well.

What a team he might have captained had he been content to
stop!
Think of TEN assistant secret'ries with brains chock full of
'shop'
All working like the deuce until they're fairly fit to drop
And I think he'd have inspired them very well, very well,
Yes, I think he'd keep them busy very well.

Or, look farther in the future when amongst those super-
men
There'll be super ladies also, even in that 'upper ten'
Can't you fancy his addressing them as 'Trixie' and 'dear
Gwen' ?
And I'm sure he could have done it very well, very well,
Yes, I'm sure he could have done it very well.

And although this cannot happen now — he's left it all
behind —
We never could forget him even were we so inclined;
Why, we cannot get a drink without a note that he has
signed!
Oh! I think he'll be remembered very well, very well,
Yes, I think he'll be remembered very well.[65]

IV

By the time that Fisher left Somerset House in the autumn of 1919, what major changes in the structure of the civil service which there were to be up to 1939 had already been made. An Establishments Department had been set up within the Treasury to develop consistent personnel policies for all of Whitehall, the reorganization of the Treasury and the appointment of its Permanent Secretary as Head of the Civil Service had been approved by the Cabinet Finance Committee, and negotiating machinery had been set up under the aegis of the National Whitley Council to see through a standardization of grades throughout the civil service. All this was done under the direction of the Treasury chiefs whom Fisher was appointed to replace, the joint permanent secretaries Sir Thomas Heath and Sir John Bradbury, although Fisher made a substantial contribution while still Chairman of the Inland Revenue. The process by which the civil service was reorganized after the First World War has sometimes been misunderstood. In order to evaluate Fisher's influence and role it is necessary to consider the changes which occurred in Whitehall in some detail.

Even before the war dissatisfaction with the internal organization of Whitehall had arisen. This crystallized in the report of the Royal Commission on the Civil Service of 1912–14, chaired by Lord MacDonnell. It pointed to the needless complexity and lack of uniformity in the grading and treatment of staff throughout the civil service. Despite the opposition of the main Treasury witness to appear before it, Fisher's mentor Sir Robert Chalmers, the commission called for increased Treasury control of departmental establishments in order to ensure uniformity and rationalisation, and thereby to pull the disparate elements of the civil service together[66].

The war prevented action on the MacDonnell recommendations, and rapid and haphazard wartime expansion created more problems of civil service organization. These were addressed in a string of reports produced between 1916 and 1919 by a committee of inquiry into 'the war expansion of government departments', by an internal Treasury committee, by the House of Commons select committee on national expenditure, by the Haldane committee on the machinery of government, and by the Bradbury committee on staffs. All emphasized the importance of the Treasury in establishments matters on grounds of economy, efficiency, and consistency, while the Gladstone committee on recruitment to the civil service suggested a reorganization of clerical grades throughout Whitehall and more extensive employment of women. At the political level some ministers, notably E.S. Montagu and Lord Milner, became very conscious of the administrative defects of the expanded civil service, and after 1918 the Cabinet collectively grew alarmed at the size and cost of government. Circumstances produced an unusual community of interest between those who wanted to improve the civil service and those who wanted to reduce the cost of running the country.

Fisher was unquestionably one of the prime movers in the drive for reform within Whitehall. It appears that, in common with the MacDonnell commission, he had come to the conclusion by 1914 that the civil service should be organized and staffed more as a unit than as a collection of heterogeneous departments each with its own way of handling and grading its employees. His practical success in the Inland Revenue once war broke out increased both his confidence and his prestige. Although in theory far down the Whitehall pecking order as the recently appointed deputy head of an unfashionable department, his achievements in organization stood in marked contrast to what had happened in most public departments and allowed him to speak with considerable authority on the problems of the civil service generally.

In evidence to the Gladstone committee in 1918, for example, Fisher stressed the importance of having 'a strong Establishments Division with a highly paid man in charge' in each department, said that there were 'far too many' clerical classes and that they were 'much too watertight' and gave no incentive to staff to work hard and to accept responsibility. He deplored the 'tendency to promote on seniority', and expressed the view that 'university women' should be employed on responsible work. The war had demonstrated that women clerical workers were 'more conscientious' than men. Women given 'the higher type of work during the war ... had done it very well.' He believed that they might 'in a decade or twenty years' be suitable for recruitment to administrative grades, though 'they had now no tradition of public work.'[67]

He developed these themes as a member of the committee on staffs chaired by Sir John Bradbury, a Joint Permanent Secretary to the Treasury. The committee took evidence

throughout 1918, and made a number of important recommendations: an Establishments Division should be set up
within the Treasury to 'maintain close personal relations with
the establishment officers of the various departments, acquire
knowledge of their office methods and act as a clearing house
for information on all staff questions.' The creation of a 'standing committee ... of the establishment officers in the principal
departments for the purpose of assisting and advising the
Treasury' was also suggested, as well as the 'appointment in
each of the larger public departments of a picked and thorougly
experienced' establishments officer, 'to be of a rank at least as
high as the heads of the principal divisions of the department
and to be responsible directly to the permanent head of the
department.' Furthermore, the committee called for the institution of regular investigations by the Treasury of 'the
actual working methods of the departments in co-operation
with the establishment officers'.[68]

Action to implement the personnel policies suggested by the
various committees which had touched on staff questions since
1916 was swift once the war ended. In February 1919 an
Establishments Division was set up within the Treasury under
Sir Malcolm Ramsay, together with 'an advisory committee of
heads of Departments', including Fisher, under the Financial
Secretary to the Treasury, Stanley Baldwin. Its job was 'to
advise the Treasury on general questions.'[69] Fisher entirely
supported a key principle enunciated by this committee, that
establishment officers should have 'the rank of assistant
secretary or at any rate high standing in their respective
departments', pointing out that the Inland Revenue 'regard the
post of principal establishment officer as one of the utmost
significance; and Barrett's [the Inland Revenue establishment
officer] authority and responsibility are probably greater than
is the case with any of his analogues elsewhere.'[70] He also
pushed for the effective working of the staff negotiating
machinery established under the National Whitley Council in
1919, and was a member of the Ramsay Bunning committee,
composed of official and staff representatives. After ten months
of discussion this group reached agreement on how civil service
regrading would proceed, and it cleared the way for the
astonishingly successful rationalization and standardization of
grades into administrative, executive and clerical classes which
followed between 1919 and 1921.[71]

While preparing its final report, the Bradbury committee on staffs had consulted a number of permanent secretaries: Murray of the Post Office, Guillemard of Customs and Excise, and Brade of the War Office. All three agreed that the Treasury should be staffed by the transfer of experienced assistant principals (the grade at which graduates were recruited) rather than by neophytes who had been highly placed in the entrance competition, and said that as things stood the department was 'out of touch' with the rest of Whitehall over whose affairs it had such influence; only Murray objected to the proposition that 'the appointment of an establishment officer should require Treasury approval'; both Brade and Guillemard thought that the Treasury should assume responsibility for the placement of all assistant principals in order to encourage 'general fluidity.'[72] Similar comments were made to the Haldane committee in 1918: Troup of the Home Office said that departments were far too numerous and too cut off from each other, suggesting that each 'should regard itself, both in theory and in practice, as standing in some relation to the other departments of the public service, and not as an isolated unit.'[73] Such evidence indicates that Whitehall was ready for a degree of change which would extend beyond consolidation of clerical classes throughout the civil service and continued experimentation in the employment of women, measures which had been put forward by the Gladstone committee on recruitment; there was also some recognition of the importance of general contact and co-operation between departments.

The surprising degree of agreement on the need for change is explained primarily by the impact upon Whitehall of the chaotic expansion of wartime, combined with widespread resentment at the way in which the Treasury habitually dealt with other departments. What is striking about the process is that it was almost exclusively an internal Whitehall affair. The main exception was the Haldane committee on the machinery of government, which reported in 1918. In the reverential words of one historian it had 'a breathtaking mandate, a splendid career, and a luciferous afterlife', and its conclusions are still routinely invoked as the epitome of rational thinking on British government organisation.[74]

Besides Haldane, the former Liberal minister who had made his name through his reorganization of the army while Secretary of State for War from 1905 to 1912, the committee included only two men with experience of running government departments, the social reformer Sir Robert Morant and Sir George Murray, a former joint head of the Treasury. The two men seem largely to have cancelled each other out, much to Morant's grief.[75] Its working papers show that, as with all such committees, there were considerable differences amongst both its members and the witnesses whom they heard on the issues they discussed; there was also general agreement that some changes in the organization of government departments were necessary. Its report, which was mainly Haldane's work, provided an agreeably symmetrical and logical framework upon which the organization of government should be based. It also called on the Treasury to concern itself more with establishment questions throughout the civil service, and to adopt a less hostile attitude towards the aspirations of spending departments.

In this it was not forming opinion but rather echoing what were already widespread sentiments in Whitehall, that the spirit in which the Treasury dealt with other departments had to change, and that uniformity in the treatment of staff was necessary. The report's originality and importance lay not in its specific recommendations, but in its attempt to look at the machinery of government as a whole. That was Haldane's particular contribution, and it was by far the most important.[76] The report itself earned the admiration more of students than of practitioners of administration — Sir Robert Fraser, who was closely involved in both the planning and the implementation of post-war reorganization of the civil service, believed it had no direct influence at all — whereas those ideas of Haldane's which underlay it were regarded with something approaching veneration by both Fisher and the Secretary to the Cabinet Sir Maurice Hankey, the two officials who did most to determine the way in which central government functioned between the wars.[77] When Haldane died, Fisher wrote that 'he had the greatest gift for administration and organisation of any man of our time; and this was the direct outcome of his realisation that thought is action and it is the spirit which animates.' He was 'a master in the field of administration and organisation.'[78] It has been said that the process of civil service integration was needlessly haphazard, unscientific and incomplete because the great men of Whitehall ignored the 'magnificently consistent and rigorously thoughtful (i.e. doomed) set of principles' embodied in the Haldane committee's report.[79] This is farfetched. The fact was that Fisher and Hankey considered themselves disciples of Haldane. It did not follow from this either that the report represented the culmination of his ideas — it did not — or that they as his adherents should have accepted it uncritically.

By the beginning of 1919 even the Treasury had come round to the view that the post-war civil service would require a great deal more direction and co-ordination than had been given before 1914. That realization was the product principally of the Treasury's wartime experience. The pre-war Treasury had been organized into six divisions, only one of which, Finance, had been established by function. The other five divisions each dealt with a somewhat miscellaneous group of departments. Each division handled all staff and organizational questions relating to the departments within its group, in addition to dealing with their spending plans and activities. Two temporary divisions had been added to help with the flood of work after 1914, but the department remained organized basically on pre-war lines. It had proved impossible to control the expansion of the civil service, which by 1919 was almost three times its 1914 size. The war had also seen the creation of a number of new departments which were not likely to disappear once peace came. In 1916 a committee of middle-ranking Treasury officials had endorsed the establishment on a permanent basis of ministries of Labour and Health, and concluded that the post-war Treasury would have to 'continue to exercise functions far wider than it did' in 'the old days of humdrum peace.'[80]

The war fundamentally altered the shape and size of British government. However, there were sharp limits to what innovations key Whitehall officials thought necessary in response. Sir Robert Chalmers told the Haldane committee that the creation of a separate Establishments Division in the Treasury would see effective control 'dissipated and weakened', while Whitleyism was regarded with suspicion as giving too much power to the staff. Guillemard believed it 'quite unsuitable for application to government departments', while Sir Thomas Heath of the Treasury hoped that 'it might be possible to confine the Whitley concessions ... i.e. to exclude the major question of pay altogether. It might also be useful to intimate that the experiment would be open to review after three (or five) years.'[81]

Heath, whom one Chancellor a dozen years earlier said was 'regarded by the other departments as the special incarnation of all that is most angular and pedantic in Treasury traditions & practices', had previously opposed the introduction of telephones to the Treasury on the grounds that they would impair the ability of officials to write concisely.[82] He was also something of a misogynist: he conducted a rearguard action in favour of the continued segregation of female from male employees in departments, and against the 'policies of the same examination and equal pay' which were being urged.[83] Furthermore, he 'would not force women on an unwilling department.'[84] Such remarks were significant and somewhat ominous, coming as they did from the Treasury official directly in charge of staff and organization questions. They begged the question of whether major changes in the civil service could take place without major changes in the Treasury itself.

V

Implementation of the recommendations which emerged from the various reviews of government organization initially attracted very little ministerial attention. This was partly because ministers had more pressing problems to deal with, partly because administrative reform was a rather technical issue. It was also an indication of the surprising degree of agreement at official level within Whitehall on the changes to be made. This in turn is explained largely by the fact that the new measures and policies would affect the lower ranks of the civil service rather than the administrative classes. It was left to individual departments to decide how to adapt their higher organization to the changed circumstances of peace.

The first significant stirrings of Cabinet interest in civil service organization came in the summer of 1919. By then there was strong public pressure for cuts in taxation and expenditure, and retrenchment had replaced reconstruction as a political priority. Determining how the cost of running the country could be reduced was left to the Cabinet Finance Committee. It had considerable authority as its members included the Prime Minister Lloyd George, the Chancellor Austen Chamberlain, and the leader of the Conservatives in the Coalition government, Bonar Law. The civil service was an obvious target for cutbacks, both because of its unplanned wartime growth and of its perennial unpopularity with the public. It was clear to ministers that a strengthened Treasury was required to enforce reductions in staff numbers and to increase efficiency in all government departments.

On 20 August 1919, at a meeting of the finance committee, 'the Chancellor ... indicated certain changes in the organisation of the Treasury which he proposed to introduce with a view to the more effective control of expenditure.' The Treasury would be divided into three 'departments', Finance, Supply Services, and Establishments, each headed by a 'Controller' with the pay and status of the head of a major Whitehall department. Above them would be a single Permanent Secretary, who would also be designated Head of the Civil Service and as such would advise the Prime Minister on civil service appointments and decorations. These proposals were welcomed by Lloyd George, who declared that 'not only in view of the state of public opinion but because of the financial situation of the country, ruthless cutting down of expenditure was imperative.'[85] Bonar Law was also satisfied with this 'very good arrangement about the Treasury.'[86] In sanctioning the Treasury reorganization, the finance committee also approved the appointment of Fisher to be its new head in succession to the Joint Permanent Secretaries Bradbury and Heath — Chalmers, from 1916 also a Joint Permanent Secretary, had retired some months earlier. On 4 September the formal approval of the Board of Treasury to the changes was conveyed in a Treasury minute which stated that the new Permanent Secretary would 'act as Permanent Head of the Civil Service and advise the First Lord in regard to Civil Service appointments and decorations.'[87] Eleven days later a circular was issued to all departments explaining 'in somewhat greater detail' what the reorganization meant.[88]

The provenance of these changes has remained something of a mystery. Some writers assumed that Fisher was responsible for the whole scheme, others that he was the begetter at least of the title of Head of the Civil Service.[89] These views were authoritatively dismissed in the 1950s by Sir Horace Hamilton, who pointed out that Fisher had said publicly that he did not know who had devised the 1919 reorganization and that he disliked it from the first.[90] This is confirmed in a minute by Fisher written in 1931, in which he told ministers that when in August 1919 the Government ... informed me of their intention to bring me across to the Treasury with effect from the following October, I was presented with a new-fangled, indeed bizarre organisation the authorship of which is still unknown to me.

I said that I would of course do my best to work it, but it was agreed that it could only be regarded as experimental, and subject to modification if the course of events showed that to be necessary.

The scheme was to some extent in outline, and with its implications resulted as follows.

The Departmental Treasury was subdivided into three so-called 'Departments' entitled 'Finance Department', 'Supply Services Department' and 'Establishments Department'.

The Permanent Secretary to the Treasury — whose title was about the only recognizable trace left of the old Treasury — was the permanent head and in general charge. In specific charge of the three so-called 'Departments' ... there was a 'Controller' with the service rank and emoluments of the Permanent Head of a First Class Department of State.[91]

Elsewhere, he wrote that the changes were approved by the Cabinet Finance Committee, 'having previously been the subject of informal consideration among ministers', while Hamilton pointed to a speech made in the Lords in 1942 by a former member of the Finance Committee, Auckland Geddes, which suggested that the reorganization had been Milner's work.[92] However, there is nothing in Milner's papers or in the Finance Committee records to suggest that he was particularly involved in reforming the Treasury, although he was close to despair at the 'fungus of mediocrity' pervading the higher civil service.[93] What evidence there is indicates that the man responsible for the scheme adopted in August 1919 was one of the serving Joint Permanent Secretaries to the Treasury, Sir John Bradbury.

On 19 August Bradbury wrote to the Chancellor, Austen Chamberlain, telling him that 'for an office like ours the dual or triple headship is not I think a suitable arrangement', although 'owing to personal reasons and the fact that we had "grown up together" ... it worked without friction in the case of Chalmers, Heath and myself.' But other departments tended to try to play off one secretary against another while 'in our domestic relations the staff always felt the absence of a single chief responsible for office arrangements generally.' Furthermore,

> the work of the Treasury has grown enormously since 1913 and will probably grow still more in the near future, and it is clearly impossible for one permanent secretary to do justice to it without a very much larger amount of devolution than has existed in the past.
>
> Under present conditions the work of the department falls into three categories which, though they overlap to some extent, can be kept fairly distinct (a) General Finance (b) Control of Establishments (c) Control of Services ... (a) is lightest in volume of work but probably most exacting in regard to complexity and importance ...
>
> I think each of these sections justifies a post with the status and salary of a Head of a Public Department and unless such an arrangement is thought likely to create difficulties in resisting claims from other departments, I should be disposed to place them on that basis.
>
> The heads of these sections might be given new titles (say) Controller of Finance, Controller of Establishments, Controller of Supply Services and I would make them directly responsible to the Board of Treasury subject to the general supervision of a single Permanent Secretary who to mark his pre-eminence might be given the additional £500 a year which that post always carried over other headships of departments up to 1913.
>
> The functions of the Permanent Secretary would be to consult with the Controllers concerned in regard to all overlapping questions (which are fairly numerous), to keep in touch with the work of the office as a whole and to have the final say (subject to Ministers) in regard to appointments, promotions and distribution of staff, to act generally as permanent head of the Civil Service and to advise the Prime Minister in regard to the bestowal of Civil Service patronage and honours.

Bradbury expressed his dislike of 'this last function', which 'has of late years fallen into desuetude.' However, 'human nature ... being what it is, it is vastly important to the prestige and influence of the Treasury and ought to be restored as soon as possible.' This would allow the Prime Minister to 'allege the opposition of the Head of the Civil Service as the reason for refusing an honour or appointment which he may not wish to make or bestow', and 'from the point of view of the Head of the Civil Service the reputation of being able to keep people out may be even more useful than that of being able to get them in.'

Bradbury acknowledged that his proposals were open to criticism:

> This, I admit, does not look like a very laborious life for the Permanent Secretary. On the other hand, I think it is important that he should have 'time for thought' and also be able to serve on committees for which the Chancellor ... himself cannot spare the time.

Bradbury could only 'speak with some diffidence ... as regards personnel', but 'if I were to stay at the Treasury, I should be prepared ... to duplicate the posts of Controller of Finance and Permanent Secretary', a tacit admission of the weakness of the Permanent Secretary in the scheme he had devised. He went on to nominate three Treasury men, Blackett, Barstow and Ramsay, for the three controllerships, to suggest that the redundant title of Assistant Secretary be given to the Treasury principal clerks as 'this ... is very desirable from the point of view of status in dealing with their opposite numbers in other departments', and to recommend that internal Treasury establishment matters be dealt with by a committee of the three controllers and the Permanent Secretary. He concluded by saying that 'we should work in the direction of making each section self-contained, promotions being made *ceteris paribus* within the section', although there should be 'free discretion to recommend transfers from one section to another', while 'the freer the circulation of officers between the Treasury and other departments both ways the better it will be for the service generally.'[94]

A day later, and apparently without any serious consideration, the Finance Committee accepted the Chancellor's recommendation that precisely this scheme should be adopted. Theirs was essentially a short term view, whereas Bradbury wanted to secure a permanent change in Treasury organization in response to the expansion of its responsibilities brought about by the war. The need for this had been acknowledged within the Treasury as early as 1916.[95] However, there are no signs that the Bradbury scheme was the product of extensive consultation within the department: it envisaged the removal of his fellow Joint Permanent Secretary Sir Thomas Heath, and his authorship of it remained unknown to Fisher and to generations of Treasury officials.[96] Bradbury may have intended to prepare the ground for his own acquisition of sole control over the Treasury, and it appears that he was given this option by the Chancellor.[97] He had every reason to expect it: he was only 46 years of age, and he had performed brilliantly on finance questions during the war. Although he was on poor terms with Lloyd George, whom as Chancellor he had served until 1915, his departure seems to have been voluntary: instead of remaining at the Treasury, he took on what proved to be a wearisome and unsatisfactory task as chief British delegate on the Reparations Commission in Paris. His motivation may have been financial: the work was very highly paid, and he is reputed to have wanted to make a great deal of money.[98] Sir Thomas Heath had a harder fate: widely regarded as pleasant but pedestrian, he suffered a spectacular demotion, being made Comptroller General and Secretary to the Commissioners for the Reduction of the National Debt.[99]

Fisher came to the Treasury at an awkward time. Although he wanted to 'break the pride and prejudice of the Treasury', he was obliged to accept the main features of a scheme of reorganization with which he profoundly disagreed. The post of Permanent Secretary as defined by Bradbury and endorsed by the Cabinet Finance Committee was completely nebulous: as a colleague later wrote, 'it looked as if his main function was to be indirect guidance and co-ordination rather than the vigorous mixture of leadership and slave-driving by which he had made his reputation.'[100] His difficulties were compounded because the Cabinet Finance Committee, with the same decision that made him Head of the Civil Service and gave him power in relation to senior appointments in all departments, tied his hands by giving the new Treasury controllerships to Bradbury's nominees. Fisher was consequently prevented from selecting his principal lieutenants in his new department, instead inheriting three experienced Treasury men each of whom expected to be treated as an independent potentate.

He later wrote of the restructured department he inherited that

> this odd organisation if allowed to proceed to its logical conclusion could only have led to a complete disintegration of the Treasury. From the first, therefore, I said that the personnel must be regarded as Treasury officials and liable to serve at any time in any of the three 'departments', and that for promotion purposes the Treasury, and not the 'departments', must be the field of choice. I further said that the old Treasury organisation by Divisions with consecutive numbers must continue and must span the three 'Departments', instead of each 'Department' having a 1st Division, a 2nd Division and so on of its own. Other steps of one kind or another have also been taken from time to time to ward off the danger; and more and more it has been brought home that these so-called 'Departments' are nothing more than a rather pompous and cumbrous — though by no means complete — method of describing the principal functions of the Departmental Treasury.[101]

Although he made it perfectly clear from the start that he was ultimately in charge of everything that the Treasury did, the existence of the controllerships may have limited Fisher's impact on areas of policy and administration, particularly finance, where he had little previous experience. It is hardly a coincidence that two of the three controllers chosen by Bradbury left fairly quickly. Sir Malcolm Ramsay was made Comptroller and Auditor General in 1921. He was replaced by his deputy Russell Scott, a long-time ally and friend of Fisher's whom he had brought over from the Admiralty.[102] Blackett left to go to India in 1922, and was succeeded by Otto Niemeyer, another Treasury financial specialist. Although Niemeyer was given a free hand, and found the job of 'Controller of Finance … as interesting … as any in Europe', he left the Treasury in mid-career. He 'could not refuse' an offer to move to the Bank of England in 1927 though 'I shall be sorry to leave H.M. Treasury'. Barstow, the Controller of Supply Services who was rather too wedded to pre-war Treasury ways for Fisher's taste, retired in the same year.[103] Fisher then brought in the Chairman of the Inland Revenue, Sir Richard Hopkins, to become

Controller both of Finance and of Supply Services, and, when Russell Scott left the Treasury to become permanent head of the Home Office in 1932, the title of 'Controller' was abolished altogether. Hopkins became Second Secretary responsible for Finance and Supply Services, and Establishments was put under the control of a senior Under Secretary.

A minor detail of the Treasury reorganization also caused some difficulty. Although Fisher recalled that when he was offered the Treasury job 'it was specifically stated in response to a specific enquiry by me that the post being offered was a sole, and not a joint, secretaryship', Bradbury in fact remained technically a Permanent Secretary to the Treasury for three years.[104] He was paid his Treasury salary in order to protect his pension rights, on condition that he returned it in full as it was received. The matter only came to Fisher's notice in 1922, when Bradbury complained that the Inland Revenue had sought 'to exact an actual payment of super tax' on this 'non-existent source of income'. The discovery that Bradbury was formally still a colleague who might seek to return to the Treasury clearly annoyed Fisher, but the matter was settled satisfactorily when it was agreed that Bradbury should be paid a yearly allowance in compensation for abolition of his post as from 1 July 1922.[105]

Fisher's appointment came as a complete surprise and as something of a blow to the Treasury. His reputation was well known, but no one in the Treasury had anticipated that an outsider would be brought in to head it, especially a man so young and comparatively junior from a department which the Treasury had long regarded with disdain. Despite wartime expansion, the Treasury remained extremely conservative and stuffy department. Sir Robert Fraser recalled that when he joined it from Oxford in 1914, there were rigid social and hierarchical divisions between the various grades of staff, and business was conducted with great formality.[106].

Fisher was not a man to worry about upsetting departmental expectations or offending Treasury etiquette. He had a dramatic impact on the Treasury's methods of doing business, introducing 'the era of bad language and Christian names.'[107] Over time, he transferred out a number of men whom he felt were too 'Treasury minded', replacing them with officials who could bring the perspective of spending departments to the conduct of Treasury business.[108] For the same reason he eventually ended the system whereby the Treasury took raw recruits as assistant principals from the civil service examinations, insisting instead that anyone coming should have some years' experience of work in another department. He placed a premium on informality, and on breaking down class barriers. More than one Treasury man got into Fisher's bad books not for inefficiency but for being stand-offish or for not participating in Treasury socials. He made a point of getting to know new recruits and of keeping in touch with them, sometimes having them in for drinks at lunchtime if things were quiet and, even when under great pressure in the late 1930s, he was extremely accessible to junior staff.[109]

Some of the changes made in his first years were less successful than others. The number of administrative posts in the Treasury was increased substantially during his first two years, from sixty five to about ninety, almost three times the pre-war total. Not all the new faces were a success, and some were eventually shipped out. In addition, a number of specialized posts were created to provide expert advice on aspects of staff organization. In 1920 Dame Maud Lawrence became the first woman to be appointed to an administrative rank in the Treasury when she was made the first Director of Women's Establishments, a post which survived retrenchment although its first incumbent was notoriously underemployed. A small section established to study the working methods of departments and to encourage them to make use of modern office machinery was also created, which again had little impact.[110]

The Treasury suffered in common with the rest of Whitehall from post-war cut-backs, and it lost a number of posts. The consequence was that for many years after 1921 promotion prospects were very poor for the more junior administrative staff. The case of Edward Bridges is illustrative. He joined the Treasury in 1919 and was promoted to principal a year later when the department was reorganized. He was quickly recognized as outstandingly able and was given various signs of favour including the secretaryship of three royal commissions, yet he did not move up a rank for a further fourteen years. There was a modest expansion in the number of posts in the early 1930s, and this facilitated a number of long overdue promotions. Despite these problems the major changes in Treasury organization and especially in attitude which Fisher imposed bore fruit in the way that the Treasury approached its

tasks, although in an era of retrenchment spending departments still found the department too inclined to say no.

Ministerial support was of great importance to Fisher in his
first years at the Treasury. Both the Coalition leaders already
knew him well and thought very highly of him: the Prime
Minister's private secretary wrote that 'Lloyd George had great
confidence in him, and I think was responsible for bringing
him to the Treasury. Bonar Law had confidence in him, and so
did Stanley Baldwin. I know. I served them all.'[111] However,
they had little interest in the long term problems which he
faced. What they wanted was quick savings, as the Chancellor
made clear within a few weeks' of Fisher's appointment: 'my
new chief Warren Fisher is working admirably, the reorganisation is justifying itself already, & the team-work is admirable
... Give me three years more & short of unforeseen
catastrophes in Europe or Asia we will have our finances in a
thoroughly sound position.'[112]

Notes

1. Entries on Fisher's birth and marriage certificates.
2. Interview with Sir Thomas and Lady Padmore, 14 Jan. 1980.
3. Information from Mr Robin Warren Fisher and from Mrs Annette Pollock (daughter of Fisher's son Captain Norman Fisher RN).
4. Fisher to Zimmern, 20 July and 5 Sept. 1902, MS Zimmern 10.
5. Information from R.W. Fisher.
6. Fro   me by Mr F.R. Wylie. Information from Mr Wylie, derived from issues of *The Draconian*.
7. From an obituary in *The Draconian*, Christmas 1948, supplied by Mr Wylie.
8. Information from R.W. Fisher.
9. Information from Mr Wylie, as in note 6 above.
10. ibid.
11. Toye, *For what we have received*, pp. 21, 23.
12. *The Wykehamist* vii (1896), p. 267.
13. ibid, p. 396. Raymond Asquith, who was killed during the First World War, was the brilliant son of H.H. Asquith. A.E. Zimmern, later Sir Alfred, became Professor of International Relations at Oxford.
14. *The Wykehamist*, 10 Nov. 1948; Fisher to Zimmern, 20 July 1902, MS Zimmern 10.
15. Hamilton, 'Sir Warren Fisher', p. 4.
16. Fisher to Zimmern, 20 July 1902, MS Zimmern 10.
17. ibid., 12 Sept. 1902.
18. ibid., 23 Aug., 12 Sept., and 27 Dec. 1902.
19. ibid., 23 Aug. 1902.
20. ibid., 20 July 1902. Fisher reversed his opinions of Oxford and London in later life, but he retained some links. He chaired a committee to fix the level of financial contributions from the colleges to the university in 1930. He was elected an Honorary Fellow of his own college, Hertford, in 1933, and received an honorary D.C.L. in the same year.
He acquired another honorary doctorate in 1937, when he was conferred with a D.Sc. by the University of Reading.
21. Civil Service Commission, *Annual Report* (1903), pp. 98–9. Sir Arthur Dixon became a senior official in the Home Office. See p. 193 for Fisher's attack on him in 1932. Sir Edward Harding and Sir Findlater Stewart became permanent heads of the Dominions Office and the India Office respectively.
22. *The Wykehamist*, 10 Nov. 1948.
23. Interview with Sir Robert Fraser. Sir Robert, a Treasury official from 1914 to 1939, was a distinguished tennis player himself.
24. Fisher to Adrian Boult, 10 Sept. 1946, BBC Archives, file marked 'Maddison, Margaret'.
25. From the text of an appreciation by Fisher of Sir Robert Johnson, Apr. 1938, in *The Draconian*, provided by Mr F.R. Wylie.
26. Text of an obituary of Fisher by W.J. Brown in *Red Tape*, Nov. 1948, Warren Fisher papers.

27. Bridge, *Permission*, p. 125.

28. Sturgis diary, 15 July 1920, PRO30/59/1; *The Wykehamist*, 10 Nov. 1948.

29. Fisher to Chamberlain, 18 June 1936, Chamberlain papers, NC 7/11/29/20; Fisher to Chatfield, 12 Nov. 1934, Chatfield papers, 3/2/25.

30. Information from R.W. Fisher.

31. Bridge, *Permission*, p. 129; Clementine to Winston Churchill, 28 Oct. 1927 in Gilbert, *Churchill Companion*, p. 1073.

32. Interviews and correspondence with former Treasury officials; information from R.W. Fisher. MacDermott, *The Eden Legacy*, p. 43, confuses the circumstances of Johnson's death with Fisher's own.

33. Fisher to Zimmern, 7 Sept. 1905, MS Zimmern 11. This is the first document discovered which bears the very distinctive flowing style of handwriting always associated with him. His undergraduate writing was square and more spikey.

It is curious that Fisher and the Cabinet Secretary Sir Maurice Hankey, the twin pillars of Whitehall between the wars, should each have had such distinctive styles. Hankey's is also instantly recognizable: it is like something that a ten-year-old schoolboy might produce.

34. Information from R.W. Fisher. In December 1987 Mr Fisher found correspondence from the 1920s and 1930s between his parents which he kindly gave the author sight of. The letters dealt with money and with other family matters.

35. Private information.

36. *Morning Post*, 24 Feb. 1926. For the attack on Fisher's position, see pp. 150–3 below. Lady Fisher lived to the age of 88, which suggests that her belief in 'the cure' was well founded.

37. *The Times*, 6 Oct. 1953. The couple were convicted of defrauding Lady Fisher of £1,400 in cash, shares, and furs. R.W. Fisher, who called in the police, says that far more had in fact been taken, including some of his property. The loss was very serious for Lady Fisher, whom Fisher had expressly excluded from his will. A copy of the will, dated 25 March 1944, was consulted in the General Register Office.

38. Bridge, *Permission*, pp. 128–9.

39. Private information from three former non-Treasury officials; interview with Sir Robert Fraser.

40. Fisher memoir, Chapter 8, Part 1, Warren Fisher papers; Bridges, *The Treasury*, p. 170; entries in the Treasury register of correspondence, 11 Sept. 1907 and 22 Apr. 1908, PRO, T2/440 and 444. The file containing the correspondence was not found.

According to Waineright, *Winchester College*, p. 526, Fisher studied for the Bar, becoming a student at the Inner Temple in 1904. No other reference to this aspect of his career has been found. The Inner Temple states that due to bombing in World War II there are no surviving admissions records for that period.

41. Royal commission on the civil service 1912, minutes of evidence, *Parliamentary Papers (PP)* (1912), xv, 166.

42. *The Times*, 2 Apr. 1945, p. 5.

43. Harris, *Not So Humdrum*, pp. 108–9. R.W. Harris was an Inland Revenue official.

44. Information from R.W. Fisher; Fisher memoir, Chapter 8, Part 1; as in note 41 above.

45. Fisher memoir, Chapter 11, Part 1.

46. ibid.; Harris, *Not So Humdrum*, p. 155; Braithwaite, *Ambulance Waggon*, passim.

47. With the exception of Salter, these all reached the rank of permanent secretary or its equivalent. Gowers also wrote *Plain Words*. Anderson became an extremely effective minister in Churchill's War Cabinet in 1940. Salter became Professor of Political Thought at Oxford, and was subsequently a junior minister in the 1940s.

48. Fisher memoir, Chapter 11, Part 1.

49. ibid.; Harris, *Not So Humdrum*, pp. 170–1.

50. Braithwaite to his wife, Aug. 1912, in *Ambulance Waggon*, p. 293. Braithwaite diary, entry headed 1913, but dated at end 31 Dec. 1912, Braithwaite papers, 1(a). Braithwaite was, like Fisher, a Wykehamist.

51. Masterman, *CFG Masterman*, p. 236.

52. Grigg, *Prejudice and Judgement*, pp. 50–1; Harris, *Not So Humdrum*, p. 147.

53. Salter, *Memoirs*, p. 71.

54. Fisher memoir, Chapter 12, Part 1.

55. Information from R.W. Fisher. Fisher's appointment as deputy chairman was not universally popular. The Inland Revenue man who expected to get the job through seniority, an Irishman named Crowly, was 'disturbed' by what happened. O'Broin, *No Man's Man*, p. 31. A.J. Sylvester to the author, 17 Mar. 1980.

56. Fisher memoir, Chapter 14, Part 1.

57. Quoted in Hamilton, 'Warren Fisher', p. 6.

58. Fisher to Law, 16 July 1918, PRO, T172/766.

59. Sir Alexander Johnston to the author, 7 May 1981. Sir Alexander was chairman from 1958 to 1968.

60. Lord Houghton to the author, 4 Feb. 1982.

61. Sir Edward Playfair to the author, 27 Apr. 1981.

62. Grigg, *Prejudice and Judgement*, p. 51.

63. Royal commission on the income tax, 1919, minutes of evidence, *PP* (1919) xxii, 286–7. The allegation — if it existed, about which members of the commission disagreed — was that Revenue officials' advice on taxation might be coloured by its impact on their own pockets. The witness involved was Richard Hopkins, afterwards Fisher's no.2 at the Treasury, ultimately Head of the Civil Service himself and a man of the utmost rectitude.

64. Lord Houghton to the author, as in note 60 above.

65. From the typescript of an original document found among Lady Fisher's papers, in the possession of R.W. Fisher. From Harris, *Not So Humdrum*, pp. 170–1, it seems likely that Harris was the composer of the song.

As secretary to the Treasury, Fisher signed banknotes until 1928 when the responsibility was transferred to the chief cashier of the Bank of England. Treasury notes had become known as Bradburys following their introduction in 1914 because they bore the signature of Sir John Bradbury as joint head of the Treasury. According to Arthur Marshall,

Times Literary Supplement, 16 Oct. 1981, p. 1195, one of the many millionaires in the stories of P.G. Wodehouse was a Mr Bradbury Fisher.

66. Royal commission on the Civil Service 1912–14, report, *PP* (1914), xvi, 20.

67. Fisher's evidence to the Gladstone committee, 17 July and 3 Nov. 1918, T1 12665/50322.

68. Final report of the committee on staffs, *PP* (1919), xi, 222.

69. Ramsay to Bradbury, 12 Mar. 1919, T1 12306/14598. This committee does not seem to have been active after October 1919.

70. Ramsay to Fisher, 3 Apr., and Fisher to Ramsay, 4 Apr. 1919, PRO, T1 12306/14598.

71. Parris, *Staff Relations*, p. 84; PRO, T163 12/7/G567; interview with Sir Robert Fraser. Sir Robert was secretary of the official side on the Ramsay Bunning committee.

72. Minutes of the Bradbury committee, 14 Jan. 1919, T1 12137/6667.

73. Sir Edward Troup's evidence to the Haldane committee, 10 Dec. 1917, Passfield papers xii, fols. 699–706.

74. Johnson, *Land Fit for Heroes*, p. 43; Ministry of Reconstruction, report of the machinery of government committee, *PP* (1918), xii, p. 20.

75. Morant to Mrs Webb, 6 Dec. 1918, Passfield papers xii, fols. 1071–81.

76. Bridges, 'Haldane and the machinery of government', p. 262.

77. Interview with Sir Robert Fraser. Sir Robert was secretary of the Gladstone committee.

78. Tribute to Haldane by Fisher, sent to Tom Jones, 5 Feb. 1929, Thomas Jones papers, O/3/10; Fisher memoir, Chapter 10, Part 1, and Chapter 13.

79. Johnson, *Land Fit for HEroes*, p. 43.

80. Draft report and report of the principal clerks' committee, Aug. 1916, T1 12226/44454. On the Treasury's wartime performance, see K.M. Burk, 'The Treasury: from impotence to power', in Burk (ed.) *War and the State*, pp. 84–107.

81. Chalmers' evidence to the Haldane committee, 3 May 1918, Passfield Papers xii, fols. 1015–19; Guillemard to Heath, 23 May, and Heath to Murray, 26 Jan. 1918, PRO, T1 12308/15674. Despite his reservations, Guillemard chaired a sub-committee to devise a 'model constitution' for departmental Whitley councils. T1 12307/36345.

82. Information from R.W. Fisher; minutes of Gladstone committee, 17 Dec. 1918, PRO, T1 12265/50322; Asquith to Sir Edward Hamilton, 27 Sept. 1907, Hamilton papers, Add MSS 48614. Heath in 1914 had married Maysie Fisher's sister Ada Thomas.

83. Minutes of Gladstone committee, as in note 82 above.

84. ibid.

85. Minutes of Cabinet Finance Committee, 20 Aug. 1919, PRO, CAB 27/71.

86. Bonar Law to Lloyd George, 21 Aug. 1919, Bonar Law papers, 101/3/136.

87. Treasury minute, 4 Sept. 1919, PRO, T199/50b.

88. Treasury circular, 15 Sept. 1919, ibid.

89. See e.g. Grigg, *Prejudice and Judgement*, p. 51, and Fisher's obituary in *The Times*, 27 Sept. 1948.

90. Hamilton, 'Sir Warren Fisher', pp. 10–11.

91. Fisher to Neville Chamberlain, Baldwin and MacDonald, 25 Nov. 1931, T199/50b.

92. Hamilton, 'Sir Warren Fisher', pp. 10–11. See also Chapman and Greenaway, *Dynamics of Administrative Reform*, p. 104, and Burk, 'The Treasury: from impotence to power', pp. 98–9, as in note 80 above.

93. Undated MS notes by Milner, [1918?], Bodleian library, Milner MS dep. 125.

94. Bradbury to Austen Chamberlain, 19 Aug. 1919, Chamberlain papers, AC 24/1/21.

95. See note 80 above.

96. See notes 90 and 91 above. All the former Treasury people interviewed confirmed this.

97. See Bradbury to Austen Chamberlain, 17 Mar. 1922, where he discusses his pension rights and uses the phrase 'if I had remained on as sole Permanent Secretary at the rate you were good enough to offer me in 1919.' PRO, T162 56/E4508.

98. Sir James Dunnett to the author, 16 Oct. 1981. Despite his financial acumen as an official, Bradbury apparently proved a poor judge of investments.

99. Interview with Sir Robert Fraser. Heath retained his Treasury salary. Contrary to what was generally believed in the Treasury, Fisher was not responsible for pushing out Heath. The decision was taken before Fisher was appointed.

100. Grigg, *Prejudice and Judgement*, p. 51.

101. Fisher to Neville Chamberlain, Baldwin and MacDonald, 25 Nov. 1931, T199/50b.

102. Information from Robin Warren Fisher; interview with Sir Robert Fraser.

103. Niemeyer to Blackett, 26 July 1926 and 9 Apr. 1927, Blackett papers, MSS Eur E 397/29; interview with Sir Robert Fraser.

104. Fisher to Bradbury, 2 June 1922, T162 56/E4508.

105. Bradbury to Chamberlain, 17 Mar. 1922, T162 56/E4508; Bradbury's pension papers, T164 26/P20298.

106. Interview with Sir Robert Fraser.

107. Lord Houghton to the author, 4 Feb 1982, quoting Sir James Grigg to him.

108. Interviews with Sir Robert Fraser and Sir John Winnifrith.

109. Interviews with Sir Edward Playfair, Sir John Winnifrith, Sir Thomas and Lady Padmore, Sir George Dunnett, and Lord Trend.

110. Interview with Sir John Winnifrith; T199/112. See Sir Herbert Creedy (War Office) to Scott, 12 Jan. 1928, paying tribute to the help given by the Treasury's office machine experts, T199/32.

111. A.J. Sylvester to the author, 17 Mar. 1980.

112. Austen Chamberlain to his wife, 26 Oct. 1919, Chamberlain papers, AC5/1/141. I am grateful to Dr Keith Jeffery for this reference.

2

Civil service reorganization, 1919–22

I

The first three years of Fisher's time at the Treasury were decisive for him personally and for the civil service. Establishments policy was made broadly uniform throughout the service, a new doctrine of financial accountability was devised and imposed, and he developed a role as an adviser on every sort of question to the Prime Minister.

On 3 September 1919 Fisher gave his general views on the financial situation facing the government to Lloyd George. He touched on a wide range of matters, from the need to charge the full cost of any services 'in so far as the state acts as a trader or common carrier or intervenes at all in relation to the public as consumers', to 'the mission of Great Britain in the world. I cannot help feeling that we may overdo the part of fairy godmother. It is with diffidence that I express these crude opinions, but it seems to me that the country can only act as a Don Quixote if it is prepared for bankruptcy.' Britain 'need not lose the advantage of the naval and military experience gained in the War, but to ensure this and to keep that experience up to date should be possible for a reasonable outlay ... instead of being bled white, we should be able to re-establish our reserve of wealth to be available if trouble hereafter recurs.' Moreover, he said, a cut in the size of the civil service and in the number of departments was vital, although 'the big money is ... in policy. The margin of difference between a government machine which is perfectly adjusted for the execution of that policy' and one 'which is too large (because of bad organisation and management or of self-importance) is — in terms of cash — insignificant relatively to the huge figures of a modern Budget.' The principal problem caused by 'swollen Civil Service establishments' was 'a moral one.' Action was also needed to introduce 'permanent improvements and safeguards' in the financial management of the Service departments, where 'the warrior has hitherto been too easily able to sweep aside any civilian control in finance.' His time on the Bradbury committee on staffs had convinced him that 'the explanation of waste and muddle in departments (so far as policy was not responsible) was nothing more subtle than the absence of the right man in charge, with time to think and power to act.' He thought departmental ministers poor judges of who to install 'in the top posts.' In conclusion, he told Lloyd George that the departmental Treasury

> has always been undermanned and hopelessly overworked. Delay and insufficiency of time to think things out or to get a conspectus have resulted, and the office has therefore been prejudiced in the discharge of its business. At the same time Ministers of other departments have been able to shortcircuit the Treasury officials; who — impotent on that account to resist unreasonable demands alike on major issues and in the staff matters advocated by those ministers — have perforce tended to direct their critical activities into somewhat meticulous channels. With ministerial support and adequate staffing I think the Treasury officials will have (to the extent admitted by policy) greater opportunities for effective control.[1]

Fisher got the support which he needed. Events were to show that the Coalition leaders were prepared to back the major changes which he wanted to introduce in civil service organization.

The Cabinet Finance Committee which agreed to appoint Fisher also directed the Chancellor to convene 'a Council of the chief financial officers of the public departments under the chairmanship of the Financial Secretary to the Treasury to serve as a clearing house for information and discussion of financial reform and administrative economies.'[2] This body, known as the Baldwin Council after its chairman, Stanley Baldwin, produced a report which, with Fisher's vital amendments, laid the basis of the system of financial accountability which still operates in the civil service.

What concerned the council was the standing of financial officers within departments. Although these were normally the accounting officers, responsible to Parliament under ministers for regularity and economy, 'in many Civil Departments the Principal Financial Officer ranks only as one of a number of Assistant Secretaries.' The council recommended that such officers be appointed or removed only with the consent of the Chancellor and Prime Minister. They emphasised that 'the relation' between the Chief Financial Officer and his permanent head 'requires very careful adjustment', as 'we think it most undesirable to encourage the idea that the functions of the permanent head are divorced from or antagonistic to finance, or that the existence of a separate Financial Department in any way relieves other officers of their duty to be economical.'[3]

Fisher was 'in agreement with the general tenor of the report', but suggested a number of changes. These were included in the Cabinet Finance Committee's acceptance of the Baldwin Council's findings, subject to four amendments:

> (a) that the permanent civilian head of the Service departments should be charged with the primary responsibility for finance and that he should have the status of a full member of the Council or Board:
>
> (b) that the Principal Financial Officer in civil departments should continue to be definitely subordinate to the permanent head of the department who is primarily responsible, under ministers, for economy:
>
> (c) that in all matters of staff organisation and machinery the officer held responsible for economy by the permanent head should be the Principal Establishment Officer:
>
> (d) that the appointment, or removal, of permanent heads of departments, their deputies, principal financial officers and principal establishment officers should be confirmed by the Prime Minister before taking effect.[4]

Fisher thought (a) to be necessary because in service departments 'the civilian is subsidiary and subordinate except in regard to finance', so it was essential that he exercised himself in the one realm of significant activity open to him. As regards (b), it was vital to avoid the position where the 'sense of responsibility in the Permanent Secretary' for economy in the policy and administration of his department might be jeopardized by 'the creation of an *imperium in imperio* represented by a

finance officer more or less independent of the Permanent
Secretary.' While it was necessary to improve the standing of
financial officers in departments, this should not be so done as
to 'undermine the position of the Permanent Secretary in his
own Department and thereby weaken or deter the official
personality; which can be the most potent of all in securing
economy.' As regards (c), the importance which he placed on
establishment work has already been illustrated. Unless departments shared a common policy in questions of pay, grading, recruitment and discipline for their staffs, the unified civil
service which he sought would remain a pipe-dream. As regards (d), he held that all these posts were of sufficient importance to warrant the Prime Minister's attention: 'Efficiency and
economy in the management of government departments as
of any other business turn on the top men, and too often as a
result of inexperience or misplaced kindness the wrong men
are appointed.'[5] He was firmly against the convention that
senior posts were normally filled from within the department
concerned, believing that the civil service as a whole offered a
far wider field of candidates, and that the best way to stimulate
departments and to lessen their isolation frequently was to
import new blood.

The decision of the Cabinet Finance Committee on the
report of the Baldwin Council was circulated to ministers on
30 January 1920 together with the text of the report and
Fisher's comments on it. A covering note by the Cabinet
Secretary, Sir Maurice Hankey, stated that 'the Prime Minister
proposes that the Cabinet shall take note of the minutes at an
early meeting, if no objections are raised.'[6] On 11 February the
Cabinet duly did so; there was no discussion of the question,
and it is obvious that its significance was not recognized. A
month later appeared the controversial Treasury circular entitled 'Control of Expenditure', which embodied the decision
so casually accepted by the Cabinet and gave two supplemen-
tary instructions: all departments should consult their financial
sections 'at an early stage' when 'questions involving finance'
were being considered, and whenever an Accounting Officer
'has, by written directions of the head of his department, made
a payment to which he sees objection, the Treasury and the
Comptroller and Auditor General should be informed.'[7] As will
be seen, the circular provoked some protest from two ministers, Churchill and Curzon, but they were very late in their

objections, having had ample time to consider the issue before the Cabinet 'took note' of the Finance Committee's decision.[8] Doubtless it was hoped that the decision would go through with the minimum of fuss, but even had it been challenged in the Cabinet it is most unlikely that it would have been changed. It had the backing of the two Coalition leaders, both former Chancellors, whose disquiet at the level of government spending had repeatedly been stressed to their colleagues. The Cabinet had itself agreed in December 1919 to the issue of an instruction by the Cabinet Secretary to all departments, in connection with what Fisher called 'the endeavour to restore that very elusive thing called "Treasury control"', the object of which

> was to prevent the short circuiting or jumping of the Chancellor and his machine by departmental Ministers. These gymnastic feats had been, & were being, successfully performed by shooting into the Cabinet without the slightest notice memoranda on all sorts of topics involving expenditure without any previous consultation with the Treasury, Ministers and officials alike.[9]

In December 1919 it was decided to attach a Treasury official to the Cabinet secretariat to make sure that no financial proposals were slipped through without Treasury knowledge.[10] Over the years the requirement of prior consultation in questions involving expenditure became, as it was intended to become, a hard and fast rule of procedure for all matters brought before the Cabinet by ministers.

By the spring of 1920, the steps necessary to the restoration of the Treasury's authority in the new circumstances of the post-war world had been taken. But one aspect of the issue which had exercised the Baldwin Council, the fostering of economy in the planning and administration of policy by departments, had yet to be fully worked out. Fisher twice discussed the question in 1920 with the Committee of Public Accounts (PAC) of the House of Commons. On the first occasion, in April, he explained that: 'I am very anxious indeed that it should not be open to any permanent head ... to say "please, Sir, it wasn't me." That is what I am anxious for. Pin it on him in the last resort and you have got him as an ally for economy.'[11]

It was not until November that he put forward 'my own feeling ... that the permanent head should be the departmental Accounting Officer', a definite development of his position as compared with his earlier statement that 'I do not attach any importance' to whether the permanent head or some other official acted as Accounting Officer, provided that the ultimate responsibility for economy lay with the permanent head in every department.[12] He suggested that he should convene a meeting of the heads of the big civilian departments, where the accounting officers remained subordinate officials, in order to 'get them together and expound what we are after, then send out a circular.' Fisher sought to persuade the PAC that the principle already accepted by the Cabinet for the Service departments — that the permanent head should be the Accounting Officer — should be applied to all large departments: 'What the Treasury wants to get into them is the feeling that they are as much trustees for the taxpayer as the Treasury is merely the co-ordinating and controlling centre, and you want them both after the same object.' He believed that 'we can provide teamwork amongst ourselves, but we have not got it yet, and that is what we want to get, and I believe that will make for an economy.'[13]

These remarks provoked an extraordinary outburst from the Assistant Comptroller and Auditor General, R.F. Wilkins. Wilkins, who was pedantic to the point of eccentricity, had been moved from the Treasury shortly after Fisher's arrival. He defended the traditional view that the best people to act as accounting officers were 'the trained expert' financial officers, who 'are persons with a long and thorough technical training, they are versed in the history of finance' ; the permanent heads, on the other hand, could only provide 'amateur evidence and it will not be the same kind of thing at all.' He argued that it would be 'a retrograde step to lower' the standing of financial officers in departments 'by ceasing to nominate them as accounting officers', and pointed out that a similar conclusion of the Baldwin Council had been omitted from the Treasury circular on 'Control of Expenditure.' He 'thought it right ... to let the committee hear the other side of the case' to ensure that 'the pros and cons have been very carefully weighed', and suggested that the views of some more officials should be sought on the merits or otherwise of what Fisher proposed.

Fisher protested that this would be giving civil servants 'the opportunity of publicly criticising the object of a Treasury circular. I am not a person to stand on any dignity — I have got none to stand on — but you cannot do business on these lines.' He went on to say that the circular embodied 'a government decision' whereupon Wilkins interjected that 'the grading down of the financial officers is not a government decision ... The circular says nothing about the appointment of the permanent heads of departments to be accounting officers.' Fisher replied that 'the general conception, to which this is considered to be one means of giving effect, is a government decision', to which Wilkins retorted that 'it is hardly fair to say that a general conception is a government decision.'[14]

While the anti-waste sentiments of MPs had ensured some lively debate on government expenditure — the Minister of Transport complained of the Commons estimates committee that 'we are treated as criminals' — this direct and public clash between two senior officials was most unusual.[15] Wilkins was in an awkward position, since his own superior clearly favoured Fisher's view on the standing of accounting officers. There was some literal justification for the points which he raised. The circular had in fact followed very closely the proposals accepted by the Cabinet in February 1920. Yet at that time, as shown by his evidence to the PAC in April, Fisher had not yet come to believe that it was necessary to make permanent heads the accounting officers for their departments. It followed that the circular could scarcely be said to embody a principle of administration which had not been devised when the circular was issued. Whether intentionally or not, Wilkins implied that Fisher had misled the PAC, and had claimed an authority from government which he did not possess. The committee may have been influenced by Wilkins' words, since they declined to endorse the application of the new arrangement to the large civil departments without 'further consideration', as 'the work is so heavy that it will be extremely difficult for the permanent head to be in any true sense specifically responsible for finance.'[16] Wilkins continued to be a minor irritant. His post of Assistant Comptroller and Auditor General was abolished in 1922 as an economy measure. Fisher then tried to make him Librarian of the House of Lords but the plan fell through, with the result that the Treasury had to take him back. In 1924 a suitable niche was finally found for him as Assistant Paymaster General.[17]

After his second appearance before the PAC, Fisher wrote to the heads of those large departments in which the committee had said that the arrangement proposed by him should not apply. He raised 'two very important questions' involved in the 'problem of controlling expenditure': were departmental heads to be regarded as trustees for the taxpayer in co-operation with the Treasury, or is this the exclusive function of the Treasury? and ... who are to be the *de facto* permanent heads of departments?' There followed an exceptionally lucid discussion of the issue.[18] He knew the value of openness and informality in trying to convert an audience, and more than once he used the device of what he termed 'a flamboyant letter to colleagues ("I", "I", "I")' to good effect.[19]

His letter on accounting officers, which was submitted as evidence to the PAC, had been carefully drafted over a number of weeks. The response was good: the Comptroller and Auditor General thought it admirable, as 'the most important function of the "Accounting Officer" nowadays is the striving after economy. You want the biggest gun for the purpose and that is the permanent head of the department', whereas 'the present type of man that fills the post in the offices you are dealing with does not with one or two exceptions carry sufficient weight.' Chrystal of the Ministry of Pensions told Fisher that 'I entirely agree with the views you express.' The head of the Ministry of Transport felt that the problem had arisen because the PAC had confused 'two allied and distinct questions — that of economy and that of accounting. They have assumed that the "regularity man" must also be the "economy man" ....' He felt that the permanent head should carry the ultimate responsibility for economy, but that as a matter of convenience the accounting officer should remain a subordinate official. Only Selby-Bigge, Permanent Secretary since 1911 of the Board of Education, gave short shrift to Fisher's exhortations:

> I think you are wrong in suggesting ... that the power exercised by the Accounting Officer in respect of regularity is relatively unimportant ....
>
> Personally I very much dislike pretending to be responsible for matters of which I know and can know nothing ...

53

I am rather puzzled by your references to "team work", and Heads of Departments working as a team .... If you mean that we ought all to be inspired by the same desire for economical and efficient administration, I cordially agree. But I do not understand how the relation to each other of the heads of different departments can be compared with that of a factory who co-operate in turning out a complex product. Except where an administrative question affects two departments, we know nothing and can know nothing of each other's methods of administration.[20]

Following a meeting called by Fisher to discuss the question, Selby-Bigge remained convinced that 'the present arrangement is the best one in the interests of the public service', but he doubted whether Fisher would 'mention my views to the PAC or ... give me an opportunity of stating them.'[21] He was right: although Fisher's letter was submitted as evidence, the question was not discussed again by the PAC. In 1925 its chairman was persuaded to say formally that 'the practice which obtains in the fighting services should be extended, as opportunity offers, also to the larger civil departments.' The Comptroller and Auditor General remarked to Fisher that 'I am extremely glad that the committee have now adopted the view which you and I have throughout held and the road is now, I trust, perfectly clear.'[22]

It is not easy to say what practical effect the new doctrine had on the civil service. However, in the 1960s one of Fisher's most eminent successors wrote that 'this arrangement, which was so hotly contested in the early 1920s, now corresponds to something quite fundamental in our way of thinking', that 'responsibility for policy and for the financial conclusions of that policy go hand in hand.'[23] Fisher himself attached the greatest importance to it, and was prepared to wait years for it to be accepted. The doctrine was manifestly intended to improve the civil service in the long term, not to produce immediate savings by bringing unruly departments to heel. Although the Treasury was involved in continuous tussles with departments to produce savings on their estimates, and on expenditure of money already voted by Parliament — a process graphically described by one Treasury official as 'scraping the butter back out of the dog's mouth' — the pressure for cuts in expenditure while recurrent was essentially transient, a response to changes in the economic climate rather than the product of a fixed idea that government should spend as little as possible.[24]

What is most striking is that Fisher was able, at a time when his department was required to enforce retrenchment, to see beyond the considerable day to day problems facing him and to conduct a major campaign for the acceptance of a doctrine which he knew would need years to take root, and which represented a departure from the Treasury's tried and trusted methods of browbeating departments into enforced economies.

II

Shortly after Fisher's appointment, the Treasury informed the Cabinet Finance Committee that, excluding industrial civil servants and Post Office workers, the numbers employed by government departments had increased by approximately 120,000, from 73,000 to 193,000, between 1914 and 1919. Of this increase, about 72,000 belonged to the six departments which had been created during the war. This left 48,000 in the older departments, of which nearly 25,000 were in the Admiralty and the War Office. The Treasury took the view that departments had not taken 'sufficiently seriously' repeated requests to reduce staffs as much and as quickly as possible, and singled out certain ministries for particular criticism: the War Office and Air Ministry had too many officials, while 'the Admiralty have actually increased their staff since the Armistice'. That they should in peace require 'a staff greater than sufficed to carry them through the war is prima facie incomprehensible.' Another department criticized was the Ministry of Pensions, although there improvement could be expected as 'a new [Permanent] Secretary and an Establishment Officer and general organiser in whom the Treasury have confidence have recently been appointed.' The Prime Minister was advised to press for a 25 per cent reduction in civil service numbers.[25]

Despite these brave words, it quickly became clear that such cuts were unlikely to be achieved. While all for retrenchment in general, ministers opposed it vigorously when its application to their own departments was attempted. For example, the

Board of Education, after repeated requests to review its staff levels from the Cabinet Finance Committee, replied in February 1920 that, after careful inspection, it had not found a single post which could be scrapped.[26] In 1921, despite post-war rationalization and all the pressure for savings, civil service numbers were only 7 per cent below their 1919 level.[27] The establishments side of the Treasury put forward a number of reasons why costs and numbers had not fallen; the most obvious of these was 'the development of new policies, and the passing of legislation involving new Governmental activity and therefore further staff', from which it followed that 'reductions of staff on a really big scale can result only from important changes in policy.' The obligation to give preferential treatment to ex-servicemen, and 'the imposition of elaborate methods alike in records, statistics and accountancy in order to meet the multifarious demands for information by the House of Commons ... and to ensure against the political criticism to be made out of trifling inconsistencies or inaccuracies' were also mentioned.[28] In January 1922 the Controller of Establishments complained that a Commons committee wanted to know 'how much the Treasury Establishments Department has been able to lop off proposals for new expenditure submitted by Departmental authorities', and warned that

> if we are to present a statement on such lines (however general in terms) I should despair of ever getting the Treasury and the Departments again to work together as a team. Such economy as we are able to secure is due primarily to a growing conviction in the minds of Heads of Departments & Establishment Officers that the Treasury Establishments Department is not out to obstruct but to help. I could not conceive of any better plan for weakening Treasury control over the organisation of the Civil Service than for the Treasury to issue a document parading its own virtues & (by implication) vilifying its partners.[29]

He also argued that 'it is really impossible to give figures to illustrate the result of our activities', and that 'we are just getting Departments to co-operate with us. I am very much afraid of antagonising them by publishing specific figures.'[30]

Such a defensive attitude was understandable. The Establishments Department had been set up with the intention of improving the civil service, and to win the co-operation of departments it had to work by persuasion rather than by coercion. This was at variance with what politicians saw as the pressing need for quick reductions in the cost of government. The regrading of the clerical and executive classes which was undertaken in 1920 and 1921 was a crucial step towards a more unified and efficient civil service, but it did not produce immediate savings.[31] The Treasury's scrutiny of individual departments was equally barren of dramatic cuts.[32] Fisher wanted 'team work between departments', believing that economy could only be secured with the consent of all concerned.[33] Furthermore, he repeatedly made the point that big savings came from changes in policy, not from chipping away at the civil service. He told Lloyd George in 1920 that

> the cost of staff and machinery generally depends on policy which settles the functions to be undertaken by Government. An exact adjustment of the machinery to its work (towards which the Treasury is continually striving) might be equivalent at the outside to 1d in the £ of Income Tax.[34]

A year later, the Treasury concluded that the 10 per cent growth 'in respect of the whole of the pre-War departments' which it noted was largely justified by the expansion of the work of those departments. Nevertheless, it was forced to admit that the result of all its efforts to foster economy and efficiency was 'frankly disappointing: experience had abundantly proved that outside pressure' on departments was insufficient. 'The matter has gone beyond the stage at which it can be left to heads of subordinate departments to argue with outside committees and officers the extent of their functions and the size of the staff which they consider it necessary to employ.' Only 'personal intervention' by ministers could secure further savings.[35] Such intervention was not forthcoming, and the Cabinet instead chose to pursue cuts in the cost of government through the Geddes economy committee, established in August 1921.

In February 1922, this committee issued detailed recommendations for drastic cuts in various areas of government spending. Amongst these were the abolition of five ministries, reductions in the pay of police, teachers, servicemen, and civil servants, and a large cut in expenditure on public health and education. Lloyd George was hardly the man to lead Britain into an era of stable austerity, but he did not want to lose power. The Cabinet ultimately accepted £64 million of the £86 million in savings suggested by the committee. Although over £40 million of these were to be made on the armed services, the Cabinet's decision was regarded mainly as a spectacular reversal of domestic policy, since the Coalition thereby substantially abandoned its committment to post-war reconstruction and social improvement.[36] The effect of the cuts on the civil service, when combined with other substantial reductions in government spending, was considerable: by April 1923 there had been a fall of almost 25 per cent in numbers as compared with 1919.[37]

Although Fisher was able to convince the government that everything possible was being done to improve the civil service, Parliament and the press remained very critical of the size and cost of bureaucracy. Attacks ranged from vague charges that the service was underworked and overpaid to a campaign against 'that most dangerous and unnecessary institution', the Cabinet secretariat.[38] It was seldom difficult to refute specific allegations, but equally it was almost impossible to dispel the general prejudice against officialdom. This was something Fisher found hard to accept. In July 1921 he sent a memorandum to Lloyd George, Austen Chamberlain, and Sir Robert Horne, after a renewed press campaign following the government's acceptance of the recommendations of the Asquith committee on the pay of senior civil servants:

> The animus and ignorance by which this attack is characterised are merely contemptible, and I am only moved to say anything by a very real fear that, if there is no public condemnation of it by the government, the regular Civil Service of future times may gradually cease to be influenced by its great traditions. For with human nature there is always more than a risk that it may tend to adapt itself to the standards which it feels commonly attributed to it.
>
> If a man is frequently treated as a pariah, he needs to have character and self respect in an unusual degree if he is not to be affected detrimentally.

He was particularly bitter about recent parliamentary criticism: 'Trumpeted throughout the land ... is the allegation that the whole regular British Civil Service is idle, incompetent, grasping and fraudulent.' Although the government could rely on the present group of officials, as 'their feeling of cynical contempt at their treatment will not make them untrue to their traditions', the 'coming generations will start and continue on an altogether lower plane of self sacrifice and of native ability.' If 'the Navy or Army were similarly attacked ... there would be no hesitation' in defending them. Yet they 'are not more conscientious, industrious, or efficient than the Civil Service', whose 'officers in controlling positions and grades' were in his experience 'alike in ability and in intelligence ... the superior of the Admiral and the General.' Fisher was not

> for a moment suggesting that the regular Civil Service of this country is perfect or that there are not directions in which it is susceptible of improvement. But for many of its defects it is not responsible, its size is primarily dictated by policy, its over-elaborate methods are the direct outcome of Parliamentary and political requirements ...
>
> My reason for submitting these observations is, as I have already said, to emphasise the danger that continued acquiescence in these series of attacks can in the long run have but one result, namely the deterioration of your regular Civil Service which, however far it may be from perfection, has been, and still is, incomparably the best in the civilized world.[39]

A few days later 'the attention of the Cabinet was drawn to the strong feeling among men in the higher ranks of the Civil Service in regard to the attitude assumed towards them in Parliament and press', remarks which were received 'with expressions of the fullest sympathy' for 'these devoted civil servants.'[40] Despite this, attacks on the civil service continued. Ministers, who shared the sentiments of Westminster as well as of Whitehall, never put up much of a fight for the service as a whole, but they defended their own departments stoutly enough. Fisher's dire warnings were not fulfilled, although the staff side of the National Whitley Council expressed some unease from time to time. Edward Bridges argued in 1928 that 'if the general public wishes to keep civil servants as a stock joke along with mothers-in-law, no amount of speeches will prevent them', a common-sense view which most officials probably shared.[41]

An American civil servant has written that 'the overwhelming weight of empirical evidence supports the ... view that reorganizations do not save money', quoting President Roosevelt as saying in 1936 that: 'We have to get over the notion that the purpose of reorganization is economy .... The reason for reorganization is good management'.[42] This was certainly true of the establishments policy adopted in Whitehall from 1919 on. It is clear from Treasury papers that it was much less difficult to make departments more efficient than to make them smaller. The successful reorganization of clerical and executive grades which took place between 1919 and 1921, principally the result of the work of that remarkably successful innovation the National Whitley Council, did not save much cash. Although it received the blessing of a government bent on quick reductions in expenditure, post-war establishments policy helped produce a better rather than a cheaper government organization.

III

The title and functions of the 'Permanent' or 'Official' Head of the Civil Service have been the subject of some controversy as a result of Fisher's career. In particular, it has been alleged that Fisher was responsible for the title, and that as its holder he claimed an unwarranted authority over the Foreign Office and the foreign service.[43] It has already been shown that neither the title nor the Treasury reorganization which went with it were of his doing, and that both were explicitly approved by the Cabinet Finance Committee, which included the three most senior ministers of the government. The committee furthermore resolved that the Prime Minister, advised by the Head of the Civil Service, should have a veto on senior appointments, and, as has been seen, their conclusion was noted without demur by the full Cabinet.

Fisher in fact developed his role in regard to appointments well beyond the letter of the 1919 decision: he had a major say in the membership of government appointed commissions and committees of inquiry, for example, and his advice was frequently sought on the filling of posts outside the civil service.[44] There was nothing illegitimate about this; it was simply that he was, by virtue of his position and his contacts, in the know about a very wide range of people. As regards the Civil Service, the questions that remain to be answered concerning appointments and decorations involve the advice which he gave, rather than his right to give it. What is of more significance is that he came to believe that as Permanent Secretary to the Treasury and Head of the Civil Service he had duties far wider than those merely of supervising the work of the departmental Treasury and of recommending who in Whitehall got what job or honour.

Fisher would admit of no distinction between the permanent secretaryship to the Treasury and the headship of the civil service; the latter was simply an explicit recognition of what had long been the case: 'The association of the (official) headship of the Civil Service with the Secretaryship to the Treasury has been an admitted fact ever since the Service was organised to meet modern conditions', that is since the middle of the previous century.[45] Historically, this was a reasonable argument, in so far as the Permanent Secretary to the Treasury had long been regarded as the most senior official in the civil service, and had received a larger salary than all other heads of departments.[46] What was more contentious was the theory he advanced in January 1924:

> The Treasury has a dual responsibility in the national administration: (a) it is the central department of government and (b) it is the financial department of government.
>
> The First Lord of the Treasury is the Prime Minister, and as the chief Minister of the Crown he is primarily concerned with function (a) above. He is the ministerial head of the Public Services and his principal official is the permanent Head of the Civil Service (the Permanent Secretary to the Treasury). The First Lord is directly interested in all questions of magnitude, domestic and overseas, in their general and financial bearings. With him rests the final say as to Public Service appointments and Honours, for which purpose the permanent head of the Service is his adviser ...
>
> The Permanent Secretary is the official head of the Treasury and also the Permanent Head of the Civil

Service in which capacity he is the principal official adviser of the Prime Minister.[47]

A number of issues arise from this. First, it was by no means generally accepted that the Treasury was the 'central department of government' except in so far as its financial powers and control over the civil service were concerned. As head of the Treasury and of the civil service Fisher's interests ranged far and wide, but it did not follow that such interests came *ex officio* for all permanent secretaries to the Treasury. While it must be said that no one head of the Treasury performed in precisely the same manner as any other, and that each developed the office in his own way, neither Fisher's immediate predecessors nor his successors had anything like his range of activities. Furthermore, the institutional relationship which Fisher described between the serving Permanent Secretary to the Treasury and the Prime Minister of the day was neither so strong nor so enduring as he professed. In 1936, he reminded the Prime Minister that a committee on ministerial salaries which reported in 1920 had shown their

> indifference ... to considerations of history and tradition ... by their reference to the office of First Lord of the Treasury as a sinecure, and their disposition to separate it from the office of Prime Minister, contrary to the advice of the then Chancellor ... speaking for the Prime Minister and himself. The Committee appear to have been quite unaware of the fact that ages before the phrase 'Prime Minister' was coined, the Chief Minister of the Crown was the Lord Treasurer — a sufficiently venerable illustration is Queen Elizabeth's Minister, Sir William Cecil.
>
> ... If it were necessary, the historical aspect could, of course, be developed in greater detail, but I should assume that the present Prime Minister and First Lord would be the last person to divorce himself from centuries-old association and tradition.
>
> Moreover, practical considerations underlie and support the argument from history. The presence of the Prime Minister on the Board of Treasury as its first member has a great moral weight of its own, and stops the mouths of those who would twit a Minister of Finance with being a mere purveyor of ways and means, insensible to

the higher range of political motives and sympathies. It also possesses the advantage, which no other expedient could furnish, of providing a Court of Appeal from the Finance Ministry within the Treasury itself to which other departments can resort, so that a decision arrived at on financial grounds by the financial authorities of the Treasury including the Chancellor ... can be reversed on political grounds by the Prime Minister and First Lord without any shock to Treasury authority, because it is done under the guise of a reconsideration, by the Treasury, of its own decisions.[48]

In fact, there had been instances where the Prime Minister had not been First Lord of the Treasury, for example when Arthur Balfour held the latter office in Salisbury's administration at the turn of the century.[49] More importantly, there is nothing in Treasury papers or elsewhere to suggest that Fisher's 'Court of Appeal' theory was seriously entertained by anyone. If the Prime Minister overruled the Treasury in favour of some other department, it was, as everyone in Whitehall knew, a victory for that department and a defeat for the Treasury. Major disputes would in any case be resolved by the Cabinet, not by the Prime Minister on his own, for the practical reason that no head of government could afford to let himself become a financial arbitrator. Otherwise he would be besieged by appellant departments, and the collective responsibility of the Cabinet in questions of expenditure would entirely disappear.

One historian has written that Fisher as head of the Treasury could 'tender advice on any subject directly, and on his own initiative' to the Prime Minister.[50] This tallies with Fisher's statement that the Permanent Secretary as Head of the Civil Service was 'the principal official adviser of the Prime Minister.'[51] But such a claim had no firmer basis than what happened to be the position for much of his time at the Treasury: he tendered advice on all sorts of subjects to successive Prime Ministers because they knew him and trusted him personally, not because he had an inalienable and recognized right to do so. Lloyd George, Bonar Law, Baldwin and Chamberlain had each worked closely with him at the Treasury before becoming Prime Minister. When a Prime Minister was appointed in 1924 who had no previous links with the Treasury or its volatile chief, Fisher found himself regarded merely as a specialist on civil service and Treasury matters. On the other hand, when Baldwin was Prime Minister from 1924 to 1929, Fisher's conception of his duties as Permanent Secretary to the Treasury drew the wrath of the Chancellor, Winston Churchill, who told him he was

> well aware that you do not regard yourself in any way responsible for assisting the Chancellor of the Exchequer and that you reserve your functions entirely for the First Lord of the Treasury. You have been careful to impress this upon me and I have not challenged your interpretation of your duties. I must say however that it is an interpretation very different from that which after nearly twenty years experience in Ministerial office I had supposed was the practice, and I cannot conceive that any of your distinguished predecessors have not been accustomed to give more constant and effective assistance to the Chancellor of the day, whether in regard to the controlling of expenditure or the framing of finance. Such knowledge as I possessed led me to suppose that the Secretary to the Treasury was the right-hand man and fellow-worker of the Chancellor of the Exchequer and the leading official figure in the whole business of the Treasury.[52]

Fisher's activities as Head of the Civil Service were determined to an extent by the way the reorganized Treasury operated. Although he evidently established his authority within the department as its permanent head, the three controllers beneath him were in extremely strong positions — in forwarding their comments on their responsibilities to the Chancellor in 1921, he hoped 'Mr Chamberlain will note that their public use requires not a little caution lest they give rise to the charge that officials have too great powers.'[53] If he was to have an effective role, he needed a wider sphere of activity than what was left to him in the departmental Treasury. His theoretical justification of the expansion of his areas of interest as permanent head of the Treasury and the civil service came well after practical necessity had brought it about.

The nomination of the Permanent Secretary to the Treasury to be Head of the Civil Service in 1919 provoked little interest at the time. It was not until 1926 that the question of his precise duties was raised in Parliament, and then solely in relation to appointments and honours.[54] There was no suggestion that the Head of the Civil Service was considered an adviser to the Prime Minister on general matters. Publicists and parliamentarians were fully occupied with the campaign to abolish the Cabinet secretariat, which was described as an iniquitous and unconstitutional creation.[55] The relative respectability of the headship of the civil service was underlined by the report of a committee on the salary of heads of departments in 1920. This committee was chaired by Asquith, a habitual critic of the civil service under Lloyd George, and included Sir Joseph Maclay, an indefatigable exposer of supposed waste and extravagance in Whitehall.[56] Their conclusion was that the heads of first class departments should be paid £3,000 a year plus cost of living bonus, as opposed to the £2,000 plus bonus paid hitherto. They recommended further that the Permanent Secretary to the Treasury should receive an extra £500 a year in recognition of his position as official Head of the Civil Service.[57]

These findings strengthened Fisher's position, and also afforded him the opportunity for a thorough classification of public departments. After the committee had submitted its report, he appeared before it to say that although it 'had really exhausted its terms of reference ... as the reassessment of salaries could not fail to give rise to a certain amount of inter-departmental heart-burning' the Treasury 'would be very considerably fortified in giving effect' to a reorganization scheme if the committee 'had first examined' it and had 'satisfied themselves' that it 'conformed to the general principles adopted by the Committee in the case of the more important Departments.' The committee agreed with Fisher's list dividing departments into four groups in order of importance, carrying salaries for their permanent heads of £3,000, £2,500, £2,200 and £1,800 — plus a cost of living bonus in each case — respectively.[58] The departments involved knew nothing of this until informed by the Treasury of the grading to which the committee had agreed. As Head of the Civil Service Fisher constantly preached the necessity for good faith and team-work amongst its members, precepts which evidently did not preclude an occasional *fait accompli*.

Notes

1. Fisher to Lloyd George, 3 Sept. 1919, T171/170.
2. Minutes of Cabinet Finance Committee, 20 Aug. 1919, CAB 27/71.
3. FC 33, undated, Dec. 1919, CAB27/72.
4. Conclusions of a meeting, 30 Jan. 1920, CAB 23/20.
5. FC 35, note by Fisher, 22 Dec. 1919, CAB27/72.
6. It was circulated as CP 561 of 1920.
7. CAB 10(20), 11 Feb. 1920, CAB 23/20; Treasury circular 8/20, 12 Mar. 1920, T162/E11353. For the text of this important document see Appendix A.
8. Ministers had eleven days in which to consider the matter. Those who overlooked it and who subsequently complained had only themselves, and their officials, to blame.
9. Fisher to the Financial Secretary to the Treasury and the Chancellor, 25 Oct. 1920, T160 639/F6064.
10. Treasury circular 11/24 of 28 Apr. 1924 strengthened procedures by laying down the rule, agreed by Cabinet on 7 Apr. 1924, that 'at least five days' must elapse between circulation of memoranda and their discussion by the Cabinet, and that each should carry a specific statement on the front page that other departments had been consulted. T160/639/F6064. Fisher to the Chancellor, 24 Dec. 1919, T199/88, and a Cabinet secretariat circular, 12 Jan. 1920, T1 12466/63122, deal with the establishment of permanent liaison between the secretariat and the Treasury.
11. Committee of Public Accounts, minutes of evidence, *PP* (1920), vi, 176.
12. ibid., pp. 175, 367.
13. ibid., pp. 368–9, 371.
14. ibid., pp. 371–3. Wilkins was believed to be the model for 'Mr Pro Hac', a stuffy, fussy civil servant who appears in the work of Arnold Bennett. Interview with Sir Robert Fraser.
15. Sir Eric Geddes to Bonar Law, 30 July 1920, PREM 1/9. Ironically, Geddes was soon to give his name to the most notorious government spending cuts seen in Britain, the 'Geddes Axe'.
16. Committee of Public Accounts, fourth report, *PP* (1920), vi, 22.
17. Fisher to Lloyd George, 21 Feb. 1922, Lloyd George papers, F/17/1/14.
18. The departments concerned were the ministries of Labour, Pensions, Transport, and Health and the boards of Trade and Education. Fisher to Masterson-Smith, 9 Mar. 1921, Committee of Public Accounts, third report, appendix 8, *PP* (1921), vi, 463–6.
19. Fisher to Tom Jones (Assistant Secretary and Deputy Secretary to the Cabinet, 1916–30), Thomas Jones papers, W/7/5.
20. Gibson to Fisher, 2 Feb.; Chrystal to Fisher, 24 Mar.; Dunnell to Fisher, 15 Apr.; Selby-Bigge to Fisher, 21 Apr. 1921, T163 109/1/G282/1. I am grateful to Mr C.J. Carey, then of the Treasury, for drawing my attention to this file in 1980.
21. Selby-Bigge to Masterson-Smith, 5 July 1921, ibid.

22. Willie Graham MP (Chairman of the PAC) to Fisher, 12 May; Ramsay (Comptroller and Auditor General) to Fisher, 9 May 1925, T163 109/1/G282/1. The decision was formally promulgated in a Treasury circular of 1 Jan. 1926, Committee of Public Accounts, *PP* (1926), v, 638.

23. Bridges, *The Treasury*, p.172. Those former permanent secretaries interviewed for this study, not all of them ex-Treasury men, supported Bridges's view.

24. Gilbert to Phillips, 26 Feb. 1931, T160 403/F12833.

25. Note prepared by Treasury, 8 Oct. 1919, CAB 27/72.

26. Correspondence between the Cabinet secretariat and the Board of Education, 20 and 27 Nov. 1919 and 2 Feb. 1920, T1 12454/56195.

27. On 31 Mar. 1919 there were 397,825 non-industrial civil servants. Using this as the base figure, by 1921 numbers were down by 7.5 per cent, by 1923 by 23.3 per cent, and by 1926 by 25.5 per cent to 296,258, the lowest total in the inter-war period. By 1938 the service had expanded again to 94.6 per cent of its 1919 size. These percentages are derived from the quarterly returns of staff employed in government departments in *PP*.

28. Unsigned memorandum, 29 June 1921, T172/1214; unsigned, undated memorandum, 1921, T172/1225.

29. Scott to Financial Secretary, 20 Jan. 1922, T162 88/E9916.

30. Undated, unsigned memorandum, by Scott [?], T162 59/E5083.

31. Parris, *Staff Relations*, pp. 83–4.

32. T162 69/E5835.

33. Fisher to Masterson-Smith, 9 Mar. 1921, as in note 18 above.

34. Fisher to Lloyd George, 16 June 1920, Lloyd George papers, F/17/1/1.

35. T172/1214; a year later, the increase in the size of the pre-war departments had fallen to 5 per cent. Unsigned, undated note [by Scott?], 1922, T172/1255.

36. Morgan, *Consensus and Disunity*, pp. 284–93.

37. The big drop in numbers came between 1921 and 1923. See note 27 above.

38. St Loe Strachey (editor of *The Spectator*) to Sir Henry Craik MP, 26 May 1922, St Loe Strachey papers, S/19/4/14.

39. Fisher to Chamberlain, Lloyd George, and Robert Horne [the Chancellor], 20 July 1921, T172/1215.

40. CAB 61(214), 25 July 1921, CAB 23/26.

41. Note by Bridges, 6 Jan. 1928, T162 136/E18914.

42. Seidman, *Politics, Position and Power*, p. 12.

43. See especially Selby, *Diplomatic Twilight*, pp. 3–6; Ashton-Gwatkin, 'Thoughts', pp. 374–8; Murray [afterwards the Master of Elibank], *Reflections*, passim; Legge-Bourke, *Master of the Offices*, passim. These eccentric works are designed to show that Fisher was the man ultimately responsible for the failures of British foreign policy between the wars.

44. See, e.g., W.H. Beveridge to Fisher, 16 Mar. 1926, Beveridge papers, V/36.

45. Fisher to Baldwin, 16 Feb. 1926, PREM 1/53.
46. This had not been the case for Fisher's immediate predecessors, presumably because they were joint permanent secretaries.
47. Note on Treasury organization, unsigned, Jan. 1924, T199/50b. From internal evidence in the file, it is clear that Fisher approved this note if he did not actually write it.
48. Fisher to Baldwin, 11 May 1936, PREM 1/199. He got his way, as the Ministers of the Crown Act of 1937 tied the two posts together for salary purposes.
49. Lord Salisbury was Foreign Secretary as well as Prime Minister, and received a salary in respect of the former post.
50. Peden, 'Fisher and British rearmament', p. 30.
51. As in note 47 above.
52. Churchill to Fisher, 1 Dec. 1925, in Gilbert, *Churchill Companion*, p. 601. Relations between Fisher and Churchill as Chancellor are discussed in Chapter 5.
53. Fisher to Gower (private secretary to the Prime Minister), 17 Aug. 1921, T199/3.
54. This will be dealt with in Chapter 5.
55. Lord Esher to Lloyd George, 29 June 1922, Lloyd George papers, F/16/1. Esher was writing in support of Hankey and the secretariat.
56. Maclay to Lloyd George, 4 Aug. 1922, ibid., F/35/3/63.
57. Treasury minute of 17 Aug. 1920, T162 24/E1552.
58. Note of a meeting, 21 July 1920, T162 23/E1461.

3

The Lloyd George coalition, 1919–22

I

It has been said of Lloyd George that, 'coming into the British system from outside, he had no respect for its traditions or accepted formalities ... Most of all, he distrusted the permanent officials.'[1] His use of the 'Garden Suburb', and what Milner described as his tendency 'to settle things that really mattered, or unsettle them, in his own favourite way — by devious methods and through anything but the regular agents', could be taken as evidence which supports this view.[2] However, it was also during his premiership that the two most important officials of the inter-war years, Hankey and Fisher, came to power. While the Garden Suburb came and went with its creator, they survived his departure with surprising ease, although Hankey suffered some anxious moments in the immediate aftermath of the election. Both men were personally devoted to Lloyd George, but both were also quite acceptable to his supplanters. The supreme individualist as Prime Minister bequeathed to his successors not the amorphous, ill-defined government machine which he had inherited in 1916, but a reorganized and relatively centralized civil service.

An important test of Fisher's authority as Head of the Civil Service came in the spring of 1920. Winston Churchill, a man with whom he seldom saw eye to eye, was Secretary of State for War, and wanted to make changes in the organization and staffing of his department. Without consulting the Prime Minister he appointed Sir Herbert Creedy to be its head, while leaving financial responsibility with another official, Sir Charles Harris. Thus he contravened the new arrangement for senior appointments in two respects, by failing to get the Prime Minister's assent, and by ignoring the principle that the permanent head of a service department should also be the accounting officer, with the ultimate responsibility in all questions of finance. He defended this action by telling Lloyd George that 'no doubt through inadvertence, which I regret, this is the first time that I have had the enclosed conclusion of the Cabinet Finance Committee of January 30th placed before me', a claim which was patently untrue since he had written a month earlier that 'for myself I am in agreement with the new scheme which provides for better co-ordination of our civil work.'[3] Fisher pointed out the inaccuracies in Churchill's argument, and remarked that his 'trouble ... is due primarily to his own precipitate action in promoting Sir Herbert Creedy', who 'is a very nice man, but lacks the qualities needed for the permanent civilian headship of a great department of state'. Fisher reiterated the general case for making heads of departments responsible for finance, and noted that

> in a service department it is the soldier or sailor who is (a) the advisor to the Minister in regard to policy and (b) responsible to the Minister for the organisation and administration of the main machinery (army or navy) for carrying out that policy. The permanent civilian element is subsidiary and subordinate except in regard to finance. But Mr Churchill's picture of the civilian head of the War Office is that he ought to continue to be (as for some years past he has been) a mere clerk of a Council, an amiable busybody, knowledgeable in formality and routine, a compound of a gentlemanlike flunkey and a soother of irascible warriors.
>
> The one large field of responsibility open to the permanent civilian head in the War Office, viz.: financial, he would relegate to an officer inferior alike in title and emolument ....
>
> The fact is that Mr Churchill is in a difficulty due to his having made a promotion wrong both as regards the individual and because the opportunity was lost of reviewing the War Office organisation.
>
> A transition period may therefore be inevitable at the War Office before the change can be applied in its entirety. But it is earnestly to be hoped that Mr Churchill can be persuaded from doing anything to stereotype the vicious War Office arrangements.[4]

Fisher and Churchill eventually reached a compromise whereby Harris was made a joint permanent under secretary along with Creedy. The office would revert to a single permanent head with financial responsibility once Harris retired. This happened sooner than Churchill had anticipated, as Harris was retired against his will at the end of 1923.[5] Creedy carried on as the sole Permanent Under-Secretary until 1939. The dispute was important because it involved the two principles central to the reorganization of the civil service. Churchill ignored both, and got away with it, although Fisher secured confirmation from his political chiefs that they were in future to be strictly adhered to, and both Chamberlain and Lloyd George supported him against their Cabinet colleague.

Neither the divided command up to 1924, nor Creedy's eventual accession to the sole permanent headship, made any apparent difference to the War Office's ways. Unlike the other service ministries, which took the view that their job was simply to get as much money as possible for the fighting men, it exhibited a 'Crimean War mentality' in its financial affairs, so much so that the Treasury could seldom find any fat to cut in the spending proposals which it made.[6] The department had a poor reputation in Whitehall, and by the late 1930s was thought to be in need of major reorganization. Creedy's last minister, the energetic and somewhat excitable Leslie Hore-Belisha, thought him a hindrance in financial matters and an obstacle to reform.[7] Whether or not this was so, and whether or not Fisher would have picked someone better had he been given the chance, is an open question. What is clear is that the appointment of Creedy, who was born and bred in the War Office, precluded for two decades the possibility of introducing new blood into the top of that department.

Another minister who gave Fisher trouble over an appointment was the Home Secretary Edward Shortt. When the headship of the Home Office fell vacant in 1922, Fisher pushed for the appointment of Sir John Anderson. Like Fisher, Anderson had established an outstanding reputation in his time with the National Health Insurance Commission, and his Whitehall career thereafter was never more than a step behind Fisher's own — in 1919 he had succeeded him as Chairman of the Inland Revenue, before being sent to Dublin Castle as Under Secretary in 1920 to rescue the Irish administration from complete collapse. He left the civil service in 1932 to become

Governor of Bengal. Six years later he was elected to Parliament and became a Cabinet minister. Despite his lack of political experience, he enjoyed great success up to 1945 as the minister who ran Britain while Churchill ran the war. Anderson was universally recognized in Whitehall as a brilliant adviser and administrator. 'Industrious without apparent effort', he was much cleverer than Fisher, as the latter was happy to acknowledge; on the other hand, he accumulated dignity with each promotion, and colleagues and subordinates found him inordinately pompous. Although there was some disappointment and apprehension in the Home Office, where there were two internal candidates, when he was made Permanent Under Secretary, 'it soon became apparent' that in him 'we had acquired a head who belonged ... to an altogether different dimension.'[8]

After securing Lloyd George's approval for Anderson's appointment, Fisher belatedly consulted the Home Secretary. He then told the Prime Minister that Shortt had planned to appoint a Home Office insider, Sir Ernle Blackwell, though he was

> in full agreement that, if none of his local geese were acceptable, Sir John Anderson was the man he himself would select outside the ranks of the Home Office. He realised that the final say is with the Prime Minister, & he admitted that for the position of permanent heads of departments the whole public service must be the field of choice & that he himself did not know enough about that field to enable an effective comparison on his part. He said he wd. think over the matter afresh in the light of what I had said ...
>
> I have heard nothing from him, & as time is beginning to press, I beg to re-submit the matter to you. There is no comparison between Sir E Blackwell and Sir J Anderson for this (or any other) post, and if Sir J Anderson were not available, the cause of public efficiency would still require the importation of fresh blood into the Home Office which still lingers in Mid Victorian days.[9]

Two weeks later, Fisher complained to Frances Stevenson, Lloyd George's private secretary and mistress, of the 'masterly inactivity of Shortt cum Troupy [Sir Edward Troup, the outgoing permanent head]'. Both had conceded that Anderson was the best man for the post, but

> they shrink from the proper inference because they say that they have 'adequate' men in the Home Office & that the introduction of an outsider would be a 'shock' to the Office.
>
> Now for the premier posts in the public service the field of choice is the whole service, &, unless each rare opportunity is seized as it arises, we shall not get the best men into the principal positions & departments so deprived will not become efficient. That was the motive of the Cabinet agreement that the final word was to be with the Prime Minister (& not with the departmental Minister) who wd. take a wider, more detached, & better informed view.
>
> Shortt will not put up any fight, and if the Prime Minister will tell him of his decision that Anderson is to be appointed, that will cut short this process of drift, & (no pun is intended) strengthen Shortt (who will really be rather relieved).[10]

Anderson was duly appointed, and remained in the Home Office for ten years. He is remembered not only as a brilliant but as an independent minded chief who stood up to the Treasury. His successor, Sir Russell Scott, was also a close associate of Fisher. Despite this, Fisher is said to have remarked in 1935 that 'I have no use for the Home Office or for anyone in it', a 'comprehensive anathema that sent a chill' down Home Office spines.[11] Putting in the right men did not always produce the right results.

Opportunities to make senior appointments were rare. For example, Fisher believed that the Board of Trade 'lacks force & practical capacity', but he could do little about its higher organization, as he complained to Chamberlain in 1921: 'Every opportunity lost for filling such posts with the right men prolongs the interval before which we can get the Civil Service under the right direction throughout.'[12] He had great hopes for the Board of Education: its permanent head since 1911, Sir Lewis Selby-Bigge, had been dismissive of Fisher's views on the responsibilities of permanent secretaries and on the need for team-work between departments. Fisher anticipated that he would be retiring shortly, and reminded Lloyd George of a recent discussion in which

> you contrasted the systems prevailing in Scotland on the one hand and England and Wales on the other much to the disadvantage of the latter. Your feeling was that, whereas in Scotland education reflects the genius of the race and is consequently a real thing, in England and Wales — apart from the great Public Schools — it is in its present form an exotic and that, so far as it can be said to be directed to anything — at all events judging by results — it is a factory of clerks and shopwalkers. Unless and until a real pride and interest in education inspires the population as a whole, the national education system must continue a bloodless, soulless mechanism, administered by a bureaucracy, full no doubt of admirable aspirations for the common weal, confident that it alone knows what is good for us all, and unconsciously opposed to the evolution which echoes the characteristics of the English and the Welsh ...
>
> Naturally my function is limited to making suggestions to you as to the appointment of officials in government service, and, though for some little time I have been pondering about this particular post, I have found it quite a problem. I entertain no doubt whatever that the Board of Education does not contain the right man: my namesake [i.e. H.A.L. Fisher, the Education Minister] is not likely to agree with me any more than I agree with his bureaucratic standpoint. There are in the public service one or two men whom I think would do well as Permanent Secretary, but they are already heads of departments and are needed where they are. And this at once plunges us into the vortex of opinion. I should like, however, to make a suggestion for your consideration.

He put forward the name of Cyril Norwood, the headmaster of Marlborough, who was said to be 'a man of force, with distinct personality, enthusiastic about education, at the same time practical and sensible.'[13] This would have been an unusual nomination in any circumstances; coming from the head of the Treasury and the civil service, and at a time when retrenchment not reform was the order of the day, it was extraordinary.

However, Selby-Bigge in fact hung on till 1925, when he was succeeded by an official of whom Fisher approved, Sir Aubrey Symons.[14]

The practice of transferring senior officials from one department to another quickly gained general acceptance. Fisher's method for finding suitable candidates was to keep in touch with all heads of departments and to learn from them who the rising stars of the service were. He described the process to the Royal Commission on the Civil Service in 1930:

> In the first place, it is completely informal; the less formal it is the greater the likelihood, in my opinion, of the eventual judgement being correct. My colleagues in Departments, whenever they come into my room, in the course of discussion sooner or later get to this question, and they are themselves looking out for people. Names are canvassed, it may be that no vacancy is in sight. Thus in the most informal way a trend of opinion gradually forms itself as to the suitability of people, either particularly or generally, for this class of post.

In such a manner, the promotions pot 'is kept simmering, instead of boiling up periodically.'[15]

Although appointments and promotions are sensitive issues in any institution at any time, even under Lloyd George, this procedure was considered legitimate. The prime ministership was virtually in commission so far as civil service matters were concerned during the lifetime of the Coalition, so that suspicion of prime ministerial patronage in appointments did not arise. In managing the civil service, Fisher dealt not only with Lloyd George but with the Chancellor and the Lord Privy Seal. The quest for economy in administration was a collective task, not a device by which the Prime Minister might strengthen his personal position.

A historian of the Coalition writing in 1979 complained of 'the encroaching control of the Treasury', and remarked that Fisher 'had a veto over appointments in other departments: new ministries like Health or Labour were in no position to resist.'[16] This is incorrect: it was the Prime Minister, not Fisher, who had the veto. Fisher could only advise, and his advice was not always followed. Another writer, Dr Rodney Lowe, has said that with the Treasury's 'control over promotion ... there developed suddenly a marked reluctance to challenge any of the Treasury's fundamental precepts'. He maintained that at the Ministry of Labour Sir Horace Wilson and the Accountant General 'felt their duty to lie not in the championing of social reform but in the effecting of Treasury control from within the department.'[17] Wilson, who became permanent head of the ministry in 1921, he points to as 'the archetypal career civil servant who fully appreciated that promotion did not lie in antagonising the Treasury.'[18] Such sweeping charges are of their nature hard to answer, but it can be said that neither by background, education nor the course of his career was Wilson the 'archetypal' senior civil servant: indeed, he was reviled for his humble origins in *Guilty Men* as the son of 'a furniture dealer', born 'in a Bournemouth back street', educated in 'the local board school', who had entered the service straight from school as 'a Second Division man', which was 'an easy standard to achieve.'[19] Furthermore, as permanent head of a first class department Wilson could scarcely have anticipated any further promotion no matter how amenable he was to the Treasury's wishes: the only service post of higher rank and emolument was that held by Fisher, which was clearly not going to fall vacant for many years.[20]

The same writer made the broader charge that the centralization of senior appointments in 1920 led to the supremacy in social departments of officials who lacked 'determined conviction and economic sophistication', and consequently 'to the standardisation of economic and social values which undermined the very departmental expertise which policy initiative required.' The 'Treasury view that all public expenditure was to be deprecated as lost investment' came to dominate. Furthermore, he complained, the appointments system ensured that generalists assumed control at the expense of departmental specialists.[21]

The inter-war social ministries were certainly staffed by men very different from the pioneers of social reform of Edwardian days. This was because the state now accepted a large degree of responsibility in such areas as health and employment; the corollary was that, as these problems became the business of government to deal with, so the government looked to its regular civil service to devise policy and implement legislation on them.

It is true that Fisher put a premium on moving officials from one department to another, in order both to introduce new blood and to dilute the traditional insularity of Whitehall offices. He practised what he preached, importing officials at both senior and junior levels from all sorts of departments to the Treasury. To staff departments with men who would do the Treasury's bidding was neither the intention nor the consequence of his appointments policy. He deprecated strongly the notion that the civil service could be made more efficient and Treasury control enhanced if the Treasury had its agents in every department. Such an idea ran contrary to everything he was trying to achieve with the service. As will be seen, he was not always right in his advice on appointments, and he undoubtedly had 'blind spots' about individuals though, in the words of a colleague, 'it was very rarely that he would not at any rate hear the arguments against his prejudices.'[22] The principles which he sought to uphold in advising on appointments did not alter, and the installation of yes-men was not one of them. Furthermore, it is quite clear that departments could, and did, successfully resist Fisher's suggestions if they had sufficient determination. This was particularly so where a strong minister or permanent head was involved.

The second charge cited above, that the centralization of appointments, the increase in importance of the status of finance officers in departments, and the responsibility laid on permanent heads as accounting officers stifled innovation and initiative in economic and social departments is less easy to dismiss. Since he first addressed these issues in the early 1970s Dr Lowe has moved from his earlier suggestion that at the Ministry of Labour Sir Horace Wilson was little more than a traitor within the gates, an ambitious hack who enhanced his career prospects by playing up to the Treasury at the expense of his department's interests. He now advances a more general and more credible argument, that in the inter-war period a mandarin consensus on the economy emerged in Whitehall which was not so much Treasury-mindedness as economic defeatism. This point owes a great deal to unprovable assumptions about how alternative policies would have fared.

Running through these criticisms is the implication that the inter-war Treasury was the sworn enemy of social improvement. There was a great disparity between the hopes held out for reconstruction during the First World War, and the experience of the post-war years. Britain emerged from the First World War with its economy in a parlous condition. The country had an enlarged empire to defend, it owed a lot of money, and its prospects for recovery were inextricably bound up with the performance of the international economy. In the immediate post-war years the Treasury was undoubtedly concerned that the government was committed to expenditure that the country could not afford. So too was Parliament, and so too, if elections are any guide, were the voters. As permanent head of the Treasury Fisher was naturally involved in efforts to keep expenditure down. It did not follow that either he or his department were opposed to social spending or to the proposition that the state had a responsibility towards the sick, the poor, the young and the unemployed. There is ample evidence that from his first day as a civil servant to his last Fisher's personal sympathies lay with social reform — this was why he worshipped Lloyd George — and it is nonsense to say that the Treasury in the 1920s and the 1930s collectively regarded all public expenditure as a waste of money. Such generalizations, made with the benefit of Keynesian hindsight, simply ignore the national and international economic and political realities of the inter-war years.

II

Lloyd George was too dynamic a Prime Minister to leave foreign policy entirely in the hands of his Foreign Secretary. To an extent he was justified: the issues were too big during the war and the treaty-making which followed it too important to be left to a single department of government. But he did not stop meddling once the Versailles settlement had been concluded, and of course, his fall in 1922 was precipitated by the fiasco of Chanak. His interest in foreign affairs was resented by diplomats, one of whom complained in 1921 that 'I have long known of the curious relations as between the Foreign Office and No. 10 and appreciate the fact that the latter tries to concentrate affairs in its hands.'[23] A more rabid critic later wrote of 'the usurpation of the rightful powers of the Foreign Office' which 'Lloyd George continued into the years succeeding the cessation of hostilities with injurious effects upon the international situation both at the time and during the difficult years that followed.'[24] These charges are similar to those made against Neville Chamberlain as Premier, and their author portrays Fisher as the leading henchman of both Chamberlain and Lloyd George at No. 10.

Even before the Cabinet Finance Committee began to speak of economy in the summer of 1919, the Foreign Office had anticipated that changes would be forced on it by the government.[25] Pressure 'to put into operation a number of long overdue reforms, which had been pressed on the office for nearly a decade by outside critics and not a few members of the Foreign Office itself', resulted in the merging of the Foreign Office with the diplomatic service.[26] The combined department found itself short of men to cope with the considerable post-war increase of work, but the Treasury was reluctant to allow any increase in staff. Quite apart from the question of economy, the Treasury 'was anxious to sweep away the existing quasi-independent status of the Foreign Office and bring it into line with the rest of the domestic departments.' The Foreign Office, having undergone its amalgamation with the diplomatic service, wished to remain separate from the domestic civil service 'on the grounds that the diplomatic function was a specialised one, unlike the ordinary administration.'[27] These issues, which remained unsettled, engendered a certain amount of tension between the Foreign Office and the Treasury.

By the summer of 1920, discontent with life under Lloyd George was rife amongst Foreign Office men and British diplomats abroad. The Prime Minister took it upon himself to play a part in the appointment of ambassadors, and 'revelled in suggesting & bringing in outsiders to important diplomatic posts', to the despair of the permanent head of the department: 'There is nothing to be done as far as I can see, for the prospects for the service are very poor.'[28] When Lloyd George appointed Lord D' Abernon to be ambassador in Berlin without consulting Curzon, his Foreign Secretary, the latter protested, very mildly, that 'the precedent is rather a dangerous one', while a disappointed diplomat concluded that 'the recent appointments in our service show clearly enough that we cannot expect advancement.'[29] Such incidents ruffled the feathers of traditionalists in the foreign service, but prime ministerial involvement in the selection of ambassadors was neither unconstitutional nor new. It was continued by Lloyd George's more orthodox successors.[30] There is no evidence to suggest that Fisher had any influence on diplomatic appointments under Lloyd George, but as Head of the Civil Service he advised on the filling of senior posts in the Foreign Office as in all other Whitehall departments. This was to be the cause of controversy in later years, and was confused by some of Fisher's critics with the separate issue of Lloyd George's interest in ambassadorial appointments.[31]

Curzon was quick to react to the Treasury circular of 12 March 1920 which detailed those appointments for which the Prime Minister's sanction was required. The application of such an arrangement to his department would, he told the Chancellor Austen Chamberlain, 'constitute a complete innovation in the practice of the office', and 'prima facie, I should have thought it most dangerous. For later on it may enable a Labour or Socialist government to obtain control by these means (though ostensibly designed in the interests of economy) of every department of state.' Chamberlain replied, in a letter drafted by Fisher, that 'the public service provides a wider field of choice than any individual department, and, although a well-managed office should often throw up the right man, this is not invariably so.' As 'a result of inexperience or misplaced kindness', the wrong men were too often 'appointed to the more important permanent positions.'

Curzon was not persuaded: 'The fact that the Cabinet "took note" of the recommendations of the Finance Committee with regard to the method of appointment to higher posts in the Civil Service (with a string of other recommendations, none of which were referred to or explained)', could not be taken 'as necessarily carrying with it the approval of the Cabinet. I do not, therefore, feel that I, or any future Secretary of State can be held to be bound by the Finance Committee's decision.' He argued that 'if a man is fit to be appointed Secretary of State for Foreign Affairs, or head of any other department of state, he must be considered competent to decide who shall fill the higher posts in the office for which he was responsible.'[32] Chamberlain responded in a conciliatory manner: the new arrangement was 'the considered policy of the Cabinet Committee presided over by the Prime Minister, and received formal Cabinet sanction.' The Foreign Office he thought an exception to most departments, where ministers had little chance of evaluating their staff: 'There have been cases where we have serious cause to regret appointments which have been made on insufficient knowledge of the men in the office, and without any enquiry as to whether there were not men of very superior capabilities available from other offices.' He continued:

> For these reasons I am sure that the new order is right, and I think you will find that the Prime Minister attaches as much importance to it as I do. At the same time I feel that you are unduly alarmed about the Foreign Office, and that in practice you will find that the authority of the Secretary of State for Foreign Affairs will decide the appointment of both the Permanent Under Secretary and his chief assistant. It is only in regard to the appointment of the Accounting Officer, if at all, that I anticipate that the Prime Minister would desire to make any representations to you in regard to your Staff.[33]

Chamberlain's prediction was not borne out by events. Curzon had a hard fight over the appointment of a successor to the permanent head of his department, Hardinge, who feared he would be replaced by 'a diplomatist or a civil servant. Nobody wants the latter .... It would make me shudder to think that a civil servant or an inferior diplomatist was in control of the office.'[34] Lloyd George was rumoured to want to install Sir Maurice Hankey, the Cabinet Secretary, in the post, but eventually Curzon had his way, and Sir Eyre Crowe was appointed. There is no evidence that Fisher played a significant part in that struggle, although he recalled Crowe as 'a truly remarkable man ... in almost every respect an exception to the standard Foreign Office type.'[35] However, it is clear that he interpreted the Prime Minister's say in Foreign Office appointments less narrowly than had the Chancellor in his letter to Curzon. This is reflected in advice he gave in 1921, when the Foreign Secretary put forward the name of Sir William Tyrrell to be deputy head of the Foreign Office. Fisher wrote that

> of the existing personnel in the Foreign Office I cannot suggest anyone who should be given this appointment in preference to Sir W Tyrrell, and I think therefore the Prime Minister need not offer objection to Lord Curzon's proposal.[36]

Quite apart from the issue of appointments, the Foreign Office was affronted by the way that the reparations negotiations were conducted by Sir John Bradbury. As chief British delegate he reported to the Chancellor, not the Foreign Secretary, an arrangement to which the Foreign Office had incautiously agreed.[37] Bradbury thought the attitude of the French government towards reparations vindictive and shortsighted, and he made a number of efforts to persuade the government to replace him by men 'who are, as I unfortunately am not, themselves convinced of the wisdom and practicality of the general policy which they are called upon to administer.'[38] In 1922 the British ambassador in Paris warned Curzon that Bradbury 'is adopting a rather independent line', and there was considerable suspicion amongst the francophiles of the Foreign Office that the Treasury was pursuing a pro-German line to the detriment of Anglo-French relations.[39] Curzon complained to the Chancellor in November 1921 of the Treasury's failure to consult his department on questions which affected foreign policy, 'a process which has grown up in the course of the last two years, which I have more than once already deprecated, and which I must earnestly request you to take effective steps to bring to an end'. Enclosed with this protest was a list of the Treasury's misdemeanours, which concluded with the observation that 'it is important that no further violations of the rule that all negotiations with foreign governments must be carried on under the responsibility of the Secretary of State for Foreign Affairs would take place.' Although the Chancellor replied that he would be happy to improve liaison between the two departments, and that there had been no 'intention of acting independently', the Treasury in fact continued to deal with reparations and other international financial questions as it saw fit.[40] The responsible Treasury officials took a uniformly hostile view of French behaviour, and pushed for strong action to protect Germany. Here financial and foreign policy issues merged, whereas the advice tendered by the two departments did not. These differences between the Foreign Office on the one hand and Lloyd George and the Treasury on the other were significant because they presaged and influenced disputes of later years. By 1922, the Foreign Office was clearly disturbed by the Prime Minister's management of foreign policy, and by the Treasury's growing involvement in international issues through its interest in reparations and inter-allied debts.

Fisher never had much time for the Foreign Office or the diplomatic service. The origins of his prejudice are unclear, but he disliked both the assumption that foreign affairs were beyond the ken of the rest of Whitehall and what he saw as the superiority complex of most British diplomats. He had some close allies in the Foreign Office and the diplomatic service — Sir Eyre Crowe and Sir William Tyrrell in the 1920s, and Sir Robert Vansittart, Sir Robert Craigie, and Sir Eric Phipps in the 1930s — but he thought little of either the machinery or the personnel of British diplomacy collectively. Long after his retirement he complained of 'the mumbo-jumbo that diplomacy was a high mystic art', and said he did not believe 'any clear distinction could be made between foreign policy and internal affairs. They were closely intertwined and reacted upon each other even when there was no apparent connection.'[41] He possibly acquired his opinion from Lloyd George, who, according to Curzon, his Foreign Secretary, 'cherished a deep hostility to the Foreign Office and all its works.'[42] Nevertheless it is ludicrous to claim, as one of Fisher's most rabid critics did, that the disasters of 1939 and 1940 could be traced back to an illegitimate hegemony exercised by Lloyd George and the Treasury over foreign policy in the early 1920s.[43]

III

In December 1919, Fisher was brought into discussion of the Irish question, when he was asked to find a job for General Sir Joseph Byrne, who had just been ousted from the headship of the Royal Irish Constabulary (RIC). Byrne had been removed ostensibly because he was tired out, but in fact because he was said to have 'lost his nerve' and to be in sympathy with Sinn Fein.[44] He had been head of the RIC since 1916, and his removal was due to his disagreements over policy with the Viceroy, Lord French, and the Chief Secretary for Ireland, Ian Macpherson. These two and their friends put it about that Byrne was a coward, and managed to convince the Coalition leaders that he should be removed.[45]

Byrne, however, put up a fight, arguing that 'the present Irish Executive had become impossible as it was not only out of sympathy, but actually out of touch with all shades of opinion. It was essential to distinguish between real crime and political crime.'[46] It was clear from what he said and how he said it that he was neither tired out nor a fool, which was more than could be said for some of his detractors.[47] The worst that could be proved against him was that he was an Irish Roman Catholic. Fisher became suspicious about the affair, the Treasury dragged its heels over the question of a pension, and a suitable post could not be found for him anywhere.[48] All this was a considerable embarrassment to the Viceroy and the Chief Secretary, and in March 1920 they sought to end the uncertainty by sending him a formal letter of supersession.[49] This move rebounded on them, however, as six days later the Irish executive was, as Fisher put it, compelled to 'eat its own words in the form of a letter to Sir Joseph Byrne ... revoking the order for his supersession.'[50] Although it proved impossible to reinstate him — a successor had already been appointed — he was paid his full salary for the post until given a colonial governorship in 1922.[51] In addition, in Fisher he found a formidable champion.

Fisher already had strong views on Ireland. He liked the country and its people, his wife was half-Irish and a Roman Catholic, he had a number of Irish friends, and he was 'a life-long Home Ruler.'[52] His enquiries into Byrne's case reinforced his convictions. Outlining the case to ministers at the end of 1921, he did not mince his words:

In the course of 1919 Lord French, Mr Macpherson, Sir John Taylor, Mr E Saunderson (secretary to the Lord Lieutenant) and Mr Watt (secretary to the Chief Secretary) had convinced themselves that the only cure for the (then) sporadic and infrequent exhibitions of force in Ireland was the total excommunication of Sinn Fein as such with bell, book and candle. The fact that Sinn Fein was a political creed ... escaped the notice of these gentlemen. They merely regarded it as a convertible term with the physical force faction which at that time — as shown by results — was quite a trifling element. So, drawing no distinction between the gunmen of that date and Sinn Fein as a whole, they decided that the Irish problem would be solved if the majority of people in

Ireland were forbidden to think, discuss, talk, write or speak the political views which they favoured.

In high places in Ireland there were some — not many — of whom Sir Joseph Byrne was one, who realised the full implication of 'proclaiming', that is proscribing in its entirety, a political creed. No attention was paid to their warnings that such procedure would reinforce indefinitely the physical force party, and would justify their methods in the eyes of the rest of the population as being the only instrument left to them. The sole result of the warning was that Sir J Byrne was believed — no doubt sincerely — to have lost his nerve and to be in sympathy with the "rebels", by which was meant Sinn Fein ....

The Irish government responsible for his treatment ... was within a month or two [i.e. in May 1920] itself replaced with the exception of the lord lieutenant .... Lord French was left, not because His Majesty's Government felt any more confidence in him than in the other three, but because he could be side tracked for all important purposes and consideration could therefore be given to the undesirability of exposing the lord lieutenant to an imputation of running away (his life had already been attempted. Nemesis had not tarried in this instance) .... In plain English, the people who had sat in judgement on Sir Joseph Byrne were themselves condemned.[53]

Fisher was in a good position to speak on the conduct of the Irish administration. In March 1920 General Sir Nevil Macready had been appointed general officer commanding the troops in Ireland, and he had sent to London a string of reports on the 'administrative chaos that seems to reign here', where 'the machine was hopelessly out of gear.'[54] Macready pressed for a committee of experienced administrators to examine the workings of Dublin Castle, a suggestion which was well received in London.[55] After some discussion, Fisher was asked to take charge of the investigation, and he took with him to Ireland two subordinates, R.E. Harwood of the Treasury and A.W. Cope of the Ministry of Pensions.[56] The three men travelled to Ireland on 4 May. While Cope and Harwood conducted an inspection of the Chief Secretary's Office, the central department of government in Ireland, Fisher sought the view of people of every political persuasion on the state of the country. Although the die-hards in the Castle at first thought him 'a treasure', it quickly became clear that his views on how the administration could be improved were very different from their own.[57] The account which he and his assistants gave to Chamberlain, Law, and Lloyd George 'disclose a condition both of administration & staff which is much worse than anything' the Chancellor had anticipated. Fisher passed on the detailed report of Cope and Harwood together with his own general observations:

> The Castle administration does not administer. On the mechanical side it can never have been good and is now quite obsolete; in the infinitely more important sphere (a) of informing and advising the Irish government in relation to policy and (b) of practical capacity in the application of policy it simply has no existence ....
>
> The prevailing conception of the post of Under Secretary — who should be the principal permanent adviser to the Irish government in civil affairs — appears to be that he is a routine clerk ....
>
> The position at the present moment is seemingly that no one in the Chief Secretary's Office, from the Under Secretary downwards, regards himself as responsible even for decisions on departmental papers, let alone for a share in the solution of difficulties in the realm either of policy or of execution.
>
> The Chief Secretary, for his part, appears to be under the illusion that a civil servant — even though he has the position and emoluments of permanent head of the Irish administration — is entirely unconcerned with the exploration or settlement of the problems which the Irish administration exists to solve.
>
> So long as these notions continue, the attainment of mere mechanical perfection has next to no value. For with the Chief Secretary skied on Olympus and his top permanent official hewing wood in the remotest valley the natural expectation is that essentials must suffer.

He supported his subordinates' conclusion that James MacMahon, the Under Secretary, was inadequate for his post. This was certainly the case: MacMahon had been cut out of all important decision-making by his deputy, Sir John Taylor, without so much as a protest from him, and was quite content to collect his salary, be polite to all and do nothing to antagonize anyone. Nevertheless his retention was suggested, as his 'appointment is a source of satisfaction to the Roman Catholic hierarchy', and as he 'quite sincerely holds views more in keeping with 20th century sentiment than those expressed by the ascendancy party and the supporters of indiscriminate coercion, and, so far as it counts, his advice would be on the side of judicious moderation'. Fisher also agreed with the suggestion of Cope and Harwood that an additional under secretaryship be created, and suggested Sir John Anderson, who 'would be quite admirable and would rapidly acquire the real control', for the post. He recommended Cope for an assistant under secretaryship, and said that 'I should allow loans of picked men from London' to staff the administration. In this way 'not only would the interior economy of the Irish civil government rapidly get right, but (what is far more important) the Chief Secretary would have first class civilian advisers and assistance in dealing with major issues.'[58]

Fisher was astonished at what he learnt while in Dublin. There, the administration had since the start of 1919 been dominated by a Unionist clique as incompetent as it was extreme. They were successful only in one respect, squeezing Roman Catholics, who had become 'objects of suspicion', out of positions of power.[59] Thus they had got rid of General Byrne of the RIC, while tolerating MacMahon only because he raised no protest at being ignored. Fisher made his opinions on this group abundantly clear to his masters, without apparently reflecting that Lloyd George had been its staunch supporter, or that Law was leader of the Unionist Party as well as Lord Privy Seal. A few days after his return from Dublin, he told them that

> with the notable exception of General Macready ... the government of Ireland strikes one as almost woodenly stupid and quite devoid of imagination. It listens solely to the ascendancy party and ... it never seemed to think of the utility of keeping in close touch with opinions of all kinds. The phrase 'Sinn Fein' is a shibboleth with which everyone not a 'loyalist' is denounced, and from listening to the people with influence you would certainly gather

that Sinn Fein and outrage were synonyms. If you ask whether it is not the case that two thirds of the Irish people and over 70 of their MPs are Sinn Fein and that the murder etc. gang are a few hundreds, they admit this to be so; they admit also that the bulk of the population has no desire to murder or be murdered, and that its passive attitude is due to impaired morale ...

In fact the ruling caste reminds one of some people in England — mainly to be found in clubs and amongst retired warriors and dowager ladies — who spend their time in denunciation of the working classes as socialists without ever condescending (or indeed being able) to analyse what they mean ...

The fact that the Sinn Fein movement includes amongst its ideals ultimate separation from Great Britain is no argument for withholding recognition of Sinn Fein as a political party. It *is* a political party, however much people may dislike it; and, if the test whether or not a political party is to be recognised is that its programme shall contain nothing anathema to people of different political complexion, then I can't imagine any party which ever could be recognised ...

The policy I advocate is not one of 'conciliation' but the restoration to the community at large of elementary human rights as understood by Anglo-Saxondom.[60]

The administrative changes he suggested were all carried out. Anderson, Cope and a number of others were sent to Dublin to reorganize the Castle and to furnish sound advice. But Fisher's words on policy were ignored, and the deficiencies of the Irish government were presented to the Cabinet as merely technical.[61] Despite the warnings of its new advisers in Dublin, the British government stepped up its efforts to defeat unrest by force alone. Fisher had recommended that the administration be removed from Dublin Castle, 'the associations of which are a heavy sentimental handicap', but in August 1920 it proved necessary to immure the new officials within its walls for their own safety, and there they lived a curious collegiate existence for the next eighteen months. When Fisher asked that they be recalled to London, on the grounds that they could achieve nothing further locked up in the Castle, his request was refused by the Cabinet.[62]

Fisher was appalled at the consequences of the government's Irish policy in 1920 and 1921. He made several trips to Dublin to visit his beleaguered colleagues, and seems to have been in touch with some of the Sinn Fein leaders.[63] Along with Anderson, who in his less flamboyant fashion was equally critical of government policy, he attempted without success to coax the Chief Secretary, Hamar Greenwood, into a flexible frame of mind. Greenwood's sole wish was to echo the Prime Minister, and Fisher was making little progress with Lloyd George, though he never gave up trying:

> It would take a highly skilled dialectician to convince me that there exists any control of the police either from outside or from inside the force. Unintelligent and un-directed brute force is no substitute for scientific well-planned operations involving leadership and discipline; and, although the blind hitting back of the Auxiliary Police and Black and Tans did at the first go off have an effect, they are now getting fully as much as they give, for the gunmen are killing them while they as often as not raid, damage, and insult inoffensive people (which is no sub-stitute for artistic killing) and in the process harden opinion in favour of the extremists and against the Crown.[64]

He also tried his hand with Law, to whom he wrote after reading a rabidly nationalistic Irish pamphlet (given to him by a British general) that 'the elimination of Ireland as a compe-titor in the field of agriculture & in that of industry over the centuries is not a chimera', and that 'for centuries we exploited the country and, when we didn't do that, we prevented her development lest it should damage our own undertakings'. It was 'no answer to say that we have now ceased doing these things', as 'the Irish have memories like horses — I am married into them & know it — & they have something to remember. They have in the past been desperately wronged — their minds dwell on that, the results remind them of it — they are revenge-ful and suspicious. Shd. not we be so?' He concluded by re-marking that

> if only Walter Long & Carson wd. read their history — not this little pamphlet which they would say was tainted —

but books by men of their own faith & stock, wd. not some realisation of 'the other man's' point of view be vouchsafed to them?[65]

After fourteen months of terror and counter-terror in southern Ireland, the Cabinet reluctantly accepted what their advisers had been telling them since May 1920, and a truce was agreed with the Irish separatist leaders. Neither side had gained much from the delay, and the fighting had ensured that Anglo-Irish relations would be strained for many years. Fisher retained his sympathies for the southern Irish, and a dislike of Unionism, to the end of his life. He attributed the course of events from 1912 to 1923 to the 'crass folly of the Castle, reinforced later on by the high treason of Sir Edward Carson.'[66] Within the Treasury's sphere of influence, he did a good deal to develop good relations with the new state. Independent Ireland's machinery of government was largely the creation of C.J. Gregg, an Irishman from the Board of Inland Revenue who was on loan to the new state for its first two years. Similarly, the ethos and procedures of the Irish civil service owed a great deal to British guidance.[67] Finally, as will be seen, in the 1930s Fisher played an important role in protracted and successful negotiations to end the economic dispute between the two countries.

Fisher's activities in relation to Ireland in 1920 and 1921 are striking in a number of ways. Firstly, he took the administrative steps necessary to secure a change in policy by installing competent and trustworthy officials in the Dublin administration. His success in this contrasted with his failure to persuade ministers that a change in political policy was necessary. His comments on coercion were directed at two ministers whom he greatly respected. It would be wrong to assume that he thought he was making a courageous and risky protest; it was rather that he saw Lloyd George and Law as national, not as party figures, open to reasoned argument whatever the colours they wore. They did not damn him for his heresies, but neither did they heed his advice except on the technical question of making the Irish administration efficient. He bore them no grudge, regarding them as prisoners of the Unionist Party where Ireland was concerned. He judged ministers by what he saw as their competence, not their politics, as he told Neville Chamberlain in 1930: 'Tho' as you know I am not a Conservative, you also know my simple creed that the true test —

whatever the label — is the man, with principle, courage & humanity.'[68]

IV

At the end of October 1921, Sir Basil Thomson resigned his post of Assistant Commissioner of the Metropolitan Police. As Assistant Commissioner he had since 1919 been head of the Special Branch and also of what was known as the 'Directorate of Intelligence', while some ministers thought him head of what they called the 'secret service'.[69] He did not go willingly, and his supporters were enraged by the news that his job had been offered to General Byrne of the RIC, whom Thomson had helped to undermine in 1919. This neat twist was Fisher's doing, and the case illustrates the considerable latitude allowed him in all sorts of questions by the Coalition leaders.

The row over Thomson's removal was the culmination of months of uncertainty concerning his activities. Following the reorganization of the Metropolitan Police in 1919, he had been given additional powers to gather domestic intelligence. These arrangements were approved by the Cabinet secret service committee under Curzon, the Foreign Secretary, and including the First Lord of the Admiralty Walter Long, who was the one minister more preoccupied by the Bolshevik peril than Curzon.[70] Thomson also remained head of the Special Branch, staffed by ordinary police detectives, which concentrated on Irish political crime in Britain. From then on he had a responsibility to the Commissioner of the Metropolitan Police for the regular Special Branch, to the Home Office for counter-subversion work in Britain, and to no one in particular for intelligence work concerning Ireland (from mid-1920 onwards he had a particularly wild subordinate in Dublin Castle). He also ran anti-Bolshevik operations in Northern Europe, and he sometimes reported to the Foreign Secretary, who thought him 'a very able and indefatigable public servant and — to us in the F.O. ... an invaluable Sleuth hound.'[71]

The secret service committee was reconstituted in March 1921 to review the workings of the various intelligence and security organizations in being, apparently to eliminate duplication of functions and confusion of responsibilities as well as, undoubtedly, to save some money. On this occasion its members were the Cabinet Secretary Hankey, the permanent head of the Foreign Office Eyre Crowe, and Fisher. Their deliberations produced a far-reaching rationalization of intelligence and security work.[72]

One of the major losers in this review was Thomson, whose non-police activities were hived off, mainly to his rivals in the Security Service, MI5. The committee was 'unfavourably impressed' by Thomson's performance, while 'those most intimately associated with the work, including the Prime Minister, thought that neither the organisation nor Sir Basil Thomson was working as effectively as they ought to and were desirous of a change.'[73] There had been trouble about the cost of his organization the year before, and there was a good deal of evidence to suggest that he had become involved in far too many areas of intelligence activity for either comfort or efficiency. At a time when economy was in vogue, some of his activities appeared farcical and expensive as well as questionable. In 1920 he had dispatched a fifteen man troupe to Poland 'under the direction of Mr Harold Shaw, the well-known producer', to 'photograph material ... for a Russian anti-Bolshevik film .... Their intention is said to be merely to photograph one or two streets and a few villages with peasants etc.', while Labour MPs, amongst his sternest critics because he spied on them, once claimed that thousands of Bolshevik newspapers carefully faked by his organization were on their way to Russia before it was discovered that the printer had complied with British law by putting his name and address on the bottom.[74]

Thomson's removal came shortly after he had been severely criticized in a memorandum submitted by his superior, General Horwood, to the Prime Minister. Horwood described 'the independence of the Special Branch' as 'a standing menace to the good discipline of the force', claimed that Thomson failed to consult him regularly although instructed to do so, asserted that he could find 'no instance' in which information supplied by Thomson had led to successful police action against political crime, and complained that Thomson's organization was expensive, wasteful, and inefficient. He reminded Lloyd George of an incident some months previously, when four Irishmen had been precipitately released by Thomson after being arrested in the grounds of Chequers, and continued:

As to its information regarding labour matters at home, I have recently called the attention of the Secretary of State to misleading and inaccurate reports by the Directorate of Intelligence to the Cabinet in regard to meetings of the unemployed in London itself ...

Sir Basil Thomson's organisation has achieved, probably undeservedly, a reputation for espionage on labour which causes resentment among a proportion of the working classes .... English public opinion ... is most suspicious and resentful of anything approaching the continental system of domestic espionage.[75]

A few days later, Thomson was 'kicked out by the P.M. without reference to the Cabinet by whom I was appointed (with the exception of Austen Chamberlain and Shortt [the Home Secretary] the latter disagreeing) .... The P.M. knew that a majority of the Cabinet would object to my going so he obtained Chamberlain's concurrence and told Fisher to do the work.' The reason, he claimed, was that Lloyd George had been angered by his handling of the Chequers incident. He was offered 'a higher pension than I could legally have claimed if I would "go quietly" (as if I were a dangerous criminal) and at once.'[76] A sympathizer thought that there was 'no doubt that you are a victim of the [Daily] Herald. Your exposure of Lenin's purchase of that paper and of the connection between the Labour extremists and the Soviets made them determined to get you .... Revolutionaries always remove obstacles when they want to kill', while H.A. Gwynne of the *Morning Post* felt Thomson was removed because 'he was the most active anti-Bolshevik in England ... it seems to me that there is always some subtle force behind the Prime Minister in favour of Bolshevism.'[77]

Thomson's account of his fall was inaccurate. Disquiet at his activities predated the Chequers incident. Furthermore, his pension was awarded under a provision of the Police Pensions Act of 1921 which Fisher had 'pressed upon' the Home Office, perhaps as a preliminary to disposing of him.[78] It was designed to meet the necessity of providing adequate pensions for senior officers who might not have many years' service towards a normal police pension and who therefore could plead poverty if asked to resign.[79]

Thomson had been involved in the campaign to remove General Byrne from the headship of the RIC in 1919. Fisher was incensed at the furore created by Thomson's parliamentary friends when it was learnt that Byrne had been offered the post of Assistant Commissioner:

> Circumstances which may be variously interpreted — not the least mischievous being undoubtedly the performance of Sir Basil Thomson, so alien to the great traditions of our service, have in the course of the past week or two resulted ... in what I believe to be one of the most tragic instances on record of injustice to a public servant ... [his detractors] have succeeded in discrediting Sir Joseph Byrne in the eyes of the world. His name conjures up in the minds of the people the defects most noxious in a servant of the Crown — lukewarmness amounting to disloyalty, irresolution hardly distinguishable from cowardice, supineness equivalent to incapacity. And disloyalty, supineness and incapacity are expressions which have actually been put into circulation by members of the late Irish Executive ...
>
> Let me end with the repetition of my most earnest plea that a limit be put to this gallant officer's tortures by an order from HM Government for an immediate and searching enquiry.[80]

Fisher's anger was all the greater because Byrne declined the appointment following the attacks on his reputation. His decision gave some comfort to Thomson's friends. The ailing Walter Long, who had already clashed with Fisher over the reform of Dublin Castle, was 'shocked and distressed beyond measure' by the news of Thomson's removal, but relieved that Byrne would not be taking over 'as I satisfied myself when I was working at this question that it is most dangerous to put a *devout* Roman Catholic in charge of the Secret Service'.[81] The post instead went to General Sir Wyndham Childs, who proved less ambitious than Thomson but no more efficient: he in turn was forced to retire in 1928 because he was deemed unbalanced.[82]

The Cabinet would not agree to Fisher's suggestion of an official inquiry to clear General Byrne's name — indeed, it would if conducted openly have been an acute embarrassment to the Coalition leaders — but he was instructed to prepare a statement expressing the government's confidence in Byrne, and this was read in the Commons in February 1922.[83] In addition, the Cabinet revived Curzon's committee on the secret service to 'go carefully into the question of the proper relationship of the Secret Service Branch to the Chief Commissioner and other Government Departments.'[84] Thomson retired into private life, though not into obscurity. He published several volumes of reminiscences, and wrote some light-hearted detective stories. In 1926 he was convicted with a Miss Thelma de Lava of indecent conduct in Hyde Park, a charge which he stoutly denied.85 He blamed Lloyd George for his removal in 1921:

> I belong now to a growing army of public servants sacrificed because they did their duty fearlessly .... The trouble is that we are not governed by a Cabinet but by one man, who now insists on making the appointments in every department. It would not matter if he were a good judge of men but look at the gang he has round him!
>
> I dare say that he found my reports especially on the Russian Trade people inconvenient. I hear that he said the other day that I dealt in 'Morning Post' stunts.[86]

Fisher continued to take an interest in the Metropolitan Police, and was largely responsible for the appointment of Trenchard as head of the force in 1931.[87] As Permanent Secretary to the Treasury he was, also, the Accounting Officer for the Secret Service Vote. The Treasury was closely involved in the various sleights of hand by which the intelligence and security services were funded, and he kept a watch on all of this. In addition, as the international situation deteriorated in the 1930s he saw quite a lot of Admiral 'Quex' Sinclair, the head of SIS from 1923 until 1939, and he also had some dealings with MI5 on security matters involving civil servants.[88] Having so powerful a friend seems to have done the intelligence services little good; until 1936 they suffered a great deal as a result of shortages of staff and money, the main cuts being made in 1921–22.[89]

V

In addition to being Permanent Secretary to the Treasury and Head of the Civil Service, Fisher held the office of Auditor of the Civil List. This was normally nothing more than a title, but he was occasionally consulted on financial matters affecting the royal family.[90] In December 1920 he informed Lloyd George that there was a deficit of over £24,000 on the Civil List expenditure for 1919, and that there was no obvious way in which economies could be made 'unless there is to be a sensible diminution in the amount of ceremonial and splendour which is associated by tradition with the British Throne.'[91] Despite these doubts, he was made chairman of a committee appointed to advise 'as to the means by which the estimated deficit for the year 1922 can best be reduced.' The other members were a leading accountant, Sir William McLintock, who was one of Fisher's City contacts, and the Lord Chamberlain Sir Frederick Ponsonby. Fisher appointed as secretary to the committee a Treasury official, R.E. Harwood, who had risen from being a Post Office telegraphist to become an assistant secretary and principal establishments officer in the Treasury. He did most of the investigating, and Fisher was amused by the contrast between the good job he did and the well-bred inefficiency which he uncovered. The committee's report disclosed mismanagement and dishonesty on a grand scale. It stated that almost all the staff of the royal household were grossly overpaid. If the accounts were to be believed, it cost six times as much per head per day to feed royal servants as it did to feed non-commissioned officers and their equivalents in the services, at the most conservative calculation and 'exclusive of the cost of liquor.' The household often paid wholesale prices in excess of the normal retail prices for its food: 'the buying has been carried out with incompetence ... the bacon must all be Irish.' Furthermore,

> we are forced to the conclusion that there is leakage, either by way of a proportion of the goods paid for not being delivered at the Palace, or by a part of the quantity delivered finding its way surreptitiously out of the Palace, or both.

About £10,000 worth of food had disappeared in this way in 1920, in addition to the money wasted on feeding all and sundry, including the delivery men. The committee recommended economies totalling £40,000, including a two-thirds reduction in the quantity of food purchased, and a halving of the price paid by competitive buying on the open market.[92]

King George is said to have been very grateful to Fisher for his handling of this inquiry, to have regarded him highly thereafter and, together with Queen Mary, to have consulted him on various matters from time to time. Fisher himself recalled that he had tried to warn off Edward VIII before the King's plans to marry Mrs Simpson became public.[93] In the absence of documents, however, it is impossible to gauge to what extent, and when, Fisher performed anything more than the normal duties expected of the Permanent Secretary to the Treasury in relation to the affairs of the monarchy. Although he was made a KCVO in 1923, and a GCVO in 1927, it is hard to know if these were signs of particular favour as they were honours which he might have expected ex officio as Auditor of the Civil List.

What is clear is that Fisher was not much interested in honours in themselves. In 1932 he waived his right as a GCB to a stall in Henry VII's chapel, writing to his fellow Wykehamist Sir Clive Wigram, the King's private secretary, that 'you and I have known each other for many years and you will appreciate that forms and ceremonies are not exactly my long suit.' Nevertheless, he might still have taken the stall were it not that, for purely technical reasons, the College of Arms refused to accept his coat of arms and wanted to prepare a new one. Fisher saw no reason to cast aside what he believed was his proper coat of arms, and declined to do so.[94] At the end of his time at the Treasury he refused a peerage offered by the Prime Minister, though this was as much on political as on personal grounds.[95]

As Head of the Civil Service Fisher was responsible for recommending officials for various honours. Lloyd George was notorious for his handling of political honours, and even those awarded to the civil service came in for some criticism from Buckingham Palace.[96] In asking the King to restrict the number of peerages and knighthoods available, however, the Conservative leader Austen Chamberlain made it clear that he was happy to rely on Fisher's judgement where the civil service was concerned.[97] Despite his disdain for honours personally, he believed that Whitehall should get its fair share. Civil service honours were settled by a committee of heads of departments chaired by him, and he became the focus for resentment amongst those disappointed. Most of the criticism made against him in relation to honours seems a product of the animosity of officials who considered themselves unfairly passed over.

Sir Walford Selby, for example, author of a string of wild charges against him which will be discussed in later chapters, listed among Fisher's sins his unwarranted interference in the award of honours to the Foreign Office and the diplomatic service. By this account Fisher was successfully beaten off by 'Austen' [Chamberlain, the Foreign Secretary] in 1924, but was later successful.[98] This story, however, is hard to reconcile with a minute written by Chamberlain early in 1926, when Fisher's role in appointments and honours came under attack in the House of Commons. The Foreign Secretary wrote that 'I need not say that I most heartily concur' in Fisher's defence of his functions as Head of the Civil Service. 'I regard the 1919 decisions as vital to the efficiency of the Civil Service.'[99] It should be said that of its nature the bestowal of honours is bound to create jealousy and excite rumour of departmental if not of personal bias, no matter how unimpeachable the integrity of those making the recommendations. It is, furthermore, also quite likely that ministers sometimes alleged Fisher's opposition to awards which they did not wish to make, as Bradbury had anticipated in 1919.

Fisher was not a prig, and he held very strongly that the private life of an official was of no concern to his employers unless it affected his work in some manner. When he was informed that the Treasury Controller of Finance, Sir Basil Blackett, could not be invited to a royal garden party because he was divorced, he told the Lord Chamberlain that 'I of course appreciate that the discretion in such matters rests with you under the direction of the King; and you for your part will no doubt appreciate that as Permanent Head of His Majesty's Civil Service I am in the position of a trustee for the members of that service.' He pointed out that 'in all the great economic and financial crises on the solution of which the recovery of the whole world depends Sir Basil Blackett is the man on whose judgement, skill, and knowledge His Majesty's ministers principally rely', and that if the government accepted Blackett's services 'he is entitled to be saved from the treatment of a pariah.'[100]

During his time as its head, the Treasury became a refuge for a succession of talented undesirables from less broadminded departments. In the most celebrated of these cases, a

War Office man who had been involved in a divorce case was told by the head of the department, Sir Herbert Creedy, that he could expect no further promotion, as the generals would not stand for it. Fisher brought him to the Treasury, where he was a spectacular success, and ultimately he returned to his first department and became its permanent head.[101]

The one politician who in Fisher's eyes could do no wrong was Lloyd George. Although he must have known perfectly well of the practice of selling honours, Fisher would never admit that the Prime Minister had behaved improperly.[102] When the Coalition fell in 1922, he did all he could to secure the futures of Lloyd George's entourage. J.T. Davies became a director of the Suez Canal company. It was one of the most agreeable sinecures in the government's gift and Fisher kept it firmly in the Treasury's grip despite the protestations of the Foreign Office and the Admiralty.[103] According to Frances Stevenson, Lloyd George's secretary and mistress, Fisher offered to make her 'a permanent civil servant in the First Class. I think I would have been the first woman to receive this honour.'[104] A few months later, A.J. Sylvester

> was invited by Lloyd George, now out of office, to rejoin him as his Principal Private Secretary in succession to Sir John Davies ... As a civil servant I consulted Sir Warren personally. He was at great pains and gave me his advice freely. This I followed, and I am mightily glad that I did: it has proved absolutely right and sound.[105]

VI

By the time the Coalition fell in October 1922 Fisher had been Permanent Secretary to the Treasury and Head of the Civil Service for three years. In that time he had achieved a good deal: the process of reorganizing the civil service was well under way, and a broadly uniform personnel policy had been applied in all departments. Although the financial doctrine which he propounded of the ultimate responsibility of heads of departments had yet to be accepted for the large civil departments, it was evident that eventually it would be. His right to advise the Prime Minister on senior appointments had been generally recognized, although where the Foreign Office was concerned it was insufficiently defined. As an adviser, particularly on the Irish question, he had displayed his complete lack of fear, and had established the habit of speaking his mind as he saw fit on various policy issues outside the Treasury's traditional purview. On the other hand, there were some unresolved questions to be dealt with. In particular, he had been unable to put the relationship between the Cabinet secretariat and the Treasury at the centre of government on a satisfactory footing, although he had taken some preparatory steps in 1921.[106] This was to occupy quite a lot of his attention in succeeding years.

Fisher was supported in his activities by the Prime Minister and by both Law and Austen Chamberlain, successively the Conservative leaders in the Coalition. They all agreed that economy in administration could only be secured by a Treasury with increased powers in questions of staff and organization. That consensus was essential if the reforms begun in 1919 were to endure, and Fisher took care to foster it by involving them all at each step. As a result, the Prime Minister's power in senior appointments was accepted from the outset as being non-political, and the Head of the Civil Service was not regarded as Lloyd George's creature. This was not simply the result of bureaucratic adroitness: Fisher took care to maintain good relations with the Conservative leaders by constant consultation, but he also spoke out in an astonishing manner against the views on Ireland which their party embodied. Yet they trusted him to serve Law's government as he had served Lloyd George. His intuitive distinction between ministers and their parties was a good one.

Notes

1. Taylor, *Essays*, p. 257.
2. Note by Milner 23 June 1921, Milner MS Dep. 125.
3. Churchill to Lloyd George, 23 Apr.; same to same, 4 Mar. 1920, Lloyd George papers, F/9/2/27 and F/9/2/11.
4. Fisher to Austen Chamberlain, 26 Apr. 1920, ibid., F/7/3/5 and 5a.
5. ibid., undated, F/7/3/6; Fisher to MacDonald (the Prime Minister) and Haldane, 7 Feb. 1924, PRO 30/69/1/192.
6. Interviews with Sir Robert Fraser and Sir John Winnifrith.
7. Interview with Sir John Winnifrith; Liddell-Hart's note of a talk with Hore-Belisha, 27 Mar. 1939, Liddell-Hart papers, 11/HB 1939/3.
8. K.B. Paice to the author, 4 Nov. 1981. Mr Paice joined the Home Office in 1929.
9. Fisher to Lloyd George, 9 Feb. 1922, Lloyd George papers, F/17/1/13.
10. Fisher to Frances Stevenson, 27 Feb. 1922, ibid., F/17/1/15.
11. K.B. Paice to the author, 4 Nov. 1981; Sir Alexander Johnston to the author, 7 May 1981. Sir Alexander joined the Home Office in 1928.
12. Fisher to Austen Chamberlain, 28 Feb. 1921, T162 56/E4424.
13. Fisher to Lloyd George, 22 Nov. 1921, Lloyd George papers, F/17/1/12.
14. Fisher and Symons shared the lease of a shoot in Wales. Interview with R.W. Fisher.
15. Royal Commission on the Civil Service, 1929–31, minutes of evidence, p. 1276, Fisher's evidence of 17 Dec. 1930.
16. Morgan, *Consensus and Disunity*, pp. 52, 94.
17. Lowe, 'State intervention', pp. 828–33; 'A graveyard of social reform?', p. 432. See also Lowe, 'Bureaucracy triumphant or denied?', pp. 291–310.
18. Lowe, 'State intervention', p. 280.
19. 'Cato', *Guilty Men*, p. 87.
20. Wilson did of course succeed Fisher in 1939, but it would be absurd to argue that he had been playing up to the Treasury for twenty years with this in mind.
21. Lowe, 'State intervention', p. 285; 'The Ministry of Labour, 1916–19: a still, small voice?', in Burk (ed.) *War and the State*, pp. 121–2, 130. Lowe and Roberts, 'Sir Horace Wilson, 1900–1935', pp. 649–51 develop the argument further in relation to Wilson. At n.11 at pp. 644–5 the authors pause to condemn the unpublished doctoral research on which the present study is based. See O'Halpin, 'British government and society', p.761, where this writer incautiously went to the aid of Wilson's reputation, thereby evidently enraging Dr Lowe. Sir Horace Wilson's extraordinary career undoubtedly merits further research, but anyone attempting it will find documentary material hard to come by.
22. Grigg, *Prejudice and Judgement*, p. 52.
23. Rumbold to Oliphant, 30 Mar. 1921, Rumbold MS dep. 26.

24. Murray, *Reflections*, p. 6.

25. Acton to Rumbold, 20 May 1919, Rumbold MS dep. 26.

26. Steiner and Dockrill, 'Foreign Office reforms', p. 138.

27. ibid.

28. Note by Curzon, 30 Nov. 1922, Curzon papers, MSS Eur. F112/319; Hardinge to Rumbold, 13 July 1920, Hardinge papers, 43/126–7.

29. Curzon to Lloyd George, 20 July 1920, Lloyd George papers, F/13/1/1–4; Rumbold to Hardinge, 28 Aug. 1920, Hardinge papers, 43/84–90.

30. See Sanderson to Russell, 6 Apr., and Kilbracken to Sanderson, 3 Apr. 1919, Curzon papers, MSS Eur. F112/214(a), on previous occasions when the Prime Minister had been involved in such appointments.

31. Murray, *Reflections*, p. 8.

32. Curzon to Austen Chamberlain, 12 Apr.; Austen Chamberlain to Curzon, 23 Apr.; Curzon to Austen Chamberlain, 3 May 1920, T1 12564/20935.

33. Austen Chamberlain to Curzon, 5 May 1920, ibid.

34. Hardinge to Ronald Graham, undated, 1921[?], Hardinge papers, 22/194–7.

35. Note by Curzon, as in note 28 above; Fisher memoir, Chapter 16, Part 1.

36. Fisher to J.T. Davies, 13 Jan. 1921, T162 24/E1551.

37. T1 12503/11228.

38. Bradbury to Lloyd George, 5 May 1921, Lloyd George papers, F/27/6/50.

39. Hardinge to Curzon, 30 Mar. 1922, Hardinge papers, 45/66.

40. Curzon to Horne (Chancellor of the Exchequer), 19 Nov.; Horne to Curzon, 22 Nov. 1921, T160 122/F4516.

41. Minutes of Royal Institute for International Affairs (RIIA) British Security group, 1 Jan. 1945, Greaves papers, coll. misc. 462/6.

42. Note by Curzon, as in note 28 above.

43. Murray, *Reflections*, p. 7.

44. Long to Lloyd George, 21 May 1919, Lloyd George papers, F/33/2/45.

45. Lloyd George to Bonar Law, 30 Dec. 1919, Lloyd George papers, F/31/1/16.

46. Lloyd-Graeme's note of a talk with General Byrne, 20 Jan. 1920, Swinton papers, SWIN 270/2/1.

47. The background to these events is described more fully in O'Halpin, *The Decline of the Union*, pp. 188–96.

48. Ibid., p. 195.

49. Byrne had been ordered to take three months leave in December 1919, and an acting Inspector General had been appointed in his place.

50. Fisher to Austen Chamberlain and Lloyd George, 18 Nov. 1921, Chamberlain papers, AC23/2/16.

51. He was governor successively of the Seychelles, Sierre Leone, and Kenya.

52. Fisher memoir, Chapter 14, Part 1.

53. As in note 50 above.

54. Macready to Long, 23 Apr. 1920, Lloyd George papers, F/34/1/19.

55. Macready, *Annals*, ii, 449.

56. Fisher to Law, 27 Apr. 1920, Bonar Law papers, 103/2/17.

57. Saunderson to Long, 7 May 1920, Long papers, WRO 947/348.

58. Austen Chamberlain to Law, 12 May; Fisher to Austen Chamberlain, Law and Lloyd George, 12 May 1920, Lloyd George papers, F/31/1/32.

59. Extracts from a draft of an unpublished memoir, *The Life of a Civil Servant*, by G.C. Duggan in my possession. Duggan worked in Dublin Castle from 1919 to 1922.

60. Fisher to Austen Chamberlain, Law, and Lloyd George, 15 May 1920, Lloyd George papers, F/31/1/33.

61. H.A.L. Fisher diary, 28 May 1920, H.A.L. Fisher papers, box 8a.

62. Fisher to Austen Chamberlain, Bonar Law and Lloyd George, 12 May 1920, as in note 58 above; the Cabinet decision of 13 Aug. 1920 to leave the officials in Dublin is in CAB48(20), CAB23/22. Mark (later Sir Mark) Sturgis, of the Board of Inland Revenue, was sent over to Ireland as Assistant Under Secretary. At Fisher's behest he kept a remarkably frank diary of Castle life, which Fisher had typed up in the Treasury. Sturgis diary, 30 Nov. 1920, PRO 30/59/1.

63. Interview with R.W. Fisher.

64. Fisher to Frances Stevenson, with a memorandum for Lloyd George, 11 Feb. 1921, Lloyd George papers, F/7/1/9.

65. Fisher to Law, 17 July 1920, Bonar Law papers, 102/5/34.

66. Fisher memoir, Chapter 5, Part 1.

67. This is examined in detail in Fanning, *Department of Finance*.

68. Fisher to Neville Chamberlain, 24 June 1930, Chamberlain papers, NC7/11/23/5.

69. The Commissioner of the Metropolitan Police called it the Special Branch, Curzon and Long the Secret Service, and Thomson the Directorate of Intelligence. Some of the confusion arose because the Special Branch and the Directorate of Intelligence were, at least notionally, entirely separate organizations although both were controlled by Thomson.

70. Curzon to Austen Chamberlain, 5 Nov. 1921, Chamberlain papers, AC23/2/1.

71. ibid.; Sturgis diary, 13 Feb. 1921, PRO 30/59/1–4.

72. Andrew, *Secret Service*, p. 232.

73. Austen Chamberlain to Long, 4 Nov., and to Curzon, 7 Nov. 1921, Chamberlain papers, AC23/2/3 and 14. The committee's remit was to 'examine the secret service expenditure'.

74. Hardinge to Rumbold, 21 Feb. 1920, Rumbold MSS dep. 26; *Parliamentary Debates*, (*Parl. Deb.*), *House of Commons (HC)*, 5th series, vol. 146, col. 2063, 3 Nov. 1921. It was said that the fake newspapers were later found locked in a cupboard in Riga.

75. Memorandum by Horwood, 26 Oct. 1921, Lloyd George papers, F/28/1/6. See Taylor (ed.) *Lloyd George*, p. 218, on the Chequers incident.

76. Thomson to H.A. Gwynne, 2 Nov. 1921, Gwynne MS 22.

77. St Loe Strachey (editor of the *Spectator*) to Thomson, 4 Nov. 1921, St Loe Strachey papers, S/19/3/12. Gwynne to Houghton, 3 Apr. 1922, Gwynne MS 7. See Andrew, *Secret Service*, pp. 263–4, on the Russian subsidy to the *Daily Herald*.

78. Note by Fisher, 5 Oct. 1928, T 164/P71229.

79. Thomson's pension had been discussed between the Home Office and the Treasury over the summer of 1921, and at the beginning of October they agreed on the amount. Thomson had raised the question himself. T164 16/P11618.

80. Fisher to Austen Chamberlain, Law and Lloyd George, 18 Nov. 1921, Lloyd George papers, F/7/4/33. Fisher had been named in the Commons as having threatened Thomson that he might lose his pension if he did not retire quietly.

81. Long to Austen Chamberlain, 2 Nov., Chamberlain papers, AC23/2/1; Long to Thomson, 28 Oct. 1921, Long papers, WRO 947/855.

82. His pension papers are in T164 78/P71229. His superior General Horwood was due to retire, and the opportunity was taken to get rid of Childs as well in the wake of the Savidge case in 1928, T164 29/P25084. Miss Savidge had been accused of indecent conduct with Sir Leo Chiozza Money, a well-known Liberal politician. She was subsequently harassed by the police. Sir Leo said he had been advising her on her career when they were both arrested in a railway carriage.

83. *Parl. Deb., HC*, vol. 150, cols. 1208–9, 16 Feb. 1922.

84. Austen Chamberlain to Long, 10 Nov. 1921, Chamberlain papers, AC 23/2/7.

85. His Labour foes did not forget him. G.D.H. and Margaret Cole satirized both him and his successor as 'Sir Basil' and 'General Bunker' in *The Death of a Millionaire* (1925). Thomson's defence in the court case was that he was carrying out research for a book on prostitution.

86. Thomson to Gwynne, 2 Nov. 1921, Gwynne MS 22.

87. Boyle, *Trenchard*, pp. 591–2.

88. Interviews with Sir Thomas and Lady Padmore, and with R.W. Fisher.

89. Hinsley, *British Intelligence*, i, 48–52; O'Halpin, 'Financing British intelligence: the evidence up to 1945', in K.G. Robertson (ed.) *British and American Approaches to Intelligence*, pp. 187–217, discusses how some intelligence costs were borne on open votes.

90. Stamfordham (private secretary to the King) to Lloyd George, 26 May 1920, Lloyd George papers, F/29/4/10.

91. Fisher to Lloyd George, 4 Dec. 1920, Lloyd George papers, F/31/1/50.

92. Report by Fisher, Sir Frederick Ponsonby, Sir William McLintock, and R.E. Harwood, 22 Dec. 1921, T160 284/E12544. Some months later Harwood was attached to the royal household as temporary Deputy Treasurer to the King.

93. Interviews with R.W. Fisher and with Professor H.R.G. Greaves.

94. Fisher to Wigram, 11 Aug. 1932, Warren Fisher papers. The problem was that whereas Fisher could trace his family, and his crest, to 1715, the College of Arms found an identical crest belonging to an Edward Fisher of Gloucestershire dating from 1628. While Fisher was happy to accept the likelihood that Edward Fisher was one of his forebears, the College of Arms was not, and wanted to charge him £77 for designing a new one.

95. Interview with R.W. Fisher; Stuart, *Reith Diaries*, p. 227, entry for 16 Mar. 1939.

96. Stamfordham to Davies, 14 May 1921, PREM2/23; Fisher to Lloyd George, 29 June 1920, Lloyd George papers, F/7/1/8.

97. Austen Chamberlain to Stamfordham, 3 May 1922, Chamberlain papers, AC23/5/12.

98. Selby to Lord Killearn (formerly Miles Lampson), 10 Apr. 1956, Selby papers.

99. Copy of note by Chamberlain, on printed note prepared by Fisher, 30 Mar. 1926, for the Prime Minister's use in answering parliamentary questions on the role of the Head of the Civil Service, Warren Fisher papers.

100. Copy of Fisher to the Lord Chamberlain, 18 July 1922, Lloyd George papers, F/17/1/16.

101. The reaction of the generals is not recorded. Interviews with Sir John Winnifrith, Sir Edward Playfair, Sir Robert Fraser, and Sir Thomas and Lady Padmore.

102. Interview with R.W. Fisher. In the surviving fragments of the Fisher memoirs there are copious references to Lloyd George, all of them extremely favourable, as well as dismissive remarks about the Marconi scandal of 1913.

103. Whether or not he actually suggested Davies for this post, Fisher could probably have obstructed the appointment had he wished. There was some indignation when Davies got this plum, inspired mainly by jealousy and by dislike of Lloyd George. Hardinge to Curzon, 1 Nov. 1922, Hardinge papers, 45/172–4. Foreign Office and Admiralty ambitions to have a say in filling the British directorship are clear from papers in T1 12501/10947 and T160 139/F5142.

104. Lloyd George, *The Years*, p. 210. It seems unlikely that this is what Fisher offered. Miss Stevenson had ceased to be a temporary civil servant on 31 Mar. 1922, when her pay and that of two other secretaries ceased to be met from public funds. Davies to Fisher, 26 Apr. 1922, T163 13/1/G577. This, 'together with the early abolition of the Garden Suburb, is the Prime Minister's contribution to the Geddes report'.

105. A.J. Sylvester to the author, 17 Mar. 1980.

106. This is discussed in the following chapter.

4

The Law, Baldwin, and MacDonald governments, 1922–4

I

The government formed by Bonar Law in October 1922 was quite unlike its predecessor. Not only the Lloyd George Liberals were gone: the great men of the Tory party were conspicuous by their absence. The general election of November confirmed that the flashy politics of Coalition days were gone for good. Law's government sought and secured a mandate to do as little as possible, to steer clear of foreign adventures and to cut public expenditure. It was the last of these that gave most difficulty.

The cuts in expenditure adopted by the Coalition after the report of the Geddes economy committee in February 1922 were so severe that there was little for anyone else to reduce, a problem that confronted Law as soon as he took office as Prime Minister. Since he had been a senior minister continuously from May 1915 until March 1921, this cannot have come as a surprise to him. In practice he wanted to ensure that expenditure did not start to grow again, rather than to introduce additional large reductions overnight. In one area, however, he was committed to definite action: the Cabinet secretariat was to go.[1]

Disbanding the secretariat was a troublesome matter. It was headed by Colonel Sir Maurice Hankey, who was also secretary to the Committee of Imperial Defence (CID), a body consisting of ministers, civil servants and service officers established in 1908 to co-ordinate strategic policy decisions. The CID had a full-time secretariat of officers on secondment from the services. The failures of British strategy in the first two years of the war were quite clearly not attributable to the CID's existence; indeed they emphasized the need for more rather than less co-ordination of national strategy. Once war broke out, the Asquith government had made piecemeal innovations in the organization of Cabinet business, first through the establishment of the ministerial War Council in November 1914, and, after the Conservatives joined in May 1915, through the Dardanelles (later the War) Committee.

The key difficulty faced by all these bodies was that in the last resort they were subordinate to the Cabinet, and that they reflected rather than avoided the differences on strategy which bedevilled the government as a whole. Because of his great ability, because the main preoccupation was with military matters, and because he was the man on the spot, Hankey was secretary to each of them in turn. When Lloyd George became Prime Minister in December 1916, he created a new body, the War Cabinet. This was unlike its predecessors in one key respect: it was effectively superior to, not subordinate to, the full Cabinet. Furthermore, Lloyd George was able to dominate it. Hankey became secretary to the War Cabinet, and was responsible for the secretariat which sprang up to service the network of committees to which detailed consideration of all the business of government, including civil matters, was delegated.[2]

The secretariat had shown its value from the day of its formal creation in December 1916, and it was patently obvious that the co-ordinating functions which it performed were essential to the discharge of government business in peacetime as well as in war. The feeling against it was based not on any coherent theory of government, but on a distrust of Lloyd George and all his works.[3] Criticism of the secretariat had grown after March 1921, when it had been given a separate vote in the estimates, and was no longer sheltered under the umbrella of the 'Treasury and Subordinate Departments' vote. Ostensibly this change had emphasized the independence of the secretariat, but Hankey bitterly resented it since it drew attention to his organization while conferring no worthwhile benefit.[4] Fisher had insisted on making the change, probably as a preliminary to an attempt to absorb the secretariat into the departmental Treasury organization. He certainly did not want the secretariat to become entirely independent of the Treasury, and equally he did not wish it to disappear. If his intention was to put pressure on Hankey, he succeeded, but the outcome of his manoeuvring was not what he desired.

After the fall of Lloyd George, Hankey took the battle for his department to Law, pledging his loyalty to the new Prime Minister and proposing a reduction 'from £37,000 to £15–16,000' in the yearly cost of the secretariat.[5] Law seemed amenable to these changes, and Hankey believed 'I have saved the ship by chucking ballast overboard.'[6] Despite this, it soon became clear that his troubles were not over: Fisher, who had earlier been 'in perfect agreement with me in regard to my office', gave him a considerable shock by 'springing on me his proposal that I should become a Treasury official. He admitted that he had been planning this for years', and 'I even suspect that the plan of a separate vote for the Cabinet Office, which I strenuously resisted, was "put over" us in order to wreck us. I felt Warren Fisher had not played quite straight.'[7] Nor was Law much help, and Hankey had a feeling that 'a lot of civil servants are in this thing against us on principle — even though personally they are good friends. I am unsuspicious by nature, but too many wisps of straw blow in the same direction.'[8]

Hankey refused to consider becoming a fourth 'controller' under Fisher in the Treasury: although Fisher 'promised me as free a hand in this position as I have had before and I believe him', the 'latitude' allowed to 'Controllers of the Treasury is granted only by Treasury Minute', and is 'liable to be revoked by a fresh Treasury Minute', and 'even if the Permanent Secretary to the Treasury could be trusted *in saecula seculorum* never to interfere with the Secretary of the Cabinet, a hostile' Chancellor 'could make his position impossible.' Hankey argued further that the secretaryship of the Cabinet and of the CID were 'inseparably linked.'[9] The fight went on for some days, and Hankey considered resigning and putting his case in public.[10] Then 'an extraordinary thing happened', as Fisher 'suddenly launched out into a brand new proposal, viz. that, in addition to continuing S[ecretary] of the C[abinet] and C.I.D. I should also become clerk of the Privy Council — practically a sinecure' (the incumbent, Sir Almeric Fitzroy, was about to resign following a court conviction, dismissed on appeal, for bothering women in Hyde Park).[11]

This was an excellent development for Hankey: it would confound the nagging argument that his involvement at Cabinet meetings was somehow unconstitutional, as the Cabinet was technically only a committee of the Privy Council. Furthermore, the additional responsibility would strengthen his position in relation to the Treasury. In the course of the next week he consolidated his gains: Law promised to 'meet me everywhere' and to defend the secretariat in the Commons. He also agreed that the office would revert to its old position as a subordinate department on the Treasury vote, and that Hankey, not the Treasury, would be in charge of all its staff.[12]

Fisher assented to these changes in a minute which stated that 'the Treasury ... is not merely the finance department but also, under the Prime Minister (First Lord) and the Cabinet, the central and co-ordinating organ of government. As such it is the natural body to provide for the secretarial needs of the Cabinet.'[13] In reality, the changes agreed represented a climb-down as compared with his earlier claims that the secretariat should become part of the departmental Treasury — it was even rumoured that he had contemplated becoming Cabinet Secretary himself should Hankey go.[14] He made it clear to Hankey that he conceded only out of respect for him personally, and did not hide his belief that the secretariat should ultimately be absorbed by the Treasury.[15]

Despite this fundamental disagreement, he and Hankey remained quite close throughout their time together in Whitehall. They were very different men, but both excelled in operating in the twilight zone between politics and administration. Hankey's expertise as an adviser was in military strategy, particularly imperial defence where, as befitted a Royal Marine, he was an important defender of the navy's interests. He had no great interest in the civil side of Cabinet Office work, and he did not generally put forward distinctive views on domestic issues to the Prime Ministers he served. He and Fisher were usually not in competition, and the influence of each depended in part on having a good understanding with the other. Frequently they co-operated to secure a given end; occasionally they clashed. Each felt he knew the other's strengths and weaknesses and in the last resort could turn them to advantage. The two did differ fairly considerably on defence policy in the 1930s, as will be seen, but they remained on good terms. After their battle in 1922, the future of the Cabinet Office did not become an issue between them again until Hankey was about to retire in 1938. By then there was little besides egoism in his views about the appointment of his successor, and Fisher secured a relatively easy victory over his old ally and adversary.[16]

Law's concern that his government should behave with the utmost propriety, in contrast to the irregular methods employed by Lloyd George, was explained by the state of feeling in his party against the way that the Coalition had been run. However, he emulated Lloyd George in bringing in a private secretary from outside the Civil Service. The man he appointed was Colonel Ronald Waterhouse, who had been his personal private secretary since 1919. Waterhouse would not have been out of place amidst Lloyd George's personal entourage.[17] He was not at all trustworthy, and Bonar Law seems to have disliked him.[18] Fisher was 'very anxious on constitutional grounds' that Law should have 'a first rate Treasury man, thus reverting to an old practice of many of your predecessors' amongst his personal staff, but he could not prevent Waterhouse's appointment.[19] When Stanley Baldwin succeeded Law in May 1923, he kept Waterhouse on.[20] It is not clear why Fisher, who in later years made sure that the Prime Minister was surrounded by career officials, took no action either in 1922 or 1923 to regularize the position. Baldwin's biographers have written that he was 'encumbered with the unreliable Waterhouse until 1928', but in fact Fisher tried to get rid of him in 1926 by proposing him to Baldwin in fulsome terms for a Suez Canal company directorship.[21] Not only did Baldwin disregard this advice, but he let Waterhouse have a copy of Fisher's recommendation.[22] He told Neville Chamberlain in 1938 that 'Warren Fisher in '25 or '26 suggested' Waterhouse for a Suez directorship, 'but I strongly suspect it was to clear him out of No. 10!', which indicates that it was Baldwin's responsibility that Waterhouse remained his private secretary.[23]

It was not until 1928 that Fisher succeeded in making the Prime Minister's private office a preserve of the career civil service, after Waterhouse had been pushed out and his successor, Sir Patrick Gower, had departed to work for the Conservatives. He then installed Robert Vansittart, who two years later returned to the Foreign Office as Permanent Under Secretary. Curiously, however, Vansittart's successors as principal private secretary at No. 10 up to 1939 did not find the job a springboard to much greater things — indeed, the post of private secretary to the Chancellor offered somewhat better prospects for ultimate advancement.[24]

Law was Prime Minister for only seven months, and was succeeded in May 1923 by Stanley Baldwin. The news prompted Fisher to shout 'Thank God', with the 'fervour of an Archdeacon.'[25] Baldwin had been a Treasury minister from 1919 to 1921, and from October 1922 onwards, and he had, nominally at least, played an important part in the effort to regain control of expenditure. Baldwin's public persona was that of a kindly, straightforward, decent provincial gentleman who had become an MP out of a sense of simple duty towards his locality, and who had been made Prime Minister almost by accident.[26] However, he already had the reputation in the Treasury of being remarkably shrewd in political affairs, and of being exceptionally lethargic about departmental Treasury matters.[27]

Baldwin had earned the respect of the Treasury in January 1923 with his handling of negotiations on the repayment of British debts to the United States arising from the First World War. Although the American ambassador in London had given the strong impression that the American institutions were prepared to make considerable concessions, the British party sent to negotiate found the American representatives had been thinking on very different lines. A Treasury official involved thought it 'just possible' that very favourable terms could have been obtained had the Chancellor been allowed more latitude in the talks. Unfortunately he had to consult the Cabinet which, misled by the American ambassador's earlier optimism, and worried that the Americans would take no account of the related problem of European indebtedness to Britain, was against additional concessions. Ultimately the Americans offered terms which 'though not generous, are not impossible' and which 'are perhaps less likely to endure than more generous terms.'[28]

When the ship bringing the delegation back docked at Southampton, Baldwin made a statement to the Press which effectively pre-empted Cabinet refusal of the American offer. This provoked a Cabinet crisis, and the Prime Minister Law took the unusual step of denouncing the settlement anonymously in a letter to *The Times*.[29] But, in the words of the Treasury Controller of Finance, Sir Otto Niemeyer, Baldwin 'dug his toes in or had them fixed in for him and eventually pulled it off'. It was 'an amazing achievement in the circumstances to have got off so cheap.'[30] An Inland Revenue official who wrote a history of the negotiations some years later concurred: the British side 'got the best terms they could have got short of default, which at that time was simply not to be considered. To say otherwise is simply to say that one is ill-informed.'[31] However, the settlement did nothing directly to ease the problems of Britain's European debtors, not that there was ever any prospect that the Americans could have been induced to take a broader view of the issues than they did.

II

For some months Baldwin combined the offices of Prime Minister and Chancellor, thereby strengthening the bond between the Treasury and No. 10. The new regime continued to worry about the cost of running the country. A perennial target for economy drives were the armed services. The financial difficulties they encountered were continuous throughout the 1920s, but they had their roots in decisions taken in the early years of the decade.

The strategic problem facing Britain was a straightforward one. As a result of the war its resources had dwindled and its obligations had vastly increased. The army was expected not only to provide garrisons and put down disorder in Ireland, the Middle East, India, and Egypt, but also to maintain sufficient strength at home to deal with civil unrest. It was also supposed to be prepared for a future war, although planning for this was not much encouraged by ministers.[32] The demands on the navy were less pressing — who was there left to fight? — yet the admirals proved far harder to control than the hapless generals.

Within a year of the armistice Barstow, shortly to be Controller of Supply Services in the Treasury, prepared a memorandum on the Admiralty estimates, and attached a note in which he remarked that 'I am afraid that in writing' on the Admiralty's plans 'I may have touched on matters of high policy outside my province: but I do not see how else the question of fleet strength can be dealt with ....' He could not 'believe that war between the United States of America and Great Britain', a spectre conjured up by the First Lord of the Admiralty, 'is anything but unthinkable', and he was equally dismissive of the likelihood of major naval confrontations with either Russia or

France, while the German and Austrian navies 'are destroyed'. He requested 'instructions as to whether naval estimates are to be examined on "policy" lines, or merely by way of "checking" ....' Two months later the Cabinet agreed on the 'ten year rule', whereby service departments were to plan on the assumption that Britain would not be engaged in a major war within the next ten years.[33] This rule, combined with the continual need for savings as the country struggled simultaneously to deal with its huge war debts, its overseas commitments, mass unemployment at home and international economic instability, meant that the services suffered a great deal in the 1920s. Under Fisher the Treasury was willing to query not only the cost of the services but the strategic and political assumptions underlying defence planning.

The Treasury regarded the Admiralty as especially obstinate, not without reason. Quite apart from the question of how large the navy should be, the Admiralty itself was held to be overstaffed. In the autumn of 1919 the Treasury complained that the number of Admiralty staff had 'actually *increased*' since the war's end; four years later a committee under a distinguished industrialist, Lord Weir, discovered the 'extraordinary fact' that while the number of sailors was 32 per cent below the pre-war level, the number of Admiralty civil servants had grown by 70 per cent in the same period. Lord Weir concluded that, whereas the other service departments were reasonably well run, the Admiralty was greatly overstaffed and needed to introduce 'modern business methods' into its dockyards. Weir also commented that 'the Naval Staff was too big, was unduly enlarging its functions, and was making unnecessary work for other people.'[34] The Admiralty dealt with these criticisms by ignoring them.

What the Treasury saw as the department's unwillingness to play the game was evident also in the matter of naval pay. In the summer of 1919, alarmed by talk of disaffection in the fleet, the Admiralty 'browbeat the Cabinet' into accepting the recommendations of the Jerram committee on naval pay, a departmental body which took no account of pay scales in the other armed services.[35] This unilateral action meant that rank for rank the navy was overpaid as compared with the army and the RAF. That comparative advantage did not prevent Beatty, the First Sea Lord, from warning in 1925 that 'I feel that I cannot remain responsible for the discipline of the Navy' unless naval officers were paid the same marriage allowances as their counterparts in the other services, although the Jerram committee had expressly rejected such allowances in favour of higher basic pay.[36] Such high-handedness antagonized the Treasury.

In June 1923 the Admiralty sought to make various commitments on naval construction to the dominions without first discussing them with the Treasury. The Admiralty argument was that the matter was 'a purely technical naval question', but that the Treasury would be brought into discussion of the financing of the proposed programme. By then, as Barstow pointed out, 'the government might well find themselves so far committed by the naval staff that it would be difficult to withdraw with any semblance of dignity.'

The Admiralty's proposals drew a sharp response from Fisher, because of their implications both for financial management and for the general co-ordination of policy. He drew the attention of the Prime Minister to

> the implied claim by the Admiralty ... that the amount available for naval expenditure is in effect to be settled and dictated by the Admiralty and that consultation with the Ministers and Departments responsible to Government and the country for national solvency — if it takes place at all — should be little more than a formal registration of a *fait accompli*.
>
> A private business run on such a principle would end in bankruptcy; and, if I may be allowed a topical allusion, I suggest that the great position of Baldwins Ltd in the industrial world would never have been attained if its direction had proceeded with such childishly arrogant indifference to business principles.
>
> The attitude of the Admiralty has always been 'hands off, we are the great panjandrums, ours must be the first and the last word, let the profane crowd beware of even so much as asking a question ....' The Admiralty claim is tantamount to saying that the technical man instead of being subject to the general manager shall be the arbiter of every issue ... the naval advisers of the Government ought not to be allowed to keep at arm's length the general and financial advisers of Government. It is the business of the public services to work together as a team and inter-

change and pool their respective points of view and knowledge; then, and by that means only, can the Government of the day obtain the necessary conspectus and be saved from running in blinkers.

Final decisions of policy are a matter for the Government, not for officials whether in blue uniforms or in black coats. The sailor, however, is allowed to dictate policy while his civilian opposite number, whose acquaintance with the sum total of the considerations on which policy has to be founded is infinitely greater than the sailor's can be, is not allowed an opportunity — until it is too late — of placing before the Government the whole story in its proper perspective.[37]

In Fisher's eyes, the Admiralty was going against every principle central to the proper working of government. While his minute laid stress on the financial implications of allowing a spending department to commit the government without proper consideration of the cost, he also believed that no one department could stand apart from the rest and claim unique and exclusive competence in a particular policy area.

Fisher played an important part in a further controversy involving the Admiralty which began in June 1923, when a sub-committee of the CID under Lord Balfour recommended that the RAF retain responsibility for all aspects of aerial warfare. Such had been the case since the establishment of the air force in 1918, when Beatty, the First Sea Lord, had for some reason agreed that the navy's entire aviation staff of 55,000 men should be placed under RAF command.[38] Once post-war retrenchment began in earnest, the navy and the army turned against the RAF, claiming it to be an extravagance which failed in what they saw as its primary function of providing aerial support for their operations on land and sea. Such attacks sharply limited the chances of constructive co-operation with the new service, which was led by a capable though belligerent officer, 'Boom' Trenchard, who believed that its main wartime task would be strategic bombing.

Fisher had shown pro-air sympathies as early as 1921, when he advised that the air minister be paid the same as those responsible for the army and the navy lest it 'be suggested that the potentialities and importance of the air were being prejudiced.'[39] He was strongly in favour of the Balfour committee's findings, as he recalled in 1937, less because of the specific issue of control of naval aviation than because it guaranteed the future of the RAF as an independent service:

> I feel no doubt that in the early post-war days the decision to reconstruct our air force as something independent of the Navy and Army was right. Initiative, enterprise, experiment would otherwise have been stifled, and the older Arms, when called upon to economise, would have sacrificed the new-comer.[40]

The Board of Admiralty reacted to the Balfour committee's report by declaring that its 'letters Patent give full authority to the Lords Commissioners in all things which concern His Majesty's Navy, and impose upon them the responsibility of seeing that the Navy is in all respects efficient.' This sententious reply was accompanied by rumours that the sea lords intended to resign, by the leakage to the press of an official paper outlining the Admiralty case, and by the priming of Conservative MPs — then, as now, of the three armed services the navy had by far the most effective parliamentary lobby. This provoked a minor Cabinet crisis, during which Fisher again put his views forcefully to the Prime Minister.[41] He told Baldwin that the Admiralty's response to the Balfour committee

> has only one meaning, that in all things pertaining to the naval service...the final authority is not His Majesty's Government but the Board of Admiralty.
> In other words the board and the naval service are not the servants but the masters of Government.
> The issue raised is of vital constitutional importance.
> If the naval service is right in this claim, then the Civil Service, the military service and the air service can make the same claim. I need not develop this in detail, but obviously it disposes of ministerial and cabinet responsibility once and for all, and public servants will in future be the government instead of the advisers of government .... At present a naval member of the Board of Admiralty as a reward for coercing the Cabinet by resignation is still eligible for a command afloat or other public employment; he remains on active service and jeopardises

nothing for himself, pay or pension. If it is right for him to usurp the functions of government without any sacrifice to himself, his colleagues in the other three public services must not be placed at a disadvantage ...

It is not material to this fundamental issue whether on merits the Admiralty or the air force view on the particular problem discussed by the C.I.D. is right ....

The leakage to the press is a subsidiary, though important matter. If confidential recommendations to the Cabinet are to reach cabinet ministers through the newspapers which are apparently being mobilised so as to coerce the Cabinet, chaos will replace government![42]

The Prime Minister defused the crisis with characteristic dexterity by making some minor concessions to the Admiralty.[43] A committee of inquiry had no difficulty in tracing the source of the leaks; the officers involved in gingering up MPs and the press made no secret of their actions, and faced with such frankness the committee took refuge in the unlikely supposition that they had been unaware that official papers could not be used in this way, which 'lends itself to great abuse and should be discontinued.'[44]

In the wake of these troubles Fisher made a determined effort to achieve a degree of co-operation between the Treasury and the defence departments, and to get the fighting services working together. He took steps to improve the Treasury's relations with the Admiralty in March 1924, when he told the First Lord in the new Labour government, Lord Chelmsford, that

I have given the Chancellor ... a summary of our talks ... and told him of your general desire for closer and more harmonious working between the Treasury and the Admiralty.

He knows my views on the subject, which coincide with your own, and appreciates fully the great advantage of real co-operation between the various services of the Crown.... He would welcome the extension to the naval members of your Board of the personal contact which now exists between the Treasury and the military and air members of the Army and Air Councils respectively as well as the civilian members. Good feeling between the non-political heads of the four Services and between the Treasury, the Admiralty, the War Office and the Air Ministry is, he agrees — as previous Prime Ministers have agreed — more likely to promote general efficiency than are endeavours to dictate. All parties will learn to understand the others' point of view, and, even when these differ, ill-feeling and friction will be avoided.

He sent a copy of this to his friend Hugh Trenchard of the RAF:

It occurs to me that you and your colleagues may care to have the relevant extract ... as the growing evidence available during recent years of good-will on the part of the air to the civil authorities has marked a definite development in the progress to our common object.[45]

He was helped in his efforts to promote good relations by his membership of the CID, where he was at pains to speak as Head of the Civil Service and not as head of the departmental Treasury. However, his attempts to instill a degree of harmony had only mixed success, and depended almost entirely on personal contacts: his conception of the 'four Crown Services' all pulling together for the greater glory of England never had much of a chance in an era of severe retrenchment and inter-service rivalries. Treasury officials did have drummed into them the message that the service departments were to be treated with respect, and relations between the Treasury and each of the three services seem to have been quite amiable. But the same could not be said for relations between the armed services themselves, which were bedevilled by long-standing enmities.[46]

As a member of the first Labour government Chelmsford lasted less than a year. Under his Conservative successor, the Admiralty again sought to achieve its objects by fair means and foul. As a result, a major row blew up in 1925 over the Admiralty's cruiser-building programme, and over the cost of development of the base at Singapore. The Chancellor Winston Churchill, himself a former First Lord of the Admiralty, complained to Baldwin that the navy 'imagine themselves confronted with the same sort of situation in regard to Japan that we faced against Germany in the ten years before the war.'

There was not 'the slightest chance' of a war with Japan 'in our lifetime. The Japanese are our allies.'

Fisher for once entirely agreed, and passed on to Baldwin a Treasury memorandum which warned that it was important to remember 'that the One Power Standard is not an aim in itself but only a means to the end' of defending the trade and territories of the empire. 'The temptation is to elevate the formula into a fetish, and to strain its meaning until it almost becomes a World Power Standard — e.g. equality with U.S.A. in Battleships and Destroyers, with Japan in cruisers, with France in submarines simultaneously.' The memorandum maintained that the navy's wish to acquire the strength to beat the Japanese in the Pacific was completely impractical, since Japan would only need only a marginal increase in her own naval power to throw an unbearable strain on Britain, which had extensive naval commitments elsewhere. In any case, 'if there was any real probability of naval aggression by Japan, we should have to cease talking of formulas, and build to beat Japan.'[47] In short, the Treasury view as expounded by Churchill, by Fisher and by his subordinates was that Britain could not hope to defend its Far Eastern interests unaided against Japan.

The Treasury was equally unsympathetic towards the Admiralty's ambitious plans to build up the Singapore naval base. The decision to develop it was not in dispute, but the Admiralty was trying to push through a large spending programme without disclosing the full cost, although Trenchard of the RAF tried to rectify this omission by providing the Treasury with what he said were the full navy and army plans for the base.[48] After a considerable political crisis, some wavering from the Chancellor (who was torn between the dictates of his Treasury brief and his affection for the Royal Navy), and much talk of navy resignations, what Fisher called 'this King Charles' head of the nautical variety', the admirals won on both counts: they got most of the cruisers they wanted, and Singapore was developed as they wished.[49] (By a curious twist, Fisher's son Norman was to serve as commander of the Singapore naval dockyard, the cost of which had caused much friction between the Admiralty and the Treasury, from 1955 to 1957.)

The Treasury's response to this run of Admiralty successes, and to the manner of their achievement, was to set up a committee to look into the expenditure of all three armed services. It was chaired by Lord Colwyn, an amiable businessman often used for such purposes, and its other members were Chalmers and Bradbury, who had served together as joint heads of the Treasury during the First World War. The committee took evidence from the three services before issuing its report, which had been prepared over a weekend in Cambridge where Chalmers was Master of Peterhouse. It was predictably hostile towards the navy. While 'the Army is on the whole prudently and economically administered', in the Admiralty

> administrative methods have got completely out of touch with up-to-date civilian administration. While the War Office has profitted largely by the advice of the expert organisers who have from time to time reported on Army administration, the professional advisers of the Admiralty have in the main directed their energies to discovering reasons why similar advice in regard to the Navy ought not to be acted upon.

The committee proposed that the government fix a total amount for defence spending each year, out of which a cabinet committee should allocate funds to the three services. It opposed the idea of a unified defence ministry, something which was to be mooted again in the 1930s, and recommended that the Admiralty Jerram pay scales be brought into line with those of the other services.[50] On the Fleet Air Arm controversy it came out firmly in favour of the RAF, whose commander Trenchard greatly impressed the committee when he gave evidence.[51] He was far from impressed with what the other services had to say to the committee:

> It is true that the Admiralty paid lip service to the principle of a separate Air Ministry but as they claimed to take over from us all units afloat and the War Office, as partners in the campaign, demanded all units ashore, it was obvious that the dismembered Air Ministry must bleed rapidly to death.[52]

Despite his complaints, Trenchard had every reason to be happy. Two authoritative bodies had ruled decisively within the space of two years in favour of an independent air force, and even the Admiralty could not press for a quick reopening of a matter which, it should be remembered, had its origins in Beatty's casual agreement in 1918 to cede responsibility for naval aviation to the RAF. Not until 1937 did the navy finally get control of carrier-borne aircraft. Fisher, who always regarded himself as 'a sort of intermediary between the contestants' in the dispute, played a part as an honest broker between the Admiralty and the Air Ministry.[53] An eminent naval historian has argued that naval aviation suffered as a result, and that British fleet commanders were denied an opportunity to grasp the potential of aircraft in warfare at sea.[54] But the navy still had its carriers, although ultimate control of the aircraft operating from them lay with the RAF.

The 1920s campaign to have all aspects of naval aviation put back under the Admiralty was led by Beatty, the same man who had relinquished control to the newly formed RAF in 1918.[55] Against the navy's case, and the parallel claim of the army to control of land-based aircraft, should be put the development of the RAF, which won Britain's decisive defensive battle in 1940. The navy's lack of aviation expertise was certainly a weakness in the early years of World War II, but this cannot be explained simply by its lack of direct control of the Fleet Air Arm.

Very little evidence has been found concerning Fisher's dealings with the other armed services and their parent departments in the 1920s. Both the War Office and the Air Ministry were considered by the Treasury to be reasonably frugal, and neither the army nor the RAF behaved as the navy did in seeking favourable government decisions. They suffered in the same way as did the navy from the continual demands for economies, but there is nothing to suggest that their strategic assumptions were questioned by the Treasury except on purely financial grounds. Fisher accepted that the army's strength was barely adequate to do its basic peacetime job of policing the empire, and he seems to have taken no active part in discussion of military strategy. Despite his friendship with Trenchard and his interest in the RAF, it too was badly hit by the cuts imposed: in 1929, shortly before he retired, Trenchard complained to Fisher of 'the pressure that I have had put on me for the last four years to go on making a paper force and yet reduce all the time.'[56] Towards the end of his life, Fisher stated that the Baldwin government of 1924–9 had brought the country to a condition of 'military impotence.'[57] He also claimed that when he was secretary to the Treasury he had fought the politicians far harder than the service chiefs had done to get adequate armed strength for the country. There had been cuts after the last war, more cuts under the Baldwin government — for though the Labour government was often blamed, it was not really responsible — and even the vitriol he had poured out could do nothing.[58]

This vitriol has long since evaporated from the records, if it ever existed. All the evidence suggests that it was only in the early 1930s that Fisher began to press for a sustained strengthening of Britain's armed forces. Prior to that, he supported successive reductions in defence spending, although he eschewed a narrowly financial approach to the issue. There is nothing to indicate that he opposed the stringent version of the ten year rule adopted by the CID at Churchill's request in 1928, whereby planning was to be on the 'assumption that at any given date there will not be a major war for ten years from that date', though the CID would review the position each year.[59] The initiative for this rule came from the Treasury, and it must have had Fisher's support. A few months later he commented that

> our margin in naval strength, the absence of anyone to fight at sea, the Cabinet instruction about no 'major war', the Kellogg Pact [an international agreement renouncing aggressive war], and our financial situation seem to me to provide in the aggregate an overwhelming argument for a drastic cut in naval expenditure.[60]

Cutting back on the armed services was probably the only policy on which Fisher and Churchill as Chancellor consistently agreed between 1924 and 1929. The conventional economic wisdom and the exigencies of domestic politics required that the government should balance its budget and that what increases there were in social spending should be offset by savings elsewhere. All three armed services suffered, though to varying degrees: the navy did best, the army worst. In the international climate of the 1920s retrenchment was justified: the Washington naval conference of 1921–2 had produced a satisfactory agreement between Britain, the United States, and Japan on naval construction and on the preservation of peace in the Pacific, and as the decade progressed the likelihood of a general disarmament agreement grew. But the degree of retrenchment enforced, and the way in which cuts were made, was shown by events to have been a major mistake. Not only the services were affected: rearmament, when it came, was greatly hampered by the weakness of the British armaments industries, which had been starved of orders in the 1920s. Within the services, reductions in spending were frequently achieved at the expense of modernization: retrenchment did not bring automatic rationalization.

The Treasury must take some of the blame for failing to ensure that whatever savings it deemed necessary were achieved with the least possible damage to the future efficiency of the armed forces and the industries upon which they depended for equipment.[61] As a member of the CID Fisher did support efforts to plan ahead, for example in air raid precautions and civil defence, but the Treasury's primary concern was to save money on defence by whatever means possible. In 1929 the incoming Labour Chancellor was advised that 'the main hope of savings' in public expenditure 'lies in armaments and it is by success or failure in this field that the government will specially be judged.'[62] Over the next two years hopes of a general disarmament agreement and economic conditions at home and abroad led the Cabinet to make further inroads into defence spending.

III

In January 1923 events in Europe took a decisive turn for the worse. The French secured a declaration from the Reparations Commission that Germany was in partial default on its reparations payments. France then exercised its right as a creditor to collect what it was owed, sending a mission into the Ruhr to collect coal, timber, and industrial equipment. It also sent in three divisions of troops. Over the following months France increased its presence in the Ruhr. French actions produced a catastrophic dislocation of the German economy.

The Treasury took the view that the Ruhr crisis was entirely the fault of the French. Bradbury, the British delegate on the Reparations Commission, thought that Germany's repayment performance in the latter half of 1922 was 'in spite of increasing difficulties, certainly no worse, and relatively actually better, than it had been.' He expressed dislike of the Reparations Commission, 'an obsolete and discredited institution.'[63] But Britain was inextricably involved in the reparations tangle, and was unable to prevent French occupation of the Ruhr. The occupation precipitated a major financial and political crisis in Europe. Fisher warned Baldwin of the possible consequences:

> I think the average Englishman would say that he wants to be on terms with all countries and to see an end to excursions and alarms.
>
> The problem then appears to be narrowed down to the means of avoiding a break with France and of restoring a measure of peace to the world. Shall we best obtain our object by leaving the French under the impression that we shall continue indefinitely to acquiesce in a policy which we believe will produce (1) early chaos and (2) eventual war. Sooner or later we shall say 'no further' and then the French will have a plausible excuse for the parrot cries of 'nous sommes trahis' and 'perfide Albion'. And then a rupture will come with a vengeance .... Writing merely as an Englishman and in no way professing to be a pundit, I would earnestly suggest that we none of us are concerned with being 'pro-French' or 'pro-German' — let us be 'pro-English' whose interests are ultimately connected with the restoration of peace and whose position is sufficiently detached from European animosities to make our judgement cooler.
>
> The French occupation of the Ruhr is held by our lawyers to be a breach of the Treaty and by everyone else to be in addition midsummer madness ...
>
> I do not pretend to have argued the question in detail — many others have done that already and I was quite aware of the security problem of which the French speak. But you are, I know, not uninterested in what the average Englishman is thinking (by which I do not mean our Prussians of the *National Review* and the *Morning Post*!) and I believe and hope I am an average Englishman.[64]

He soon returned to the question, after the French had refused to take part in an inter-allied conference on the crisis unless Germany gave an undertaking that passive resistance to the occupation would cease immediately. British acquiescence in this condition, he argued,

> involves the triumph of French policy which every think-ing Englishman knows can have but one result viz: the indefinite postponement of the reconstruction of Europe. However intelligible the motives of the French may be — whether fear, revenge, or desire for money — are we not bound to consider the world problem as a whole, and are we not in a better position to do so than France. France is self-contained, we are international in our interests: France is under the influence of emotion, our judgement is cooler and more detached ...
>
> Is it not fairer and more candid to let the French know that if there is to be an inter-allied conference, it must be without prior dictation of conditions either by them or by us?[65]

Baldwin's biographers credit Fisher with persuading him to take a firm stand, but the results were disappointing, and the crisis dragged on.[66] Fisher told the Prime Minister a month later that 'I am an Englishman and quite devoid of sentimental predilections for foreigners collectively, Germans or other-wise', but 'we are ... in the position of trustees, directly by reason of the Treaty and generally because of our English heritage of fair play', and could not allow France to hit a defenceless Germany 'below the belt.' He continued:

> I have read principally as a pastime and partly for ex-aminations at Winchester and Oxford a good deal of history; and, while I admit that the French from 1870 to 1914 had their tails well down and therefore assumed the veneer of moderation, during the whole of the rest of their centuries old existence they have played the part of bullies whenever they had or could make the chance. And they are doing so now. This view is neither anti-French or pro-German — it arises solely from regard for English self-respect ....
>
> We have a moral responsibility, which we emphasised by urging Germany to make proposals, to see that the ring is at least fairly kept.[67]

The Ruhr crisis was the first important issue of foreign policy on which Fisher tendered advice. He was undoubtedly entitled to do so since it involved the problem of international debts, although he was clearly more interested in the broader political issue. The Treasury and the Foreign Office appear to have co-operated amicably in advising on the crisis, since they agreed that France was in the wrong. The Foreign Office was anxious not to offend the French needlessly, and it was, correctly, pessimistic about Britain's ability to restrain its ally.[68] In December 1923 the respective governments finally reached agreement on the device of a committee of experts, headed by the American General Dawes, to determine Germany's capacity to pay. Its report, accepted by the countries in the summer of 1924, brought stability to reparations payments for a number of years. But Germany's currency and finances had collapsed completely as a result of France's action, and this hardened the francophobe attitude of the Treasury, whereas the Foreign Office, once the diplomatic tension was resolved, reverted to its normal pro-French attitude. Thereafter up to the final settlement of the problem in 1932 the two departments tended to push in opposite direction on the reparations issue.

Fisher was not a financial or economic expert, and from Treasury papers it seems that he had little distinctive to say on such matters. He left this work to successive Treasury controllers of finance and their subordinates.[69] His own contributions were he maintained based simply on common sense, giving the view of the 'average Englishman' and the 'man in the pub'.[70] This of course was important, in so far as he sought to convey to ministers the likely political consequences of particular decisions. He spent a lot of time in assessing the trend of opinion outside Whitehall: he had a wide range of acquaintances in industry and the City from whom to get advice and ideas, amongst whom were his friends Montagu Norman and Reginald McKenna, two men who differed continually on financial issues.[71] He was, therefore, an informed and experienced layman, not a dilettante incapable of independent judgement. On reparations, as on other economic issues, his advice was a composite of expert opinion and his own view of what national honour and the national interest dictated.

Between October 1922 and December 1924, Fisher worked with four chancellors, Baldwin, Neville Chamberlain, Snowden and Churchill. With all but the last of these he got on well. Baldwin had been a somewhat indolent ally since

1919. When Labour came to power in January 1924, Philip Snowden became Chancellor. He turned out to be an obstinate but extremely effective minister, who knew what he wanted and how to get it, regarded by some insiders as the best the Treasury had between 1914 and 1939.[72] Winston Churchill, however, who came to the Treasury in November 1924, was in Fisher's view a 'lunatic', 'an irresponsible child, not a grown man', whereas Neville Chamberlain could do no wrong.[73] When Chamberlain became Chancellor in August 1923, his half-brother Austen told him that 'you will like Fisher', and Fisher certainly liked him.[74] After the general election of December 1923, Neville Chamberlain had a talk with Fisher which

> depressed me profoundly. He said that he had had a long talk with S[tanley] B[aldwin] in which he had impressed upon him the necessity of having in opposition a lieutenant on whom he could rely. Once again he urged that [J.C.C.] Davidson though perfectly straight and honest was a fool and a bad counsellor whilst others ... were first and foremost out for their own interests. He must therefore take counsel with the one man whose motives were disinterested & whose judgement could be relied upon, viz. the Chanc. of Exch. ... S.B. had agreed with everything either actively or more frequently passively but W.F. said: 'It's not enough to agree. You must definitely tell N.C. that he is your lieutenant & is to act as such. Otherwise you will get nothing from him for he is as reserved as you and will never push himself forward'. To this S.B. appeared to give assent but evidently W.F. thought he wouldn't act upon it and he said: 'He wants you but you have got to go against your own inclinations and operate on him or you will find him with his inability to make up his mind vacillating till the last moment & then having it made up for him by the coarsefibred energetic self-seekers, the Worthys, the Lloyd Graemes & the Jixes'. What depressed me so was first the conviction that what W.F. said was true & second that I feel myself so totally unable to follow his advice. I am not & never can be a pusher through. I may act for a brief period like one.[75]

While out of office, Chamberlain kept in touch with Fisher, who wrote to him in July 1924 in characteristically mawkish vein:

> I am indeed touched by your letter.
> My feelings towards yourself are no less warm, &, brief tho' our time together was, you had given me the hope that I might think of you as a friend — a word full of meaning ...
> If I may ... I will ring up & find out what time you are free when I will come along with joy.[76]

Fisher regarded himself as the fount of official rectitude. It is, accordingly, all the more surprising that he should have tried to be a go-between for two outgoing ministers, particularly as the incoming government was such a novelty. Admittedly his advice was entirely personal, and it was quite in character for him to pour out his opinions on all sorts of subjects to those whom he trusted, be they civil servants, soldiers, politicians, or relatives.[77] Haranguing the lethargic Baldwin was second nature to him, and it implied no disloyalty to his new Labour masters. His sentimental attitude towards Neville Chamberlain was matched by his feeling for the man whom above all others Chamberlain despised, Lloyd George. In September 1925 Fisher spent a week visiting the former Coalition leader and his mistress, 'an ideal illustration of the harmony which gives life its meaning.'[78] The 'fun, the atmosphere of friendliness, the naturalness of it all, & the setting combined to give us as it were a peep into heaven.'[79]

IV

The first Labour government gave no cause for alarm to its civil servants or even to most sections of the opposition. MacDonald's cabinet made only modest changes in the policies it inherited from the Conservatives. Its more grandiose ambitions were held in check, partly by Philip Snowden, whose nonconformist radicalism was allied to an ingrained thriftiness and dislike of extravagance, and partly by the fact that it was a minority administration. Unlike his predecessors, MacDonald found a balance between adventurism and isolation in his conduct of foreign affairs, while his Cabinet demonstrated their commitment to the empire when for once they outvoted Snowden and sanctioned a larger naval building programme than Baldwin had been willing to allow.[80]

MacDonald was the first Prime Minister whom Fisher had served who did not regard him as a general adviser. There were a number of reasons for this. Unlike his predecessors, he had not worked with Fisher before becoming premier. Furthermore, he seldom saw eye to eye with his Chancellor Snowden, and Fisher could scarcely act as an adviser to both at the same time. Besides all this, MacDonald was Foreign Secretary as well as Prime Minister, and naturally he tended to rely on Foreign Office officials more than on the Treasury. Despite his Socialist pedigree, he was very popular at the Foreign Office. The man he succeeded there, Curzon, although quite successful had been 'difficult ... to please' and 'a bully'.[81] MacDonald was a more pleasant man with an equal grasp of foreign affairs. Being Prime Minister he gave them considerable prominence, and he was able to impose the Foreign Office view in Cabinet in a way that Curzon had sometimes been unable to do. MacDonald had a sharp disagreement with Snowden over the terms of the Dawes plan for the resumption of reparations payments, but in general his sway in foreign policy was uncontested.[82]

Amongst the Labour ministers was a man whom Fisher revered, Lord Haldane. As Lloyd George was his greatest political hero, so Haldane was his administrative one. Alone of politicians, in Fisher's view, he could think rationally and systematically about the organization of government. In a fulsome tribute, Fisher wrote that Haldane was 'an illustration of the truth that as a man thinketh in his heart, so is he; his whole being was expressed at all times, whether externalised in the re-modelling of the Army or [in] a discourse on metaphysics.'[83] Despite this, the development of British government between the wars bears few obvious signs of Haldane's influence, but quite a lot of Fisher's and Hankey's, the two key men in Whitehall. In 1924 both were enthusiastic about Haldane's proposals for a 'Committee of Economic Enquiry', which would deal with 'questions of a technical but civil character' just as the CID did with military matters.[84] The Labour Cabinet agreed in principle, although it did not last long enough to bring it into being. It was left to Baldwin's government to set up a 'Committee of Civil Research' a year later under Lord Balfour, like Haldane an intellectual but a rather more effective party politician.[85] The committee was not of great importance, and its functions were never satisfactorily defined. It was a useful forum for the co-ordination of work on technical matters affecting more than one department, but it did not have the influence on economic policy that Haldane had apparently envisaged.[86] Its significance lay in its existence, not its activities. It was the result of the first of a number of efforts to improve the quality and breadth of the material upon which the Cabinet took decisions. One problem was that it existed only on the sufferance of Whitehall. For example, although he had co-sponsored its creation and was anxious that use should be made of it, Fisher was not willing to permit the committee to become a source of economic advice independent of the Treasury.[87]

Towards the end of its time in office, the Labour government was gravely embarrassed by the Campbell case. In August two Anglo-Russian treaties were signed as part of a modest effort to improve relations between the two countries. In the same week John Campbell, the acting editor of the *Workers' Weekly*, the sort of newspaper usually read only by its own contributors and by the Special Branch and MI5, was charged with incitement to mutiny. This followed the appearance of an article urging troops not to fire on their fellow workers if ordered to do so. Campbell had been seriously wounded and decorated for valour in the war, and it was unlikely that a jury would take a severe view of a couple of inflammatory paragraphs in an obscure broadsheet. The ill-considered prosecution was withdrawn, and the opposition reacted with largely synthetic indignation at this supposed demonstration of Labour's toadying to Bolshevism. The Prime Minister made matters much worse with a misleading statement to the Commons, and he subsequently tried to throw the blame for this on Hankey's deputy Tom Jones.[88] The Liberals, on whose support the minority Labour government depended, seized on the episode as the occasion for a vote of confidence, and they forced a dissolution.[89] Some years later MacDonald told his party colleague Hugh Dalton that the crisis had arisen because Chelmsford, the First Lord of the Admiralty and a Tory, leaked a Cabinet memorandum on the case which 'was all around the West End Service Clubs & in the Middle Temple the day after circulation [to ministers].' In his diary Dalton linked this episode with a much more confused and emotive issue: 'Noel-Baker has suspected an Adm[iralty] leak over Zinoviev from the start.'[90]

The Zinoviev letter was supposedly sent by the President of the Comintern to the Communist Party of Great Britain, exhorting his British comrades to a renewed burst of subversion. Its content was entirely predictable. Ever since it came into office MacDonald's government had been worried about externally inspired Communist activity, and the Prime Minister was waiting for clear-cut evidence to use in an official protest to the Soviet government. The letter appeared to give this, and MacDonald had the Foreign Office draft a protest note, the text of which was to be released to the press. He received this draft while away campaigning in the general election, and made substantial changes to it by hand, the thrust of which was to strengthen the protest. The Foreign Office incorporated these amendments and, on 25 October, issued the protest after satisfying itself that the letter was genuine. MacDonald was astonished that his officials should have done this without explicit directions, but it is clear that the Permanent Under Secretary, Sir Eyre Crowe, in the absence of directions to the contrary, understandably took MacDonald's amendments to the draft protest as confirmation that he was to go ahead and issue it. Furthermore, Crowe told Fisher on 24 October that he was going to publish the note and the text of the Zinoviev letter, not to discredit the government but to forestall charges that MacDonald was refusing to act against subversion; by then the text of the letter had come into the hands of the *Daily Mail* and of the Conservative Central Office, who were bent on using it against Labour.[91]

Despite Crowe's prompt action, however, the Conservatives were able to use the letter to great effect during the campaign, largely because of the confusion in Labour ranks — most ministers knew nothing about it.[92] Its effect on the voters is hard to gauge: Labour's vote actually increased, and the main losers in the election were the Asquithean Liberals, who, having precipitated it through withdrawing support for the Labour government, were decimated.

A lot has been written about the Zinoviev letter, dealing with its possible authenticity, with the intentions of the Foreign Office officials involved, and with its effect on Labour's electoral fortunes.[93] In dealing with it here, the good faith of Sir Eyre Crowe and J.D. Gregory of the Foreign Office is assumed. This conclusion was reached also by the committee of inquiry into the 'Francs Affair' of 1928, which resulted in Gregory's dismissal for currency speculation.[94] The committee reported that 'one of our number' — obviously Fisher, who was chairman — had confirmed that Crowe acted as he did only to save the government from embarrassment, and on the assumption that the Prime Minister had authorized the action which was taken.[95] They were amply justified in this belief by the actions of the Tory press, as the newspapers had clearly been primed by people connected with the intelligence services.[96]

Stories about the affair abound, few of which are more far-fetched than that told by Walford Selby, who was private secretary to successive foreign secretaries from 1924 to 1932:

> Sir Wyndham Childs who was commissioner of the Police in 1924 ... wrote me a letter [in 1942] ... saying he thought the 'curious' story of the Zinoviev letter should be placed on record.
>
> Sir Wyndham said our Police knew the letter to be a forgery. He declared his services had been liquidated by Sir Warren Fisher for refusing to declare the letter as otherwise than a forgery. Sir Wyndham added that subsequently the Police seized some very curious correspondence in an Office in the City — he mentioned the name of Im Thurn — exchanges between Im Thurn and Warren Fisher in regard to 'services rendered'. He said he was standing as a Conservative candidate at the time and had given the correspondence to Mr Baldwin who said it was 'very honourable of him'. Mr. Baldwin added that he always thought the letter was a forgery.[97]

Selby said elsewhere that Fisher 'brought in another authority from our Secret Service to declare the letter genuine, "a disgraceful piece of poaching on my preserves", declared Sir Wyndham', and that 'it was Warren Fisher who passed it as genuine across the Cabinet.'[98] This astonishing tale was repeated by Lord Noel-Baker in a letter to *The Times* in 1966, although he refrained from naming Fisher.[99]

Selby's story is riddled with inaccuracies, and the letter from Childs on which he said it was based cannot now be located. Contrary to what Selby says, the Cabinet were not consulted about the letter at all. Childs was in fact assistant commissioner in charge of the Special Branch in 1924. He states in his memoirs that he presumed the letter to be a forgery, but that neither he nor his organization were consulted about it at the time.[100] Furthermore, he was not pushed out until November 1928, when the Home Office took advantage of his superior's retirement to get rid of him in the wake of the Savidge case. Sir John Anderson wrote that although his 'disability no doubt falls short of physical unfitness in a medical sense', the 'effect upon a man of a naturally highly strung temperament' of the pressures of work 'is such as in the deliberate opinion of the Secretary of State to render him unsuitable for the duties of an office which calls in an exceptional degree for a balanced judgement and great reserve.'[101] The police did not at any time (so far as is known) raid the office of Donald Im Thurn, a former MI5 officer who had passed the text of the letter to Conservative Central Office, but his house was burgled after his death.[102] By then Childs had retired, and could therefore have been involved in Conservative politics.[103] It later came out that Im Thurn had been paid £5,000, a payment which was only explained in 1966, when J.C.C. Davidson said that as an officer of the Conservative Party he had issued a cheque for that amount for payment to Im Thurn.[104] This money was to go to the mysterious 'X', Im Thurn's informant who supposedly risked life and limb to tell the British government and the Conservative party of the Zinoviev letter.[105] It has been argued that this was in reality payment for the forgery of the document; whether or not this is so, the fact is that Davidson took full responsibility for the transaction.[106]

Selby provided no coherent explanation of why Fisher should have wanted to bring down the government in 1924. However, Selby did say that 'the forgery resulted in the breach of our relations with Russia just at the moment when we were engaged in bringing Germany to order', a reference to the fact that the Labour government fell before the two treaties negotiated with Russia could be ratified.[107] The implication of this is obvious: he saw Fisher as pro-German, and described his activities in terms in which he appears as nothing less than a traitor, continually thwarting the aims of his masters in order to prevent the adoption of an anti-German policy. As is clear from an earlier part of this chapter Fisher and the Treasury did feel that Germany was being harshly treated by the French in 1923 and 1924. So did most informed people in Britain at that time. Selby is imposing on the events of 1924 the Germany of 1939 when he says that 'we were ... bringing Germany to order.'

It is nonsense to suggest that the government saw its negotiations with Russia as an integral part of a process of containment of Germany, and it is absurd to argue that Fisher brought down the government to stop that happening.

Walford Selby was obsessed by Fisher, whom he held responsible for the outbreak of the Second World War. In his retirement he and his friends Lord Elibank, Frank Ashton-Gwatkin and Harry Legge-Bourke MP produced a string of accusations against Fisher, and his book *Diplomatic Twilight* is frequently cited in relation to Fisher's alleged interference in the running of the Foreign Office, the distribution of warnings about Hitler's intentions, and the formation of foreign policy generally.[108] His published attacks, though sharp, are curiously brief. This has lent them a credibility which they would not otherwise possess. Only in private correspondence did he make his charge that Fisher was behind the Zinoviev letter affair, and that he was also responsible for the fall of the second Labour government in 1931.[109]

In so far as they can be tested, most of Selby's allegations are false. His animus against Fisher arose partly from the latter's attempts to bring the Foreign Office into a common fold with the rest of the domestic civil service, and partly from what he believed were the consequences of Fisher's activities on his own career. In 1940 Selby was ambassador in Lisbon. After the fall of France, it was decided to move Sir Ronald Campbell, previously in Paris, to Portugal, which had through circumstances become an extremely important post. Selby was moved out five months short of his sixtieth birthday, when he could have retired in the normal way. Ironically, the Treasury proved surprisingly sympathetic to his plight, and pressed the Foreign Office to give him some notional job in London for the remaining months so that he could serve out his time with dignity, get his full pension rights, and not be tarred with the 'dud diplomat' brush — a title given to a number of ineffectual British officials who had been compulsorily retired on grounds of inefficiency once war broke out. Selby was not regarded as a dud, but the circumstances of his removal made him appear one. He was deeply hurt by the treatment accorded him, and seems to have blamed Fisher for inventing what he called the 'retire at 60' rule.[110] As usual he was wrong: it was left to departments to enforce the rule as they saw fit.

Lord Noel-Baker, a veteran pacifist who as a Labour MP was Parliamentary Private Secretary to the Foreign Secretary from 1929 to 1931, told the author that he 'fully shared Walford Selby's view' of Fisher, and was 'strongly opposed to Warren Fisher's attitude on armaments and the League of Nations ... he was a most dangerous hawk who worked closely with the leading and most dangerous hawks ... Vansittart and ... Hankey.'[111] Noel-Baker was quite right: Fisher had no faith in the League of Nations or the panacea of disarmament and he thought Germany a menace. However, Noel-Baker's complaints about Fisher are rather difficult to reconcile with Selby's central thesis, that Fisher was blindly pro-German.

Fisher thought in national, not in political terms. He had no axe to grind so far as Labour were concerned: from the Treasury's viewpoint, they performed rather well in government.[112] But he did not establish any rapport with MacDonald and seems to have had surprisingly little direct contact with him.[113] The proud claim of January 1924 that the 'Permanent Head of the Civil Service' was 'the principal official adviser of the Prime Minister' depended entirely on who the Prime Minister was.[114]

Notes

1. Blake, *Unknown Prime Minister*, p. 501.

2. Turner, 'Cabinets, Committees and Secretariats: the higher direction of war', in Burk (ed.) *War and the State*, pp. 57–83.

3. Esher to Lloyd George, 29 June 1922, Lloyd George papers, F/16/1.

4. Hankey to Fisher, 5 Mar. 1921, quoted in Hankey papers, HNKY 8/24.

5. Hankey diary, 21 Oct. 1922, HNKY 4/14.

6. Hankey to Esher, 22 Oct. 1922, ibid.

7. Hankey diary, 23 and 27 Oct.; Hankey to Esher, 26 Oct. 1922.

8. Hankey to Esher, 27 Oct. 1922, ibid. Hankey was no innocent abroad himself. A subordinate described him in 1934 as 'a proper little snake! An artist at "slipping round the corner" ....', Pownall diary, 4 Jan. 1934. This passage does not appear in Bond, *Pownall Diary*.

9. Memorandum by Hankey, 7 Nov. 1922, HNKY 8/24.

10. Hankey diary, 27 Oct. 1922.

11. ibid. Fitzroy's superannuation papers give the more demure explanation 'on grounds of age', T164 35/P29774.

12. Hankey diary, 29 Oct. 1922.

13. Fisher to Baldwin and Bonar Law, 7 Nov. 1922, T199/65.

14. Hankey diary, 27 Oct. 1922.

15. Hankey diary, 8 Nov. 1922.

16. Roskill, *Hankey*, iii, 352–4. This is dealt with in Chapter 8.

17. Blake, *Unknown Prime Minister*, p. 402.

18. ibid.

19. Hankey to Bonar Law, 23 Oct. 1922, Bonar Law papers, 111/21/99.

20. Blake, op.cit., pp. 520–5. Middlemas and Barnes, *Baldwin*, pp.162–5.

21. Middlemas and Barnes, ibid., p.172. Fisher to Baldwin, 27 Apr. 1926, Baldwin papers, 161/95–6.

22. Waterhouse to Baldwin, 1 Apr. 1928, ibid., 174/107.

23. Baldwin to Neville Chamberlain, 4 Apr. 1938, Chamberlain papers, NC 7/11/31/7.

24. Waterhouse, *Private and Official*, p. 359. Jones, 'The prime ministers' secretaries', p. 29, says Waterhouse was forced to resign in January 1928 because of his involvement in an 'extra-marital entanglement'. This would normally not have been sufficient grounds for resignation. However, Mrs Baldwin had very strong views about divorce, and several civil servants in her husband's private office had to be moved on when they got into marital difficulties. One of these was promoted prematurely by Fisher to principal in order to give him a valid reason for leaving Baldwin's office which would not damage his career. Sir Edward Playfair to the author, 3 Apr. 1982. In the autumn of 1928 Waterhouse secretly married Mrs Baldwin's secretary. Waterhouse, op. cit., pp.15, 360–1. Waterhouse continued to live up to his reputation as an intriguer. See Dalton diary, 12 Feb. 1935, for a curious meeting.

25. Middlemas, *Whitehall Diary*, i, 237.

26. See Middlemas and Barnes, *Baldwin,* on the Prime Minister's complex personality.

27. Interview with Sir Robert Fraser; interview with Sir George Dunnett.

28. Rowe-Dutton to Blackett, 21 Mar. 1923, Blackett MSS Eur E397/29.

29. Blake, *Unknown Prime Minister*, p. 491; Middlemas and Barnes, *Baldwin*, pp. 135–49. Blake, op. cit., pp. 492–3, points out that Law was concerned not merely at the terms of the settlement, but that it had been agreed without reference to the related problem of the debts of Britain's European allies to her.

30. Niemeyer to Blackett, 20 Mar. 1923, Blackett MSS Eur E397/29.

31. Sir Edward Playfair to the author, 27 Apr. 1981. Sir Edward had 'access to all papers and most survivors.' When he wrote the history he had no idea that one day he would become a Treasury official.

32. For the conflict between the government's imperial and external commitments and its desire to save money see Jeffery, *The British Army and the Crisis of Empire*, pp. 11–30.

33. Note by Barstow, 29 June 1919, T1 12469/3873.

34. Memorandum for the Cabinet Finance Committee, 8 Oct. 1919, CAB27/72; report of Lord Weir's committee on Admiralty estimates, 20 Jan. 1923; Sir Russell Scott to the Chancellor, 17 Dec. 1924, T162 95/E11019. Weir, a Scottish shipbuilder, had been brought into government during the war. Thereafter he was used constantly as an adviser on industrial matters.

35. Hankey to Baldwin, 3 June 1925, Baldwin papers, 2/211–20.

36. Beatty to Bridgeman (First Lord of the Admiralty), 27 June 1925, ibid., 2/196.

37. Note by Barstow, undated; Fisher to Joynson-Hicks and Baldwin, 27 June 1923, T160 639/F6064.

38. Roskill, *Naval Policy*, i, 237–8. This was the result of in-fighting over the convoy question. Captain Roskill points out that the navy lost 55,000 officers and men, who were transferred to the RAF in April 1918. This number is somewhat deceptive, since the navy's aviation staff would in any event have been drastically cut when peace and retrenchment came.

39. Note by Fisher, 15 Apr. 1921, T162 58/E4818.

40. Fisher to Simon, 28 July 1937, in support of the Inskip report recommending the transfer of the Fleet Air Arm to navy control, T161 736/S22793/2.

41. T172/1309. Middlemas and Barnes, *Baldwin*, p. 321.

42. Fisher to Baldwin, 30 July 1923, Baldwin papers 2/237–8.

43. Middlemas and Barnes, *Baldwin*, p. 323.

44. Report dated 2 Aug. 1923, T172/1309.

45. Fisher to Chelmsford, 7 Mar., and to Trenchard, 10 Mar. 1924, Trenchard papers, MFC 76/1/184. Hamilton, 'Sir Warren Fisher', says Fisher and Chelmsford were particularly friendly.

46. Interviews with Sir John Winnifrith and Sir Edward Playfair; Sir John Laing to the author, 3 Nov. 1981; Sir Clifford Jarrett and Sir

Richard Powell to the author, 22 Oct. 1981. Laing, Jarrett, and Powell joined the Admiralty in 1923, 1934, and 1931 respectively.

47. Churchill to Baldwin, 16 Dec. 1924; Fisher to Baldwin, with Barstow to Fisher, 3 Feb. 1925; Barstow to Fisher, 26 Mar. 1925, Baldwin papers, 2/26–33.

48. Hankey to Baldwin, 15 Sept. 1925, Baldwin papers 2/102–3; Churchill to Baldwin, 22 Mar. 1925, T161 201/S18917/02. Trenchard did this in support of his claim that increased use of the RAF for imperial defence would make financial and strategic sense. Trenchard to Churchill, 23 Mar. 1925, T172/1440; Trenchard to Fisher, 26 Sept. 1925, Trenchard papers, MFC 76/1/184.

49. Fisher to Baldwin, 3 Feb. 1925, Baldwin papers 2/249.

50. Colwyn committee report, 23 Dec. 1925, Baldwin papers, 4/221–57.

51. Interview with Sir Robert Fraser. Sir Robert was secretary to the committee.

52. Trenchard to Baldwin, 4 Feb. 1926, Baldwin papers, 2/253–5.

53. Fisher to Simon (Chancellor), 28 July 1937, T161 736/S22793/2.

54. Roskill, *Naval Policy*, i, 237–8.

55. See Roskill, *Beatty*, pp. 305–17 for a sympathetic account of Beatty's position. For the navy case as put forward by Admiral Sir Roger Keyes, who orchestrated the 1923 campaign, see memorandum by Keyes, with Keyes to Chatfield, 7 Feb. 1937, Chatfield papers CHT 2/7/126, 129–32. For the army attitude see Milne (Chief of the Imperial General Staff) to the Secretary of State for War, 10 Feb. 1933, Milne papers, box 3.

56. Trenchard to Fisher, 4 Oct. 1929, Trenchard papers, MFC 7/1/184.

57. Fisher, 'Civil defence', p. 212.

58. Minutes of RIIA British Security group, 14 Aug. 1944, Greaves papers, coll. misc. 462/8.

59. Hopkins to Churchill, 1 May 1928, T162 136/E18938; CID minutes, 5 July 1928, CAB 2/5.

60. Undated note by Fisher, on Hopkins to Fisher and Churchill, 20 Nov. 1928, T161 292/S34216; Gilbert, *Winston S Churchill*, v, 311–13.

61. There is no evidence to suggest that Treasury officials had these considerations in mind during the 1920s.

62. Hopkins and Phillips to Snowden, undated, T172/1684.

63. Bradbury to Bonar Law, 19 Feb., PREM 1/23; Bradbury to Baldwin, 13 Mar. 1923, Baldwin papers, 159/15. Bradbury remained British delegate on the reparations commission until 1925.

64. Fisher to Baldwin, 11 June 1923, Baldwin papers 125/141–4.

65. Same to same, 12 June 1923, ibid., 125/165–7.

66. Middlemas and Barnes, *Baldwin*, p. 184.

67. Fisher to Baldwin, 19 July 1923, Baldwin papers, 127/115–6.

68. Fisher to Tyrrell (Foreign Office), 24 Aug. 1923, F.O. 371/8651/c14673/1/18; Cassels, 'Repairing the entente cordiale', pp. 133–35.

69. The rank of Controller was suppressed in January 1932, when Sir Richard Hopkins was made Second Secretary.

70. 'The man in the pub' makes frequent appearances in Fisher's remarks to the RIIA British security group in 1944 and 1945.

71. Clay, *Lord Norman*, p. 296; Lady Norman to the author, 9 Aug. 1981; interview with R.W. Fisher. It is always difficult to know whether people whom Fisher regarded as dear friends felt quite so strongly about him. Amongst financiers and industrialists he often consulted were, besides Norman and McKenna, Lord Weir, Sir John Cadman of what became British Petroleum, and Sir William McLintock.

72. Grigg, *Prejudice and Judgement*, pp. 136–7; interview with Sir Robert Fraser.

73. Neville Chamberlain diary, 1 Nov. 1925, Chamberlain papers; Cross, *Snowden*, pp. 197–8.

74. Austen Chamberlain to Neville Chamberlain, 28 Aug. 1923, NC 1/27/73.

75. Neville Chamberlain diary, 13 Jan. 1924. Davidson was J.C.C. Davidson, a Conservative MP and confidant of Law and Baldwin in turn, 'Worthy' was Sir Laming Worthington Evans MP, 'Jix' was Sir William Joynson-Hicks MP, and Lloyd-Graeme became firstly Cunliffe-Lister, and then Lord Swinton, Secretary of State for Air from 1935 to 1938.

76. Fisher to Neville Chamberlain, 4 July 1924, NC 7/11/17/7.

77. Interview with R.W. Fisher.

78. Fisher to Frances Stevenson, 30 Sept. 1925, Lloyd George papers, G/8/1/3.

79. Fisher to Lloyd George, ibid.

80. In forming his government MacDonald had given Chelmsford a specific pledge that the defence of the empire would not be neglected. Chelmsford to Haldane, 13 Jan. 1924, Haldane papers, MS 5916/74.

81. Rumbold to Lorraine, 16 Aug. 1923, MS Rumbold dep. 31; Hankey diary, 22 Mar. 1925, following Curzon's death.

82. In July 1924 Snowden helped to negotiate the agreement on reparations, then attacked it in a newspaper article as being too favourable to the French and Belgians. This predictably enraged the French, but MacDonald managed to smooth things over, and the agreement stood. Lyman, *Labour Government*, p. 167. For MacDonald's standing with the Foreign Office, see Murray to Isaacs, 15 Dec. 1924, Elibank MS 8808/165–8.

83. Tribute to Haldane by Fisher, sent to Tom Jones, 5 Feb. 1929, Thomas Jones papers, O/3/10. After Haldane's death in 1928, Fisher wrote to Miss Haldane:

> Like your brother, I believe Life to be Deathless & that union with our friends who have passed from mortal sight is as real as ever because Thought, which is living, is not subject to any break.
>
> He is, as he was, a very great expression of the true Being & Quality which is Good; & his influence, & therefore his reality, is more potent than ever before.

Fisher to Elizabeth Haldane, 18 Sept. 1928, Haldane papers, MS 6034.

84. Haldane to Tom Jones, 4 July 1924, Thomas Jones papers, W/9/95; Middlemas, *Whitehall Diary*, i, 284.

85. Hankey to Miss Haldane, 19 Feb. 1931, HNKY 4/23; Hankey to Fisher, 15 July 1924, Thomas Jones papers, B/3/8/1–2; Haldane, *Autobiography*, pp. 331–2.

86. The Treasury was in principle sympathetic to medical and scientific research throughout the inter-war period, although Boyd Orr, *As I Recall*, p. 111, complains of its attitude.

87. Fisher to Tom Jones, 28 Aug. 1929, Thomas Jones papers, W/7/5, says he was 'pondering ... whether the suggestion might not be made for a flamboyant letter to colleagues ("I", "I", "I") ... leading up to the request that they would consider the production of suitable topics for enquiry ....' See also Hankey to Tom Jones, 19 June 1925, HNKY 4/17, saying Fisher 'is not only favourable but very enthusiastic and anxious to push' the committee 'all he can'. There was 'suspicion and hostility' among the Treasury controllers, however.

88. Marquand, *MacDonald*, pp. 365–77. MacDonald had in fact seen and approved the Cabinet minute on the affair. Middlemas, *Whitehall Diary*, i, 286–93. Fisher was a friend and ally of Jones. See also PREM 1/45.

89. In the election which his group precipitated, Asquith himself lost his seat.

90. Dalton diary, 12 Mar. 1928, Dalton papers, 1/1/10. See note 80 above on Chelmsford's reasons for serving in a Labour administration.

91. Grigg, *Prejudice and Judgement*, p. 152; Report of the Board of Enquiry appointed by the Prime Minister to investigate certain statements affecting civil servants, *PP* (1928), vii, p. 531, referred to hereafter as 'Francs report'.

92. This account draws heavily on Andrew, *Secret Service*, pp. 302–13.

93. See especially Chester *et al.*, *Zinoviev Letter*.

94. This will be dealt with on pp. 160–5. Gregory had lost over £20,000 in currency speculation, and it was logical for the committee, having investigated his financial probity, to look at his behaviour in such a *cause célèbre* as the Zinoviev affair.

95. 'Francs report', p. 531.

96. Chester *et al.*, *Zinoviev Letter*, passim. Waterhouse, *Private and Official*, p. 318.

97. Note by Selby, 26 Feb. 1957, Selby papers.

98. Selby to George Glasgow, 10 May 1955, ibid.

99. *The Times*, 22 Dec. 1966. Lord Noel-Baker was a Labour MP for many years. He was a convinced pacifist, and like his mentor Arthur Henderson, a passionate supporter of the League of Nations.

100. Childs had been appointed in 1921 after General Byrne had refused the job, as described on pp. 91–4. Childs, *Episodes and Reflections*, pp. 246–51. On p. 246 he mentions that he won £500 plus costs in an action against a 'certain journal' which had said he was involved in authenticating the letter.

101. Anderson to Fisher, 5 Oct. 1928, T164 78/P71229. Note by E.W.H. Millar, 21 Aug. 1928, ibid. A Home Office man told him that the Home Secretary 'wants to get Gen Childs ... to resign at the same time as General Horwood', the Commissioner.

102. Chester *et al.*, *Zinoviev Letter*, p. 182.

103. The question then arises of how he came to be in possession of police documents.

104. Chester *et al.*, op. cit., p. 178.

105. ibid.

106. ibid. Lord Davidson's papers are in the House of Lords. Rhodes James, *Memoirs of a Conservative*, uses them extensively.

107. Selby to A.L. Kennedy of *The Times*, 20 Oct. 1955, Selby papers.

108. Selby, *Diplomatic Twilight*, pp. 3–7, 184. See Chapter 3, note 43 for the works of the others named.

109. Selby to Elibank, 29 Nov. 1956, Selby papers. Elibank was in some ways even more absurd. On 20 Sept. 1955 he told an unidentified friend that 'the longer-term repercussions' of Fisher's dealings with the Foreign Office included the Burgess/Maclean affair. Elibank papers, MS 8817/300–21.

110. Selby's superannuation papers are in T164 193/P2/88966.

111. Lord Noel-Baker to the author, 21 Feb. 1980.

112. Grigg, *Prejudice and Judgement*, pp. 133, 137.

113. There is almost nothing of interest concerning Fisher in MacDonald's papers in the Public Record Office, or in the PREM papers for the time he was premier. In Marquand, *MacDonald*, Fisher is barely mentioned.

114. Note on Treasury organization, unsigned, Jan. 1924. T199/50b. This document was discussed in Chapter 2 above.

5

The Baldwin government, 1924–9

The election of October 1924 brought Baldwin back to power as Prime Minister. Less happily for Fisher, it also brought Winston Churchill to the Treasury as Chancellor. Clementine Churchill wrote that her husband quickly became 'immersed in thrilling new work with the Treasury officials, whom he says are a wonderful lot of men.'[1] In March 1925 the momentous decision was taken that Britain should return to the gold standard, a move which the Treasury had favoured since 1919. Fisher played no important part in the technical debate which preceded the move, but he supported it wholeheartedly.[2] Churchill also showed himself eager to fight the Admiralty over its shipbuilding plans, although when it came to the crunch Beatty could always talk him round, and he was generally an ardent proponent of cuts in expenditure.[3] From the start he was a very troublesome minister for his officials. This was partly because of his unpredictable enthusiasms for new ideas, partly because he seemed unsure of what he really wanted to do, and partly because of the manner in which he dealt with Treasury business, the 'thrilling new work' which so attracted him.

Churchill had no detailed knowledge of his new department, nor of economic affairs. He was unperturbed by this, evidently believing that a few weeks' familiarization were all that was required. He soon began not simply to question the advice of his officials, but to devise alternative policies based on nothing more substantial than his own musings. These were communicated to his officials in sonorous edicts which did not invite refutation. The subjects they covered ranged from tax cuts to 'the method of preparing Minute papers and files', as 'the present method of presenting official papers at the Treasury is not convenient to the swift despatch of business.' He was an energetic, even a restless Chancellor, who disliked a cautious approach to anything. In some respects he resembled Lloyd George as Chancellor from 1908 to 1914, except that the latter had had a very clear idea of what he wanted to achieve, whereas Churchill oscillated between the Treasury view and his latest theories.[4]

Churchill and Fisher did not get on well. In March 1925 Fisher warned Baldwin of 'the oft-repeated threat ... by Winston that in spite of everyone, he is going to seize & divert from debt exemption any surplus there may be from the present year', and his disquiet about the Chancellor grew as time passed.[5] Before a meeting of the Cabinet Economy Committee, set up for the familiar reason of seeking a reduction in the budget deficit, Fisher drew Neville Chamberlain aside. Chamberlain's diary records Fisher's warning that 'the present position showed a deficit for 1926/27 of £36 million' which 'was entirely due to Winston who ought to be in the dock himself instead of putting other ministers there'. A few days later Fisher visited Chamberlain

> & we talked for an hour. The conversation left me very depressed. W.F. is evidently thoroughly miserable and out of sympathy with his chief ...
>
> He declares that all the heads of depts. have lost heart. They never know where they are or what hare W.C. will start. In October when he came in the finances were in a thoroughly healthy condition but he was warned that everything pointed to a stand easy budget ... The budget as finally presented to us was nothing compared to what W[inston] had been working on, but even so he was warned that it was risky and could only be justified if no further expenditure was agreed to. Instead of that he had allowed further concessions ... And now in the mess he had just got himself into he was proposing the maddest ideas e.g. to cut all Govt. servants down by 5% including civil service, fighting services, postmen, police and teachers.
>
> Or, alternatively, to cut down all Govt. Establishments by 25% of their number ... 'If you don't have him out, he will bring you down', he said, 'and indeed I am not sure that he won't bring you down anyhow whether out or in'....

He then went on to discuss S[tanley] B[aldwin]. He had warned him innumerable times of the danger but S.B. wd. never say anything & nothing *happened*. That was what he meant by saying that S.B. was getting under W.C.'s influence. W.C. required sitting on constantly. Only one man cd. do that, viz. the P.M., and he was not doing it. Once more he urged me to keep more in touch with S.B., but once more I explained that that was not a game that *one* could play at and that I cd. get no response .... W.F. said [of Baldwin] 'I do not know whether he is unable to concentrate. What I do know is that he does not concentrate'.

He said he had poured out all his troubles to Austen [Chamberlain] who had been 'horrified' but who took a very detached view.[6]

Amery, the Colonial Secretary, also found Fisher 'very much upset by the way Winston is splashing about and by the kind of thing he is contemplating doing with the Civil Service and the upset it would cause'.[7]

Fisher's prediction about Churchill's plans was correct. Towards the end of November, the Chancellor addressed a peremptory minute to his officials: 'the present standard of staffing in the Civil Service must be reduced', by means which included 'simplification of office routine ..., devolution downwards of responsibility', and the acceptance 'by the public of a lower standard of service, e.g. in the Post Office'. He made no reference to the work which the Treasury had been doing since 1919 both to streamline the civil service and to reduce its costs, if indeed he knew of it.

The response was not encouraging: Sir Richard Hopkins of the Inland Revenue 'had ... been fully persuaded that considerable economies would be found practicable', but after investigating the question 'I am driven ... to the conclusion that on the whole it would be unwise to disturb existing arrangements, except, of course, the introduction of machinery ... & the elimination of any superfluous routine.' Fisher prepared a memorandum for the economy committee which went through all the Treasury's arguments about the size of the service being dictated primarily by policy, cited the Anderson committee of 1923 which concluded that the service was neither too large nor overpaid, and outlined where savings could be made.[8] Churchill capitulated and signed a similar document, although he felt it 'very adverse to change.'[9] It stated that 'it would not be possible to have a major cut in numbers', but that 'we must intensify the effort to reduce numbers' by cutting 'staff overheads' and other measures, including an eight hour day for those civil servants not already on one.[10] This was a far cry from a 25 per cent cut, but if the Chancellor felt thwarted, it was his own fault for issuing instructions on a matter of which he knew little, in such a fashion that any demur from his officials appeared to be wilful obstruction. Churchill returned to the theme of staff reductions two years later, and again expressed disquiet at the Treasury's attitude to the question.[11]

The Chancellor was quite as critical of Fisher as Fisher was of him. In December 1925 he rebuked Fisher in resonant terms for criticizing his tax proposals. Churchill accepted that Fisher did 'not regard yourself in any way responsible for assisting the Chancellor', but

> I do not think that a Minute such as you have addressed to me is couched in a tone which should be used by an official, aloof from the labour and anxiety of financial business, to the Minister who, whatever his shortcomings, has actually to conduct it. Had you chosen, and I should have welcomed it, to throw yourself wholeheartedly into the stress and strain of our work, you would not have found me at all averse to remonstrances or implied censure; but in the circumstances which actually exist, I do not consider that such fitful interventions on your part rest upon a sufficiently solid foundation of aid and guidance.[12]

On the face of it, this was an extremely serious reprimand. However, the Chancellor used the same magisterial tone for everything he wrote, and he invariably put more thought into composition than into content. A few months later, he addressed another stern minute to Fisher. This commented that 'the use of locked boxes for the conveyance of secret papers is indispensable', and asked how it was that 'Memoranda and Minutes which are more informative and more able than any I have seen in any Department, should be circulated in such a happy-go-lucky fashion.' Churchill had some grounds for complaint: although the Treasury registry had been reorganized in

1920, files continually went astray. Ironically in the department responsible for urging modern office methods on the rest of the civil service, the Treasury adopted the expedient of having a messenger visit all its rooms each day in a systematic trawl for missing files. Unfortunately, Counter, the man employed on this work, hit on the idea of selling financial information gleaned from these waifs and strays to a newspaper.[13]

The similarity in language and disparity in importance between the two minutes illustrate the difficulty of assessing how seriously at odds Churchill and Fisher were. Nevertheless, there clearly was friction. In May 1926 the Chancellor threatened to obtain 'a Treasury Minute defining our relationship precisely' unless Fisher gave a clear answer to 'perfectly plain questions' about 'the functions of the Permanent Secretary in relation to the Chancellor of the Exchequer.' He also complained that Fisher had issued a Treasury minute without consulting him, the Prime Minister 'or, I need scarcely say, the Treasury Board. In other words you exercised some independent authority which you conceive to be resident in your office. This is obviously unconstitutional.'[14] The two men appear eventually to have established a more satisfactory *modus vivendi*, although Fisher continued to criticize Churchill's financial plans, and in December 1927 advised Neville Chamberlain on how to deal with the Chancellor's de-rating proposals when they came up in cabinet.[15]

Churchill's difficulties with Fisher raise a serious issue: to whom did Fisher hold himself answerable? There seems little doubt that he maintained that he was responsible to the Board of Treasury — rightly described by Churchill as 'a fiction' — and to the Prime Minister as First Lord.[16] But the fact was that he was also briefing the two Chamberlains, former Chancellors, it is true, but not members of the Board of Treasury. The Chancellor had every right to protest, if Fisher's attitude was what Churchill said it was. Furthermore, Fisher's relationship to the Prime Minister was based not on an immutable principle, but on the fact that he got on better with Baldwin than with Churchill. When Snowden and Neville Chamberlain were at the Treasury, he happily worked to them — indeed from 1929 to 1935 he had little to do with the First Lord, MacDonald, except when advising on appointments. There was no hard and fast doctrine governing the relationship between the Permanent Secretary to the Treasury, the Chancellor and the

Prime Minister. In so far as Fisher said otherwise, he was only stating in an abstract form what happened to be the position which existed for much of his time at the Treasury — he was trusted by the Prime Minister of the day.

II

On 24 November 1924 Fisher had a talk with Leo Amery, the new Colonial Secretary, on the future of the Colonial Office. Amery wanted to introduce a number of reforms, in particular 'the division of the Colonial Office into two independent Departments each in the charge of a Permanent Under Secretary', to deal with 'Imperial Relations' and 'Colonial Affairs' respectively.[17] This was anathema to Fisher, who told Baldwin that 'Winston' was convinced that 'provided the Dominions are assured of the formal fact that no one under the degree of the Prime Minister is regarded as the opposite number of a Dominions Prime Minister', they would have no interest in a change in 'the machinery to which they are accustomed'. He continued:

> I am neither qualified nor is it my job to express any opinion as to this: my concern is limited to preventing, with your support, wrong business organisation in the Public Service. And *two* official Heads or General Managers as a *permanent* arrangement in a single Department is the negation of every business principle.[18]

At Fisher's suggestion, Amery was asked to provide Baldwin with a detailed statement of his proposals. He responded by presenting the plan he had already put for the creation of a separate secretaryship of state for the dominions, to be held by himself in addition to the colonial secretaryship. The Colonial Office would be divided along the same lines, with a permanent head for each of the two departments. Fisher opposed this, as it 'involved one Minister (of the Pooh-Bah variety) & two Permanent Under Secretaries of State' in what he claimed would still be a single department. This 'is the negation of all business principle & organisation, & if one Minister is to be indulged in this fallacy, why shd. not all Ministers?'[19] He asserted that the dominions wanted no change, and incautiously proposed that they be consulted. They were, of course, delighted at the idea of a separate department.[20] Amery refused to budge from his plans, but he did agree to Fisher's proposal of a committee of inquiry into 'the higher establishment of the Colonial Office'. The committee was made up of men close to Fisher, and its findings were predictably a compromise.[21] It recommended that a deputy permanent under secretary in a unified Colonial Office be given responsibility for dominions affairs. Fisher hailed these 'conclusions, after impartial enquiry, of three of the most experienced & practical men of affairs in the Public Service', but Amery was unmoved: 'A month or more was wasted while certain worthy fellows who knew nothing about the Colonial Office when they began, and not very much when they finished, produced a report which really added nothing to the question.'[22]

Amery's refusal to accept the committee's findings eventually won him the day. Churchill, who had 'personally found the Colonial Office very much quieter and easier' than any other public office he had held, reluctantly agreed to the creation of a separate secretaryship of state for dominions affairs, and to the appointment of a Deputy Permanent Under Secretary to be responsible for dominions business.[23] The Cabinet approved this arrangement, with the proviso that the new deputy 'should be only of slightly lower rank and stature than the Under Secretary and should have direct access to the Secretary of State.'[24] This decision did not end the matter, however, as Amery and Fisher disagreed about what it meant. Fisher insisted that 'the Permanent Head of a Government Department is responsible to the Minister and the Government for the efficiency of the Department and his subordinates are not permitted to exercise an *imperium in imperio*.'[25] This was a central tenet of his thinking about the civil service; in the dispute with Amery, it seems to have led him to accept a complete defeat in preference to the Cabinet's vague formula. Amery complained to Baldwin that

> Fisher wants to defeat the whole essence and purpose of the scheme, first of all by refusing to allow the Deputy Secretary for Dominion Affairs to have any higher pay or status than an ordinary Deputy Under Secretary, and secondly by insisting that the Permanent Under Secretary

for the Colonies should exercise a control over the work of the Deputy Under Secretary for Dominion Affairs ....

I only mention this not to bother you but because I am afraid from the tone Fisher is taking up that he will make an effort to obstruct matters.[26]

On 10 June, Fisher and Amery finally agreed that, instead of a Deputy Under Secretary of uncertain status, dominions affairs should be looked after by a Permanent Under Secretary, whose department would be on a separate vote from the Colonial Office.[27] It was a comprehensive victory for Amery, though he had to haggle about the salaries of the two permanent heads.[28] He also got his nominees appointed to the two posts: Sir Charles Davis took charge of dominions affairs, while Sir Samuel Wilson became head of the Colonial Office. Fisher had given Baldwin a list of candidates for the latter job with comments on each: one was 'too clever: undiplomatic: judgement uncertain: strong character: bad mixer', while Wilson was 'easy to get on with, tactful and considerate: quite competent and not deficient in character: not at all conspicuously qualified for the permanent headship'. Fisher favoured Sir Hugh Clifford, 'head and shoulders the best among Colonial Governors (simply in need of a short holiday).'[29] Amery, however, felt Clifford was 'in a state of nerves from overwork' and was 'too much of a bull in a china shop as well as a little too oriental'; he preferred Wilson, who was duly appointed. This was probably just as well. Clifford was certified as 'of unsound mind' in 1930.[30]

Fisher put a brave face on his defeat to Baldwin:

You will be relieved to be quit of this troublesome subject .... The personnel is not ideal, but short of advising the transfer of indispensable men from other Departments (which I cannot do), it is probably not too wrong, & I submit therefore that you approve the names proposed.[31]

Amery continued to have his differences with Fisher and the Treasury. He disliked their attitude to the Empire Marketing Board and to colonial development, where finance was a perennial problem.[32] By 1929 he believed that he had achieved 'all that ... is possible' while the 'blight of Winston at the Treasury' persisted.[33] Nevertheless, he frequently consulted

Fisher on questions of appointments, honours, finance, and organization. Sometimes they agreed, sometimes they did not: although 'all with him on general principle', Amery resisted Fisher's proposal to push out the deputy head of the Dominions Office once he reached the age of 60 in favour of 'Montgomery of the F[oreign] O[ffice] as a man of the world', since this would be 'hardly fair' to the incumbent 'after his long and devoted service.'[34] On the other hand, Amery thought Fisher's suggestion to him for the post of high commissioner to Canada 'a very good choice', and appointed him.[35] When he decided that a powerful inquiry into the organization of the colonial service was necessary, he took good care to make sure that Fisher was sympathetic, and appointed him chairman of the inquiry committee.[36] The Colonial Office man most concerned was told: 'convince Warren and your battle is won. No one will dare to question his recommendations', and so it proved. The committee's conclusions, 'the Magna Carta of the modern Colonial Service', were entirely on the lines favoured by Amery and his civil servants.[37]

Amery's dealings with Fisher are interesting in themselves; they are significant also in providing the fullest illustration available of Fisher's relations with a non-Treasury minister.[38] This is largely chance: Amery kept a detailed diary, and there happen to be relevant official records.[39] Fisher's interests and activities were somewhat eclectic, so it cannot be presumed that Amery's experience is representative, though it may well be.[40] What can be said is that he handled Fisher sensibly, and as a result got what he wanted.

III

In February and March 1926, a number of questions were asked in the Commons about Fisher's standing as Head of the Civil Service. In forwarding a draft reply to a question by Sir Henry Craik MP as to the 'nature of the instrument by which in 1867 the title of principal officer of the Civil Service was conferred upon the Secretary to the Treasury', and as to whether it carried with it any right of 'interference in regard to appointments to other departments', Fisher told Baldwin that this is by no means the first time that Sir Henry Craik has evinced uneasiness that the Constitution is being jeopardised in this respect.

Sir H. Craik was himself a Civil Servant from 1870 to 1904, during the last nineteen years of the period being Secretary to the Scottish Education Department. He conceived that position as one of great importance and the contemporary Treasury (unfortunately) never seems to have disguised its view that neither Sir Henry nor his post was of any particular importance.

Hence an abiding resentment on his part in particular against the Treasury and in general against the Service.

The King is, as Sir H. Craik rightly suggests, the sovereign or supreme Head of each and all the Services of the Crown. The Prime Minister is the Political Head of the Civil Service, and the Secretary to the Treasury is the permanent or official head. So far from any constitutional innovation or any infringement of business or of Service organisation being involved, the association of the (official) headship of the Civil Service with the Secretaryship to the Treasury has been an admitted fact ever since the Service was organised to meet modern conditions of government .... The decision in 1919 of Mr Lloyd George and Mr Bonar Law to reorganise the Treasury on its present basis made no changes so far as the position of the Secretary to the Treasury in his relationship to the Service is concerned; all that they did on that point was to include a specific reference to it in the Circular issued to the Service over your signature in September of that year.[41]

Craik was not mollified by Baldwin's reply and wrote to *The Times* that many of those 'familiar with the traditions and ways of the Civil Service' were 'profoundly stirred by this new and ill-founded claim to independent authority beyond his own Department for a Civil Servant.' He implied that it was impossible to secure a satisfactory discussion of the issue in Parliament, but eventually he did get a debate, on 14 April 1926.[42]

Fisher provided Baldwin with a lengthy brief for this debate. It included all the usual arguments in favour of Treasury control of the civil service, cited the MacDonnell, Haldane, Asquith, and Anderson committees, and attacked Craik's claim that a minister was 'responsible for his own Department to the King and to Parliament'. As Fisher pointed out, there was no room in this assumption 'for the ultimate responsibility of the Prime Minister or for the collective responsibility of the Cabinet'. He continued:

> The title of a Prime Minister, so long as he continues to be Prime Minister, and as the Minister *ultimately* responsible for everything, to insist on being consulted by his colleagues, and on having the final say, with regard to any subject or subjects he chooses has always been inherent in his position, and appointments to the more important posts in the Public Service have at no time been admitted as an exception to this principle. Prior to the commencement of 1920, no systematic procedure had been laid down in this connection.

But the brief had one considerable weakness: it assumed that 'the status dates from before 1872, and it is probable that it is contemporaneous with the introduction in 1867 of the title Permanent Secretary to the Treasury. The 1867 papers have, however, long been missing.' Craik and his allies made much of these missing papers; they would have made more had they known that the documents did not confer the title of Head of the Civil Service on the permanent head of the Treasury.[43] As it was, the debate was of little value: Craik made a meandering and pompous speech, saying of the disputed title that there was 'to an old member of the Civil Service ... besides its palpable lack of constitutional foundation, something ludicrously absurd in this new-fangled piece of mountebankism'. Sidney Webb, John Simon, Ronald McNeill, and Lloyd George all defended the present arrangement on grounds of practicality and efficiency, and Lloyd George stated that when he was Chancellor the Prime Minister had consulted the secretary to the Treasury about civil service appointments.[44]

This attack was easy to repel because those MPs who criticized the post of Head of the Civil Service did so in such a petty manner — indeed, one of Craik's parliamentary questions coincided with publication by the *Morning Post* of a ludicrous interview given by Fisher's estranged wife at a health farm, the object of which was plainly to discredit him.[45] The debate fizzled out in irrelevance: it was of no practical

1: Warren Fisher aged two.

2: Warren Fisher c.1900.

3: *Warren Fisher's wedding, April 1906. The bride's father Major Thomas is at the back on the right-hand side. His parents did not attend the ceremony because it took place in a Roman Catholic church.*

4: Warren Fisher in his thirties.

5: *Family holiday at Lossiemouth, 1921. Fisher is sitting beside Russell Scott of the Treasury. Maysie Fisher is immediately behind Scott. To the right of Robin and Norman Fisher is Bunny, the family nanny who later became Fisher's housekeeper.*

Lady Fisher (centre), wife of Sir Warren Fisher, whose signatur

6: *A cutting from an unidentified newspaper, February 1926, when Lady Fisher was interviewed at a health farm.*

7: Warren Fisher at the age of 54, in April 1934.

6, TREBOROUGH HOUSE,
GREAT WOODSTOCK STREET,
MARYLEBONE,
W.1.

24th March 1930

My dear Nan

Will you get
some little thing with
the enclosed for my
god-child in honour
of the 26th? I hope for
a good cheerful, as you
do indeed deserve to.
I got your little memento
of the 17th, & I really
ought to reciprocate for

8:    *An example of Warren Fisher's handwriting, 1930.*

importance whether the phrase 'Head of the Civil Service' was used first in 1867 or in 1872, though the Prime Minister, on Fisher's advice, made it a central point of his argument. There was ample historical justification for the title in the role which the Treasury had played since the mid-nineteenth century as the maker of regulations on discipline, appointments and pay in public departments. There were few references to the process by which appointments were in practice made, and none at all to the question of whether the Head of the Civil Service was entitled *ex officio* to advise the Prime Minister on general policy. Yet these were the crucial issues which arose from Fisher's career. It was perhaps just as well that Churchill did not speak in the debate, since, as has been seen, the Chancellor was himself greatly dissatisfied with Fisher's quasi-theological definition of his function of principal official adviser to the First Lord of the Treasury.[46]

Fisher was extremely sensitive to attacks on the civil service, although years of experience should have taught him that they mattered very little.[47] When Lord Midleton alleged in 1927 that there was 'undoubtedly room for greater decreases in the Civil Service', that 'I could tell you cases of young fellows who are ordered to extend their luncheon hour from 1–2 p.m. as there is nothing for them to do', and that 'three of the most responsible officials who have ever served the country' were 'behind me' in calling for an 'expert body' to comb out departments, Fisher reacted sharply: 'You will observe that, let alone his judgement, he is frequently at sea on his facts.'[48] His irritation at Midleton's remarks was probably heightened by his knowledge of Churchill's own fondness for such talk.[49] When Midleton returned to the charge two years later, Fisher told the Chancellor Philip Snowden that

> argument with Lord Midleton is [a] complete waste of time: he has not, & never has had, any intention of listening to anything that doesn't agree with his particular craze; & I am sorry to have to agree that, not only is he deficient in intelligence, but that he has proved himself quite indifferent to scruple.[50]

He was equally contemptuous, with less justification, of a speech by Lord Oxford (Asquith) in 1927 calling for the abolition of four ministries and the transfer of their functions to other departments. These proposals annoyed Fisher, partly perhaps because he was never able to make much headway himself with the reorganization of the boundaries of departments which he always maintained was necessary. Although 'a practical man, and apparently more up to date in my information than Lord Oxford', Fisher in fact agreed that ideally the Department of Overseas Trade, and the ministries of transport and mines should go: 'I see an important advantage in ending the vicious principle that a single industry should have ... a special Department ... for its particular affairs. This has encouraged the politicalisation [sic] of the coal industry.' However, he poured scorn on the suggestion that the Ministry of Labour should be scrapped: 'such a trifle ... as the fact that the insured population of 1912 numbered between 2 and 3 millions, whereas today it numbers between 12 and 13 millions, seems to have escaped' Oxford's notice.[51] A fortnight later, the government took the decision in principle to abolish three departments, mines, transport and overseas trade, though ultimately only the first of these disappeared.[52]

The general strike of May 1926 was the most dramatic event of the Conservatives' term in office from 1924 to 1929. Thanks largely to Sir John Anderson at the Home Office, the government was well prepared. There is nothing in published work or in official papers to show the part that Fisher played in forming policy on the strike, although his son believes that he was in the thick of it.[53] Most of Fisher's work was done informally and by word of mouth; the absence of documents need not mean an absence of activity. His only significant intervention of which there is a record concerned Churchill's 'precipitancy towards the union legislation and funds' — the Chancellor was in his element in the emergency, and was urging punitive action. Not for the first time Fisher disagreed with his minister. He and other officials thought anti-union laws might lead to Baldwin being 'pulled down from his pedestal.' Neville Chamberlain recorded him as saying that a

> number of civil servants to whom he had been talking all with one accord felt that it was wrong now. They were satisfied that we must hold out to the last against 'concurrent' concessions but he seemed to take the view that if we thoroughly beat the General Strike as to which

he entertained no doubt legislation would not be necessary.[54]

When the draconian Trade Disputes Act was passed a year later, the Treasury gave departmental establishment officers an unusually broad hint to ignore it in their dealings with staff associations.[55]

An important issue arose from the strike after Labour returned to power in 1929. Pressure was brought to bear on the First Lord of the Admiralty to review the cases of some Admiralty dockyard workers, who had forfeited part of their pension rights as a result of taking part in the strike. Fisher wanted the question discussed by the Cabinet, as it 'is not a mere departmental concern; it is nothing less than whether the state is in times of crisis to be liable to be thrown over by its Public Service. On this there can in my opinion be no compromise.' Three weeks later he told Snowden that

> it appears to me axiomatic that for a State servant no suggestion of 'divided allegiance' can at any time be admitted. We, whether we be civilian or military employees of the State, are the instruments thro' which HMG operates & HMG has the elementary responsibility to the community that its existence should be ensured. For this purpose HMG must know that its agents can be relied on, without any possibility of doubt, to make effective that responsibility of government.
>
> Condonation of a strike by State employees at any time negatives the essential principle on which civilian govt. (& the country for which it is a trustee) rests; condonation of such a strike in times of emergency is the first step towards suicide.
>
> (It is of course quite immaterial to the principle in what branch of the Public Service the strike may have occurred.)

Although the Cabinet at first agreed that the penalties imposed in 1926 should not be withdrawn, some months later a committee of ministers was appointed to look into the question. Fisher hoped that 'this vital issue of the responsibility of the services of the Crown may not be jeopardised by a reversal' of the previous decision. Nevertheless, the committee resolved to restore full pension rights to the men concerned.[56] Fisher maintained that this breached a key principle, but the Cabinet's decision did not have the adverse effect which he feared.

It should be said that Fisher was not anti-union, although he thought both strikes and lock-outs were 'merely methods of barbarism' which should be replaced by 'a sense of co-opera-tion and partnership'. He cultivated union leaders as he did businessmen. He was particularly friendly with W.J. Brown, the maverick general secretary of the Civil Service Clerical As-sociation, who thought him 'a great Secretary to the Treasury and a remarkable human being' — on one occasion Fisher entertained Brown, the left-wing Labour MP James Maxton and the miners' leader A.J. Cook to dinner in his flat, present-ing his guests with 'three vivid red carnations' so that they could wear their true colours.[57]

Fisher was closely associated with sport in the civil service. He believed that sport could break down barriers of rank and department, and also that it increased a sense of common identity in the service as a whole. The founders of the Civil Service Sports Association were allowed to use offices in the Treasury for their meetings, and in 1921 he launched an appeal among his fellow heads of departments to raise £150 towards the cost of establishing the new body. In 1925 he persuaded the government, despite Churchill's objections, to give a grant of £200,000 over four years to finance the purchase of suitable grounds.[58] This was announced by Austen Chamberlain at the annual civil service dinner on 12 February 1926. Leo Amery, who attended the dinner, doubted 'very much whether this is the right moment for such a concession and I think the doubt is widely shared.'[59] The unpopularity of the grant was soon apparent, and the Cabinet quickly withdrew it.[60] Fisher was predictably incensed at what he saw as a craven concession to popular prejudice against the civil service:

> If the government do not intend to give the £50,000 a year as promised, there seems to be nothing to be said for vague references to the future. They certainly would carry no conviction; indeed they would as certainly confirm a suspicion throughout the whole Service that what has happened will happen again.[61]

The sports council nevertheless raised sufficient money from its members to buy grounds at Chiswick, which were formally opened by the King in February 1926. Fisher continued to be an active patron. He presented the council with a trophy to be awarded annually to the best 'all-round sportsman in the service' — further evidence, perhaps, of his generalist values. He subsequently gave one of the council's leading lights, Noel Curtis-Bennett, a new post as civil service sports adviser in the Treasury, an appointment which understandably raised some eyebrows, and he did everything he could to further the council's interests. In 1938 the government finally agreed to support civil service sport, instituting an annual grant of £20,000.[62]

The council was rather more successful than another innovation with which he was associated, the annual civil service dinner. This was attended by representatives of all grades and departments, and by guests from the royal family, the armed services and the political world. It was addressed by a senior cabinet minister or the like — in 1930 the guest of honour, the American ambassador General Dawes, planned to talk on the workings of the United States Bureau of the Budget, a novel theme for an after-dinner speech — but the event never really caught on although for some years it was carried live to a wider audience by BBC radio.[63]

Fisher had other more esoteric plans to foster *esprit de corps* and improve morale. While standing at his Treasury window overlooking Horse Guards Parade one day he saw 'a stream of men moving out to lunch from the Treasury, Home Office, Foreign Office and various other Civil Service Departments'. He was struck by the contrast between these officials 'slouching along out of step, trousers uncreased, suit unpressed and cut for any figure but its wearer', and the men who emerged from the War Office and Admiralty, also in civilian clothes but moving with the crisp and confident stride of the warrior. 'I asked myself whether in the public interest Parliament might not ... provide a small sum annually so that Civil Servants — of course excluding volunteers — might be sent, say to Paris, to see "life".' The colleagues he consulted 'were clear that the thing was unthinkable; and so went west another of my bright ideas for "humanising" the Civil Service (which, after all, is what the public is always shrieking for).'[64]

IV

By 1925, foreign affairs had ceased to be controversial. The Dawes plan for reparations payments operated smoothly and without fuss, and the Locarno treaty, signed in December, demonstrated the calm which pervaded international relations following the crises of the early 1920s. The League of Nations came into its own as a forum for settling disputes, although not everyone had faith in it. Amery was 'horrified' by Austen Chamberlain's reliance on it, while Hankey was worried about Britain's 'military spirit ... in some parts of the country the history text books used at primary school teach nothing but internationalism and are contemptuous of patriotism as we know it.'[65]

In Fisher's view, Britain's foreign policy from 1924 to 1929 was along the right lines. It was stable, even-handed and under the direction of a man whom the Treasury respected, Austen Chamberlain. Fisher later said that 'the league had had a pretentious facade with an ill-constructed house behind it', but at the time he appears to have kept his views to himself.[66] He did, however, become friendly with the American ambassador, A.B. Houghton, who was rumoured to be hostile to it and in favour of the major powers affirming 'their will to peace by a plebiscite ... He is very much in earnest about it, uses many religious terms, and declares that he means to devote the rest of his life to peace.'[67] Houghton, Fisher, and Tom Jones combined in 1928 to press Baldwin to overrule a Foreign Office draft reply to Kellogg's proposal of a pact renouncing war in favour of something 'which could be understood in the Middle West.'[68] Fisher was friendly also with Houghton's successor, General Dawes.[69] More importantly, he was close to the senior professional diplomat at the American embassy from 1927 to 1937, Ray Atherton. (He acted as best man when Atherton married in 1928.)[70] When considering his 'fierce anti-American views' of the 1930s, these links should not be forgotten.[71] He disliked only the United States Congress, which he thought chauvinistic and capricious, not the American people.

It was in this period that Fisher began to take a distinct interest in the affairs of the Foreign Office. When the Prime Minister's secretariat was put on a proper civil service footing in 1928, Fisher had Robert Vansittart of the Foreign Office appointed as Principal Private Secretary.[72] Another move evidently intended to lessen the Foreign Office's isolation from the rest of Whitehall was his suggestion that one of its senior men, Sir Hubert Montgomery, be made deputy head of the Dominions Office in 1929.[73] He is alleged also to have suggested the appointment of Miles Lampson to be Deputy Under Secretary in 1925, in preference to the candidate nominated by Sir William Tyrrell, the head of the department. This story comes from Walford Selby, whose unreliability has already been shown.[74] Selby claimed that Tyrrell 'immediately perceived a Treasury intervention', and threatened to resign unless his man was appointed. 'In the face of this attitude', Fisher 'did not press his point.'[75] It is quite possible that Fisher proposed Lampson, who was much younger and less hidebound than Tyrrell's choice, Sir Victor Wellesley.[76] It is most unlikely that Tyrrell took exception to this intervention, or that he threatened to resign. Fisher had been consulted about an appointment to the same post in 1921, so his interest could not be described as unprecedented.[77] Furthermore, the two men were on very good terms, and in 1942 Tyrrell went out of his way to deny explicitly the charge of his former colleague Lord Perth that Fisher had interfered improperly in the administration of the Foreign Office.[78] In any case, even in Selby's version of events Fisher gave way in 1925 without much fuss, which belies the charge that he imposed unwanted men on the Foreign Office.

The officials of the Foreign Office and the foreign service were a small and homogeneous group. With the exception of William Strang and one or two others who came in by the special examinations for demobilized officers following the war, they shared a common background in education, family and fortune. They were quite different from the staff of other government departments, and they perceived themselves as such. While there was an inordinate amount of personal enmity and bitterness within their ranks, they were united in their dislike and suspicion of moves to put them on a par with the administrative civil service. This Fisher attempted to do, because he did not believe that diplomacy was beyond the ken of ordinary civil servants, and because he felt that the main difference between the home civil service and the Foreign Office was that the latter were, with some honourable exceptions, a collection of well-connected snobs. He obtained a fresh insight into the ways of British diplomats through his investigation in 1928 of the 'Francs affair'.

In January 1928, Mrs Aminta Bradley Dyne was taken to court by a firm of currency brokers. She had been speculating in foreign currencies for over five years, and judging by her debt of over £38,000 had been remarkably unsuccessful. The debt had been contracted by gambling in futures, a fairly painless way of losing money since nothing had to be paid until the settlement date, and if a client's credit was good the brokers might allow further speculation to make up losses rather than press for a balancing of the account. In the course of the court action, it came out that Mrs Bradley Dyne had been speculating in partnership with J.D. Gregory of the Foreign Office, and that other Foreign Office men had made similar forays into the currency market. As a result of this disclosure, a committee was set up to investigate 'certain statements affecting civil servants'; Fisher was chairman, and its other members were the Comptroller and Auditor General Sir Malcolm Ramsay and Sir Maurice Gwyer, the Treasury Solicitor.[79] The Foreign Office was alarmed, as the British minister in Ecuador heard:

> As you can imagine the whole Office & indeed all London is in a ferment about it — what the outcome of it all will be nobody knows, but the pundits say Sir Warren Fisher is out for blood. The only question is to what extent he will be allowed to get it.[80]

A diplomat in Madrid was also pessimistic:

> This Gregory business is most unfortunate and I do not know what will be the outcome. Gossip says that the enquiry will take 3 weeks as there are ramifications which means, I suppose, that other persons are involved besides those already mentioned. Meanwhile Gregory is not working at the F.O. pending the result of the enquiry and I hear that there is pessimism as regards his fate .... If it is found that other members of the F.O. or diplomatic service are also involved in similar transactions the difficulty will be where to draw the line as regards disciplinary action. All this is nuts to foreigners who can now cast stones at Anglo-Saxon rectitude.[81]

Owen O'Malley, an official mentioned in the court case, told his wife that he did not know 'what line the enquiry is going to follow or whether they'll want to give me the sack for having dealt in francs', and that 'I shall keep away from Don [Gregory] and Aminta till it's over and I don't want to be called into their counsels.' After appearing before the board, he felt it 'unlikely that they can give me the sack. There is no rule against civil servants buying & selling anything ... It's all a question of degree & taste.' But O'Malley had not been entirely frank with the board, and this had a bearing on their findings.[82]

The board's conclusions were severe. It recommended that Gregory be dismissed, O'Malley be permitted to resign, that Maxse, another man involved, lose five years' seniority, and that Miles Lampson, who had once bought and sold francs as opposed to gambling in futures, be severely reprimanded. All were exonerated from any hint of corruption or of using official information to their own advantage.[83] The board also investigated and emphatically rejected the allegation that Gregory's actions during the Zinoviev letter crisis had been connected with his financial speculation. The Foreign Secretary Austen Chamberlain and the Prime Minister endorsed these findings, and action was taken accordingly.[84]

The penalties imposed were amply justified by what the board had uncovered. In addition to the impropriety of civil servants, especially those responsible for foreign affairs, gambling in the currencies of other countries, the amounts involved were disturbing. Gregory had lost around £20,000 — about ten times his salary — and Maxse £3,200. O'Malley had dropped only a few hundred, but he was the victim of his own evasiveness and was treated as one of the instigators of the speculation.[85] In addition, it was evident that Mrs Bradley Dyne was Gregory's mistress. This, combined with the huge debts the pair had contracted, made Gregory an obvious candidate for blackmail. What is most curious is that, while there was no protest at the disciplinary measures taken, few people in the Foreign Office appeared to believe that those punished had done anything questionable.

The Francs report was, in the words of Geoffrey Dawson, the editor of *The Times* who had been briefed in advance by Fisher, 'an admirably written document with some weighty words for Civil Servants.'[86] Its authors stated that they wished to enunciate general principles, which we do not seek to elaborate into any detailed code, if only for the reason that their application must necessarily vary according to the position, the Department and the work of the Civil Servant concerned. Practical rules for the guidance of social conduct depend as much upon the instinctive perception of the individual as upon cast-iron formulas; and the surest guide will, we hope, always be found the nice and jealous honour of Civil Servants themselves.

The report argued that a civil servant

is not to subordinate his duty to his private interests, nor to make use of his official position to further those interests, is to say no more than that he must behave with common honesty. The Service exacts from itself a higher standard, because it recognises that the State is entitled to demand that its servants shall not only be honest in fact, but beyond the reach of suspicion of dishonesty .... A Civil Servant is not to subordinate his duty to his private interests; but neither is he to put himself in a position where his duty and his interest conflict. He is not to make use of his official position to further those interests; but neither is he so to order his private affairs that a trust has been abused or a confidence betrayed.[87]

These precepts were distributed to all departments as a Treasury circular. For decades it served as the definitive statement of the obligations of all government employees. Fisher later commented that the 'standards of conduct' specified had 'existed long before' 1928 'and apply ... equally to all' civil and military servants of the crown.[88] Nevertheless, the circular ruffled some feathers in the foreign service: one ambassador refused to be bound by anything based on 'Treasury rules and minutes' which he claimed did not apply to the foreign service.[89] His objection stemmed from resentment, not from principle: the circular contained nothing novel or unfair, and it had the full backing of the Foreign Secretary, who had always been particularly strict about civil service discipline.[90] But the Foreign Office and the diplomatic service saw themselves as a breed apart, and some saw a threat to their independence in the outcome of the Francs affair. Whatever their claim to separate treatment in regard to appointments, they had no grounds for complaint at Fisher's attempt to impose uniform standards of discipline.[91]

O'Malley resigned as required, although 'I don't think people in general think I'm in the least disgraced. Plenty may think I'm a bloody ass.'[92] This crisis came at a bad time: he was short of money, and two of his children were seriously ill.[93] Furthermore, his wife, the novelist Ann Bridge, was with their convalescent son in Switzerland.[94] Help came from where he least expected it: two days after the report came out, a Foreign Office friend invited him to lunch with Fisher. O'Malley found his former inquisitor

> exceedingly friendly — I think he's genuine.
>
> The substance of what he said was this. I get no pension, but ... all the service believe in me & want very strongly to help me. He said 'You must wait & do nothing for the moment. Live from day to day ... I promise to leave no pains unspared to see you through eventually; for the moment you are not normal in mind or body, tho' you may think you are. You *must* trust me, altho' it's the hardest thing of all to do'...
>
> It was something to find trust & sympathy & genuine desire to help in one's hangman ...
>
> Of course this didn't take two hours to say — we started off at lunch with Portia [Bland, wife of Neville Bland who was hosting the lunch] on general principles of life, my sort of quasi-metaphysical stuff.[95]

Fisher left 'in tears', having realized that O'Malley had done himself an injustice in his evidence to the inquiry. That afternoon, he sent O'Malley a copy of *Verba Christi*, which 'is, to me, a wonderful ever deepening philosophy of life — Life itself — not in any sense what is currently spoken of as "religion" ....' He drew O'Malley's attention to various passages in the book, and concluded: 'All things to constitute real happiness are added unto us, I deeply believe, if we have trust in our Father, who is Love.'[96] A week later, Fisher wrote to Ann Bridge in Switzerland:

> This little line is written — not by the official who was Chairman of the Board of Enquiry — but by one who in

his private capacity has, I hope, a human understanding of your distress. And it is written to assure you that even among the officials, whose conclusions and advice must, I fear, seem to you severe, there is personal friendship to you & your husband. This is not play-acting on our part, &, if I may, I wd. like quite simply to say that you & he have friends who will stand by & see you through, & your children, during this time of strain, & for the future are keeping their eyes open so that no chance of work ... may be lost to him. In the meantime, will you try, please, to have trust & confidence & not to be afraid.[97]

He advised O'Malley on the terms of his letter of resignation, and urged him to 'have faith, have faith, have faith in love & courage & nothing can hurt you'. It was clear that he was working for mitigation of the penalty originally imposed, but that this was likely to take some time.[98]

Ann Bridge returned from Switzerland to help her husband. Her melodramatic book *Permission to Resign* tells how she persuaded Fisher of the justice of her husband's cause, and gives a very full account of all the people she lobbied on his behalf. It is clear however that Fisher, who had already declared his intention of helping her husband, would have secured at least a reduction of the penalty imposed without any help from her. Within two months she was able to tell her husband that 'we have pulled it off, after a fashion — a year *en disponibilité* & five years' loss of seniority.'[99] This was based on official acceptance that O'Malley was not so important a figure in the speculation as his evasive manner towards the board of inquiry had suggeted .

Ann Bridge made her most important contribution to her husband's cause a month later, when she mentioned to Fisher that O'Malley had not been suspended prior to appearing before the board. This came as a complete surprise to Fisher, who argued that 'the failure' to suspend him, and thereby to put him on notice that he was suspected of serious wrongdoing, 'was and is a very serious matter.' Had Fisher known of this when revision of 'the original sentence ... was under consideration, I should ... without any doubt' have urged that the revised sentence be limited to 'a year *en disponibilité*.' [100] He tried unsuccessfully to persuade both Chamberlain and his successor as Foreign Secretary to reduce O'Malley's punishment.[101]

When O'Malley himself tried in 1930, none of the five senior officials asked for an opinion — Fisher's two companions on the board, and three permanent secretaries — thought he deserved any further remission, and they all felt he had been treated very leniently.[102]

The O'Malleys remained friendly with Fisher, though their recollections of him show that they both looked down on him a little. Ann Bridge wished she could have 'snapped my fingers at Warren, & told him we didn't want his ruddy intervention' in 1928, but when her husband wanted the post of high commissioner in Dublin ten years later, it was of course to Fisher that he turned.[103] O'Malley thought Fisher

an elusive and enigmatic character; but I could state quite categorically that he was a good man. His superficial attractions were obvious — good looks, extreme readiness in speech, openmindedness, toleration, patience, and scholarship. A model civil servant — courageous and emphatically *not* dishonest in personal or official relationships.

Why I originally got into trouble with him was because he was not intelligently sensitive to the characters of other people who were quite unlike himself. He was educated, it is true, at the Dragon School and at Winchester, but never moved as a member of it in that large upper middle class society of which ... my parents on both sides and all my aunts and uncles were typical ...

Outside official life we should have been most unlikely to meet. I was and, I suppose, am an old-fashioned snob, born and brought up in the country, and consequently at ease with all classes of society, particularly the top and bottom strata. The class of society with which I was least at ease is precisely the class to which Warren appeared to belong ...

I became, and remained, very fond of Warren. He was much cleverer than I — cleverer than almost everyone — frighteningly clever. Just a little too clever .... On the whole a good man, who worked like a tiger.[104]

Ann Bridge described Fisher as 'a small man — slim, alert, and spry, with grey hair and a youthful unworn face. Something rather sweet about the eyes and mouth. Bad, weak, obstinate hands. Very smart and natty in his dress, very smooth and urbane in his speech.' He apparently developed a dog-like affection for her, and enjoyed 'spreading love and peace over one like treacle'; in return she writes of him with an airy condescension.[105] She thought 'there was something about Fisher that was not quite genuine — not really honest to himself, and therefore not able to be honest to or about other people.' But she approved of his

> simple, earthy taste for low not to say vulgar humour. After his long strenuous days conducting public affairs at the Treasury with some of the most highly-trained intelligences in the country, his favourite recreation, back in his rather featureless little flat, was to settle down after supper in a chair by the fire with a glass of port.

She thought his fondness for the songs of Harry Lauder and George Formby 'perfectly wholesome; I felt that these simple tastes of his were completely genuine.'[106] The O'Malleys' depiction of Fisher as a dapper and quick-witted clerk whose ability has taken him above his social station is malicious nonsense. However, what Owen O'Malley wrote about Fisher's character rings true. The entire episode casts light on a number of his traits: his insistence on an extremely high standard of conduct by public servants, his openness and decency in private, his knack of developing intense but transient friendships, and the inspiration and consolation he derived from his spiritual beliefs. This last is the hardest element of his character to describe, let alone to understand. He regarded himself as a non-Christian, yet *Verba Christi* was his bible and he believed, rightly or not, that in everything he did he was trying to follow its precepts. Those who fell foul of him would have found this hard to credit.

Some British diplomats feared that after the Francs affair 'we shall never hear the end of it from the French and other people too', but in fact the episode was quickly forgotten.[107] Curiously, although it was an open intrusion into Foreign Office affairs neither Walford Selby nor his friends ever made much of Fisher's conduct of the inquiry. This was probably because it was the Foreign Secretary, not Fisher, who was most severe on those involved. But there is no doubt that his intrusion was somewhat resented in the Foreign Office, where it was generally believed that he had a strong prejudice against both the department and the diplomatic service and wanted to bring them to heel.[108] Foreign Office suspicions about Fisher's intentions have sometimes been confused with the separate question of his views on foreign policy. Both kinds of issue are discussed further in succeeding chapters.

V

In December 1927, the Prime Minister asked Fisher to act as chairman of the Industrial Transference Board, set up to consider how workers, especially miners, could be moved from decaying to expanding industries. After consulting Neville Chamberlain, he took on the job.[109] The board involved Fisher in consideration of questions which did not normally come his way, including the effect on people of long-term unemployment, but, like his Treasury colleagues, he could find no easy solutions. One of the ideas which the board considered was the encouragement of emigration to the dominions. In June 1928 Leo Amery, the Dominions Secretary, met the board and afterwards noted that

> beyond denunciation of the stickiness of the Dominions with regard to overseas settlement Fisher and his colleagues had very little to say while Winston [Churchill] who was in a very naughty mood could only denounce all action and say that the miners had better go out and find some work as things improve.[110]

A pessimistic report was finally produced. It eschewed consideration of proposals which went against the government's stated financial and trade policies, and concluded that without unacceptable expenditure and a change of attitude on the part of the dominions, the government could do little to assist the ailing heavy industries.[111] In the autumn Baldwin appointed a further 'secret Committee with Warren Fisher in the chair ... to see what, if any, special measures can be taken to reduce unemployment during the winter.'[112] Fisher was still keen on overseas settlement as a long-term solution to chronic unemployment, but his hastily convened committee could only recommend the expenditure of '£20 millions in the next three years on roads etc.' as a stopgap.[113]

Even this, however, went against the grain for the Treasury. Fisher was deeply concerned about unemployment, which by 1928 stood at something over 10 per cent of the working population, but he took the orthodox line that the situation would only be made worse if the government overspent.[114] The Treasury's fatalism about mass unemployment in the 1920s and 1930s has frequently been castigated by historians writing with the benefit of Keynesian hindsight. These tend to exaggerate the potential impact of alternative expansionist policies, to underestimate the reality of the country's fragile financial position after the First World War, and to ignore the broader international economic environment and the far grimmer experience of other industrialized countries. In Britain mass unemployment was made bearable and politically acceptable by the provision of a minimal level of state assistance, and by piecemeal improvements in social reform.[115] It was not a glorious record, but neither was it a contemptible one.

When Baldwin's government resigned in May 1929, Fisher had been Permanent Secretary to the Treasury and Head of the Civil Service for almost a decade. At the age of 49, he had achieved a great deal of what he had promised in 1919. The most important and contentious of his plans for changing the civil service were well in hand by 1923, and provided little controversy thereafter. He had no great policy or grand design to push for, and he had little to offer on the central questions of economic policy which beset the government. Had he chosen, he could have left Whitehall with honour and found work in the City: he was not a wealthy man, and his income of £4,000, over a quarter of which went to his estranged wife, was only a fraction of what he could have earned outside the civil service.[116] Yet he stayed at the Treasury for another ten years, despite his belief in giving youth its head and in preventing people from going stale. The principal reason that he did so was that the civil service was his life. He had few interests outside it and he lived alone. Also, he was intensely patriotic, a sentiment he expressed in characteristically soapy language; being chairman of an insurance company or director of a bank held no attraction for him as compared with serving his monarch and country. Besides all this, of course, he was

Britain's most senior and — with the possible exception of Hankey — most powerful official, and power is not something which men lightly relinquish.

Notes

1. Mrs Churchill to Lindemann, 27 Dec. 1924, in Gilbert, *Churchill Companion*, p. 316.
2. Interview with R.W. Fisher. Moggridge, *British Monetary Policy 1924–1931*, covers this question. Churchill's main advisers were Niemeyer of the Treasury and Montagu Norman. See Churchill to Niemeyer, 21 Jan. 1925, T171/246. The most frequently cited consequence of the return to gold at the level chosen was to push up export prices by about 10 per cent, with a consequent decrease in competitiveness.
3. See pp. 118–9 above on the cruiser crisis. Interview with Sir Robert Fraser. Grigg, *Prejudice and Judgement*, p. 208, is quite open about Churchill's lack of negotiating skills, a significant weakness for a Chancellor.
4. Churchill to Fisher, 23 Jan. 1925, in Gilbert, op. cit., p. 353.
5. Fisher to Baldwin, 13 Mar. 1925, Baldwin papers, 3/146.
6. Chamberlain diary, 1 Nov. 1925. Fisher's remark about Baldwin's concentration was apropos of Chamberlain's story of how, while giving evidence to the economy committee, he saw Baldwin pass a note to Churchill as to whether the Chancellor still had his matches 'lent at 10.30 a.m.'. This incident is described in Feiling, *Neville Chamberlain*, pp. 164–5.
7. Amery diary, 3 Nov. 1925, in the possession of the Rt Hon Julian Amery MP.
8. Churchill to Fisher, Scott, Hamilton (Chairman of the Customs and Excise) and Hopkins (Chairman of the Inland Revenue), 24 Nov.; Hopkins' note, undated; Fisher to McNeill (Financial Secretary) and Churchill, 18 Dec. 1925, T162 153/E26565.
9. Churchill to Scott, 12 Jan. 1926, ibid. Fisher frequently cited conclusions of the Anderson committee on civil service pay. The body was 'representative of the whole commercial, financial, manufacturing etc. community', he told Baldwin on 10 Aug. 1923, T162 105/E12677.
10. Memorandum for economy committee, submitted on 13 Jan. 1926, ibid.
11. Churchill's minute, 1 Dec. 1927, T162 281/E19850/1. Over the eight years from March 1919 to March 1928, the size of the non-industrial civil service had shrunk by around 25 per cent, so the Treasury's resentment of Churchill's generalisations is easily understood.
12. Churchill to Fisher, 1 Dec. 1925, in Gilbert, *Churchill Companion*, pp. 600–3. See also Chapter 2, p. 64.
13. Churchill to Fisher and Scott, 28 Mar. 1926, in Gilbert, op. cit., pp. 681–2. Despite the Counter episode, Treasury officials did not mend their ways. The worst hoarders of files were said to be A.P. Waterfield and R.G. Hawtrey. Hawtrey's room was one of the first places to look since, even if the particular file sought was not there, a search would be bound to uncover other missing papers. Interviews with Sir John Winnifrith and Sir Robert Fraser.
14. Churchill to Fisher, 30 Apr. 1926, op. cit., pp. 689–90.

15. Fisher to Churchill, 20 Dec. 1927, op. cit., pp. 1147–8; Chamberlain diary, 17 [or 19?] and 22 Dec. 1927.

16. As in note 14 above.

17. Fisher to Churchill, 25 Nov. 1924, T162 950/E15158/1.

18. Fisher to Baldwin, 25 Nov. 1924, PREM 5/32.

19. Same to Churchill, 16 Dec. 1924, T162 950/E15158/1.

20. Same to Churchill and Baldwin, ibid. Bruce (Prime Minister of Australia) to Amery, 6 May, and Amery to Baldwin, 23 May 1925, PREM 5/32.

21. These were Scott, Hamilton, and Hopkins, as in note 8 above.

22. Fisher to Baldwin, 27 Feb., Amery to Baldwin, 23 May 1925, PREM 5/32. Amery ignored the report, but bemoaned his carelessness in not insisting that Hankey or Murray of the Admiralty be chairman. Amery diary, 19 Jan. 1925.

23. Churchill to Baldwin, 13 Mar. 1925, PREM 5/32.

24. T162 950/E15158/1.

25. Fisher to Amery, 20 May 1925, T161 256/S27823.

26. Amery to Baldwin, 23 May 1925, PREM 5/32.

27. Fisher to Amery, 11 June 1925, T161 256/S27823. Amery, according to his diary, suggested this on 10 June 1925.

28. Garner, *Commonwealth Office* (1978), pp. 13–14, criticizes the Treasury for dealing in bureaucratic terms with what was essentially a political question. This is reasonable so far as it goes, but he takes no account of the genuine *imperium in imperio* question which Fisher raised. On p. 142 he wrongly states that until 1950 the Dominions Office head got the pay of a deputy head of 'any other Department.' He in fact received the salary of the head of a second class department, as approved by the Asquith committee in 1920.

29. Amery diary, 16 and 25 June; Fisher to Baldwin, 30 May 1925, Baldwin papers, 8/134. Such papers on appointments are few and far between. Presumably most of them are in the PREM appointments series, under a 75- or 100-year rule.

30. Amery diary, 27 May 1925. Clifford's pension papers are in T164 174/P83889. Shortly before he was certified, the Webbs had a visit from him. He 'talked incessantly' and 'as a finale ... read aloud some verses of Kipling.' Sydney Webb was then Colonial Secretary. Webb diary, 23 Nov. 1929, Passfield Papers 43.

31. Fisher to Baldwin, 25 June 1925, T161 256/S27832.

32. Amery diary, 29 June 1926; 16 June 1927; 7 Mar. 1928.

33. Amery diary, 26–31 Dec. 1928; Amery to Neville Chamberlain, 4 May 1929, NC 7/11/22/1.

34. Amery diary, 19 Feb. 1929. The official concerned eventually went in July 1931, T162 255/E15158/01.

35. Amery diary, 23 Mar. 1928. See also PREM 1/65. This was Sir William Clarke, who was considered a great success. Sir Neil Pritchard to the author, 18 Jan. 1981. Sir Neil joined the Dominions Office in 1933.

36. Amery diary, 17 Dec. 1928.

37. Furse, *Aucuparius*, pp. 218, 238–40. Furse had an outstanding reputation as head of recruitment for the colonial service. The remark

about Fisher came from Ormsby-Gore, Amery's parliamentary under secretary. I am grateful to the late Sir John Martin for the reference to *Aucuparius*. Jeffries, *Colonial Empire*, p. 55.

38. By 'non-Treasury' is meant a minister who never served in the Treasury while Fisher was there.

39. Other inter-war ministerial diaries of some use are those of Dalton, Sankey and Neville Chamberlain.

40. In the absence of a Fisher diary or any Fisher papers of substance, finding out what he was interested in at any one time is a hit or miss process.

41. Fisher to Baldwin, 16 Feb. 1926, PREM 1/53.

42. *The Times*, 3 Mar. 1926.

43. Brief prepared by Fisher for Baldwin, 30 Mar. 1926, Warren Fisher papers; Wright, *Treasury Control*, pp. 367–8.

44. *Parl. Deb.*, H.C., vol. 194, cols. 289–334, 14 Apr. 1926.

45. *Morning Post*, 24 Feb. 1926. See pp. 10–11 above on this episode.

46. See p. 64 above.

47. See Bridges's sensible comment on p. 59 above.

48. Midleton to Churchill, 27 Mar.; Fisher to Churchill, 13 Apr. 1927, T162 119/E16587.

49. See pp. 145–6 above.

50. In so far as Midleton had factual material, he drew on the Anderson committee of 1923, which as Fisher pointed out to Snowden on 6 Dec. 1929 reached conclusions diametrically opposed to Midleton's own. T172/1655.

51. Fisher to Baldwin, 26 Mar. 1927, Baldwin papers, 8/2–6. Unlike Oxford, he wanted pensions to remain a separate ministry.

52. Fisher to Sir Horace Wilson and Neville Chamberlain, 15 May 1939, Warren Fisher papers; note by Fisher for Baldwin's signature, 8 Apr.; Fisher to Baldwin, 9 July 1927, and subsequent papers, Baldwin papers, 8/12–13, 70–102. Baldwin had announced his intention to scrap the mines ministry as early as April 1926, T162 119/E16587.

53. Interview with R.W. Fisher. Jeffery and Hennessy, *States of Emergency*, pp. 102–42 deal with civil contingency planning for the General Strike and other emergencies and with Fisher's part in it.

54. Chamberlain diary, 11 May 1926; Middlemas, *Whitehall Diary*, ii, 45–6.

55. Minutes of establishment officers' standing committee, 27 July 1927, T162 300/E11650.

56. Fisher to Grigg, 14 Aug., and to Snowden, 6 Sept. 1929; minute by Fisher, 4 Mar. 1930, T164 125/P52410. See also PREM 1/79, and T162 147/E22792.

57. Fisher memoir, Chapter 7, 'Part 1: December 1905 to August 1914'; TS text of W.J. Brown's tribute from *Red Tape*, Nov. 1948, Warren Fisher papers. Brown was a Labour MP from 1929 to 1931. He joined Mosley's New Party, but did not win a seat. From 1942 to 1950 he sat as Independent MP for Rugby. He paid another warm tribute to Fisher in *So Far*, pp. 220–1.

58. Churchill to Fisher, 1 Dec. 1925, as in note 12 above; 'Twenty one years of achievement: the Civil Service Sports Council, 1921–

1942', p. 5 (Civil Service Sports Council records). Representative matches were arranged in various sports against the other services, but the civil service was not allowed to participate in the annual inter-service competitions. Interview with Sir Robert Fraser, who played tennis for the civil service for many years.

59. Amery diary, 12 Feb. 1926.

60. Amery diary, 26 Feb. 1926.

61. Fisher's note, 23 Feb. 1926, T172/1540.

62. Undated note by Miss Culhane, 1940, T162 956/E41132/1; *Civil Service Sports Journal*, ii, 16 (Jan. 1925), p. 53 (Civil Service Sports Council records).

63. Dawes, *Journal*, p. 277, 25 Jan. 1931. The dinner was held each year in the Connaught Rooms. BBC Archives, OB Connaught Rooms, File 1. At the 1926 dinner, Amery was seated near the writers Rose Macaulay and Canon Hannay, 'George A. Birmingham'. Amery diary, as in note 59 above.

64. Fisher memoir, Chapter '—', part 2: 'Bureaucracy'.

65. Amery diary, 24 June 1925; Hankey to Austen Chamberlain, 21 Aug. 1925, AC 24/7/16.

66. Minutes of RIIA British security group, 3 July 1944.

67. Robert Cecil to Austen Chamberlain, 22 Apr. 1925, AC 52/152. Cecil, of course, was an enthusiast for the League.

68. Middlemas, *Whitehall Diary*, ii, 136–7.

69. Dawes, *Journal*, pp. 55, 277. There is nothing of interest in Dawes's papers in Northwestern University, Illinois, USA. His diary is precisely as published.

70. Atherton married Miss Maude Hunnewell, 'the prominent American golfer.' From an undated newspaper cutting in the possession of R.W. Fisher.

71. Thorne, *Limits of Foreign Policy*, p. 97.

72. See pp. 110 above. Fisher to Baldwin, 3 Mar. 1928, Baldwin papers, 163/113. Prime Ministers continued to bring in their own secretaries, but only to augment, not to replace the regular civil servants.

73. See p. 150 above.

74. See pp. 132–5 above.

75. Memoir entitled 'Mr Ramsay MacDonald', undated, Selby papers.

76. Lampson, later Lord Killearn, had a distinguished career in the 1930s and 1940s.

77. See p. 81–2 above.

78. *Parl. Deb.*, H. of L., 5th series, vol. 125, col. 276, 26 Nov. 1942.

79. Despite the title, holders of the office of Treasury Solicitor had since the early 1800s always been barristers.

80. Christopher — ? to Clark-Kerr, 2 Feb. 1928, Inverchapel papers, unsorted.

81. Rumbold to his mother, 12 Feb. 1928, MS Rumbold dep. 35.

82. O'Malley to his wife, 3, 4, 8, and 11 Feb. 1928, O'Malley papers, MS 21685(6).

83. 'Francs report', p. 523.

84. The original of the minute carrying the board's recommendations and Chamberlain's and Baldwin's assent is on T162 138/E19377.

85. As an assistant under secretary, Gregory would have earned at most about £2,000 a year including cost of living bonus. O'Malley would have earned less.

86. Geoffrey Dawson to Sir Harcourt Butler, 7 Mar. 1928, Dawson papers; Dawson diary, 26 and 27 Feb. 1928, Dawson MS 32.

87. 'Francs Report', pp. 535–6.

88. Text of a talk on 'The British civil service', undated, Warren Fisher papers. This and a further talk on 'The Treasury' were broadcast by the BBC in April and May 1946 in the series 'London calling Europe'. Correspondence on these is in 'A–Z Contributors Warehouse', BBC Archives.

89. Waterfield, *Professional Diplomat*, p. 243.

90. See for example his note to Fisher, 20 Oct. 1920, on civil servants in the House of Lords. T162 122/E17110.

91. For a penitent reaction to the affair, see Villiers to Austen Chamberlain, 27 Feb. 1928, AC38/3/70.

92. O'Malley to his wife, 19 Mar. 1928, O'Malley papers, MS 21685(6).

93. The children had been taken ill while the family were stationed in China. His wife set two of her books, *Peking Picnic* (1932) and *The Ginger Griffin* (1934), in China.

94. Bridge, *Permission*, gives a highly coloured account of the whole affair. Interview with Miss Jane O'Malley, her daughter.

95. O'Malley to his wife, 29 Feb. 1928, O'Malley papers, MS 21685(6).

96. Ann Bridge to 'Angus', 5 Feb. 1928, O'Malley papers, MS 21688(2); Fisher to O'Malley, 29 Feb. 1928, enclosing *Verba Christi* (J.M. Dent, 1925). No author or editor is named in this book, which is with the O'Malley papers, MS 21690(1). Fisher's own copy is now held by his granddaughter.

97. Fisher to Ann Bridge, 9 Mar. 1928, ibid.

98. O'Malley to his wife, as in note 95 above.

99. Ann Bridge to O'Malley, 16 Apr. 1928, O'Malley papers, MS 21690(1). O'Malley spent his year off as a well paid research assistant to Churchill.

100. Fisher to Lindsay (permanent head of the Foreign Office), 15 July 1929, O'Malley papers, MS 21688(2).

101. Fisher to Ann Bridge, 17 Dec. 1929, O'Malley papers, MS 21688(2).

102. Notes by Gwyer and Ramsay (who had been on the board), 2 Feb.; by Horace Wilson, 22 Dec.; by Ernest Gowers, 19 Dec.; and by Herbert Creedy, 29 Dec. 1930, ibid.

103. Ann Bridge to Strang, 22 Nov. 1929, O'Malley papers, MS 21691(6); O'Malley to Cadogan (permanent head of the Foreign Office), 29 Oct. 1938, MS 21687(1) said he had already asked Fisher.

104. Bridge, *Permission*, pp. 131–2, quoting her husband. See also O'Malley, *Phantom Caravan*, p.148.

105. Curiously, a fondness for Ann Bridge was about the only thing which Fisher had in common with W.H. Beveridge, whom he detested and who detested him. A row between them is discussed on pp. 204–5. Beveridge proposed to Mary Ann Sanders, as Ann Bridge then was, on the top of a London omnibus in 1913. Their correspondence is in the O'Malley papers, MS 21691(8).

106. Bridge, op. cit., p. 131. R.W. Fisher says his father's flat was in fact very handsomely furnished. Fisher was very fond of music, and in the 1940s was honorary treasurer of the Royal College of Music. He made no secret of his preferences, telling Adrian Boult on 10 Sept. 1946 that his friend Sir Hugh Allen (Professor of Music at Oxford) 'when asked years ago by me why the amateur English intellectual in matters musical was so snooty about Sullivan, the descendant here in the tradition of Mozart, simply replied "because they are b—y fools".' BBC archives, file on 'Maddison, Margaret 1940–1962'.

107. Lord Newton to Rumbold, 2 Mar. 1928, MS Rumbold dep. 35.

108. Lord Inchyra to the author, 14 June 1981; interview with Lord Sherfield; interview with Sir Robert Fraser, who said Fisher usually spoke of the Foreign Office 'with contempt' which he made no attempt to disguise. Lord Inchyra was a private secretary to the Foreign Secretary from 1934 to 1938; Lord Sherfield joined the Foreign Office in 1928.

109. Chamberlain diary, 17[?] or 19[?] Dec. 1927; Fisher to Baldwin, 5 Jan. 1928, Baldwin papers, 12/403. The other board members were his friend Sir John Cadman, a mining expert, and Sir David Shackleton, a former cotton worker, Labour MP and permanent head of the Ministry of Labour. In his evidence to the committee on ministers' salaries in 1930, he mentioned that his Transference Board work was not Treasury or civil service business. Report of the select committee on Ministers' remuneration, *PP* (1929–30), vi, 308.

110. Amery diary, 12 June 1928.

111. The report was circulated in July 1928. The Thomas Jones papers include material concerning it on C/13/12–14, and C/13/19.1–157.

112. Middlemas, *Whitehall Diary*, ii, 146.

113. Amery diary, 11 Oct. 1928; Middlemas, op. cit., p. 115.

114. Fisher's note of 18 Jan. 1929, T162 143/E21171/04; Fisher to Jones, undated, Feb. 1929, Thomas Jones papers, C/11/55.

115. Stevenson, *British Society 1914–1945*, gives a useful account of changes in economic and social conditions between the wars. O'Halpin, 'British government and society', pp. 753–61, tilts at the Blame the Treasury school of economic, military, and political historiography at some length.

116. For example, T160 25/F866 has papers on the £10,000 salary of the chairman of the Anglo-Iranian Oil Co. Fisher's gross salary was £4,000 in 1929, since he received the civil service cost of living bonus up to a ceiling of £500.

6

The years of the slump, 1929–33

I

Labour returned to power in 1929 with higher hopes than in 1924. Philip Snowden was again Chancellor, to the delight of his officials, but elsewhere the portents were less auspicious for the Treasury.[1] Unemployment, which for five years had been relatively stable, began to rise sharply, and the world economic situation worsened rapidly in the autumn following the American stock market collapse in October. At the same time, the Liberals' radical economic proposals, which Treasury experts abhorred, greatly broadened the terms of debate about unemployment; although the new government showed little inclination to stray down Keynesian paths, it was undoubtedly dissatisfied with the conventional wisdom offered by the Treasury and the Bank of England.[2]

In October, the government decided to appoint the Macmillan committee on finance and industry, to see how the financial strength of the City could be mobilized to promote industrial development and reduce unemployment. The committee included strong advocates of the economic status quo, such as Bradbury, and of radical change, such as J.M. Keynes. Snowden was warned that it might become the vehicle for a sustained attack on Montagu Norman, the powerful Governor of the Bank of England who was thought by some to be far too concerned with financial stability and insufficiently interested in the domestic economy. In fact the committee's main achievement was that it provided an open forum for extremely technical debate between economic policy makers and their critics.[3]

In the same month, following the American financial crash, two significant proposals were made to ensure that the government got more information and better advice on economic affairs: Oswald Mosley, then a junior minister, advocated 'a body working directly under the Head of the Government and giving continuous consideration to long term development and reconstruction problems', while an official of the Ministry of Labour, H.B. Butler, suggested three new pieces of machinery: an 'economic general staff', chaired by the Prime Minister, including all ministers connected with unemployment problems, which would decide on policy; standing committees of civil servants, industrialists and economists who would study and advise on the main areas of economic policy; and a secretariat, which would co-ordinate the work of the committee and would gather information from departments.[4] The suggestion of an 'economic general staff' provoked intense discussion. No one opposed the idea outright, but there was no consensus on what such a body should do. Fisher wrote that

> a Council of Economic Research could be set up for the initiation and encouragement of fundamental research in the economic sphere, the supervision of investigation into, and compilation of, material for the examination of specific problems, and generally the survey and analysis of economic facts and tendencies and the statement of the conclusions to be derived therefrom.[5]

He disliked the idea that the 'economic general staff' should consist of 'a few whole-time salaried economists who would be regular civil servants' subject to the 'constitutional rules and practices governing the conduct of Crown Servants', as this would preclude their having untrammelled discussion of economic problems with colleagues outside the government service.[6] Hankey supported this limited view of the purpose of such a body, and suggested that to prevent overlapping it should be placed under the existing Committee of Civil Research in the Cabinet Office.[7] Both he and Fisher were clearly concerned to prevent the development within the machinery of government of an institution which could tender economic advice to the government independently of the Treasury; at the same time both were anxious to promote the Committee of Civil Research — originally conceived of by Haldane as a 'Committee of Economic Enquiry' — which since its creation in 1925 had been dealing with matters of only marginal importance.[8]

MacDonald, who had no definite idea of what he wanted, followed the line of least resistance. In January 1930 he announced the creation of an 'Economic Advisory Council' under his chairmanship. It had fifteen full members, a mix of businessmen, economists, and trade unionists, and a secretariat headed by Tom Jones.[9] The status and functions of the council were unclear, while its composition ensured that its members could never agree on the crucial economic issues of the day. It faded into virtual oblivion after the 1931 crisis, but its secretariat, amongst whom was a distinguished economist, Hubert Henderson, performed useful work throughout the 1930s as a branch of the Cabinet Office.[10]

It would be wrong to read too much into the fate of the advisory council. The intentions and views of those concerned with it were so diverse that it was bound to fail. It did not perform even the modest task allowed it by Fisher of co-ordinating economic research, while only the Cabinet could be expected to take what were clearly political decisions on how the country should be managed. If it was to confine itself to purely technical questions it could scarcely justify either its existence or the muddled faith which MacDonald reposed in it. Alternative economic policies to those advocated by the government's traditional advisers already existed, and the gathering together of spokesmen for the various economic points of view was unlikely to provide anything new. There is no reason to think the council could ever have been anything more than a talking-shop. Nevertheless it was of some political importance to MacDonald; like some of his successors, he appreciated the value of appearing willing to consult with everyone, sponsoring the idea of a national response to economic problems.

II

Towards the close of 1929, a royal commission under Lord Tomlin was established to inquire into the civil service, with particular reference to conditions of service and to the employment of women.[11] Although it was only fifteen years since the MacDonnell commission had reported, the intervening time had seen enormous changes in the way that the service was organized and in the tasks it was asked to perform. When called to give evidence, Fisher took the opportunity to expound his views with characteristic dash and clarity. In a written statement he said that

> until relatively recent years the expression 'Civil Service' did not correspond either to the spirit or to the facts of the organisation so described. There was a series of Departments with conditions of service which in quite important respects differed materially; Departments did not think of themselves as merely units of a complete and correlated whole; and in the recognition by each Department of the existence of others there was, from time to time, an attitude of superiority, of condescension, of resentment, or even suspicion.
>
> Such departmentalism is, of course, the antithesis of a 'Service'. And clearly, for the efficient conduct of the country's business, an isolationist and capriciously disposed set of entities could not compare with a Service inspired by a larger *ésprit de corps* and cooperative sense and informed by the spontaneous interchange of experience and knowledge.

For the top posts in departments 'the field is now the Service, and not the individual Department; and co-operation between the Permanent Heads is continuous, understanding and informal.' The developing sense of teamwork in the service was best illustrated, he believed, by the success of his beloved sports council, 'and the new custom of Service sides entering for matches with the three other Crown Services.' He contrasted 'Service' with 'Bureaucracy':

> Essentially the two ideas are opposed: a Service which is right in spirit and personnel realises that its sole *raison d' être* is to give service alike to its Government and to its country; a Bureaucracy on the other hand is the instrument of an Executive intent on forcing the citizen to digest the contents of the cornucopia so mystically associated with state action.

He defended the 'informal discussion' between himself and other heads of departments by which men for senior posts were chosen, and deplored 'the constant stream of innuendo ... sometimes broadening out into open attack' on the service. Fisher then moved on to another of his most familiar themes:

> Instead of 'Treasury Control' it is right to speak only of the Chancellor's control of finance; and nothing in that is inconsistent with the view that ... his purposes may most usefully be achieved, not by a body of watchdogs with orders to bite, but by a Service animated by a common understanding of the objectives of its Government including the objective of economy, and by a common desire to obtain those ends ...
>
> It is not only members of the public who have been misled by the phrase 'Treasury Control'; there have been times when even officials of the Treasury have, to its solemn refrain, conjured up a picture of themselves as the singlehanded champions of solvency keeping ceaseless vigil on the buccaneering proclivities of Permanent Heads of Departments.
>
> A not unnatural result has been an attitude of mutual suspicion ...
>
> Happily this state of affairs is fast becoming a memory; and I only refer to it here to express the sincere hope that it may be finally relegated to the limbo appropriate to shibboleths.[12]

This forthright statement evidently won over the commission, since there followed a very amicable discussion of it with Fisher. He was sincere in what he said, but the commission might have pressed him harder on his more airy assertions. When asked about the Treasury's relations with other departments, he replied that 'I am not prepared to say that you have reached Utopia', an understatement with which his listeners were evidently content.[13] He was more convincing on personnel matters and on questions concerning the service as a whole, where he took a reformist but practical view of the principal issues raised. He was in favour of more equitable treatment of women civil servants, and believed that 'there is still a good deal of prejudice ... based on fear.' Nevertheless, while 'in my Service I think I am regarded as feminist ... even I do not think we can march too fast ahead of the general public.' He poked fun at the Foreign Office witness who 'made your hair curl by the picture of a woman diplomat dealing with some gentleman of a primitive or oriental habit of mind', and said that women should of course be employed in the foreign service, 'but experimentally and quietly. To bring down a guillotine and to say that it is impossible for women to do this work is ... absolute nonsense.'[14]

Fisher was equally frank about the National Whitley Council, which no longer had 'much relation to practical business ... if you got an independent Chairman you would lose him pretty quickly; he would be bored stiff.' He rejected the idea of an appeal board in disciplinary cases, arguing that staff associations, Whitley councils, 'and also the High Court of Parliament' provided adequate safeguards.[15] He gave an illuminating description of how men were selected for the most senior posts, and warned: 'Let us guard ourselves against the idea that the permanent Head of a Department should be an expert; he should not be anything of the kind'. 'The man of fifty will have to compete with the man of forty' for such posts, he informed his listeners. Fisher then rejected the suggestion, based on the fact that fourteen out of twenty permanent heads of first class departments were not 'natives' of their departments, that his overriding concern since 1919 had been to be fair to the service as a whole, and implicitly to establish a principle, rather than simply to pick the best man.[16] On the question of pay, he felt that the salaries of heads of departments could not be compared with outside posts, and advised the commission not to recommend any pay increase for the lower ranks in the prevailing economic climate. On the functions of the Treasury, he said that

> to do its job [it] ought to be a sort of clearing house, or general staff. I see every disadvantage in the Treasury taking people straight from the administrative class examination. If you do that, they then get to work and take their little pens in their infant hands and they write away little criticisms of every sort and kind, very clever ones, no doubt, but there is no training for constructive work, or work that would enable them to get the practical experience that might make Heads of Departments. Again, their relations with Departments will be of the academic

order. Now I want the Treasury to be staffed by a continual
flow and circulation of principals with seven or eight years'
training in other Departments.[17]

Fisher's evidence to the commission was extraordinary in its
breadth, lucidity and spirit. He had recently returned from a
long holiday in the United States, and the break must have
done him good.[18] He clearly found the job of explaining his
ideas to the commission invigorating, and it may be that he
seized the opportunity for an exercise in proselytism and
exhortation. He appears to have been successful: the commission's report contained no great shocks for the civil service,
and its recommendations were thoroughly considered as soon
as they appeared by all heads of departments in conference.[19]

Fisher and his colleagues split into five groups to deal with
the main findings of the commission. He was in the promotions
group, and with two colleagues dissented from the proposal it
adopted that the Treasury should have the right to force departments to take experienced assistant principals from other
departments if they had failed to import a certain number
voluntarily. The permanent secretaries agreed on a broad
range of principles of civil service management in the wake of
the report, including a policy of transferring assistant principals from one department to another, the filling of
administrative posts in the Treasury by transfer and not by
direct recruitment, development of the Treasury's capacity to
conduct 'organisation and methods' studies for departments,
enforcement of the 'retire at sixty' rule for senior posts to
continue to be at the discretion of the individual departments,
and equal opportunities for women civil servants, though not
equal pay.[20] These conclusions were the result of agreement,
not of Treasury dictation. They are compelling evidence that
Fisher had by 1932 succeeded in his aim of promoting a
corporate spirit at least in the highest echelons of the civil
service.

Fisher was involved with two other noteworthy inquiries in
the early 1930s. The select committee on ministers' salaries
heard him argue in favour of uniform pay for Cabinet ministers
and a considerably increased salary for the Prime Minister,
whose existing income he thought 'gross underpayment.'[21] He
also served on the Donoughmore committee on ministers'
powers, set up in response to *The New Despotism*, in which

Hewart, the Lord Chief Justice, made an intemperate attack on the civil service, accusing it of usurping judicial functions. This reached the comforting conclusion that 'we see nothing to justify any lowering of the country's high opinion of its Civil Service or any reflection on its sense of justice.' During committee deliberations Fisher consistently pushed libertarian arguments, questioning whether Parliament was in fact capable of defending citizens from 'the arbitrary discretion of the Executive', while Sir John Anderson defended the bureaucratic position.[22] Another member of the commission, the left-wing Professor Harold Laski, was most impressed. He subsequently wrote a glowing profile of Fisher in the *Daily Herald*, saying of him that he 'really cares about the liberty of the subject' and that 'there is not an atom of red tape about him.' The commission seems to have achieved its object: within a few years Lord Hewart had changed his mind completely about the issue of bureaucratic powers.[23]

III

The period from 1929 to 1933 saw a transformation in international politics, culminating in Hitler's accession to power in Germany. The complex events of those years have been boiled down by some to the simple lesson that 'if it was the fault of any one individual, it was the fault of Sir Warren Fisher.'[24] The origins of this charge merit some investigation, if only because too much credence has been attached to it over the years.

In 1929 and 1930, Philip Snowden adopted a very hard line at successive conferences in the Hague on the Young plan for the adjustment of reparations payments and the evacuation of the Rhineland. His abrasive and obstinate attitude irked the French, and infuriated the Foreign Office, but he got what he wanted and gained great popularity at home.[25] It was a vindication of the Treasury's belief that the only way to deal with the French was to be blunt and uncompromising, although it should be said that the country which suffered most at Snowden's hands was Germany.[26] In 1931 the Treasury and the Foreign Office differed still more sharply on international affairs, as will be discussed below. Two other episodes should first be considered, the appointment of Vansittart and the row over the creation of an economic section in the Foreign Office.

An important study of the foreign policy of the 1929–31 Labour government states that the Treasury succeeded in 'curbing Henderson's [the Foreign Secretary] powers ... The decisive point came when MacDonald, acting on the advice of Fisher rather than on that of Henderson, appointed Vansittart as Permanent Under Secretary for Foreign Affairs.'[27] The statement is based on charges made by the ubiquitous Walford Selby.[28] The available evidence indicates that Henderson had been uncertain about who to appoint and had provisionally thought of Sir Eric Drummond, but that MacDonald had suggested Vansittart instead. Selby's unpublished accounts of this say that Henderson had hoped to make Drummond ambassador in Washington, until the Archbishop of Canterbury objected on the grounds that Drummond was a convert to Roman Catholicism! Selby also wrote that Henderson 'practically promised' the job of Permanent Under Secretary to Drummond as a sop, which must have caused him acute embarrassment when MacDonald chose Vansittart instead.[29]

Fisher undoubtedly thought Vansittart the better man, but as mentioned earlier he had little influence with the Prime Minister.[30] MacDonald himself had personal knowledge both of Drummond and of Vansittart, who was his private secretary, and he was still keenly interested in foreign affairs.[31] It seems likely therefore that he did not need Fisher to tell him who to appoint, while his distrust of Henderson may have spurred him to exercise the power in senior appointments which had been the Prime Minister's explicit prerogative since 1920.[32] Besides all this, from Hugh Dalton's diary it appears that there was no great crisis over the appointment and that Henderson was pleased with and got on with his new permanent head.[33] Selby's contention that the appointment was somehow outrageous rests on his bizarre belief that Vansittart was a fool and a knave, a pliant tool of Fisher's who allowed him to impede the development of an anti-German foreign policy throughout the 1930s.

In December 1930, Sir Victor Wellesley, the Deputy Under Secretary in the Foreign Office, proposed the formation of an economic section within the department. The idea found favour with Henderson, Dalton and MacDonald, but for two years no action was taken, because such a section was not a priority and because opinions differed as to what was required.[34] In March 1932, it was decided that a Foreign Office official, Frank Ashton-Gwatkin, would assume responsibility for the co-ordination of economic information supplied by missions abroad.[35] For almost a year Ashton-Gwatkin laboured alone at his task, although Selby unofficially lent a hand while awaiting his posting to Vienna.[36] Together they produced a circular for all missions outlining the information to be supplied, and despite criticism of it within the Foreign Office it was distributed to all government departments in October 1933.[37]

This initiative brought a sharp response from Fisher, who according to Wellesley 'had the absurd notion that I wanted to put the Treasury in my pocket. Anything more idiotic it is hard to imagine.'[38] Fisher said that the Treasury should have been consulted both as the economic department of government, and because a new section had evidently been created by the Foreign Office without Treasury sanction.[39] Wellesley, in charge of the Office in Vansittart's absence, refused to withdraw the circular, and argued that no new section had been created. He composed a ferocious letter to Fisher on these lines for the Foreign Secretary's signature, but Sir John Simon refused to sign it.[40] Once Vansittart returned, he and Fisher quickly reached agreement; the latter told MacDonald that he and Vansittart both welcomed 'this "partial awakening in the Foreign Office", but [were] worried by its "amateurish attempts ... to play Pooh-Bah in the Mikado" ... '[41] At their suggestion an inter-departmental committee was set up under Sir Frederick Leith-Ross, the Treasury's expert on international finance, to draft instructions and to ensure effective distribution of the information acquired.[42] Vansittart thought this 'not unsatisfactory', and Ashton-Gwatkin was also pleased. He told Selby:

> It is just a year since you joined my nest and laid that egg [the circular]. It is not hatched yet, but it is still warm. I am told that the Great Men (Warren Fisher, Leithers [Leith-Ross] & Co) sat in judgement upon me last Tuesday ... ; and that as a result, the Economic Section will not only continue, but will be further strengthened ....
>
> I think Van must have handled the situation quite skilfully.[43]

Although Wellesley commented that the replies furnished by missions were 'generally far more suited for articles in magazines than for officials', Ashton-Gwatkin's section was considered a success.[44] Throughout the 1930s he worked closely with Leith-Ross and was on good terms with the Treasury.[45] It was only after he was put out to grass as an appeaser in 1940 that he began to blame Fisher 'for the disaster of 1939', claiming that his intervention to block Wellesley's proposals in 1931 had ensured that the government

> plunged into the great Conferences of 1932 ... without adequately co-ordinated preparation and without adequate realisation of the degree to which all the issues involved were interconnected .... The seeds of war, sown by the Crisis [of 1931], were fertilised at Lausanne ...
> All this was due to a failure of the machinery of Government .... In this failure, all the blunders that were to follow in the next eight troubled years were conceived.[46]

Broadly speaking, this charge can be dismissed. The Foreign Office could certainly have done with more economic expertise in the 1920s and 1930s, but the question was not even raised until December 1930, and that was not Fisher's fault. What he would not tolerate was the Foreign Office appropriating to itself the final say on international financial issues.[47]

Another allegation made against Fisher was that he interfered in the 'submission and non-submission of Foreign Office advice to the Cabinet', and prevented 'Foreign Office warnings about Germany' from reaching the Cabinet 'in an effective form.'[48] The only factual basis for this charge is that in November 1931 he objected to a draft memorandum circulated by the Foreign Office which discussed the 'interlocked problems' of economic and political instability in Europe.[49] Vansittart was away, and Wellesley refused to withdraw the document, which he had clearly circulated without his chief's knowledge.[50] The incoming Foreign Secretary, Simon, 'went out of his way to deprecate responsibility' for the memorandum at a Cabinet meeting, and Fisher eventually persuaded Vansittart to have it withdrawn.[51] It was obviously a contentious document in which the Foreign Secretary had no faith, and it was withdrawn in the proper manner by the head of the department. Like Walford Selby's allegation that 'none of my warnings from Vienna [after 1934] had reached the Cabinet in proper form' due to

Fisher's machinations, it is based entirely on the premise that Vansittart was Fisher's puppet, and it is nonsense.[52]

IV

In March 1931, alarmed by the prospect of a large budget deficit, the government set up a committee under Sir George May to recommend economies. Fisher advised a broad remit on the lines given to the Geddes committee in 1921, though 'if for political reasons it was deemed desirable to avoid exact repetition of these terms no doubt the necessary guidance ... could be conveyed to the Committee in other words.'[53] By mid-July its report was ready, but it was not published till the end of the month. In the meantime, there was a dramatic run on the pound, due to fears about British liquidity following the moratoria declared by central European countries on 15 July.[54] By 31 July, with the help of the French and Americans, the situation seemed under control. On that day, however, the Treasury perpetrated 'a monumental blunder' by publishing the report without any 'accompanying policy proposals.'[55]

The Treasury fully shared the May committee's principal assumption that the country was living beyond its means.[56] On 27 July Sir Richard Hopkins told the Chancellor that 'the gold exodus is unprecedented', and that unless action was taken 'there is real danger of our being driven off the gold standard.' He continued: 'Of two things one. Either the May Report must be the beginning of our recovery, or it will mark a long step in our downward career.' He said that its publication should be accompanied by the announcement of a cabinet committee which would consider its recommendations and present to Parliament after the recess 'proposals designed to repair the budgetary position and render it sound.'[57] The government did as Hopkins had advised in publishing the report. Somewhat to their surprise, its alarmist conclusions gradually impressed themselves upon financial circles at home and abroad, and confidence in sterling ebbed again as doubts grew whether the Labour government had the political will to tackle its budgetary problems head on. By the third week of August, Britain was embroiled in a political crisis, with the Cabinet split over the nature and extent of economies acceptable. On 24 August MacDonald, Baldwin and Samuel agreed that a

'National Government' should be formed 'to deal with the present financial emergency.'[58] Labour's second term of office was at an end, but the financial crisis was not.

The day before the pound's troubles began in mid-July, Arthur Henderson had gone to Paris to discuss disarmament with the French. He hoped to persuade them to accept a settlement of the reparations issue in return for political concessions from Germany.[59] Disarmament was his abiding passion, and he saw in Germany's difficulties the chance to force her to abandon her claims to military parity. This policy was directly contrary to that proposed by the Treasury and by the City, which held that the immediate aim of the government should be to restore faith in German finances by disposing once and for all of the reparations issue. MacDonald was suspicious of Henderson's manoeuvring, and managed to arrange a conference of the countries involved despite the Foreign Secretary's activities in Paris.[60] It took place in London from 20 to 23 July, but was reduced to 'a nullity' by French insistence on political concessions from Germany in return for an international loan.[61] This outcome was a mortal blow to the hopes of Snowden and the Treasury that the reparations question could finally be settled.[62] Despite this, by the end of July the fortunes of the pound had improved, until the May report produced a new panic. It recommended an immediate cut of £97 million in government expenditure, almost two-thirds of which would come from a 20 per cent reduction in the level of unemployment benefit and changes in entitlements.[63] The cabinet committee which considered these conclusions could not agree on how much of the recommended savings to adopt, and were greatly alarmed by Snowden's information that the May report had underestimated the government's probable deficit by as much as £50 million, a claim which turned out to be completely wrong.[64] The full Cabinet split on how to handle the crisis, with a majority of ministers resigning on 24 August 1931 rather than accept a 10 per cent cut in unemployment benefit.[65]

Fisher had no doubts about the necessity for action. His advice on the broad financial issues at stake was important but not distinctive during the crisis. He supported absolutely the view taken by Treasury officials, and he pressed it strongly on ministers. In relation to public service pay, he did have a particular point to make: he complained that, although the

May committee had acknowledged that, as civil service pay did
not rise with that of industry in good times, it should not be
proportionately cut during a slump, the committee had nevertheless called for a 5 per cent cut in the civil service cost of living
bonus. He thought this could only be justified on 'general
economic' and not on 'fair wage' grounds, and he asked the
government to make this clear.[66] On the pay of senior public
servants, he told the Prime Minister on 18 August that

> I have had this morning a meeting representative of the
> four Crown Services. They fully appreciate the gravity of
> the situation in which the country is and are quite ready
> for the necessary sacrifices on their own part as their
> contribution to a scheme of national economy from which
> no section of the community can claim to be exempt.
> All officers of the four Services in receipt of substantive
> pay of £2,000 a year and upwards would contribute ... 10%
> or 12.5% of their pay

while those below the £2,000 mark would suffer the reductions
recommended by the report. Judicial salaries over £5,000
would be cut by 20 per cent.[67]
A friend met Fisher some days later, just after the Labour
government had resigned:

> Warren is foregoing his holiday & was I thought most
> apprehensive about the future. 'If Henderson's Gang gets
> in in October it's just Goodbye to England as we know it'
> was the burden of his song. And all because people can't
> understand what it's all about.[68]

Despite the resignations of most of his Labour colleagues,
MacDonald stayed on in Downing Street at the head of a
cross-party National government. Although the new administration initially restored a degree of international confidence
in British finance, this was swept away by news of the Inver-
gordon mutiny on 16 September. The pressure on the pound
became unmanageable, and five days later Britain was forced
off the gold standard as the run on sterling continued.[69] Only
a week earlier, Fisher had reacted violently to a journalist's
suggestion that this might happen: 'He could scarcely contain
himself. He got to his feet, his eyes flashing, his face flushed

with passion', and said that 'any such suggestion is an affront to the national honour' and 'is quite unthinkable'.[70] A few days later he was preparing the ground for precisely such a step. On 18 September he assured MacDonald that 'as regards food stocks ... the situation was well in hand.' Provision was made for declaring bank holidays, should depositors panic following the fateful announcement. On the evening of 20 September, he saw the ambassadors of the United States and France, who found him 'worn out with work and much depressed', and who 'most willingly agreed' to ask American and French banks in London to co-operate 'in restricting purchases by British citizens of foreign exchange.'[71]

The departure from gold went very smoothly. On the day the decision was taken, however, the Cabinet heard 'extremely disquieting rumours' of more trouble in the navy, and acted to forestall it by reducing all pay cuts for the services, teachers and police to a maximum of 10 per cent.[72] Fisher was incensed:

> In capitulating to disorderly elements in the Fleet, and in extending to the Army, Air Force, Police and Teachers the benefit which the sailors have extracted by misconduct, I assume that the Government have had present to their minds the following considerations:
>
> (1) a mutiny of the whole fleet would not at the present moment be a fundamental danger to us in the material sense, for no foreign country proposes to attack us by armed force at sea.
>
> (2) psychologically the fleet has done all the harm in its power by completing the process of bringing us off the gold standard.

He complained that 'this panic concession involves unjustified and unnecessary discrimination' since 'the vital postal services ... are to be excluded from the benefits of bolshevism in the fleet.' He was concerned less with this inconsistency than with the government's lack of resolve, which had resulted in a decision costing around £3,540,000.[73] Fisher had a point: the navy had suffered no worse than other services by the original cuts announced, but its officers had failed to maintain discipline amongst their men. The naval historian Captain Roskill concluded that 'truly the intricacies introduced under Treasury pressure in 1925 came home to roost with a vengeance six years later', but this is a gross oversimplification.[74] The intricacies of 1925 were imposed only because the Admiralty had in 1919 bullied the Cabinet into accepting pay scales thought up by the navy itself.[75] Furthermore, in the middle years of the 1920s the admirals had set a precedent with their outrageous behaviour over naval expenditure: in 1931 it was the turn of their men to make trouble for the government.[76]

Calm had descended on the money markets by the end of September, when Fisher prepared 'a brief note of the measures in existence, or in the Treasury view requisite, for the safeguarding of the £'. Most of what he wrote was straightforward Treasury thinking, although he began by mentioning 'confidence in settled Government at home and abroad (I understand the question of an election on national lines is now under consideration)' as one of the 'fundamentals of the situation.'[77] This was certainly so, but in stating it he made his own preference clear enough. For him party politics were at best irrelevant: it was the quality of the ministers, not their labels, that mattered.[78] Although Snowden was warned that 'we are not yet out of the wood', things remained stable, and the National government swept to victory in the general election of 27 October.[79] Snowden departed to the Lords, and Neville Chamberlain took over as Chancellor. He and Fisher were already on excellent terms, and for the next five years they were of one mind on most of the issues that arose.

The Tories exerted their predominance in the new government to force Snowden and the Liberals to swallow the bitter pill of protection, in the shape of the Import Duties Act of 1932. Fisher had been a free trader in his day, but times had changed. He wrote Chamberlain a mawkish letter of congratulations: 'My dear Neville, I have been thinking much about this afternoon, and rejoicing in your joy. With fond love, Warren.'[80] He sent the Chancellor an equally slushy note in June 1932, after the announcement of the conversion of the war loan from 5 per cent to 3.5 per cent, another action which would have been anathema a year before: 'As I listened & looked around this evening, I felt you had a sympathetic House ... that was because courage always appeals & you have taught us always to expect that quality from you. With fond love, W[arren].'[81] By the end of the year, the Treasury was contemplating the unthinkable, repudiation of the American debt. There was talk of sending Fisher and Leith-Ross over for a confrontation with the

Americans, although the ambassador in Washington reminded Vansittart that 'Fisher is a close friend of Atherton who has doubtless passed on his views. Administration here therefore regards British Treasury as "completely hard-boiled" ....'[82] Six months later the debt was duly repudiated.

Fisher proved less flexible, or more consistent, on another matter which arose out of the 1931 crisis. Both the police and the judiciary voiced discontent at the pay cuts imposed, the latter being supported by *The Times*, which pointed out the 'severe hardship' encountered by many judges. Although the law officers advised that the government was within its rights in cutting judicial salaries, the judges did not agree. A year later the Lord Chancellor noted that they were still 'behaving foolishly & unpatriotically.'[83] Eventually a compromise was agreed: in return for a voluntary cut the government promised to legislate to make it impossible to impose a salary reduction on the judiciary.[84] The effect of this was marred by a further row after a Treasury official was reported to have accused the judges 'of "squealing" over the cuts', a sentiment which Fisher undoubtedly shared, but the accord survived.[85]

The trouble over police pay was more serious. It arose out of an ambiguous statement in the Commons in September 1931 by the incoming Home Secretary, Herbert Samuel, from which it appeared that the police might be exempted in 1932 from the second 5 per cent cut to be imposed all round.[86] Fisher warned MacDonald that 'all four Heads of Services were clear that their own people would not stand quietly by if the Police were to get away with cuts less than their own men had suffered', while 'the people whose dole was cut by 10% would undoubtedly also have a good deal to say.'[87] He returned to the charge after Samuel had proved 'very difficult' about the issue in cabinet, saying that 'the ramifications of a surrender to the police might well be disastrous to the country whose economic equilibrium is still far from assured', and that 'the public ... would interpret it as an authoritative sign that the lean period was over.'[88] Fisher was supported by Hankey, who said that the navy feared another mutiny if the police received preferential treatment. He told the Prime Minister that Fisher 'fully realises how important it is for political reasons to find a solution', but 'has not succeeded and is faced with the same sort of difficulties' with the other groups affected by the cuts.[89]

Despite pressure from MacDonald, Samuel refused to admit that the concession would vitiate the policy of equal treatment for all public servants, arguing that administrative economies achieved since September 1931 should be offset against the anticipated reduction in police pay.[90] This did not commend itself to Fisher, who pointed out that such economies were a separate matter.[91] On 21 September MacDonald approved the circulation of a cabinet paper by Fisher outlining the Treasury case, 'but he wished Sir Warren Fisher to know that he did so reluctantly, feeling that "this correspondence should now cease" and that there was no point in multiplying these counterblasts', as 'every member of the Cabinet is properly acquainted with all the facts of the situation.'[92] This did not prevent Fisher saying a week later that once Samuel resigned from the government, as he was about to do on the issue of free trade, he would claim they had reneged on a commitment made in 1931: 'it is important to pin down this lie of his before he leaves office.' The Prime Minister wearily replied that 'this can not very well be done, I am afraid.'[93] Fisher was further angered by the suggestion of Arthur Dixon, a Home Office official, that the Treasury had in fact agreed to alter the savings required in police pay by the original White Paper of September 1931:

> The fact is that Mr Dixon cannot see straight on the subject of the police, being largely instrumental for [sic] the bad advice originally given to Sir Herbert Samuel. He now has the impudence falsely to imply that police expenditure should be relieved of its stipulated saving.[94]

On 28 September the Cabinet agreed to postpone the cut for a month, after hearing contradictory statements from Samuel and from MacDonald on whether the Treasury had previously agreed to an alteration in the amount required.[95] It is clear from Treasury papers that the Treasury was entirely in the right. The Home Secretary had either been given the wrong information by his department, or had decided to try to force a concession from the Cabinet by making a public declaration that one would be forthcoming. This, and the fact that throughout the 1920s he had urged a policy of generous treatment of the police as an acceptable premium for public order — 'a cheap — & indeed the only — insurance for the body politic' — may explain the vehemence of Fisher's denunciations of the Home Secretary.[96]

The full 5 per cent reduction was imposed from 1 November, without provoking any trouble in the police forces. Hankey thought that 'the question of Police pay' had 'as much to do' with the resignations of Samuel and Sinclair, the two Liberal ministers, 'as the Ottawa Conference [where the last vestiges of free trade were abandoned].'[97] On the facts of the matter and on the principle involved, Fisher was entirely correct in the view he took. Nevertheless, the strident manner in which he put the Treasury case can scarcely have enhanced MacDonald's confidence in him. It may be that the strain of his work was beginning to tell: as will be seen, he was ill for most of the following summer.

Fisher was involved in another matter affecting the police in the autumn of 1931. Both MacDonald and Samuel wanted Trenchard, the former RAF chief, to become Commissioner of the Metropolitan Police, and Fisher undertook 'as an intimate friend' to persuade him to take the job.[98] At Fisher's insistence, Trenchard was treated very generously by the government. He was paid £3,000 a year in addition to his RAF half pay, and received an assurance that he would be permitted to resign should 'his life's work on the Air Force' be in danger at any time.[99] As Commissioner he received considerable help from Fisher, who in 1933 chaired a Treasury 'Metropolitan Police Reorganisation Committee'.[100] This produced a remarkably favourable report on Trenchard's proposal to change 'what I considered fundamentally to be wrong' with the London police.[101] The report said of his fairly grandiose plans that 'even in existing conditions, no financial considerations exist which should preclude the consideration of the schemes ... on their intrinsic merits.'[102]

By the start of 1932, it was obvious, as the Lord Chancellor noted gloomily, that 'the Tories are getting the upper hand' in the Cabinet.[103] This was illustrated in the selection of a committee of inquiry into the Post Office. MacDonald objected to the suggestion of Willie Bridgeman MP as chairman: 'The terms of reference and the committee will undoubtedly be regarded as an indication that the Government wishes to receive a report against Government control.' Bridgeman 'was always regarded' in the Commons 'as a decent stiff-necked diehard.' However, the Prime Minister found himself out-manoeuvred by the Postmaster General, Kingsley Wood.[104] As it happened, Bridgeman's committee proved very sympathetic to the existing Post Office organization, but the incident showed how much MacDonald's authority had slipped since the 1931 crisis. The power now lay elsewhere. Fisher had no doubts about who was the key figure in the government, as he told the convalescent Neville Chamberlain in May: 'It wd. be comic, if not so pathetic, that gout shd. determine whether H.M.G. shd. have a backbone, for, when it keeps N.C away, there's not a soul with a spine of his own, excepting Philip [Snowden]'.[105]

Abroad the clouds were gathering. The disarmament conference finally got under way in February 1932, but few in official circles expected much of it.[106] The League of Nations was already in acute difficulties over Japan's aggression in China, and there was no reason to think that a conference convened under its auspices would be any more successful in tackling the huge international issue of disarmament. In Britain, the government was starting to think in terms of strengthening the nation's defences, after more than a decade of cutting them. In February 1932 the CID recommended the abandonment of the ten year rule. In April a Treasury official wrote that 'the cost of defence has been steadily squeezed down year after year. It has only been possible to bring it to the present figure by exceptional measures which cannot be repeated.'[107] A month earlier a cabinet committee had concluded that Britain's strength in the Far East should be built up, a decision which Fisher supported, and by the summer the Treasury was resigned to increased expenditure on Singapore.[108] Japanese expansion into China seemed a threat to British commercial interests, and was clearly contrary to the spirit of the League. On the other hand, there was a feeling that there was some practical justification for Japan's action, and that Britain could not afford to antagonize Japan lest it turn on the virtually defenceless empire. The Cabinet accordingly resolved to stay strictly neutral in the dispute between Japan and China, an attitude which effectively favoured the former as the stronger power.[109]

The uncertainty in the Far East was matched by events in Europe. Scarcely six months after the Lausanne conference of June 1932 finally put an end to reparations, Hitler came to power in Germany. In the course of 1933 it became clear that the new German leader had the strength and determination to make his country once again a major power. In the summer of that year, Fisher endured 'a long illness, during which I had leisure to observe the contemporary rise of Hitler to supreme power.'[110] (There was speculation that he suffered some form of breakdown. In fact he had an illness of the nervous system resembling an acute form of shingles, and he was in great pain for some months.)[111] He eventually returned to work in September convinced that Hitler's Germany would become a mortal threat to Britain, and he started to press for a 'review of our defensive position' accordingly.[112] He also began to push for a definite understanding with Japan, on the argument that Britain could not fight both Germany and Japan simultaneously and unaided in the future. Preparing for war in Europe, and avoiding it in the Far East, were henceforth his predominant concerns.

Notes

1. Grigg, *Prejudice and Judgement*, p. 136.
2. For the Treasury's attitude to the Liberal proposals, see T161 303/S40504.
3. Grigg (private secretary to the Chancellor) to Snowden, 11 Oct. 1929, T160 426/F11548.
4. Note of a conference of ministers, 28 Nov. 1929, PREM 1/70; Skidelsky, *Politicians*, p. 89.
5. Memorandum by Fisher, 3 Dec. 1929, PREM 1/70.
6. ibid.
7. Memorandum by Hankey, 14 Dec. 1929, ibid.
8. See pp. 129–30 above; Skidelsky, *Politicians*, p. 136.
9. Skidelsky, ibid.
10. For an account of the EAC, see Howson and Winch, *Economic Advisory Council*.
11. For papers on the setting up of the commission, see T162 259/E21858/3.
12. Royal commission on the civil service, 1929–1930, minutes of evidence, pp. 1267–70.
13. ibid., p. 1278.
14. ibid., pp. 1281, 1286.
15. ibid., pp. 1278, 1280.
16. ibid., pp. 1284, 1291.
17. ibid., pp. 1283, 1290. The Treasury does not seem to have got this flow of experienced principals. Most of its recruits in the 1930s came in as assistant principals after two or three years in other departments. Of the men interviewed since 1979, other than Sir Robert Fraser who joined in 1914, Sir John Winnifrith came from the Board of Trade, Sir Thomas Padmore and Sir Edward Playfair from the Inland Revenue, and Sir George Dunnett and Lord Trend from the Board of Education. None of these had more than a few years' experience when they joined the Treasury.
18. Fisher had had a rare holiday in the autumn of 1930, when he and Tom Jones spent six weeks in the United States as guests of A.B. Houghton. For plans for the American visit, see Houghton to Jones, 14 Jan. and 3 July 1930, Thomas Jones papers, W/10/3 and 5. A.B. Houghton's family knew of no relevant papers.
19. The heads of departments first met on 27 July 1931 to consider the report, and appointed five committees to go into the various findings. The chairmen of these were Creedy (War Office), Robinson (Health), Scott (Treasury), Hopkins (Treasury), and Anderson (Home Office). T162 284/E26475/05, and T162 284/ANNEX.
20. ibid.
21. Report of the select committee on ministers' remuneration, *PP* (1929–30), vi, 279.
22. Report of the committee on ministers' powers, *PP* (1931–32), xii, 13, 14, 24, 353; interview with Sir Robert Fraser, who was secretary to the committee.

23. H.J. Laski, 'The chief civil servant', *Daily Herald*, 26 Nov. 1932 (cutting in the possession of R.W. Fisher). According to Jackson, *The Chief*, p. 216, Hewart had completely changed his views by the late 1930s. In the early 1930s, he made wild attacks on the Lord Chancellor, Sankey, and the permanent head of the Lord Chancellor's department, Sir Claud Schuster. Heuston, *Lord Chancellors*, pp. 519–20; Kent, *In On the Act*, p. 36. Schuster, who seems to have been an ally of Fisher, had an astonishing career, being permanent head of his department from 1915 to 1944.

24. Ashton-Gwatkin, 'Thoughts', p. 376.

25. Skidelsky, *Politicians*, p. 137; Carlton, *MacDonald versus Henderson*, p. 55; Dalton diary, 10–19 Aug. 1929.

26. Grigg, *Prejudice and Judgement*, p. 230; Carlton, op. cit., pp. 60–3.

27. Carlton, op. cit., p. 23.

28. See pp. 132–5 above.

29. Dalton diary, 4 Nov. 1929; Selby to Elibank, 5 July 1946, Elibank papers, MS 8809/115. From a note signed by Selby, undated, and Elibank, 8 Oct. 1955, it appears that Henderson had only 'practically promised the job' of permanent head to Drummond. Elibank papers, MS 8817/207–12.

30. See p. 129 above; Rose, *Study of a Diplomat*, pp. 69–70.

31. Dalton diary, 4 and 8 Nov. 1929, mentions the appointment of Vansittart. Hugh Dalton, a junior minister at the Foreign Office, was very hostile to the Treasury and presumably would have noticed and recorded any improper Treasury intervention. His view of the Treasury, and the Treasury's view of him, both changed substantially when he became Chancellor in 1945.

32. The two men were certainly at odds, as indicated by the title of Carlton's book, *MacDonald versus Henderson*. Henderson had his critics as Foreign Secretary. He was said to spend too much time on party work, Carlton, op. cit., pp. 22–3. A senior Foreign Office man described him on 20 Dec. 1929 as 'constitutionally lazy', Sargent to Phipps, Phipps papers, PHPP 2/8. Lord Sherfield, who joined the Foreign Office in 1928, said that his recollection of Henderson's reign was that the Foreign Secretary gave no clear direction and would take no decisions, and that his private office 'abdicated' and would do nothing about it. Interview with Lord Sherfield.

33. Dalton diary, 4 and 8 Nov. 1929, 7 May 1930.

34. Dalton diary, 15 Mar. 1930; memorandum by Wellesley, 1 Dec. 1930; Henderson to MacDonald, 13 Mar.; MacDonald to Henderson, 17 Mar. 1931; Vansittart to MacDonald, 14 Mar. 1932, PRO 30/69/1/286. Wellesley was the official who had been promoted to deputy under secretary against Fisher's advice in 1925. See p. 159 above.

35. Boadle, 'Foreign Office economic relations section', p. 926.

36. ibid., p. 929.

37. ibid., pp. 929–30.

38. Wellesley to Ashton-Gwatkin, 11 Sept. 1942, Selby papers.

39. Boadle, 'Foreign Office economic relations section', pp. 930–1.

40. ibid.

41. ibid.

42. ibid.

43. Vansittart to Selby, and Ashton-Gwatkin to Selby, both 11 Jan. 1934, Selby papers.

44. Wellesley to Selby, 31 Oct. 1934, ibid. Hinsley *et al.*, *British Intelligence*, i, 61, says that by 1936 the Berlin embassy's coverage of the German economy was so extensive that its annual economic review appeared as a separate print.

45. Ashton-Gwatkin to Selby, 30 May 1935, Selby papers; Sir Lawrence Collier to Martin Gilbert, undated, Collier papers, coll. misc. 468/M.1187.

46. Ashton-Gwatkin, 'Thoughts', p. 376.

47. This is what Sir Victor Wellesley demanded in his *Diplomacy in Fetters*, pp. 193–4: 'When there is a conflict between domestic and foreign policy' it is the foreign secretary's duty 'to stress the overriding considerations of foreign policy in the interests of peace. If he is to substantiate his case he must have at his disposal the necessary independent machinery and, provided they are sound, his views should prevail over lesser considerations'. This was a recipe not for co-operation but for confrontation with all the domestic departments.

48. Ashton-Gwatkin, *British Foreign Service*, p. 26.

49. Selby to Ashton-Gwatkin, 11 Apr. 1958, Selby papers.

50. Wellesley to Ashton-Gwatkin, 11 Sept. 1942, ibid.

51. As in note 49 above. It must again be stressed that everything Selby says is suspect, and the only accounts of this incident come from him and his friends.

52. Note by Selby, 12 Dec. 1955, Selby papers.

53. Fisher to Snowden, 16 Feb. 1931, T160 398/F12414.

54. Fisher to Snowden, 24 July 1931, T172/1741; Skidelsky, *Politicians*, p. 337.

55. Carlton, *MacDonald versus Henderson*, p. 215.

56. As in note 53 above.

57. Hopkins to Snowden, 27 July 1931, T175/51.

58. Herbert Samuel was the Liberal leader. Memorandum by Samuel, 24 Aug. 1931, Samuel papers, A/78/11.

59. Carlton, op. cit., pp. 200–11.

60. ibid., pp. 201, 209; Marquand, *MacDonald*, p. 605.

61. Skidelsky, *Politicians*, p. 342.

62. ibid.

63. Sir Walford Selby claimed that Fisher leaked the report through 'concern for our outstanding credits in Germany', and told Henderson's son that Fisher 'panicked the cabinet in 1931 and brought down your father.' Note by Selby, 23 May, and Selby to Arthur Henderson, 15 May 1956, Selby papers.

64. Skidelsky, *Politicians*, p. 357.

65. Fisher to MacDonald, 18 Aug. 1931, PREM 1/134.

66. Fisher to Snowden, 24 July 1931, T172/1741. The committee had advised cuts in police pay of 12.5 per cent, and of 20 per cent in teachers' salaries. The committee got this argument from the Anderson committee of 1923 on state service pay. The cost of living bonus was a supplement paid to compensate civil servants for price rises since

1919. It was conceived as a temporary measure, and the government were prone to cutting it in stringent times. This was reasonable in that the cost of living did fall considerably during the 1920s, a point which the May committee also took into account. In 1932 the bonus was consolidated into new pay scales.

67. As in note 65 above.

68. Gertrude Grigg, wife of P.J. Grigg, to Tom Jones, 28 Aug. 1931, Thomas Jones papers, W/9/3:1–3. Henderson's group had no alternative policy to speak of, but could not stomach the cuts in unemployment benefit, and preferred to save Labour's honour by abandoning office.

69. The mutiny, such as it was, began on 14 September. By the next day the men were completely out of hand, and this caused a reaction in the financial world on 16 September, Roskill, *Hankey*, ii, 555.

70. Williams, *None So Strange*, pp. 104–5.

71. Note of a meeting, 18 and 19 Sept.; Fisher to Snowden and MacDonald, 20 Sept. 1931, PREM 1/97; Dawes, *Journal*, p. 394.

72. Neville Chamberlain diary, 22 Sept. 1931.

73. Fisher to Fergusson (private secretary to the Chancellor), 21 Sept. 1931, T172/1742.

74. Roskill, *Hankey*, ii, 558.

75. See p. 113 above. The Colwyn committee recommended that post-1925 entrants should be paid on a new and lower scale. The navy got the Cabinet to agree to the Jerram scales in 1919 when the Treasury was very weak, and when widespread unrest in the armed services was anticipated if concessions on pay were not made quickly.

76. See pp. 113–21 above.

77. Fisher to Snowden, 30 Sept. 1931, Chamberlain papers, NC 8/12/3. Since a copy of this reached Chamberlain, it is likely that he was being briefed to take over from Snowden in due course.

78. See his comment at pp. 90–1 above.

79. Hopkins and Fisher to Snowden and Chamberlain, 3 Oct. 1931, Chamberlain papers, NC 8/12/2.

80. Fisher to Chamberlain, 4 Feb. 1932, ibid, NC 8/17/18.

81. Same to same, 30 June 1932, ibid., NC 7/11/25/10. See Howson, *Domestic Monetary Management*, p. 88, for the successful outcome of this measure. See also Hopkins to Fergusson, 4 July 1932, T172/1796B.

82. Lindsay to Vansittart, 26 Dec. 1932, F.O. 371/16663/c51/1/62. For his friendship with Atherton of the US embassy, see p. 158 above.

83. *The Times*, 7 Jan.; Fisher to Baldwin, 13 June 1932, T162 318/E5577/01; Sankey diary, 5 Apr. 1933. The 'hardship' consisted of a 20 per cent cut in salaries over £5,000, and a 10 per cent cut in those below that figure.

84. ibid.

85. Sankey diary, 26 July 1933. The official involved was Sir Alfred Hurst. Heuston, *Lord Chancellors*, p. 519, says that the judges were probably correct in law.

86. The 10 per cent cut was in two parts, the second to take place a year after the first.

87. Fisher to MacDonald, 20 Aug. 1932, T162 287/E27434/2.

88. Sankey diary, 27 Aug.; Fisher to MacDonald, 5 Sept. 1932, ibid.

89. Hankey to MacDonald, 2 Sept. 1932, PREM 1/121.

90. MacDonald to Samuel, 9 Sept. 1932, Samuel papers, A/85/7.

91. Fisher to MacDonald, 14 Sept. 1932, T162 287/E26434/2. A Treasury circular, T.C. 12/32 of 8 July 1932, instructed departments to seek administrative economies wherever possible. T162 288/E27871.

92. Note by Duff, private secretary to the Prime Minister, 21 Sept. 1932, PREM 1/121.

93. Fisher to MacDonald, 26 Sept.; note by MacDonald, 26 Sept. 1932, ibid.

94. Fisher to Strohmenger (Treasury), 26 Sept. 1932, T162 287/E27434/2. Lord Allen, who was in the Home Office during the 1930s and who later became its head, has written that there 'was always a Home Office tradition ... that Dixon had blighted his career by being caught out over misleading the Treasury. I doubt in fact whether it is true that Dixon's career was blighted ... He was a most distinguished individual and a forceful administrator, but I doubt if ... he would have risen higher than the senior Under Secretary post he achieved.' Letter to the author, 23 Aug. 1981.

95. Cab. 7(32), 28 Sept. 1932. From the papers on T162 287/E27434/2, it is obvious that the Treasury was entirely in the right.

96. Fisher to Churchill, 24 Feb. 1925, T162 91/E10545/02. See also his comments to Baldwin on 26 Feb. 1926 and 7 Oct. 1927, and to Churchill on 22 Feb. 1928, Baldwin papers, 161/93, and T162 149/E23606.

97. Roskill, *Hankey*, iii, 55.

98. Samuel to MacDonald; MacDonald to Samuel, 29 Sept. 1931, Samuel papers, A/85/1; note by Fisher, 5 Oct. 1931, T162 362/E26852. There is a copy of this in the Trenchard papers, MFC 76/1/304.

99. ibid.; Anderson to Trenchard, 14 Nov. 1931, ibid., MFC 76/1/304.

100. Fisher persuaded the War Office to second an officer to be Trenchard's personal assistant while continuing to pay his salary 'to relieve the Home Office votes', Creedy to Fisher, 24 Nov. 1931, T162 286/E27048.

101. Trenchard to Fisher, 26 Jan. 1933, T162 311/E32815/1.

102. T162 311/E32815/2; Fisher to Trenchard, 4 Feb. 1933, Trenchard papers, MFC 76/1/308.

103. Sankey diary, 6 Jan. 1932.

104. Note by MacDonald, and by Miss Rosenberg (his personal secretary), 19 Feb.; by Duff (principal private secretary), 22 Feb. 1932, PREM 1/122. See also Fisher to Chamberlain on the personnel of the committee, 5 Feb. 1932, T162 333/E27284.

105. Fisher to Neville Chamberlain, 27 May 1932, Chamberlain papers, NC 7/11/25/9.

106. Sankey diary, 11 Jan. 1932.

107. Undated memorandum by Gilbert, Apr. 1932, T175/67.

108. Fisher to Chamberlain, 18 Mar. 1932, T175/48; Grieve (Treasury) to Fisher, 28 July 1932, PREM 1/152.

109. Sankey diary, 27 Feb. 1933.

110. Fisher to Neville Chamberlain, 1 Oct. 1938, Warren Fisher papers.
111. Peden, *British Rearmament*, p. 55; interview with R.W. Fisher, who said it was 'a swelling of the nerve ends' under the skin.
112. As in note 110 above.

7
Home affairs, 1933–8

I

This chapter deals with Fisher's activities in domestic policy and administration in the five years from the first talk of rearmament to the Munich agreement. The separation of this material from issues of foreign policy and defence which arose in the same period is to an extent artificial, since from 1933 onwards his overriding purpose was to help to meet the threat of war from Germany. However, he continued to involve himself in many other matters great and small, from the prosecution of Mr Bishirgian, who in 1935 tried to corner the world market in pepper, to the abdication crisis of 1936, when he and a number of other officials tried to 'stifle the crisis on their own initiative', to the granting of a new charter for the BBC, where he praised the 'imagination, enthusiasm, energy and sagacity of the first order' of its management, and tried to loosen Post Office control over its operations.[1]

Many of these episodes, while interesting in themselves, mainly confirm what should already be apparent, that throughout his time at the Treasury he was something of a bureaucratic magpie. He acted as a combination of troubleshooter and policy goad for the national government from 1931 onwards. Strikingly, although a great deal of his energy went in to work which related either to the management of the civil service or to general policy questions, he had virtually nothing to do with the First Lord of the Treasury and Prime Minister from 1931 to 1935, Ramsay MacDonald. Between 1931 and 1937 Fisher reported extensively and routinely to two ministers, Neville Chamberlain as Chancellor and Stanley Baldwin who, until 1935, was merely Lord President of the Council. The latter office had not received even so much as a mention in the semi-mystical argument Fisher had devised in the early 1920s to justify his interest in general policy in terms of the relationship between the Permanent Secretary to the Treasury and the First Lord.

As international tension increased and rearmament began, preliminary steps were taken to prepare government departments for war. In 1935 Fisher was a member of a CID sub-committee which considered the creation of an information ministry should war break out. Vansittart wanted such a ministry to be under Foreign Office control, while the Admiralty representative was worried lest naval security be compromised. Fisher insisted that 'an independent Minister with an independent Ministry was essential', and his views carried the day. He did, however, reluctantly agree to the establishment of the British Council under Foreign Office auspices, complaining to Vansittart that whatever goodwill it would generate abroad would be rapidly dissipated by the ineptitude of the British diplomatic service.[2]

Another CID sub-committee planned the establishment of a food department. This produced a notable row in 1936. W.H. Beveridge of the London School of Economics, later to earn lasting fame for his seminal 1942 report on social insurance, was asked to work full-time on plans for food control. He 'thought I had as good as left the School. But the negotiations with the Treasury hitched and, under what appeared to me incredible circumstances of inefficiency and rudeness ... I was told ... that the plan had been changed and I wasn't needed.'[3] The trouble was that the Treasury was prepared to give Beveridge only the salary of the head of a first class department, £3,000, plus the necessary yearly contribution to maintain his academic pension rights. He would also continue to receive £1,000 a year from the state for chairing the Unemployment Insurance Statutory Committee, making him by far the highest paid official in Whitehall.[4] These were generous terms, but Beveridge turned them down. He afterwards claimed that Fisher wanted 'to spoke my wheel.'[5] Evidently believing that welfare begins at home, he had asked for a salary of around £8,000, a fantastic amount of money at that time. Fisher was shocked at what he saw as Beveridge's profoundly unpatriotic piece of haggling, and there was unanimity in Whitehall that his demands could not be met. Hankey commented that 'his persistence' in pressing them 'aroused some doubts as to whether he would be the right man to handle permanently a question involving inter-Departmental questions of some delicacy.'[6] Instead the work was given to French of the Ministry of Agriculture, who made a success of it.[7]

Other plans were devised for the dispersal of government departments and for the evacuation of civilians from the cities: despite Fisher's belief that adequate preparations could not be made 'if secrecy had to be maintained', the schemes worked out were technically satisfactory, although the assumptions underlying them were soon proved false once war broke out.[8] In 1935 a start was made in civil defence planning when Hodsoll was moved from the CID to the Home Office to work on air raid precautions, but two years later a committee chaired by Fisher, whose report 'formed one of those surveys of the problem which constitute a landmark, at least for the historian', found that very little had been achieved. The Home Secretary remarked of their grim conclusion that 'there are some people who will say that the problem is so vast & intractable that it is not worth doing anything at all.'[9]

In May 1938 Fisher and Hankey recommended the creation of a 'Ministry of Home Security' in wartime, and 'the organisation of the country at the outset of war into a number of Divisions, and the delegation of a considerable measure of executive responsibility to the persons selected for the charge of these Divisions.' They feared that 'the national will to resist might be broken' at the outset of war by mass bombing 'if the situation in the devasted areas cannot be got under control at once.'[10] Fisher told the CID that 'the "Divisional Commanders" were the pivot of the scheme and must be persons of outstanding ability and experience.'[11] He took personal responsibility for putting the plan into operation, and in May 1939 he quit the Treasury to become regional commissioner for the northwest, based in Manchester. There he learnt how wrong he had been about the importance of such posts.

As Head of the Civil Service Fisher was involved in a sensitive security exercise which was the precursor of the extensive post-war vetting of government employees begun in 1947. In 1936 the Cabinet approved a new method of dealing with 'untrustworthy persons in the Defence Departments' worked out by him with Sir Vernon Kell, the head of MI5. It was not easy to reconcile MI5's call for action with elementary principles of natural justice. The system devised by Fisher and Kell provided that the case of each individual suspected by the security services of subversion or sabotage was to be reviewed in secret by a committee consisting of the permanent head and the establishment officer of the department concerned, together with a representative from the Treasury. The employees under investigation were not to be informed that such a review was in progress, still less to be shown the evidence against them.[12] The first dismissals made under this procedure caused an uproar in January 1937, when the Admiralty fired five dockyard employees believed to be engaged 'in dangerous subversive propaganda, and not merely in the doctrinaire preaching of Communism as a political creed.'[13] The First Lord of the Admiralty found himself on 'a very sticky wicket' when he tried to explain the action to Parliament, and his task was not made easier by Fisher's warning that it was

> of vital importance that extreme care should be taken not to give rise to any impression that any general system has been established in this matter or that any general instructions have been issued. If any impression of this is allowed to arise it is bound to tend not only to widen the field of agitation but to increase its intensity ... if at all this investigation should be mentioned as an ad hoc step in the process of satisfying yourself in the matter and not as forming part of a regular procedure.[14]

The row died down after the Prime Minister confided in Ernest Bevin of the Transport Workers' Union.[15] There is very little material in Treasury papers on such subjects, but it can be assumed that investigations and removals of staff continued discreetly although nothing resembling the post-war system of 'positive vetting' was introduced.[16] Ironically, Fisher was to find himself apparently the victim of official espionage in 1942, much to his indignation.[17]

II

The dismissal of Sir Christopher Bullock from the civil service in 1936 was one of the most controversial episodes of Fisher's career. Although sacked for soliciting a job from an organization with which he had official dealings, Bullock later claimed that he had been unfairly treated. The affair merits investigation because it illustrates the extremely high standard of conduct expected of officials between the wars. It also raises questions about Fisher's judgement and impartiality as Head of the Civil Service.

Bullock was sacked by Baldwin at the end of July, following the report of a board of inquiry which investigated 'certain discussions engaged in' by him.[18] He was fired because of the impropriety of approaches he had made in 1934, 1935, and 1936 to the chairman and the managing director of Imperial Airways, when he had raised the question of his becoming a member of the board of the company should he decide to leave the civil service. Civil aviation was an obvious outlet for a man of his experience and background, which could be 'utilized, not only for his own advantage, but also in directions likely to be of Service to the State', and it had long been his intention to leave Whitehall while he was young enough to make another career for himself in the City.[19]

Although he said he was motivated by a desire to strengthen the management of the firm, there is no question that Bullock grossly mismanaged his overtures to Imperial Airways. When he first raised the matter in 1934, he intimated in the course of the same conversation that an honour might shortly be bestowed on its chairman, Sir Eric Geddes, in recognition of his services to aviation over the years.[20] This was, at best, remarkably inept.[21] A year later he renewed his efforts to secure himself a directorship with the firm, although he got an unequivocal warning from Geddes that such talk should cease: whilst 'the contractual relationships between Imperial Airways and the Government are under discussion and you and I are the negotiating partners, any discussion and/or understanding between us on matters affecting our individual and personal interests are most undesirable. I know you agree with me on the ethics of this point.' Bullock afterwards claimed that Geddes had written this letter 'for production in due course' and at Fisher's behest: even if that was so, the fact was that in 1935 he received what was an extremely plain written warning from Geddes not to raise personal matters again.[22]

Despite a promise that he would not discuss the question with anyone else, Bullock brought it up again in June 1936 in a talk with the managing director of the company. Following complaints about this, a board of inquiry was set up. It consisted of Sir Richard Hopkins of the Treasury, Sir Evelyn

Murray of the Customs and Excise, and L.A. Granville Ram, the Second Parliamentary Counsel. It heard a number of witnesses, including Geddes, Fisher, and Bullock, who was allowed to cross-examine those who appeared and to call people to testify on his behalf. During the proceedings it emerged that Imperial Airways was not the only firm to which Bullock had made overtures. In 1934 he had arranged a directorship for himself with the North British and Mercantile Insurance Company, with which the Air Ministry had dealings, and had tried to get a peerage for its managing director. The board made no reference to this in the published report, but it may have influenced the conclusion that Bullock had displayed 'a lack of that instinct and perception from which is derived the sure guide by which the conduct of a civil servant should be regulated.'[23] A few days afterwards Baldwin dismissed him. In later years Bullock alleged that the board had mishandled his case, that Hopkins, its chairman, had a 'guilty conscience' about it, that its other two members were personal enemies, that Granville Ram was his junior in rank, which 'on a Court-Martial is ... precluded, if officers of equal or superior rank are available', and that 'in the Courts of Law' the omission of material from the report which he thought relevant 'would afford unchallengeable grounds for an Appeal ... and for quashing of the sentence' because of 'serious misdirection.'[24]

These arguments are irrelevant. There was nothing wrong with the way the board went about its business: if an injustice was done to him it was not the board's fault. He later complained that the report was 'only able to form an indictment by meandering into questions of taste and abstract propriety', but this was precisely the board's task: he was not accused of any crime.[25] The report exonerated him from any suggestion of corruption, but found that he had not acted in accordance with the traditions of his service. To emphasise the point an extract from the Treasury circular issued after the 'Francs affair' of 1928 was included.[26]

There was some surprise at the severity of the treatment meted out to Bullock, although the editor of *The Times* — who had been briefed by Fisher — asked a colleague to 'bear in mind that, as in so many of these cases, there is a good deal more behind this report.'[27] Bullock, nicknamed 'Napoleon' because of his size and temperament, had had an outstanding career in the Air Ministry, culminating in his appointment as Permanent

Secretary at the age of 39 in 1932. He was an ambitious and pugnacious man, and his forceful manner made him extraordinarily unpopular in Whitehall. In February 1934 Fisher had described him as

> a very clever young man, but most argumentative and singularly gifted in rubbing people up the wrong way; he never knows when to stop nor the limits of his own or other people's affairs (I am very disappointed in the absence of any sign of his maturing or mellowing).[28]

Whether justly or not, Bullock had the name both inside and outside the Air Ministry of being extremely difficult to deal with. At the end of 1935 the Secretary of State for War 're-marked that the heads of the Army had become very hostile to the Air Ministry — ascribed it partly to Bullock's manner of handling questions.'[29] His reputation and the report of the board of inquiry seem to have convinced most civil servants that he had been, as Lord Trend put it, at least 'incredibly foolish' and that he had received treatment which was 'severe' but 'not unjust.'[30] However, others felt differently: Lady Grigg, an indefatigable Whitehall gossip, commented that 'given a complete megalomaniac like Bullock I think it is all quite understandable', and 'I ... think the sentence unnecessarily harsh', while Barrington-Ward of *The Times* thought him 'fool rather than knave.'[31] Over the years this view was to gain considerable currency: in 1938 Londonderry, Bullock's minister until June 1935, reproached Baldwin with having 'destroyed little Bullock ... the victim of the inveterate hatred of a Civil Servant, who never should have been allowed to encompass his downfall as he undoubtedly did' (although this was but a minor part of a lengthy and reproachful tirade directed at his former leader); during the war, he was offered the headship of a department; and in 1946 he persuaded twelve distinguished former officials including Hankey, Vansittart and Grigg to sign a memorial to the Prime Minister asking that 'his dismissal ... should be reconsidered', as 'most of us were of the opinion that the penalty was out of proportion to the alleged offences as recorded in the Report'. However, while Bullock 'feels that the handling of his case ... was not free from at least unconscious prejudice ... we would emphasise that we are in no wise concerned with this aspect and do not wish to be taken either as

assenting to, or dissenting from, this possibility.'[32] Baldwin and
Swinton (who had been Secretary of State for Air in 1936) also
wrote to the Prime Minister asking for a review of the original
decision to dismiss him.[33]

The problem with Bullock's case was, as everyone recognized, that the report alone was scarcely enough to justify
dismissal: he could have been asked to resign, perhaps, or
publicly reprimanded so that his resignation would be inevitable and understood. It was well known that Fisher had for
some time been greatly angered at his behaviour, and from this
some inferred that Fisher had been waiting for Bullock to step
out of line in order to get rid of him. To an extent this was true.
What was not true was the imputation that Fisher acted unfairly. Prior to his importunacy with Imperial Airways, Bullock's
activities had already given cause for grave concern. He himself later boasted that in 1932 and 1933 he

> had (in the interests of the Royal Air Force and, I thought
> and think, in the wider national interest) to take steps
> which were barely consistent with my duty as a Civil
> Servant to the Government of the day. I will not be
> indiscreet enough to detail all the courses into which I was
> reluctantly forced; but I can well remember that for a
> period I had to proceed with such secrecy that I could not
> use my office telephone for much of the business that was
> passing, and had to slip out and use public call-boxes!
> And I had to ask the recipients to destroy most of my
> letters. I certainly 'stuck my neck out' at this time in the
> interests of the Royal Air Force — and could not have
> complained if I had been at least severely reprimanded.

He prepared a resolution critical of government policy for the
parliamentary air committee, and although this was later discovered he 'heard no more in the matter' from his superiors.
He drafted 'countless Parliamentary Questions for our supporters to put, wrote scores of speeches for them to deliver, [and]
organised Parliamentary Debates in both Houses.'[34]

Most importantly, in December 1934 he was involved in a
dispute with his minister, the outcome of which was a clear
warning from Fisher and from Baldwin that 'any deviation
from loyalty' to his minister 'in the future ... will be met by
summary dismissal.'[35] The dispute concerned the status within

the Air Ministry of the Director of Civil Aviation. Londonderry, the Secretary of State for Air, decided that the post should be upgraded; Bullock, who would brook no brother near his throne, disagreed. He later said that Fisher 'butted in improperly & unconstitutionally behind my back', and had persuaded the minister to make this change.[36] It is probable that Fisher did favour the change and sought to have it made; he was undoubtedly worried about the way that civil aviation was being handled, and he chaired two important committees designed to change this, those on the empire air mail scheme in 1935 and on international air communications in 1936–7. There was nothing 'unconstitutional' about this, as the Treasury had always claimed the right to consultation on major questions of organization in departments as the management department of the civil service. What form Bullock's opposition to his minister took can only be guessed at, but that it was serious is shown by the action taken against him.[37] On 8 December Fisher told Londonderry that he and Baldwin had agreed on a number of steps: Bullock would 'in writing fully acknowledge' that the decision upgrading the Director of Civil Aviation to Director General would stand, and would 'apologize for his unwarrantable activities over the last few days against his own Minister'. He would 'promise that in future he will in this and all other regards act with loyalty to his Ministers', and Baldwin would shortly speak to him 'like a Dutch uncle' about his behaviour. The

> effect of this course of action is to give Bullock the opportunity of learning a much needed lesson; and I think that is fair, though whether or not he is capable of learning the lesson, and consequently his fortune in the Service, are matters which the future alone can show.[38]

This incident, and Bullock's behaviour generally, were clearly a consideration when the decision to dismiss him was made. It was to his advantage that the published case against him was by comparison relatively slight, since it gave the impression that he was being punished unduly for an isolated indiscretion.

Bullock at first accepted his fate, although privately he said he felt the penalty was 'extraordinarily harsh.'[39] He said that the board 'showed me patience, consideration and impartiality'; by the 1940s he believed their report sought to 'pillory me with falsehoods.'[40] Hankey told him that 'its perspective is all wrong'. It should have started by setting out 'your great services to the state, and ... end[ed] by pointing out how trivial were these matters ... they found against you in comparison with these services.'[41] This was nonsense: the report did Bullock an immense favour by concentrating entirely on his wooing of Imperial Airways. Had it listed his 'great services' generally, it could scarcely have avoided mentioning his previous misdemeanours including his dealings with the North British and Mercantile Insurance Company.

The case was reviewed after the war, but the result was inconclusive. Jowitt, the Lord Chancellor, went through all the papers and correspondence available, including the transcript of the inquiry. He came to the conclusion that the board had been properly conducted, and expressed surprise at the manner in which Bullock was pressing his case. However, although not prepared to say that Bullock had been wronged, he did think that the penalty had been too severe. In his view Bullock should have been allowed to resign.[42] Bullock found this response unacceptable:

> I have a right to make the whole truth made known. Whilst, therefore, I have not yet taken any decision and shall not do so for some time, I think it almost certain that I shall resolutely decline to be a party to a series of half-truths which amount to *suppressio veri*, and unworthy wriggles & evasions with a palpable *suggestio falsi*.[43]

Despite Jowitt's findings, Sir Edward Bridges, the Head of the Civil Service, remained uneasy about the original dismissal. He consulted a number of retired and serving officials familiar with the case, including Hopkins and Ram who had been on the board of inquiry. In what was perhaps his oddest activity as Head of the Civil Service he then engaged in protracted discussions and correspondence with Bullock, who proved remarkably adept at extracting concessions with a mixture of cajolery, appeals for justice and threats that he would initiate a public controversy. However, Bullock did not get the full vindication he demanded. In the summer of 1950 Bridges' tentative proposals for a settlement were rejected out of hand by ministers, who were very critical of Bridges for allowing the discussions to go so far. Bullock continued to press for complete rehabilitation without success, although he did persuade Bridges to help him in his search for a bank directorship in 1953.[44]

Bullock did get rehabilitation of a sort after his death. His memorial service in 1972 was attended by a personal representative of the Prime Minister, a junior defence minister and the permanent head of the Ministry of Defence, and RAF representatives. In addition, the then Head of the Civil Service, Sir William Armstrong, wrote in *The Times* that 'while in the eyes of the management of the service at the time' the dismissal was 'no doubt a salutary lesson to all concerned', for Bullock and his wife 'it was a great personal tragedy which clouded the rest of his life.'[45] He also told this writer that, although the affair happened before he joined the civil service, he believed Bullock had not been properly treated. He based this on his study of the papers dealing with the post-war re-examination of Bullock's case.[46] Others who were involved in the re-examination after the war disagree. They say the case can only be understood in terms of the very strict standards of probity which Fisher insisted on in the pre-war civil service.

Sir William Armstrong's comments notwithstanding, there is no question that Bullock's conduct as a civil servant was outrageous, that his overtures to Imperial Airways, at a time when he was negotiating with the company and even after the chairman had *written* to him asking him to desist, were monumentally foolish, and that he was quite devoid of judgement where his personal interests were concerned. Within three years of his dismissal, he seems to have had hopes of employment with one of the Air Ministry's major contractors, Hawker Siddeley.[47] In regard to a somewhat similar case in 1921, Fisher had said that 'clearly there are degrees and shades; but the factor that to my mind is determining is decency.'[48] The Treasury circular issued after the 1928 Francs affair stressed that the state 'is entitled to demand that its servants shall not only be honest in fact, but beyond the reach of suspicion of dishonesty', and a year before that was issued Fisher had forced a retiring Treasury colleague to defer taking up a number of directorships because of his official dealings with the firms concerned.[49] There is no question that Bullock's conduct in pressing his attentions on Imperial Airways was improper, however oblivious he may have been to that fact. It was doubly so because he was the head of the Air Ministry, where officials involved in rearmament were particularly exposed to temptation because of the necessarily close links between the department and its suppliers in the aircraft industry.

Fisher had no doubts about the case at all: when Imperial Airways complained in June 1936, he wrote to the Chancellor in an extraordinarily bitchy vein. Bullock could expect no sympathy from him:

> Neville Dear — I did enjoy getting a little note from you — it gives such a cosy feeling. Bless you.
> That's a truly delightful paper about Bullock, isn't it? But there's no escape from the consequences.
> With fond love, Warren.[50]

Fisher defended the dismissal in robust terms. On 1 August 1936 he wrote that 'it is a mere insult to the Service to excuse any official — let alone the Permanent Head of a great Department of State — by saying that he has not been corrupt or grossly negligent' in performing his official duties. 'In the judgement of his peers, Bullock has been guilty of a complete and inexcusable violation of the standard laid down for Civil Servants' in the circular issued after the Francs affair of 1928, and 'even if his own instinctive perception is insufficient to guide him, he has had this code publicly brought to his notice' through that circular. 'Officials far subordinate in rank to Bullock have been dismissed, and will again be dismissed, for infringements of that code far less than Bullock's has been.' As head of a department Bullock had the responsibility of 'giving and maintaining the highest example, and therefore the degree of culpability when he betrays that trust is infinitely greater.'[51]

Be that as it may, two questions arise about Fisher's part in the case. Firstly, was Bullock fairly treated before June 1936? Geddes had informed Fisher in 1935 of Bullock's approaches to Imperial Airways. Fisher did not caution Bullock about the impropriety of this, as he might have done, although Geddes did write to Bullock warning him off. On the other hand, Bullock was a very senior civil servant and he was well versed in the ethics of his profession. Furthermore, he had been on a final warning about his conduct since December 1934. If he persisted in behaviour which was at best incredibly headstrong was Fisher under an obligation to caution him once more? The

answer, surely, is no. Although Bullock's downfall was predictable, there was no entrapment — except by himself.

The second question is whether Fisher was an appropriate
person to give impartial advice on what action to take against
Bullock. He had long been exasperated by Bullock's behaviour
and he had clashed with him on a policy matter. That is
presumably why he did not sit on the board of inquiry, as he
had done after the Francs affair, instead appearing as a witness
to give evidence about his dealings with Geddes. But if his
involvement in the case prevented him from serving on the
board, surely it should also have disbarred him from proposing
a specific penalty to ministers in the light of the report. It was
inconceivable that Bullock could have remained a civil servant
in the light of what the report said. But the report also commented that Bullock honestly believed he had behaved quite
properly, and this ought to have been taken into account in
deciding how to discipline him. The action taken has been
described as 'tough but fair', a conclusion with which this writer
agrees.[52] It would, however, have been wiser as well as more
compassionate to allow Bullock to resign.

III

In October 1936, Fisher appointed an internal Treasury committee to review the department's organization 'in the light of
the present and prospective development of Treasury business.'[53] This was the only such formal review which he spon-
sored, although in 1932 he had taken considerable pleasure in
ending the tripartite division of functions imposed in 1919 'in
so far as it was inconsistent with the principle of official responsibility for a Department of State'.[54] Fisher duly appeared
before this committee: he was 'particularly interested in the
question of recruitment of Treasury staff', and believed that
the present method of recruitment from other departments
should be continued 'and perhaps developed'. The aim should
be

> to make of the Treasury a 'general staff' with the recog-
> nised right to recruit at any grade from other Depart-
> ments; in this way a 'corps d'elite' might be formed to
> which the Departments in turn would often look to fill

their top posts. Such a state of affairs would greatly facilitate the proper filling of the posts of Heads and Deputy Heads of Departments.

He said that the Treasury 'is becoming increasingly concerned with foreign affairs (which are nowadays largely economics, finance and armaments); should some new division be created to bring together various aspects of foreign policy?'[55]

These were ambitious proposals, and paralleled closely his conception of his role as Head of the Civil Service. It is not surprising that the others who gave evidence were less sweeping in their recommendations. Edward Bridges suggested that 'a standing inter-departmental Committee to keep the Foreign Office in touch with the views of the Treasury, Board of Trade etc.' might be created, as

> one difficulty in the way of the exercise of the coordinating function on foreign policy by the Treasury itself was that many of the questions involved gave rise to no expenditure, and therefore the Treasury had often no official concern with them and no opportunity to take a hand.[56]

The committee steered clear of Fisher's ideas. They found no reason 'to recommend any drastic alteration in the present structure of the Treasury. There was indeed a striking unanimity of opinion in the evidence given ... that the existing arrangement is, in its main outlines, well adapted to the needs of the work of the Treasury.'[57] Given his remarks to the committee, this was scarcely Fisher's view, but he appears to have accepted the findings without demur. The most significant change in Treasury organization came well before the committee reported, when Edward Bridges was promoted and his division, 5D, was relieved of responsibility for a miscellaneous collection of questions and allowed to concentrate on defence.[58]

In May 1938, Hankey decided to retire in order to take up a government directorship on the board of the Suez Canal company.[59] This reopened the question of the proper place of the cabinet secretariat, on which he had defeated Fisher sixteen years earlier.[60] Hankey argued that the two posts of Secretary to the Cabinet and to the CID should continue to be held by one man, who should be drawn from the armed services. The obvious candidate in his view was his deputy, 'Pug' Ismay.

However, he suspected that Ismay would prefer to take only the CID post, so he also approached Pownall, Ismay's predecessor, to ask 'was I prepared to stand in' as otherwise 'the Services would lose the post since Warren Fisher was now pressing for the combined job to be in the hands of a civilian — Bridges of the Treasury.'[61]

Running two candidates rather than one weakened Hankey's position in the battle with Fisher: he was forced to rely more on the highly questionable argument that the combined posts were somehow better held by a military man than on the reasonable point that he had a competent deputy on hand to take over. He told the Prime Minister that Ismay had 'an infinitely wider experience than Bridges' and was 'his equal in all respects', said that 'it was not an ordinary Civil Service appointment on which the Secretary to the Treasury is the best judge', and pointed out that 'a Treasury appointment would be a terrible slap in the face for me.'[62] He also warned that 'if [the] person selected as my successor was not in the public interest' he would 'if necessary, ask permission to ... retain my present appointment', an extraordinary threat for a civil servant to make.[63] He was glad to learn that the Prime Minister, 'knowing how Warren Fisher got worked up about these things ... had instinctively a complete mistrust of any suggestion he made' ; nevertheless, it was decided to make Bridges Cabinet Secretary.[64]

Ismay remained a deputy secretary in the Cabinet Office although he became secretary of the CID.[65] Hankey professed himself delighted with the arrangement, but as Pownall observed, 'what has happened is that in this battle Warren Fisher has won and Hankey lost. His last big fight!'[66] In fact Bridges was the choice not only of Fisher but of Sir Horace Wilson and of the Prime Minister, who were well aware of his outstanding abilities. Against this body of opinion Hankey had only his inordinate vanity to sustain him: neither of the two candidates he ran actually wanted to be Cabinet Secretary.[67] The wisdom of Bridges's appointment was never in doubt.[68] Fisher had long sought a fusion of the Cabinet Office and the Treasury, and the appointment of Bridges was a step in that direction. However, although in 1945–6 Bridges combined the posts of Secretary to the Cabinet and Permanent Secretary to the Treasury, this end was never quite obtained.[69] The reason was simply that the tasks were too big: the Treasury was already responsible for the national economy and for management of the civil service as a whole. Whatever Fisher may have believed, it could not do everything.

IV

Fisher was exasperated by Baldwin's lethargic approach to the problems of government and his refusal to take difficult decisions, an attitude which contrasted sharply with Chamberlain's strong performance as Chancellor.[70] In June 1936 Fisher told Reith of the BBC that he was 'longing for his three more years to pass', and that 'every department chief was, as he is, more disgusted than ever before' with the Cabinet. Baldwin he described as 'completely ineffectual.'[71] News of the Prime Minister's impending retirement cheered Fisher up somewhat in January 1937. He wrote to Chamberlain in his usual worshipful vein:

> Neville Dear — at last, at last, & thank God. There is reform and positive action required in almost every direction; & even matters which superficially might be accounted small may turn the scale in this ill-poised world. These as well as more obvious things need clear thinking, courage, & decision. And it is these qualities that we are now going to have in action.[72]

He was 'horrified' to learn in March that Sir John Simon and not Hoare would be the new Chancellor, but he believed that 'the machine was now so strong that they could carry' Simon 'for some time', and he remained confident about the coming Chamberlain government.[73] His optimism was misplaced: the new government was scarcely more inspiring than the old, and his last two years at the Treasury saw a steep decline in his personal influence, despite the fact that 'Neville Dear' was now Prime Minister.

This decline had a number of causes. Fisher had always been highly strung, or, as he put it in 1926, 'an impatient, irritable sort of fellow.'[74] This was no great handicap, since the politicians he served from 1919 onwards quickly became accustomed to his habitual outspokenness and his excitable ways. There is no doubt however that as he grew older so his voice grew shriller. It was not his energy or his strategic grasp that failed him in the late 1930s — on the contrary, his energy seems to have grown, and Chamberlain had confidence in his practical capacity at least until 1937 — but rather his judgement.

While the inert Baldwin was Prime Minister Fisher at least had the ear of Chamberlain, by far the strongest man in the government. Once he was Prime Minister, however, Chamberlain looked increasingly to Sir Horace Wilson for advice. Fisher's advice to ministers grew steadily more alarmist in content and strident in tone, but his influence on Chamberlain rapidly waned. As his intimacy with the Prime Minister diminished, and as Chamberlain became more and more preoccupied with the pursuit of a foreign policy success which would head off war, so Fisher became increasingly frantic about the drift of events. At the end of 1937 an acquaintance wrote that 'Warren seems to be interfering quite unnecessarily in heaps of things.'[75] Sir Frederick Marquis (later Lord Woolton), who first met him in 1938, observed that 'he was ruthless in his dealing with either civil servants or Ministers — including the Prime Minister — if he thought that their actions were not contributing to his conception of Britain's proper position in the world.'[76]

Marquis first met Fisher while serving on the Cadman committee on civil aviation. This had been set up after parliamentary pressure for an inquiry into the disappointing performance of Imperial Airways in developing and operating long-range routes. The Commons had grown restive about aviation generally, and the government was handicapped by the fact that Swinton, the very able Secretary of State for Air, was a member of the Lords. The committee as originally constituted would have consisted of Cadman, Fisher and Sir William Brown, the permanent head of the Board of Trade. Brown had once been Swinton's private secretary, and the two were on good terms. This, and Fisher's own presence, suggests that the committee was not designed to pillory Swinton. The nomination of two civil servants was a major blunder on someone's part, because in its excited state the Commons would have none of it. The government was forced to find three outsiders, two trade unionists and a businessman, to replace Fisher and Brown.

Fisher primed the reconstituted committee extensively, with the intention of alerting the government to the state of the aircraft industry. In a very curious episode he visited Marquis and briefed him on problems in the aviation industry, beginning the interview with the tearful announcement that he was about to break the Official Secrets Act and could properly be prosecuted for doing so. The committee decided to produce two reports, one for publication in accordance with its brief, the other a confidential paper on aircraft production for the government.

Marquis hailed Fisher's patriotic belief that 'the protection of the country was more important than a rigid adherence to the regulations that should govern his conduct as a civil servant', but the fact remains that the most tangible outcome of the committee's published report was to hasten the sacking of Swinton, who was one of Fisher's 'heroes.'[77] The new air minister was Kingsley Wood, who proved to be a success: while not as able an executive as Swinton, he brought to the post the political touch which it needed, and he defended the department robustly from Fisher's attacks on it.[78]

While Fisher's influence with the Prime Minister waned that of Sir Horace Wilson grew. He had been given the nebulous title of Chief Industrial Adviser to the government in 1930, and thereafter served as a floating permanent secretary working on trade, industrial and commercial questions. In 1935 Fisher put him into No. 10 to keep things moving while Baldwin was Prime Minister. He spoke of Wilson as 'my angel' because of the work he did there.[79] Wilson expected to be moved once Baldwin departed but Chamberlain, who as early as 1926 had noted his 'cool head', retained him in Downing Street.[80] He played a controversial role during Chamberlain's premiership. He was deeply involved in foreign policy, and he played a prominent and rather public part as an adviser and emissary during the Munich negotiations. He became an object of loathing for opponents of Chamberlain's policies, and in the recriminatory years after 1939 he was pilloried as an arch-appeaser and a knave.[81]

Although violently opposed to the foreign policy which Chamberlain and Wilson pursued, Fisher was angered by attacks on his colleague. He told the Prime Minister in November 1938 that

the relationship between Ministers & Crown Servants is conditioned by the recognition that the position of the

latter is in the wings & that the foot-lights are the monopo-
ly of the politician who is constitutionally the sole responsible authority ... There has been of late years a wholly
detrimental tendency in the Press & occasionally even in
Parliament to talk about individual serving officials, civil
& military; & unless this is checked the position of Crown
Servants vis-a-vis Ministers & the Public will be
misunderstood & the effective working of the machinery
of Govt. impaired.[82]

Although no post-war advisers to prime ministers ever had to
endure the obloquy to which Wilson was subjected in his
lifetime, a number of senior civil servants undoubtedly suffered through being publicly identified with particular policies.
Despite this, Fisher's dire prediction does not seem to have
come to pass. The relationship between ministers and civil
servants does not appear fundamentally to have altered much
since the 1930s, for all the new management jargon which has
entered the Whitehall vocabulary in the last decade.

Chamberlain as Chancellor had been the most powerful and
decisive member of the Cabinet, and he remained so as Prime
Minister. Edward Bridges wrote of him that 'to me the
dominating feature of his make-up was not merely his power
of analysis but also the ruthlessly realistic judgement of
affairs and of the action to be taken which followed the
analysis.'[83] In Horace Wilson, Chamberlain found an adviser of similar temperament to himself. It is not surprising
that he came to rely on him more than on the increasingly
frantic and prophetic Fisher.

Notes

1. Bishirgian's firm contracted to buy almost all the world's pepper crop for 1935. When his scheme went wrong, causing a 'pepper crisis', he sold the firm without disclosing to the buyer its huge commitment. Fisher thought he could be charged with 'forestalling and regrating' under an ancient anti-hoarding law, but in fact he was convicted of the more mundane crime of issuing a false prospectus and sentenced to a year in jail. Sir Harold Kent to the author, 26 Apr. 1981; *The Times*, 12 Feb.–19 Mar. 1936; Middlemass and Barnes, *Baldwin*, p. 896; Fisher's evidence to the Ullswater committee, 31 May 1935, T162 370/E41413.
For more on his role in the abdication crisis see Stuart, *Reith diaries*, pp. 188–91. For his support of Reith's views on the BBC charter against Kingsley Wood, the Postmaster General, see ibid., pp. 116, 118–19, 170, and 210. There is more material in the PREM and T162 series.

2. CID minutes, 14 Oct. 1935; minutes of a sub-committee, 1935–6, CAB 16/127. It was decided to make Sir Stephen Tallents of the BBC the Director General designate. Fisher to Reith, 27 Oct. 1936, BBC archives, 910 TAL. Interview with R.W. Fisher.

3. Beveridge to Mrs A. Gardner-Dunn, 28 Feb. 1937, Beveridge papers, viii: 11.

4. Rae to Beveridge, ibid. Fisher was also antagonized by Beveridge's demand that he be allowed to select a private secretary. Interview with Professor H.R.G. Greaves.

5. Beveridge, *Power*, p. 241.

6. Hankey to Inskip, 16 Nov. 1936, CAB 104/147. Compare this with Beveridge, *Power*, p. 142, where he says Hankey and Inskip thought his terms fair. For an unlikely bond between Fisher and Beveridge, see p. 175 above, note 105.

7. Woolton, *Memoirs*, p. 169. Interviews with Sir Thomas and Lady Padmore, and with Sir George Dunnett. Sir George Dunnett also commented that Ernest Twentyman of the Treasury deserved more credit than had been given for his work in this area.

8. CID minutes, 23 Mar. 1936, CAB 2/6; report of a committee of heads of departments, dated 12 Nov. 1938, CAB 16/190.

9. Hoare to Chatfield, 8 Aug. 1937, Chatfield papers, CHT 3/1/173–4; O'Brien, *Civil Defence*, pp. 55, 92–9, 110–13.

10. Memorandum by Fisher and Hankey, 23 May 1938, CAB 104/1; O'Brien, op.cit., pp.116–17.

11. CID minutes, 2 June 1938, CAB 2/6.

12. Carter to Rae, 3 Nov. 1936, T162 424/E13264/04.

13. Report of a committee, 4 Nov. 1936, ibid.

14. Notes by Hoare, undated, spring 1937, Templewood papers, ix: 3; Fisher to Hoare, 14 Jan. 1937, T162 424/E13264/04.

15. Note of a meeting, 9 Feb. 1937, ibid.

16. Andrew, *Secret Service*, pp. 370–1 and 432 deals with two important cases where government employees were discovered to be actively engaged in espionage for the Soviet Union. The Fisher/Kell procedure would, clearly, not apply to such cases where there was hard evidence.

17. This odd episode is discussed in Chapter 9.

18. Report of the board of inquiry to investigate certain discussions engaged in by the permanent secretary to the Air Ministry, *PP* (1935–6), vii, 461–79, cited hereafter as 'Bullock report'.

19. 'Bullock report', pp. 464–5.

20. ibid., p. 466. Bullock had his minister's permission to discuss an honour.

21. Geddes did not in fact get the honour he had expected.

22. Geddes to Bullock, 16 Sept. 1935, in 'Bullock report', p. 477. Sir Christopher Bullock, 'On the case of Sir Christopher Bullock', undated, p. 26, Liddell Hart papers, 1/129/210. This interesting pamphlet puts Bullock's side of the case very fully. The extent of its circulation is not known.

23. 'Bullock report', p. 476; Chapman, *Ethics*, p. 178.

24. Bullock to Monckton, undated, Monckton MS 58; private information; Bullock, 'On the case', pp. 62 and 64. As regards the composition of the board, it is impossible to prove that they were not hostile to him. Bullock generally sought to portray Hopkins, the chairman, as being upright but overworked, just as the Treasury Solicitor, Sir Maurice Gwyer, was a member of the 1928 'Francs Affair' board. Granville Ram was presumably chosen for his legal knowledge. As regards the 'Courts of Law' argument, see the chapter on 'natural justice' in Wade, *Administrative Law*, from which it is clear that tribunals do not have to follow strict legal rules. On p. 213 Wade says how a tribunal should proceed: the board in the Bullock case acted correctly. The tribunal was neither a court of law nor a court martial.

25. Bullock's summary of the affair, 22 Apr. 1947, Liddell Hart papers, 1/129/142A.

26. See pp. 161–2 above.

27. Dawson to Barrington-Ward, 28 July 1936, Dawson papers. There is no doubt that *The Times* editor had been tipped off: a censorious editorial appeared on the day that the report was published. Dawson diary, 31 July 1936, MS Dawson 40.

28. Quoted in Peden, *British Rearmament*, p. 31.

29. Liddell Hart's note of a talk with Duff Cooper, 14 Dec. 1935, Liddell Hart papers, 11/1935/115.

30. Interview with Lord Trend.

31. Lady Grigg to Tom Jones, 18 Aug. 1936, Grigg papers, PJHGG 7/7/5. Barrington-Ward to Dawson, 9 Aug. 1936, Dawson papers.

32. Copy of the memorial, undated, MS Monckton 58; Londonderry to Baldwin, 29 Dec. 1938, Baldwin papers 171/178–92 (this has been quoted in Bullock's defence, e.g. by Hyde, *British Air Policy*, p. 387, but it is only a small part of a fourteen-page letter of reproach and recrimination in which Londonderry lists all the unkind blows dealt to him by fate and by Baldwin, complaining amongst other things that 'when the post of Viceroy of India was vacant, it was quite open to you to have sent us there.' Thus had sycophancy turned to recrimination.)

33. Bullock to Monckton, 28 June 1946, MS Monckton 58; Bullock to Liddell Hart, 25 Jan. 1946, Liddell Hart papers, 1/129/108. There is no mention of the Bullock case, or of a change of heart by Baldwin,

in Middlemas and Barnes, *Baldwin*. As regards Swinton, see Bullock to Tizard, 4 Oct. 1947, Liddell Hart papers, 1/129/152A, from which it appears that Swinton was in fact less willing to help than Bullock had earlier maintained. See also Cross, *Swinton*, pp. 150–2, which does not fully support Bullock's claims. Bullock was prone to exaggerate both the strength and the nature of support for him: see his letters to Hankey, 21 Feb. and 20 Mar. 1939, Hankey papers, HNKY 4/31. In the first of these, he attributes a favourable remark to Sir John Cadman; in the second, after Cadman had evidently denied to Hankey that he had said any such thing, Bullock denounces him as a friend of Fisher's.

34. Bullock to Templewood, 24 Oct. 1955, Templewood papers, xviii. Same to same, 23 Jan. 1956, ibid.; see also his letter to Weir, 25 Nov. 1932, in which he attached a draft letter to the press on the RAF for Weir's signature, Weir papers, 13/3. See also Bullock to Liddell Hart, undated, Mar. 1930, Liddell Hart papers, 1/129/13.

Bullock had served as a pilot during World War I, so his enthusiasm for the RAF was not based simply on departmental considerations.

35. Fisher to Londonderry, 8 Dec. 1934, Baldwin papers, 169/194.

36. Bullock to Hankey, 21 Feb. 1939, as in note 33 above.

37. A misleading account of a meeting between Londonderry and the parliamentary air committee found its way into the press. The committee denied that any of its members were responsible, and it may be that Bullock was suspected. PREM 1/147.

38. Londonderry did not find Bullock's first attempt at an apology 'at all satisfactory ... I shall be glad to know whether you have dispelled from his mind any illusion that we are incapable of dispensing with his services.' Londonderry to Baldwin, 10 Dec. 1934, Baldwin papers, 169/196–7; Fisher to Londonderry, as in note 35 above.

39. Bullock to Hoare, 29 July 1936, Templewood papers, ix: 2.

40. *The Times*, 6 Aug. 1936; Bullock to Tizard, 4 Oct. 1947, Liddell Hart papers, 1/129/49 and 152A.

41. Extract from Hankey to Bullock, undated, MS Monckton 58. It should be said that Hankey regarded himself as a military man, not as a civil servant. This is illustrated in the fact that, after the First World War, he accepted a parliamentary grant of £25,000, one of a number paid to very senior officers who had provided distinguished services during the war.

42. Chapman, *Ethics*, pp.163–4. In his study of the post-war work of Edward Bridges as Head of the Civil Service Chapman deals extensively and sympathetically with the Bullock case at pp. 142–85, drawing on official records which were not available until 1987.

43. Bullock to Tizard, 4 Oct. 1947, Liddell Hart papers, 1/129/152A.

44. Chapman, *Ethics*, pp. 165–73.

45. *The Times*, 22 May 1972.

46. Interview with Lord Armstrong. On the other hand, Sir Thomas Padmore, Sir Edward Playfair, Sir John Winnifrith and Lord Trend, all of whom served in the Treasury before the war, said that few in that department at the time doubted the justice of the penalty imposed on Bullock. Sir Edward and Sir Thomas, who were successively private secretary to Sir Richard Hopkins in 1936, denied une-

quivocally that he had a guilty conscience about the affair, as Bullock later claimed. Some former officials of the Treasury and of other departments with whom this writer was in touch came to believe that Bullock's punishment was excessive. None of these were aware of the earlier dispute with Londonderry and the warning given then. Sir Folliott Sandford, who was in the Air Ministry at the time, felt that Bullock 'dug his own grave.' Sir Folliott Sandford to the author, 11 Oct. 1981.

47. Bullock to Hankey, 20 Mar. 1939, Hankey papers, HNKY 4/31. Hankey's interest once he had retired may have been connected with the circumstances of the struggle over who was to succeed him in 1938. He became a strong critic of the Treasury in the 1940s. Lord Geoffrey-Lloyd and H. Montgomery Hyde, both of whom were connected with the Air Ministry in the mid 1930s, felt that Bullock had been very badly treated. Neither of them were civil servants. H.M. Hyde to the author, 27 Nov. 1979.

48. Note by Fisher, 18 Apr. 1921, T162 387/E14862. This was the case of Sir Arnold Wilson, who left the Indian civil service in order to work in the oil industry in the Middle East. He was so shocked at Bullock's treatment that he offered him thirty pages in the periodical *The Nineteenth Century*, which he owned, in order to state his side of the case.

49. 'Francs Report', p. 535. Interviews with R.W. Fisher and Sir Robert Fraser. The official involved was Sir George Barstow, who was much put out by the temporary prohibition.

50. Fisher to Chamberlain, 18 June 1936, Chamberlain papers, NC 7/11/29/20.

51. Fisher to Findlater Stewart, 1 Aug. 1936, quoted in Chapman, *Ethics*, pp. 157–8.

52. Private information.

53. Minute by Fisher, 17 Oct. 1936, T199/50c.

54. Insertion by Fisher into the draft report of the committee, 1937, ibid.; see p. 36 above for Fisher's views on the 1919 scheme.

55. Minutes of Treasury organization committee, 2 Nov. 1936, ibid. It consisted of Fisher's three immediate deputies at that time, Hopkins, Rae, and Barlow.

56. ibid., 1 Dec. 1936.

57. Report of the organization committee, p.3, ibid.

58. Fisher to Baldwin and Chamberlain, 20 Jan. 1937, T199/188. In the same year the post of director of women's establishments, created in 1920, was upgraded to assistant secretary level. T199/112.

59. Roskill, *Hankey*, iii, 352–3.

60. See pp. 107–9 above.

61. Bond, *Pownall Diary*, i, 132, 2 May 1938.

62. Hankey's notes for a conversation with Chamberlain, 18 May 1938, Hankey papers, HNKY 8/36.

63. Hankey diary, 16 May 1938.

64. ibid.

65. Ismay, *Memoirs*, p. 88.

66. Bond, *Pownall Diary*, i, 149, 30 May 1938; Hankey diary, 23 May 1938.

67. Ronald Wingate, *Ismay*, p. 30. Ismay dealt with the military side of Cabinet business with great distinction before and during World War II. He and Fisher remained on excellent terms.

68. For an account of Bridges' career, see Winnifrith, 'Bridges', pp. 37–56.

69. In 1922 Fisher was rumoured to be thinking of becoming Cabinet Secretary himself. Hankey diary, 29 Oct. 1922. See p. 109 above on this.

70. See Fisher to Chamberlain, 12 Dec. [1934], Chamberlain papers, NC 7/11/27/14, on his hope that Chamberlain would become Prime Minister after the next election.

71. Stuart, *Reith Diaries*, pp. 211–12, 23 June and 2 July 1936.

72. Fisher to Chamberlain, 18 Jan. 1937, NC 7/11/30/48.

73. Notes by Hoare, undated, spring 1937, Templewood papers, ix: 3.

74. Clark, *A Good Innings*, p. 273, Lady Lee's diary, 3 Dec. 1926.

75. Lady Grigg to Tom Jones, 12 Dec. 1937, Grigg papers, PJGG 7/9/16.

76. Woolton, *Memoirs*, p. 139. Marquis was created a peer as Lord Woolton in 1939 in order to allow him to serve as a minister. From his *Memoirs*, p. 162, it seems Fisher had a hand in this.

77. ibid., p. 139; interview with Sir Thomas and Lady Padmore; Cross, *Swinton*, pp. 202–3. Sir Folliott Sandford, who was Swinton's private secretary in 1937–8, described the published report of the reconstituted committee as 'one of the worst I have ever seen'.
Letter to the author, 11 Oct. 1981.

78. As Postmaster General Kingsley Wood had crossed swords with Fisher and Reith, and won, over the BBC charter. Stuart, *Reith Diaries*, p. 170 and Briggs, *Broadcasting*, ii, 476–80.

79. Interview with Sir Thomas and Lady Padmore.

80. This was at the start of the general strike. Chamberlain diary, 3 May 1926; Petrie, *Powers Behind the Prime Ministers*, p. 173.

81. See especially 'Cato', *Guilty Men*, passim.

82. Fisher to Chamberlain, 11 Nov. 1938, T162 788/E37837.

83. Bridges to Templewood, 6 Jan. 1954, Templewood papers, xix: 12.

8

Defence and foreign policy, 1933–8

Fisher had been interested in the substance of defence and foreign policy, as well as its cost, since the early 1920s. He took his membership of the CID very seriously, and maintained that he was there to represent the civil service, not to fight the departmental Treasury's battles. It was a distinction which the armed services probably found rather hard to fathom until the early 1930s. In October 1933, after pressure from Fisher, Vansittart and Hankey, the CID set up a sub-committee to consider how the worst deficiencies in Britain's defences after more than a decade of cut-backs could be made good, in the light of growing unease about developments in Europe and in the Far East.

The Defence Requirements Committee (DRC) consisted of the three men who had pressed for it to be set up, together with the chiefs of staff of the three armed services. Hankey characteristically claimed the credit as 'the instigator of the creation of that committee', but it is quite clear that Vansittart and Fisher were just as much responsible and just as much concerned at the state of the country's defences. Indeed, in 1945 Fisher reminded Chatfield, who was in a position to know whether he was being accurate, how 'I had with great difficulty induced a supine & uninterested government' to establish the committee.[1]

The causes for Fisher's alarm were twofold: Japan's expansion into China, and the new regime in Germany. Many years later he wrote that 'in 1933 there was no excuse for ... ignorance' about the German threat because 'our Authorities in the 1930s and before had full knowledge' that ever since 1919 'semi-military formations had been sedulously fostered in Germany.'[2] In fact, in 1933 there was no reliable intelligence on what Germany's armed strength actually was, on its industrial and financial potential to expand its armed forces, on its plans to do so, or on its strategic intentions.[3] The British armed services were, however, well aware of their own deficiencies. With the exception of the navy, they found it very difficult to address those deficiencies in terms of war against a particular country, and they had no clear idea of what form a potential enemy's arms build-up would take.

The history of the DRC is unusual. Before it began its work Fisher and Vansittart had each come to the conclusion that Germany was the enemy to be faced. In addition, Fisher also believed that Britain could not afford, and should never need, to get embroiled in hostilities with Japan in the Far East. The activities of both men on the committee were, therefore, partly devoted to getting agreement on fundamental strategic assumptions. It is clear that they also wanted to shock the Cabinet into realization of the country's weakness, and thereby to provoke the necessary political action to increase defence spending and to educate the public about the danger. Finally, in order to get a report on the lines they wanted, Fisher and Vansittart were willing to argue the toss with the service chiefs on quite technical military issues, particularly in relation to air defence.

From the start of the DRC's deliberations in October 1933 it was the civilians, not the warriors, who demanded the biggest increase in expenditure. Fisher recalled that 'I said to the Committee that we shd. regard ourselves as a team of experienced colleagues to think out together our country's interests, & that we were not here each to fight a particular corner', a claim borne out by the diary of the committee's secretary, who noted after the first meeting that Fisher was 'very much for putting up what the Services think right without much consideration of political and financial difficulties. The Chiefs of Staff are more wary and, I think, more intelligent. It must be within the "realm of possibilities" ....'[4] Of the chiefs of staff, only Chatfield, the First Sea Lord, was a formidable figure, and Fisher became a firm friend. Montgomery-Massingberd was an unexceptional soldier, while Ellington of the RAF was in Fisher's view particularly ineffectual. Whether or not this was a fair assessment, the two men could never agree on anything.[5] It may be that the army and the air force were so conditioned by years of retrenchment that their commanders found it impossible to think in terms of further expansion. The navy, on the other hand, which had done best in the lean years of the 1920s, was ably represented both by Chatfield and by Hankey. Fisher and Vansittart took it upon themselves to make the running for the air force.

Fisher had simple views on the strategic dilemma with which Britain was faced, and he put them to his colleagues very forcefully. He argued that 'the fundamental danger would come from Germany', that Britain had to avoid being 'tempted into a war with Japan', and that 'it is our bounden duty to shape our policy towards Japan independent of the bluster and chicanery of the United States of America.'[6] He circulated a number of papers supporting his case, including extracts from a memorandum by a former army chief which maintained that good relations with Japan were a prerequisite to a successful defence policy.[7] Fisher was 'in favour of continuing work at Singapore, but not on account of any immediate menace from Japan, but rather to indicate that we proposed to put our house in order and show a determined front.'[8]

Fisher's proposals did not meet with a warm response. Hankey 'rather inclined towards bracketing the menace of Japan and Germany as equal', and prepared a draft report along those lines without consulting his colleagues.[9] He told a subordinate that Fisher was

> rather mad. Apparently he has some mysterious nerve disorder and his judgement is affected thereby. The papers he occasionally puts in are astonishing, long tirades far removed from the point and irrelevant to the Committee's terms of reference.[10]

Some months later Hankey told Baldwin that he did not think Fisher 'is a fit man or that his judgement is at its best. Moreover he has never been sound about the Navy or understood the defence question in the Pacific.'[11]

It is difficult to say whether Fisher's 1933 illness had affected his judgement. He certainly got very worked up about defence issues after 1933, but he had always operated in that fashion. Hankey's comments probably reflect rivalry as much as anything else: he was an outstanding official, but throughout his years as Cabinet and CID secretary he tried to keep a personal grip on defence policy. He was, furthermore, a professional military man, and Fisher was not. Most importantly, he and Fisher differed fundamentally on imperial defence and on Japan. Fisher never fully accepted the assumption that Britain could defend all her overseas interests by force, and he believed that Britain should avoid war with Japan at all costs. He was also inclined to the view that it was hard to justify retention of some of Britain's overseas possessions: in 1944 he remarked that British control of Hong Kong 'has always seemed to me the most inexcusable bit of territorial rape'.[12] The war bore out the validity of Fisher's assumptions rather than Hankey's more grandiose conception of British power.

Hankey had trouble also with Vansittart, who believed the report should recommend a further twenty-five squadrons of aircraft for home defence over and above the increase of ten squadrons which the committee had agreed. Vansittart later wrote that 'gratifying support came from Fisher; it was heartening to find the Head of the Treasury ready to face the immensity of our need, but the experts remained immovable', and he did not carry his objections to the length of submitting a separate report, a decision he subsequently bemoaned as 'Fisher would have been game.'[13] The DRC secretary noted that 'the civilians, whose presumable line was to keep down impossible service demands, have continuously been the alarmist party, demanding quicker and heavier rearmament whatever the price', a remark which, with the minutes and papers of the committee, rather belie the observation of one historian that Fisher 'gave high priority to the limitation of expenditure to what was possible within the limits of a balanced budget' (as though Hankey and the service chiefs were themselves Keynesian visionaries).[14]

Eventually, and with 'infinite difficulty', Hankey 'achieved a unanimous report' which proposed additional expenditure of £77 million over the next five years, and a further £16 million in subsequent years.[15] After some consideration by ministers, the Chancellor Neville Chamberlain suggested in June that overall increased expenditure should be cut back to £59 million over five years. Within this reduced amount, the allocations for the army and navy would be sharply cut, while the RAF would get more money. His paper argued that thirty-eight squadrons, instead of the DRC's ten, should be added to the RAF's home defence strength, but that no new squadrons should be formed overseas except three at Singapore. The net result of these changes would have been only one extra squadron above the DRC's recommendations, but the emphasis was switched almost entirely to preparing Britain for aerial warfare against a European power.[16] Despite Hankey's best efforts, a cabinet sub-committee broadly agreed with Chamberlain; the army as usual fared worst in the revision, having its allocation cut by half to £20 millon.[17] Fisher would have preferred the Cabinet to authorize a higher level of spending overall, but there is no doubt that he supported the distinct alteration in priorities which these changes represented, including the attenuation of army modernization, and extra spending on the RAF.

Chamberlain and Fisher shared the belief that the greatest threat to Britain came from Germany. They shared too the assumption that Britain could not possibly deal with such a powerful enemy in Europe if she was also threatened in the Far East by Japan. Since 1919 the Treasury had argued that Britain could not hope to win a Far Eastern war unaided, and that viewpoint seemed doubly sound once the German danger emerged. Although there was 'increasing anxiety' in the Cabinet about both Germany and Japan, Chamberlain was impatient at his colleagues' reluctance to come to grips with the problems facing them.[18] Neither he nor Fisher was prepared simply to find the money for defence; both wanted to get the Far East out of the way by reaching an accommodation with Japan. Since no other minister seemed willing to take the initiative in preparing the way for such an understanding, Chamberlain took it upon himself to do so. He and Fisher believed that Japan could be won over if treated fairly on two important issues: naval armaments, and China.

II

A naval conference involving Britain, Japan and the United States was due to begin in London at the end of 1934. In the months preceding it Fisher, who was on the British delegation, argued strongly for a conciliatory attitude towards Japan. In July he told Chatfield that

> what we should not do is to antagonise the Japanese, for in a potentially hostile Japan will be Germany's opportunity. This of course does not entail truckling to Japan or

being indifferent to our own needs; but it does mean being
constantly on our guard against being manoeuvred by the
Americans into a position which, though doubtless admirable from their point of view, might prove calamitous
from ours ...

In my opinion you underestimate the German danger
and from a purely naval point of view not unnaturally; but
from my point of view the danger from Germany is
directly and intimately proportioned to the degree of good
will or ill will that exists between Japan and England ...

[We must] be prepared to sacrifice our respective Service prejudices and *amour propre*, and must be ready to look
at the facts of today and tomorrow untrammelled by any
anachronisms ... In the sense known to our forefathers, we
have not got at this moment 'command of the seas', and
we cannot under any circumstances regain it with all its
old implications.

Even if it be conceded — tho' I do not concede it — that
we can ever have command of the sea of Japan, we could
only have it at the cost of abandoning the command of
European waters (and our lines of communication); and
unless we maintain this — dependent as we are for survival
on sea borne traffic — we shall find our sources of supply
and our means of transport cut off and all that will be left
of our England will be an epitaph.

He thought priority should be given to doubling 'the *centrally
situated* air strength of this country', and said that the navy was
adequately equipped already for a conflict with Germany.[19]
Chatfield's response was friendly but firm: while Britain should
not antagonize Japan, neither should it offend the United
States. The DRC had had to consider not 'the security of this
country alone, but imperial defence'. Since the days of Anson,
it had been British naval policy to 'maintain in a central
position a Force which was capable of being sent to any
position which was being threatened so as to be enabled to meet
an enemy there with a chance of a successful issue.' Chatfield's
'own personal view ... was that I did not think the German
menace was so serious as had been represented by the Foreign
Office papers.'[20]

With Chamberlain's consent, Fisher also sounded out Matsudaira, the Japanese ambassador, about the prospects for the

conference: on 24 October they had 'a very frank talk ... They did not apparently touch on China but Japan said M[atsudaira] would have had no difficulty in coming to an agreement with us if U.S.A. were not in the way.'[21] This was a tempting prospect for the Chancellor, as 'all the evidence indicates that it would be easier and simpler to come to an agreement with Japan than with Germany.'[22] Fisher tried to prod the Foreign Secretary in the same direction:

> The stakes for the United States and for Great Britain are wholly different; at the most what is involved for America is national vanity, while for us the issue may well prove a matter of life and death. For if we now earn the undying hatred of the Japanese, when the new German version of 'Der Tag' comes to be staged we cannot hope to survive if Japan takes that opportunity for revenge. And in that event a second generation of young Englishmen will be blown to pieces, and all in vain ... At some future date Germany intends, when she is ready and the opportunity is favourable, once more to fight for the domination of Europe; she knows that her success in this aim pre-supposes the defeat of England. She very nearly won the last war with almost the entire world in arms against her and the whole resources of England and her Empire available for our defence. What is likely to be the case if on her next venture of this character she could find England distracted simultaneously with a hostile Japan?[23]

A fortnight later he complained that 'the whole trouble is due to the baseless demands and the equally baseless terror ... of the Americans' felt by Baldwin and Sir John Simon, the Foreign Secretary, and he denounced Craigie, the Foreign Office expert at the conference, as pro-American.[24] This was a rather odd charge, as Craigie was recognized to be very sympathetic to Japan, and seems to have been more or less in Fisher's pocket. Fisher subsequently unsuccessfully pushed for him to be made Deputy Under Secretary in the Foreign Office, and in 1938 Craigie was appointed ambassador in Japan, where he strove unavailingly to avoid 'the catastrophe of war.'[25] Fisher's hostility towards the United States is more understandable: he did not believe that Congress could be trusted to honour any undertakings which American negotiators might make, although he became friendly with the leader of the American delegation, Captain [later Admiral] Thomas Standley.[26] He also remained on close terms with Chatfield, although the First Sea Lord's views were so different from his own. According to one historian 'Chatfield's strong stand against compromise with Japan' eased the fears of the American naval representative at the conference 'of a British sell-out to Japan.'[27] Fisher appears gullible as well in his discussions with Matsudaira; although the ambassador was supposed to be in touch with important circles in Japan, neither he nor his successor Yoshida had any influence with the Tokyo government.

The conference collapsed in December, when Japan gave notice that she would not renew the Washington and London naval treaties when they expired in 1936. Despite his earlier warnings about such an outcome, Fisher was surprisingly optimistic in its wake: 'My inference ... is that Tokyo has been thinking throughout too parochially. Our European problems, known by now to the Japs here but insufficiently emphasised by them to Tokyo and quite overlooked there, must somehow be brought home to them.' The best policy was to continue to emphasize Britain's desire for good relations with Japan, and 'to keep on pegging away at their education' about Britain's need for a navy capable of defending her interests everywhere: 'On these lines and with patience we shall eventually get somewhere not too unsatisfactory for ourselves and the Japs.'[28] One reason for this sanguine outlook was that he and Chamberlain had already taken steps to reach an understanding with the Japanese over China. This was to result in considerable confusion in Japan, China, and London.

In the summer of 1934, a delegation of British businessmen visited Japan to discuss trade. They could make little headway: Japan wanted access to the markets of Britain and her empire, while the delegation were primarily concerned to protect British investment in China and to ensure that British firms got a share of the growing Chinese market.[29] Since Britain had no intention of allowing Japan unfettered trading rights within the empire, it was unlikely that the Japanese would be willing to make concessions to British commerce in China. Nevertheless the delegation returned home convinced that political and trading relations between Britain and Japan could somehow be improved.

One of their number, A.H.F. Edwardes, was a man with a somewhat shady background who was employed from time to time by the Japanese embassy in London to promote informal contact with government departments.[30] For some reason Fisher decided that Edwardes was a reliable authority on Japan and China, and in November 1934 showed him the text of a letter from the highly respected commercial counsellor in Tokyo, G.B. Sansom. This warned that 'we are far more likely to obtain concessions and favours from Japan if we *keep her guessing* than if we relieve her anxieties', and that 'this is not a country to make bargains with, unless they are very favourable, very explicit and very easily enforced.' Fisher remarked: 'Write in "U.S.A." for Japan and I shd. regard the document (it's in any event slightly hysterical) as generally applicable.' Nor was Chamberlain 'impressed by this letter', while Edwardes wrote a point by point memorandum refuting its arguments: he expressed his 'frank opinion that Mr Sansom's letter was written a little unadvisedly.'[31] Fisher later observed that Sansom 'has for the last year or two been disgruntled and labouring under a sense of grievance against the Japanese', and described Orde, the head of the Foreign Office Far Eastern department, as

> a pedantic ass, admirably suited to join the eclectic brotherhood of Oxford or Cambridge. His pedantry is obviously equalled by his quite obvious ignorance of human nature, and at the same time he is obsessed with the fixed idea that original sin is monopolised by Japan, and our only proper attitude is, therefore, never to soil ourselves with such impiety.[32]

Orde was not highly thought of within the Foreign Office, as demonstrated by his eventual posting to Riga.[33] Sansom, however, was rightly considered a great authority on Japan.[34] Fisher's comments on the two can partly be explained by his irritation at the entirely fatalistic and negative attitude which the Foreign Office adopted towards Japan. His words were nevertheless foolish: he was displaying a startling 'ignorance of human nature' himself in treating the equivocal Edwardes and the lightweight Matsudaira as reliable authorities on what Japan really wanted, a reliance which is all the more peculiar when it is recalled that his excellent personal contacts with

American diplomats did not prevent him from advocating an anti-American policy on the grounds that, while their officials might be reasonable men, their politicians were not to be trusted.[35] The conclusion must be that his judgement was impaired by his overwhelming desire to reach a settlement with Japan. This is borne out in the history of the Leith-Ross mission to China.

At the end of 1934, the Chinese requested international aid to help stabilize their currency. Britain gave a friendly refusal, as 'we have felt unable to regard the proposal put forward as being likely to afford any real or lasting remedy to China's monetary difficulties.' Fisher told Chamberlain that this reply offered a chance 'for us all to put our heads together', and that Matsudaira agreed.[36] Edwardes had already said that 'the actual goal to be aimed at by co-operation is clearly the reconstruction of China' by tripartite action from Japan, Britain and America.[37] These sentiments were echoed by Chamberlain's private secretary Donald Fergusson, who urged that a cabinet committee be set up to consider the question as

> it seems quite clear that, if we were to adopt the sort of attitude indicated in the Foreign Office memorandum and allow things to drift, the results might well be incalculable. If we refuse to consult and co-operate with Japan (bringing in America, of course), and China sinks into economic chaos, an isolated Japan may take military measures there, and whether she does so or not what is to happen to our vast trading interests and our employment at home?[38]

Fergusson's question illustrated the contradiction in the Treasury's thinking on China and Japan. The importance of China lay in her potential as an export market, not in her past performance as a purchaser from Britain.[39] An accord with the Japanese was necessary if Britain was to increase her share of the Chinese market, but Japan had nothing to gain by any such arrangement except political goodwill: there was no question of her being allowed to penetrate the markets of the empire in return. In any case, she already controlled much of China, and her interest in that country was not merely one of trade but of military and political domination.

Fisher thought the Japanese were ready to co-operate in saving China's currency, and he pressed for a financial mission to China to accomplish this. He sounded out the ambassadors of interested countries to see if their governments would participate in such a mission, but quickly found that they would not. Nevertheless, it was announced in June 1935 that Sir Frederick Leith-Ross, the misleadingly titled Chief Economic Adviser to the government who was in fact an overseas finance expert, would be going to the Far East for talks with the Chinese and Japanese governments on China's economic difficulties. The Chinese were delighted to have such an important visitor; the Foreign Office, which had been kept largely in the dark by Fisher, was flabbergasted.[40]

Leith-Ross set off in August, travelling to Japan via Canada. The Americans declined a suggestion that he should visit Washington on his way, much to Fisher's relief.[41] He must have been less pleased by what Leith-Ross found in Tokyo, where the Japanese made it clear they would not participate in the proposed action: they were 'genuinely sceptical as to the possibility of any solid reform in China', and the Japanese press was deeply suspicious of his mission.[42] Despite this uncooperative attitude, Leith-Ross went ahead with his plans. The Chinese government accepted his financial advice, and by the end of 1935 had stabilized their currency remarkably successfully.[43] This fiduciary triumph was not at all to Japan's liking, since it strengthened the position of the Chinese government. The British ambassador to China, Sir Alexander Cadogan, pointed out the local political realities to Leith-Ross, who quickly came to see that Japan was not going to change its line. He warned Fisher that 'you are too optimistic in thinking that the passage of time is likely to alter substantially the Japanese policy in China', and his messages clearly had an effect. In July 1936 Fisher wrote that

> while we must accept geography, and therefore a larger degree of Japanese interest, it is quite a different thing to acquiesce in Japanese monopoly or to accept the view that China can for all time be dragooned into 'brotherhood' i.e. subordination by Japan against China's wishes.[44]

The outcome of the Leith-Ross mission was a thorough vindication of the Foreign Office's fatalistic attitude towards Japan. It took some time for the lesson to sink in: Chamberlain gave a friendly welcome to proposals in the latter half of 1936 by

Yoshida, the new Japanese ambassador, aimed at improving relations between Britain and Japan. Yoshida gave offence to the Foreign Office in not approaching it first.[45] More significantly, as Cadogan, by then back in the Foreign Office as Deputy Under Secretary, wrote, he 'is a complete half-wit', who 'agrees with all one says, or says he disagrees with his Govt. But what's the good of that? I'd much sooner deal with a fire-eating Major General.'[46] Nothing came of this initiative except further confusion. In the summer of 1937 came the outbreak of war between China and Japan. Dubbed 'Leithers' war', the only war ever started by a civil servant, by some Treasury officials, it put an end to dreams of Anglo-Japanese co-operation.[47]

There is no doubt that Neville Chamberlain and the Treasury dominated the formation of British foreign policy in the Far East between 1934 and 1937, and that this was somewhat resented in the Foreign Office.[48] Both departments wanted good relations with Japan, but only the Treasury put forward a positive policy. This was a comprehensive failure. Neither Fisher nor Chamberlain appreciated the peculiar political circumstances in Japan, where military influence was growing and not, as Matsudaira told Fisher, declining.[49] As a result, they took the conciliatory attitude of successive Japanese ambassadors to be indicative of how the Tokyo government felt (Hankey fell into the same trap with ambassador Shigemitsu in 1939–41).[50] Besides this, there was a fundamental contradiction between British and Japanese aims: both wanted more trade in the Far East, and the only place where this was possible was China. Since Japan by 1935 controlled much of China, it had nothing substantial to gain by allowing Britain an increased share of the Chinese market. Nor did Japan want the Chinese government strengthened through the stabilization of its currency, since this increased its capacity to resist Japanese expansion. The best that can be said for the Treasury initiative is that it had little effect on Anglo-Japanese relations, while helping China a good deal. But this was not what Fisher and Chamberlain had intended, and they would have done well to pay more attention to what the Foreign Office said about political conditions in Japan. While Yoshida was being pacific and conciliatory in London, the much-maligned Sansom wrote from Tokyo that

we are in the middle of a crisis here, which may develop
into war of a serious kind. At present the Japanese seem
to be crazier than the average of humanity, which is saying
a good deal. They are on the verge of the kind of hysteria
which I remember as a boy, during the early part of the
Boer war. But they are worse off than we were then,
because nobody dare utter an anti-war sentiment.[51]

His prediction of war was fulfilled within a month.

The failure of the Treasury's initiative in the Far East did
not persuade Fisher to alter his view that war with Japan had
to be avoided. In June 1938 he was considerably alarmed by a
proposal which found some favour in London that Britain
should give the Chinese government a loan or credit, in return
for the rights to strategic metals produced by China. He told
Simon and Chamberlain that the issue was

a perfectly clear one — are we prepared to support China
financially in her resistance to Japanese aggression (& to
be of any use the assistance wd. have to be on an effective
scale)? If so we must face the consequences & recognise
that we shall earn the undying hostility of Japan who
sooner or later — perhaps at a time when we are at
death-grips with Germany — will take her revenge. Thus
to risk our country's security, indeed survival, wd. be
nothing short of a crime, equalled only by the folly of it as
... the trumpery odds & ends of help that have been
mentioned simply cannot be a determining factor & cd.
only result in the worst of every world, infuriation of the
Japanese against ourselves & no real benefit to China.

To be effective scores of millions wd. have to be contributed; indeed, except in form, we shd. have to range
ourselves & our resources on the side of China. Do the
protagonists of China favour this? So far all that they have
advocated is backstairs provision of a pittance, useless to
China & provocative to Japan.

Despite this protest, the Cabinet agreed to offer a loan of £5
million if America would agree to participate.[52] Fisher probably overestimated the dangers of such aid, as the Japanese
were already alienated from the western powers. In later years

he acknowledged this in saying that Britain had made a mortal enemy of Japan, at American insistence, in the early 1920s.[53]

III

On 4 March 1935 the government published a White Paper entitled 'Statement Relating to Defence'. It made reference to rearmament by a number of countries, but was clearly directed towards warning the public about the growing danger from Germany.[54] It created a considerable stir in Parliament, where the Labour Party expressed alarm at the government's intention to increase defence expenditure. After his retirement Fisher said

> that in 1935 the Government ... was well informed about the fantastic extent of German rearmament. Yet the Opposition front bench were allowed to know nothing about it. But to tell them would not have been revealing anything to the Germans that they did not know. Had this information been given it would have made a great deal of difference to opinion in the House on both sides ... he had asked the Government's permission to inform the leaders of the Opposition about certain facts. Permission had been refused on the grounds that the information would be misused. His view was that if you distrusted your fellow countryman as much as that, you might as well go Nazi and be done with it.[55]

It is difficult to know whether telling the Labour leaders what the government knew about German rearmament would have made much difference. Although the pacifist George Lansbury was replaced as party leader by Clement Attlee in 1935, the party remained wedded to an outdated internationalism for some years. Hugh Dalton, who was in touch with Vansittart and other Foreign Office men he had known when a junior minister, commented in his diary in July 1936 that 'the Hitler rearmament goes on. Few people in the Labour party seem to know or care anything about it.' Fisher was so struck by this phenomenon that in retirement, 'though he had no great love of Standing Committees of the House of Commons', he thought one should be established on foreign affairs.[56]

Fisher felt that the published White Paper did not convey an adequate warning to the public. Before it appeared, he complained to Baldwin that some of the amendments made to it by the Cabinet 'seem to me to ignore the purpose for which that document was intended', and that

> the consideration which principally influenced those of us who were responsible for suggesting ... a White Paper was that our own British public should be educated as to the vital necessity of putting our defence in order ... We are so convinced (a) of the reality of the danger of war, (b) of the profound ignorance of our own people, (c) of the degree to which they have been misled by so called pacifist propaganda, that we feel that if any document is to serve a useful purpose it must be downright in its expression, and avoid all half-hearted or unconvincing phraseology.
>
> Any document whatsoever, however mealymouthed, if it contains one scintilla of truth cannot fail to tickle up the Germans, who, as we know perfectly well, are set on making themselves the most powerfully armed European state, and are in this mood not for mere display but for action when they think the time has arrived. The choice then seems to be between no document at all if we are to be primarily concerned with foreign and in particular German reactions, and having one which warns our own people in simple, unvarnished language.[57]

Hankey's biographer thought it 'a fair guess' that Hankey 'inspired this protest.'[58] The evidence indicates otherwise. Hankey naturally claimed the credit for the White Paper, telling Liddell Hart 'privately, that he had written' it, 'not J.R[amsay]M[acDonald, the Prime Minister] as signed, nor a collectivity.'[59] However, a year later he told the ambassador to Berlin that 'although I was the author of the rest of the White Paper', as 'I think you know, the passages about which Germany took umbrage ... were inserted against my repeated and emphatic protests.'[60] It was Fisher and Vansittart, not Hankey, who were obsessed with the danger from Germany.

As 1935 progressed, information on German rearmament grew steadily more alarming. Dissatisfaction with the Air Ministry developed correspondingly in Whitehall.[61] In April Chamberlain's private secretary told him that Fisher 'doubts whether the Chiefs of Staff Committee is a suitable body' to consider the air problem, as he felt Ellington of the RAF could not 'hold his own even with his colleagues', and feared they would declare that 'we must have increased naval and military as well as air preparations' immediately. Fergusson concluded by remarking that 'so far as I know, nobody who is acquainted with the Air Ministry has confidence in the present direction of leadership either civil or military', and that it was 'lamentable that we should not have men of the highest calibre at the head of the Air Ministry and the Air Force.'[62] This was apparently a reference to two men, the permanent head of the ministry, Sir Christopher Bullock, and the RAF chief, Ellington. Fergusson's observation may also have been intended to apply to the Secretary of State for Air, Londonderry. He was a vain, querulous and indecisive minister, while Ellington was, in Treasury eyes, hopeless.[63] When pressed by Chamberlain, Baldwin agreed that Londonderry 'will certainly have to be changed', and he was duly replaced by Philip Cunliffe-Lister (referred to hereafter as Swinton) in June 1935.[64] Ellington did not depart until September 1937. Sir Christopher Bullock, dismissed from the civil service in 1936 for a personal indiscretion, as has already been seen, was replaced by Sir Donald Banks, an appointment in which Fisher certainly had a hand.[65] Banks, previously Director General of the Post Office, had a reputation as a good executive, and was said to have impressed Fisher by his work on the war loan conversion in 1932 and the empire air mail scheme three years later.[66] But he was not a success at the Air Ministry, where the political pressure on his minister was intense.[67]

Fisher deserves credit for the many good men whom he spotted and advanced in the public service. He must equally be held responsible for those appointments which were unsuccessful, and it was unfortunate that some of these occurred in the key service ministries in the years leading up to war. Each had an outsider brought in to head them. This worked out well only in the War Office. Banks came to the Air Ministry in 1936 to replace Bullock, but he was pushed aside two years later. Grigg joined the War Office early in 1939 on the retirement of Sir Herbert Creedy, who had been permanent head since 1924. Sir Archibald Carter of the India Office was brought over to the Admiralty by the First Lord Sir Samuel Hoare, after the death of the formidable Sir Oswyn Murray, the permanent head since

1917 and a long-time adversary of Fisher's. Hoare knew Carter well from his own time at the India Office, and he probably asked for him. Fisher thought Carter 'an excellent choice'. Despite his amiable personality, however, Carter never won the full confidence of his new department, where it was felt he never fully understood the navy and its problems.[68]

In the middle of 1935, Chamberlain concluded that Britain would 'have to hurry our rearmament': planning was being overtaken by events.[69] Although they did not dispute the need to rearm, the Treasury's financial experts ensured that the cost and consequences of increased defence spending were not forgotten. In addition to the financial difficulties it imposed, it placed great strain on industry, which had neither the productive capacity nor the skilled labour to absorb the increased demand immediately. Between 1935 and 1939 it fell to the Treasury to tackle these problems in addition to strictly financial questions.

Even within the financial limits set by the government, demand for arms from the three services continually exceeded supply; some form of rationing or system of priorities was required, and the service chiefs had made it clear as early as February 1934 that they were unwilling to provide it themselves.[70] The DRC and, from 1936, the Minister for the Coordination of Defence were able to introduce some order into the planning for expansion of the three services, in terms both of finance and of strategy, but it fell to the Treasury to see how the money was spent, as well as to say what the country could afford. To individual departments it appeared meddlesome and obstructive, but it was the one place where decisions were governed by an overall appreciation of the industrial, financial, economic and strategic consequences of rearmament. The Treasury was damned for its pains by even an intelligent service chief like Chatfield, but the argument that it impeded rearmament has been somewhat undermined in the last decade.[71] In his authoritative study of the question G.C. Peden has put the case for the Treasury, pointing out that

> unanswerable arguments can be advanced by military men for increased armaments, if each service is taken in isolation, and if over-all financial, industrial and political aspects are ignored. The Treasury did not ignore these aspects, and rightly brought them to the attention of those

responsible for policy. Far from being paralysing, the Treasury's use of the power of the purse forced ministers and military men to come to decisions about priorities, and thereby ensured that essential elements in Britain's defences were completed first.[72]

The developing European crisis brought with it calls for the appointment of a Minister of Defence. This was largely the work of men such as Churchill, Trenchard, and Liddell Hart, each of whom imagined himself as the ideal person for the post.[73] Hankey had been fighting off such a development for many years. Fisher wrote a formidable memorandum supporting him, though he thought there was 'one element in the present situation which ... could be usefully dealt with on a purely ad hoc basis ... the organisation of industry so that it can turn over readily and swiftly from peace to war requirements.' This 'particular ad hoc job should be committed to the charge of an outstanding industrialist, who would naturally be Lord Weir', who could 'gather up all the existing threads and convert plans into action; and in everything but name he would be a peace-time Minister of Munitions.' This would be 'quite different' from a minister supervising work already adequately done 'under the aegis' of the CID.[74]

Despite the reservations expressed by Fisher and Hankey, the Cabinet were well aware that some change was a political necessity. In February 1936 Hankey, who had earlier hinted that he might resign over the issue, came up with 'a compromise' whereby the proposed new minister would chair the CID and the chiefs of staff committee but would not interfere with strategic planning.[75] Baldwin was 'satisfied that we must accept this proposal, otherwise we should be swept away'. He offered the post to Chamberlain, who refused it.[76] Instead it went to Sir Thomas Inskip, a political lightweight whose appointment caused some surprise.[77] Despite the fact that some of the officials assigned to help him were not considered particularly able, and that his authority was very limited, Inskip proved his worth over the next two years in adjudicating on interservice disputes and proposing priorities in defence policy.[78] This calls into question the argument of Fisher and Hankey that such an appointment was not really necessary.

In common with most ministers, Fisher took the view that aerial rearmament was the first priority for Britain.[79] The navy was sufficiently well led and supported politically to look after its interests in the face of this assumption, but the army undoubtedly suffered. Until its strategic functions were decided upon, this was inevitable. In the autumn of 1936 Fisher told Chamberlain that 'being an island, and defended by the navy from military invasion, we can concentrate on this new arm [air] to a greater extent than a land power which must in any circumstances maintain a large army'. He said that the army should be brought up to the strength recommended by the DRC in 1935 of about 600,000 men in all, properly trained and equipped, but thought this should be 'our maximum war standard'. He therefore hoped that 'we shall avoid any premature decision about an expeditionary force' until the size of the army had definitely been settled. Even then,

> as to how we may use our army it seems to me that we ought to keep our hands quite free; and the French should be made to understand that we have no intention of military (i.e. army) intervention on the scale of the last war, and that we ourselves must decide how our army can be most usefully employed.[80]

His attitude towards the army changed somewhat once Leslie Hore-Belisha became Secretary of State for War in May 1937. Hore-Belisha was a talkative and impetuous man, whose judgement did not always match his enthusiasm for reform.[81] Soon Fisher, who thought him 'brilliant', was 'in H-B's pocket.'[82] The most tangible fruit of their friendship was contained in the report of a committee on conditions of service of officers in the defence services. The committee was chaired by Fisher, who led it firmly to the conclusions he had suggested at the outset: as a result, the pay of army officers was brought into line with that of their counterparts in the other services, half pay was abolished and the retirement age was lowered.[83] These changes enabled Hore-Belisha to pension off unwanted generals and promote new men, and in the long term provided a greatly improved career structure for all ranks of officers.

While Hore-Belisha's rapport with Fisher probably produced other benefits for the War Office, Fisher's views on the army remained broadly unchanged. While by 1939 he did not object to the principle of sending troops to aid France in the event of war, he maintained that the army's first duty was to provide adequate anti-aircraft defences for Britain. He also expected that one of the main jobs of an expeditionary force would be to defend airfields from which bombers would operate against Germany — after the war he commented that 'no one cd. have foreseen that ... France wd. collapse in 4 or 5 weeks & thus we shd. lose bomber bases in that country.'[84] In retirement he also argued that 'from our point of view, in matters of defence, the army was a second stage weapon: the initial weapons were sea power and air power. So ... in order of preparation, the navy and air force, in the first period of war, came before the army.'[85]

Fisher's views on aerial strategy changed a good deal between 1934 and 1938. In 1935 he sat on a CID sub-committee on air defence research, and Swinton subsequently 'cultivated' him 'to great effect in connection with the development of radar', the defensive possibilities of which the Treasury were very quick to see.[86] Two years later he was a member of another committee which looked at air raid precautions. By that time he had lost faith in the concept of bombers as the first line of defence. Although he still accepted the Trenchard doctrine that a war could rapidly be won by mass bombing, he became convinced that in a conflict Germany would be much better placed than Britain to carry out such attacks. Furthermore, although he was still on good terms with Trenchard, described by a disgruntled admiral as 'that evil genius of imperial defence ... and arch intriguer', he no longer believed that a large British bomber force would be an effective deterrent to Germany. In addition, he and the Treasury were well aware that the aircraft industry was incapable of meeting the RAF's ever-growing demands. It followed that Britain should concentrate on defending herself from the German air force, and should build up her strength with this in mind. He wrote to the Chancellor in December 1937:

> Our policy ... should be to concentrate in the first days or weeks on smashing the morale of the German pilots on their way to and over England, bringing down say 20% each attack instead of the 3% thought of by the Air Staff. We could at the same time be dropping a certain amount of bombs on Germany to keep her interested. But let us

attack and down the attackers first, and subsequently we can do more and more to agitate the civil population of Germany.

He maintained that 'because individuals may wear a uniform and are called e.g. the Air Staff, it does not follow that they are infallible guides. In regard to major principles experienced laymen have a role to play.'[87] Two months later he wrote that 'my military colleagues of all three Defence Services desire our survival as much as I do; but they are just as fallible as I am, the difference being that my fallibility and their supposed infallibility are both exaggerated.'[88] In April 1938 he wrote to the Prime Minister accusing the Air Ministry of doling out 'soothing-syrup and incompetence in equal measure', adding that 'for the first time in centuries our country is (and must continue to be) at the mercy of a foreign power.'[89] He warned the American ambassador that 'Germany is building an air force designed to demolish London in one fell swoop', and that the war would be decided 'within thirty days.'[90]

Fisher's attacks on the Air Ministry were understandable but not entirely fair. Apart from anything else, he bore some responsibility for the state of affairs in the ministry. As has been seen he had introduced Sir Donald Banks into the department, an appointment which had not worked out, although by the same token he installed Sir Arthur Street, 'a triumphant success', as deputy head two years later.[91] Aerial rearmament progressed at a very disappointing pace for a number of reasons, many of which he appeared to ignore in the very crude measures of output which he used. In fact he made much the same error as he lambasted the air staff for: equating quantity with strength. The successive expansion schemes approved by the Cabinet from 1934 on took insufficient account of industry's capacity to produce, and they placed a premium on aircraft numbers rather than on quality and improved designs. The Air Ministry faced acute difficulties in its dealings with the aircraft industry, where many manufacturers saw the sudden rush of orders partly as an opportunity to recoup losses made in the lean years of the 1920s and were not inclined to risk money on developing new aircraft.

Where Fisher had most grounds for complaint was this: the RAF clung to the view that its main role would be offensive, and it consistently favoured expansion of its bomber strength over fighters even when the bombers being built were already obsolescent and modern fighter designs were available. When, at the height of the Munich crisis, the RAF suddenly requested clearance for an order of one thousand Hurricane fighters, Fisher assented at once, commenting that he hoped it implied that the air force was 'seriously reconsidering the relationship between bombers and fighters from the point of view of this country being the aggressee.'[92] Two months later, after it became clear that the air staff had ignored the recommendation of the Inskip report on defence priorities that they should give increased priority to fighter production, the Cabinet issued directions that bomber production be restricted, 'a victory in principle for the Treasury.' Fisher continued to take on the Air Ministry, querying its technical evaluation of a new heavy bomber, but he made no headway.[93] As it happens, he was right about the new bomber, the Stirling, which proved an unsatisfactory fighting aircraft once it went into action.

Fisher's importance in relation to aerial rearmament was threefold: as a member of the CID and, until 1937, as a trusted adviser to Neville Chamberlain, he was able to press his views on the necessity of giving aerial rearmament priority; as head of the Treasury he was able to ensure that his department played a constructive part in the expansion of the RAF; and from 1937, when he became convinced that defence against air attack was the first priority for the RAF, he played an important part in getting the air staff to order enough modern fighters.

Unlike the Air Ministry, the Admiralty encountered relatively little criticism from Fisher. Once his hopes of a rapprochement with Japan evaporated, some of the strength went out of his arguments against the navy's long felt desire for a two-power standard.[94] The Admiralty in fact got most of what it wanted, within the financial and industrial constraints common to the three services. In 1937, the Fleet Air Arm controversy was finally settled when the government decided to transfer control to the navy, a decision which Fisher supported; his friend Chatfield, the First Sea Lord, had earlier nominated him 'as a perfectly impartial person' to act as an arbitrator in the dispute.[95] The Admiralty's major problems in building up the navy's strength after 1933 arose not from want of cash but from a shortage of raw materials and of industrial capacity. Duff Cooper's much publicized attack on the Treasury in 1938, after his resignation as First Lord of the Admiralty, was a characteristically confused business: what was at issue was not lack of money, but the rationing of existing industrial productive capacity between the three armed services, a task which had to be done no matter what funds were available.[96]

There can be no doubt that Fisher played a considerable part in the formation of British defence policy from 1933 onwards. At least until 1937 he had the ear of Chamberlain, the most powerful member of the government. He also had the weight of his department behind him, since it fell to the Treasury to advise on the cost and the consequences of rearmament. As Head of the Civil Service he regarded himself as on a par with the heads of the three defence services — in his final advice to Chamberlain in May 1939 he suggested the inclusion 'in the Chiefs of Staff Sub-Committee of the C.I.D.' of 'the official Head of the Civil Service' — and he believed that civil just as much as military servants of the crown had national defence responsibilities.[97] It is not surprising that he became involved in defence questions; what is striking is that his appreciation of what Britain would need to avoid defeat in a war with Germany was, sometimes in contrast to the assumptions of the heads of the fighting services, from 1933 onwards fundamentally sound.

IV

In his memoirs, Anthony Eden said that when he was Foreign Secretary in 1935 Fisher had claimed that recommendations for senior posts abroad had to be submitted through him to the Prime Minister for approval. Eden complained to Baldwin and Chamberlain, and 'after a few more exchanges, it was finally accepted that the appointments were my own and I could show them to the Prime Minister if I wished, before submitting them to the King.'[98]

This story had often been used against Fisher, and it merits examination. In the first place, it must be asked whether Fisher took any interest in the appointment of ambassadors to key missions abroad. He did, but Eden's imputation that Fisher wanted to advance appeasers and pro-Germans is nonsense. Next, it should be asked whether there is any evidence that Fisher played or sought to play any formal part in the appointment of ambassadors, and the answer, Eden's story apart, is that there is not, although it is highly likely that he expressed strong opinions as to who should go where. It is also worth recalling that Eden's predecessor, Sir Samuel Hoare, wrote of Fisher that 'I am ... certain that while I was Foreign Secretary, there was no foundation for the charge that he interfered in the administration of the Office, still less that he dictated foreign policy to anyone.'[99]

Eden's memoirs are by no means accurate about Fisher, and the most likely explanation of the story above is that he confused two separate issues, the appointment of ambassadors, where Fisher had no power, and top appointments in the Foreign Office itself, where he had. Eden made other charges about Fisher in his memoirs which are similarly difficult to verify. In attacking Fisher he perpetuated the idea that during the late 1930s the Foreign Office (and himself) were hemmed in on every side by appeasers in government and in Whitehall. He was on safe ground in making his allegations, since by the time his book appeared the charges of Selby, Ashton-Gwatkin, Legge-Bourke and Elibank had long been in circulation. He traded gratuitously on Fisher's controversial reputation to protect his own, in such a way that he did not have to make any general and contestable statement about Fisher's relations with the Foreign Office. It also helped him to slide around an embarrassing fact. From the autumn of 1936 on he had been trying to rid himself of Vansittart, his Permanent Under Secretary, who even more than Eden, and with more justice, became 'the hero of the anti-appeasers.'[100]

When Sir Eric Phipps was appointed ambassador to Paris in 1937, Fisher told him:

> Wonders never cease, do they? You know what I've thought was right from the day of W[illiam] T[yrrell]'s departure. And I have cursed and expostulated in vain. Suddenly when I had almost decided to give up hope, they belatedly and surprisingly have done the obvious thing. You really have nothing to credit me with, for normally if the Foreign Office think I think a thing is right, they do the opposite![101]

Hankey was less modest, telling Phipps on the same day that 'it is always a delicate business for me to butt in in this kind of thing ... But I adopted a steady policy for months, if not years, in carefully sowing the seed and tending it as it neared the moment of possible harvest.'[102]

Fisher's comments to Phipps reflected his discontent with the Foreign Office. Following the fiasco of the Hoare–Laval pact in December 1935, it had been expected that Vansittart, who was 'regarded as the villain of the piece' for his precipitancy, would be sent abroad when a suitable replacement for him as head of the department could be found. Fisher would barely speak to Vansittart for some time after this debacle. Vansittart eventually learnt that this was due not to the outcome of the talks in Paris but to the fact that he had carelessly allowed himself to be photographed in a chair while his minister was standing beside him.[103] Hankey told Phipps that there had been 'a tendency to "head-hunt" over Sam Hoare's escapade in Paris', and that Vansittart was under pressure. 'Warren Fisher and I and other friends will stand by him', but 'after a decent interval, it may be thought that a change would be beneficial.'[104]

The return of Sir Alexander Cadogan from China to be Deputy Under Secretary and heir apparent, an appointment which Fisher reluctantly agreed to on the understanding that Sir Robert Craigie would also be promoted to an additional post at that rank to 'bolster' Cadogan, increased the likelihood of Vansittart departing.[105] There were various rumours about a successor, including one that Fisher wanted to install Leith-Ross, but Vansittart remained.[106] Fisher sent Chamberlain an indignant note on the matter in September 1936:

> What I'm going to tell you is surprising enough, but there's nothing, at all events for the moment, requiring intervention.
>
> You will remember that (? in July) Halifax, you, S.B., H.J. [Sir Horace Wilson] & I had talks about the Foreign Office, Anthony Eden coming in a day or two later. The outcome was nil, & the matter went into cold storage. Now, if you please, Anthony gets hold of Van last Friday, informs him that it is vital to have at Paris an outstanding figure, tells Van he is the man, offers him a Peerage, & adds that the proposal ... has the support of the P.M.
>
> What of course is clear is (1) that after Van's recent outing in Germany (Van has been a fortnight in Germany & Eric Phipps tells me — as well as Van himself — that the

German theory of Van's *personal* hostility has been corrected) & establishment of agreeable personal relations with Hitler & Co., the immediate removal of Van from the F.O. wd. be interpreted in Germany as disapproval by H.M.G. of this personal improvement; this interpretation wd. be strengthened by his transfer to Paris in view of Van's previous reputation in Germany as pro-French.

(2) Paris is at present of no real importance, whereas Berlin (& Rome) are.

The fact is that the German visit of Van's must inevitably *postpone* the reform of the F.O., tho' my views about the need remain unchanged.

I see in all this the hand of Alec Cadogan who is anxious to become Permanent Under Secretary ... himself; & Anthony — who is & always will be very light metal — has been party to the folly of providing us with the worst of every world.

Van has definitely refused Paris, as he sees thro' Anthony's motive.

None of us can at present endorse any change at the F.O. for some appreciable time, for the German reason I've already mentioned. But when the time comes Alec Cadogan is out of the question; and if nothing else will prevent it, I shall have to ask the Government to put me there, tho' this wd. mean a step down in rank for me & a loss of £500 a year. These two things wd. not affect my peace of mind; what I shd. dislike wd. be the divorce from my present colleagues, surroundings & job.[107]

It can be seen from this that it is absurd to write of 'Eden, robbed of the support, help and advice of Vansittart.'[108] Eden was, on the contrary, more anxious than Chamberlain, Baldwin or Fisher to get Vansittart out quickly, a fact which he managed to gloss over in his memoirs where he omitted to mention that he offered Vansittart the Paris embassy in the autumn of 1936.[109] Of Fisher's extraordinary suggestion that he should become head of the Foreign Office himself there is not much that can be said in extenuation of its foolishness: assuming he was serious, it appears to be what Sir Samuel Hoare called 'one of the occasions when his judgement went off at a tangent.'[110] By the late 1930s these were quite frequent.

In his memoirs Eden also recounts how, in May 1937, his newly appointed Parliamentary Private Secretary, J.P.L. Thomas, had a conversation with Fisher and Sir Horace Wilson. In the course of this they expressed their dissatisfaction with Vansittart because of his obsessive anti-German outlook, and his reluctance to make overtures to the dictator states, said his influence over Eden was too great, and told Thomas they hoped he would be a 'bridge' between the Foreign Office and Downing Street.[111] This is a very puzzling episode. It is quite likely that both Fisher and Wilson spoke of the desirability of moving Vansittart out — as has been seen, Eden had tried to do so himself nine months before — but Eden's imputation, that Fisher was anxious to rid the Foreign Office of an anti-appeaser, is simply not tenable. Fisher equalled Vansittart in his mistrust both of Germany and of arguments that she could be accommodated without a complete abrogation of Britain's responsibilities as a democratic country. However, he thought that Vansittart had burnt himself out as Permanent Under Secretary, and that he was no longer fully in control of his department.

Vansittart eventually departed in December 1937, when he accepted the new post of Chief Diplomatic Adviser to the government. Fisher told Chamberlain that 'I've just had over an hour's talk with Van's wife', who was 'against a peerage, but for a GCB as something which would appeal to Van & be favourably noticed abroad.' She went off 'to impress on Van that, if his country is his creed, he will prove it by undertaking his new post in the spirit of service.'[112] Vansittart told Hugh Dalton a few months later that Eden 'had been trying to edge him out for a long time', had 'been jealous of him, thinking he had too much of the lime light', and had 'brought back Cadogan from China with the object' of making him head of the Foreign Office.[113]

This evidence contradicts the many claims later made that Vansittart was removed because his influence over Eden was too great, and that Fisher in trying to get him out was seeking to convert the Foreign Office to a policy of appeasement.[114] Vansittart's memoirs describe Fisher as 'the best friend that I ever had in adversity, less good in better days. We do less than justice to our kind in supposing that fortune attracts solicitude', an apparent reference to their falling out in the 1940s. He dismissed the claims of improper interference in the Foreign

Office, commenting that Fisher had been 'a great public servant ignorantly traduced by small fry', observations which his first biographer, the journalist Ian Colvin, chose to ignore.[115]

Vansittart was replaced by Eden's man Cadogan, to whom Fisher was bitterly opposed. Fisher's prejudice against him was based less on an estimation of his abilities than on the fear that as head of the Foreign Office he would seek to distance it from the home civil service, whereas Fisher favoured integration. Cadogan had no time for Fisher's belief that foreign policy could no longer be left to the Foreign Office: as ambassador in China, he had had personal experience of the Treasury's ineptitude in wooing Japan. Nevertheless, he was willing to discuss reform; shortly before he took over, he

> had 'tea' with Warren Fisher. He was trying to put across me [a] Committee of investigation (or 'overhaul') in F.O. I cdn't. commit myself. He suggests himself, me, Creedy, Hankey & Horace Wilson. I don't mind but said I was a newcomer, & might want support from my Service & suggested an ex-Ambassador. He suggested W[illiam] T[yrrell] & I agreed in principle. (He's a slippery customer!).[116]

Four months later, Cadogan brought up the question of a committee again, but by then Fisher was in retreat. Although 'all in favour' of exploring the question of Foreign Office reorganization, Fisher felt it needed a committee 'with a somewhat wider membership than you suggest'. He also had the 'feeling that, by reason of the very many urgent matters claiming attention at the moment ... the setting up of the Committee' should be left 'until the end of this year or the beginning of the next.'[117] Having thus called Fisher's bluff, Cadogan proceeded unilaterally with his plans for his department, and in 1941 succeeded in obtaining Cabinet approval for reform entirely on the lines that he favoured: the diplomatic and consular services and the Foreign Office were eventually merged into a single foreign service entirely separate from the home civil service.[118] This was a comprehensive victory for him, and is ample proof of the bureaucratic skills which helped to make him a success as the head of his department.

Despite his complaints about the inertia of the Foreign Office, Fisher seems to have had little to say on British policy towards Europe. There was no Treasury initiative there as there had been in the Far East, although he took some interest in 1937 in the proposed cession of African territories to Germany in return for restraint in Europe.[119] He assumed that Germany and Britain would eventually fight, but favoured putting off the evil day until the country was prepared. He had little faith in the League of Nations, as was shown in his advice in the summer of 1935, after Italy had been successfully courted at Stresa, a triumph for Vansittart over the hesitancy of his minister Sir John Simon.[120] In June, the Anglo-German naval agreement was concluded, a pact which Vansittart and Fisher both thought satisfactory.[121] Britain's Stresa allies, France and Italy, expressed alarm at the agreement, but their new-found accord was more gravely damaged by the Abyssinian crisis. Fisher thought it futile and dangerous to contemplate armed intervention, asking whether Britain was 'really prepared not merely to threaten but to use force, and is she in a position to do so effectively?' If she did, would it be for the sake of the League of Nations, or because of Britain's African interests? If the former, why had it not taken action against Japan on behalf of China in 1931? He felt that 'the threat or use of force in the present emergency has nothing to commend it', and that Britain should concentrate on seeking a peaceful settlement between the warring countries. Britain 'cannot make the League a reality by spasmodic resort to force where we think it may safely be applied; that only serves as evidence that we refrain from force whenever it is too dangerous.'[122]

This memorandum was a fair reflection of opinion throughout Whitehall — indeed it was stating the obvious. The government took the same line, and contented themselves with supporting the protests of the League. A committee under Fisher was appointed to consider the question of economic sanctions, which the League was expected to call for once Italy actually invaded Abyssinia. The committee found little to commend in most of the measures discussed: it was unlikely that central European countries would observe any prescribed sanctions for long, and it was feared that Britain's export trade would suffer. Furthermore, Italy was believed to have 'considerable reserves of all strategic materials, sufficient to maintain a war of limited effort for several months without further imports.'[123] Fisher said in 1944 that his committee had been told that any sanctions imposed must not be too severe or some great powers, such as the U.S.A. or Germany, might not play. It was obvious that a true economic blockade must be worldwide to be effective, but what actually happened was that the pundits of the departments had thought up some rotten little sanctions, which might have begun to tickle Italy in about three years' time. Then the question of an effective sanction, oil, came up. It was not correct that it was really United States opposition that prevented it: in fact she was not consulted but it was just assumed that she would not agree. Our own Government itself had run away from the imposition of sanctions.[124]

While it is true that Chamberlain was advised that oil sanctions would be 'rapid and decisive in their effect', it is an open question whether Fisher actually favoured their adoption.[125] Hankey told Hoare that 'all the official world outside the F.O. (and many within it) are against sanctions, and especially the oil sanctions.'[126] In any event, the government chose to pursue a settlement through the more traditional ways of secret diplomacy, and the Hoare–Laval pact was the eventual result.

Fisher played a considerable part in improving Anglo-Irish relations in the late 1930s. As we have seen, he had strong sympathies for Irish nationalism. He kept in close touch with the Irish High Commissioner in London, J.W. Dulanty, who had briefly served in the Treasury in 1920.[127] Relations between the departmental Treasury and the Irish finance ministry were also good, despite the economic dispute between the two countries, and there is little doubt that this had some bearing on British policy. Fisher pushed consistently for generous treatment of southern Ireland, and he resisted financial concessions to Ulster which he felt would decrease the likelihood of eventual Irish unity.[128] In September 1936 Fisher, Horace Wilson, and Harding of the Dominions Office had talks with Dulanty on the shape of de Valera's proposed new constitution. Fisher emphasized the government's friendly attitude towards Ireland, but was unable to get any concessions from Dulanty, who could give no 'satisfactory reply' to his question of 'what was the use of [de Valera] ... having a provision in his new Constitution inviting Northern Ireland to come in, if the form of the Constitution was such that it was certain they would never come in?'[129] Fisher reported that there was 'no hope' of dissuading de Valera from doing as he wished, and complained that the talks had been 'a very imperfect method of negotiation' because the British officials were unclear how far their government would go to meet Mr de Valera's requests for help in promoting Irish unity in return for concessions in his new constitution.[130]

When the 1938 Anglo-Irish agreement was being negotiated, his sympathies were again apparent: angered by the attitude of the Northern Ireland government, he wrote that 'blackmail & bluff (oddly enough called "loyalty") have for many years been the accepted methods of Northern Ireland. It is high time these parochial die-hards were made to face up to a touch of reality.' He also mentioned 'the present wholly uneconomic partition.'[131] At a delicate point in the negotiations Fisher arrived unannounced one night at the hotel of John Leydon, the secretary of the Irish Department of Industry and Commerce. In a midnight walk in Green Park he asked Leydon what the Irish government would actually settle for, and these were the terms eventually agreed.[132] The agreement was of some strategic significance for Britain, since it deprived the navy of the southern Irish ports — a point much emphasised by Winston Churchill.[133] In 1938, and again in 1945, Fisher made it clear he thought the concession worthwhile, on grounds of security as well as justice:

> Eire's neutrality was easily explained. If Mr de Valera had come in against German tyranny, he would have had a civil war on his hands and we should have had a quarter of a million fewer fighting men .... Mr de Valera's detestation of Prussianism was as great as anyone's: but there was the 20% minority which would cause trouble.[134]

V

Fisher was a better defence planner than he was a diplomat: that much is clear from his career. P.J. Grigg has written that by 1934 Fisher 'had already become alarmed — indeed almost obsessed — with the dangers of the growing German rearmament.' Thereafter he 'took less and less interest in his proper Treasury functions.'[135] This is somewhat unfair: he had always been interested in defence questions, and as Head of the Civil

Service he had never failed to speak his mind on general issues.[136] He concentrated on defence after 1933 because that was the great problem with which the government was faced.

It could be argued further that he was discharging his 'proper Treasury functions' to an unusual degree. He previously had little to contribute to economic and financial policy other than support for his experts, whereas on rearmament he gave a definite lead to the Treasury: Britain had at all costs to be able to defend itself against its enemies. This basic assumption had a profound influence on his department.[137] Equally important was his influence on defence strategy; it was not that he always got his way, or that he was always right, but that he continually challenged the assumptions of service chiefs, ministers and officials, and forced them to think about policy and priorities. Professor Watt's judgement that 'Fisher, Air Marshal Dowding and Sir Robert Watson-Watt's radar saved Britain in 1940' may seem rather sweeping, but there is no doubt that, in one way or another, he did a great deal to prepare Britain for war.[138]

Fisher had little influence on foreign policy, the Leith-Ross mission apart. Like Vansittart, his views were straightforward in the extreme: at some time in the future, Britain and Germany would fight. The Treasury's attempts to reach an understanding with Japan were based on this assumption. The Leith-Ross mission achieved precisely the opposite of what was intended, and it was an infringement on traditional Foreign Office preserves. But it should be said that the Foreign Office itself had no positive policy to offer, and that for most of its officials, including Vansittart, the Far East seemed scarcely to exist.[139] Fisher was regarded with some suspicion by the Foreign Office, it is true, but this had little to do with foreign policy. He was rightly believed to want to bring the department within the domestic civil service fold, was known to have a poor opinion of many of its senior staff, and took no trouble to disguise this.[140] In the 1930s it was his personality and his methods, not his views on foreign policy, which aroused hostility.

Notes

1. Quoted in Roskill, *Hankey*, iii, 90; Fisher to Chamberlain, 1 Oct. 1938, Fisher papers; CID minutes, 9 Nov. 1933, CAB 2/6; Fisher to Chatfield, 18 Mar. 1945, Warren Fisher papers.
2. Fisher memoir, Chapter 13 (continued).
3. Peden, *British Rearmament*, p. 8; Wesley Wark, 'Intelligence prediction and strategic surprise: reflections on the British experience in the 1930s', in Robertson (ed.) *British and American Approaches to Intelligence*, pp. 93–5.
4. Fisher to Chatfield, 18 Mar. 1945, Warren Fisher papers; Bond, *Pownall Diary*, i, 24–5, 14 Nov. 1933.
5. Peden, *British Rearmament*, p. 32; Sir Folliott Sandford to the author, 11 Oct. 1981.
6. DRC minutes, 4 Dec. 1933, and memorandum by Fisher, 17 Feb. 1934, CAB 16/109.
7. Note by Hankey, 10 Nov. 1933, circulating an extract from a memorandum by Sir George Milne, 28 Oct. 1932, CAB 16/109.
8. DRC minutes, 4 Dec. 1933, ibid.
9. ibid.; Bond, *Pownall Diary*, i, 34, 18 Jan. 1934.
10. ibid., p. 36, 15 Feb. 1934.
11. Hankey to Baldwin, 23 Aug. 1934, Baldwin papers, 1/40–7.
12. Minutes of RIIA British security group, 3 Apr. 1944.
13. Vansittart, *Mist Procession*, p. 443.
14. Bond, *Pownall Diary*, i, 37, 28 Feb. 1934; Roskill, *Naval Policy*, ii, 168. For Hankey's economic views, see his letter to MacDonald, 5 Apr. 1933, PREM 1/152, in which he complains that while Britain was neglecting Singapore it spent money on 'roads used mainly for joy-riding, swimming baths, recreation grounds, town halls, and artificially anticipated works of various kinds (such as the sewerage works in my own Parish)'.
15. Hankey diary, 4 Mar. 1934.
16. Peden, *British Rearmament*, pp. 6–8, 119.
17. ibid., p. 9.
18. Sankey diary, 25 Apr.; Chamberlain diary, 25 Mar. 1935.
19. Fisher to Chatfield, 11 July 1934, Baldwin papers, 131/189–97.
20. Chatfield to Fisher, 16 July 1934, ibid., 131/99–203.
21. Chamberlain diary, 25 Oct. 1934.
22. Draft cabinet memorandum by Chamberlain, Sept. 1934. It was not circulated as he and Simon agreed to submit a joint one instead, NC 8/18/1.
23. Fisher to Simon, 30 Oct. 1934, National Maritime Museum, Chatfield papers, CHT 3/2/17–19.
24. Fisher to Chamberlain, 12 Nov. 1934, ibid., CHT 3/2/27–29.
25. Stuart, *Reith Diaries*, p. 211, 23 June 1936; Craigie to Templewood, 4 Oct. 1954, Templewood papers, xix (14).
26. Interview with R.W. Fisher. Fisher later spoke of Standley as his 'friend', minutes of RIIA British security group, 13 Nov. 1944. There is nothing concerning him directly in Standley's papers in the University of Southern California.

27. Berg, 'Admiral William H. Standley', p. 225.

28. Fisher to Chatfield, 1 Jan. 1935, Chatfield papers, CHT 3/2/31. There is no trace of his activities at the conference in the British delegation's records in CAB 29/157, but his son says he played a considerable part and that Craigie, the chief British negotiator, looked to him for instructions. Interview with R.W. Fisher.

29. Trotter, *East Asia*, pp. 119–22.

30. ibid., pp. 117, 192; Endicott, *Diplomacy*, p. 74.

31. Copy of Sansom to Crowe (Department of Overseas Trade), 12 Oct. 1934, PRO 30/69/273; notes by Fisher, Chamberlain, and Edwardes, 17, 19, and 26 Nov. 1934, T172/1831.

32. Fisher to Neville Chamberlain, 15 and 21 Jan. 1935, ibid.

33. Cadogan diary, 30 June 1937, C.C.C., Cadogan papers, ACAD 1/6; Eden to Halifax, 1 Aug. 1937, Halifax papers, A4/410/21. Endicott, *Diplomacy*, p. 80, says Orde was Fisher's 'one-time protégé', because Fisher was 'responsible for civil service appointments and promotions.' This is wrong: the only posts Fisher had a formal say in were those listed in the circular of 12 Mar. 1920.

34. Hall-Patch (a Treasury man who worked overseas as an attaché and adviser) to Clark-Kerr, 18 Nov. 1938, Inverchapel papers, unsorted. Clark-Kerr had just been appointed ambassador to Japan. Sansom subsequently received a knighthood for his services.

35. See Chapter 5, p. 158 above.

36. Fisher to Chamberlain, 21 Jan. 1935, T172/1831.

37. Note by Edwardes, 14 Jan. 1935, ibid.

38. Note by Fergusson, 15 Jan. 1935, ibid.

39. Trotter, *East Asia*, p. 18; Endicott, *Diplomacy*, p. 19

40. Trotter, ibid., pp. 141, 147. From 1932 Leith-Ross held the post of Chief Economic Adviser to the government, with offices in both the Treasury and the Board of Trade, but for practical purposes he remained a Treasury official.

41. Note by Fisher, 18 July 1935, T160 619/F14233/1.

42. Trotter, *East Asia*, p. 166; Leith-Ross to Fisher, 11 Nov. and 29 Dec. 1935, T188/118 and 122.

43. Trotter, ibid., p. 166.

44. Note by Fisher, 31 July 1936, T188/118.

45. Agbi, 'Yoshida's bid for rapprochement', pp. 173–5.

46. Cadogan (now deputy head of the Foreign Office) to Knatchbull-Hugessen (his successor in China), 28 Jan. 1937, Knatchbull-Hugessen papers 2/46; Cadogan diary, 14 Dec. 1936, ACAD 1/5. For Chamberlain's view of Yoshida, see his diary, 25 Oct. 1936.

47. Sir Edward Playfair to the author, 27 Apr. 1981.

48. Wellesley to Ashton-Gwatkin, 11 Sept. 1942, Selby papers. Despite his Treasury links, Leith-Ross was popular with Foreign Office officials, including Cadogan.

49. Chamberlain diary, 25 Oct. 1934.

50. Roskill, *Hankey*, iii, 41–51, 515–16.

51. Sansom to Pethick-Lawrence, 10 July 1937, Trinity College, Cambridge, Pethick-Lawrence papers, P-L 3/184.

52. Fisher to Simon and Chamberlain, 18 June 1938, PREM 1/303. Leith-Ross was in favour of such a loan.

53. Minutes of RIIA British security group, 17 Apr. 1944; Fisher, 'Civil defence', p. 212.

54. Statement relating to defence, *PP* (1934–5), xiii, 803.

55. Minutes of RIIA British security group, 1 Jan. 1945.

56. Dalton diary, 27 July 1936; minutes of RIIA British security group, 17 Apr. 1944.

57. Fisher to Baldwin, 26 Feb. 1935, Baldwin papers, 1/80 a–c.

58. Roskill, *Hankey*, iii, 149.

59. Liddell Hart diary, 25 Mar. 1935, Liddell Hart papers, 11/1935/67.

60. Hankey to Phipps, 14 Feb. 1936, Phipps papers, PHPP 3/51/2.

61. Sargent to Phipps, 26 Apr. 1935, PHPP 2/10; Liddell Hart's note of a talk with Duff Cooper (Secretary of State for War), 14 Dec. 1935, Liddell Hart papers 11/1935/115.

62. Fergusson to Chamberlain, 27 Apr. 1935, T172/1830.

63. Bond, *Pownall Diary*, i, 14, 6 Apr. 1933.

64. Fisher thought very highly of Swinton. Interview with Sir Thomas and Lady Padmore. Neville Chamberlain diary, 29 Apr. 1935.

65. See pp. 206–15 above. On Bullock's reputation, see also Grigg (in India) to Trenchard, 22 Apr. 1935, Hankey papers, HNKY 4/27; Roskill, *Naval Policy*, i, 381, and 385, mentions Bullock's attitude towards the navy during the 1920s.

66. Interview with Sir James Dunnett; Findlater Stewart (India Office) to Grigg, 20 Feb. 1936, Grigg papers, PJGG 2/20/24.

67. Sir Folliott Sandford to the author, 11 Oct. 1981.

68. Fisher to Baldwin, 18 July 1936, T162 540/E1518. Sir Richard Powell and Sir Clifford Jarrett to the author, both 22 Oct., and Sir John Laing to the author, 3 Nov. 1981.

69. Chamberlain diary, 2 Aug. 1935.

70. Hankey to MacDonald, 3 Mar. 1934, PREM 1/153.

71. Peden, *British Rearmament*, passim; Parker, 'Treasury, trade unions and skilled labour', pp. 306–43.

72. Peden, ibid., p. 184.

73. Shay, *Politics and Profits*, pp. 67–9.

74. Fisher to Baldwin, 13 Jan. 1936, PREM 1/196. Fisher thought Weir a paragon of industrial wisdom.

75. Bond, *Pownall Diary*, i, 100, 3 Feb. 1936; Hankey to Baldwin, 14 Feb. 1936, PREM 1/196. There may have been an element of personal animosity in the campaign for a minister of defence, as some felt Hankey was too powerful. On 19 Jan. 1936 Chamberlain noted that he 'does not scruple to put down as conclusions of our committee [considering the third report of the DRC] what he would like us to decide instead of what we have decided. I have had to express my dissent from some of his "conclusions" today.' Chamberlain diary.

76. Chamberlain diary, 16 Feb. 1935.

77. Roskill, *Hankey*, iii, 207.

78. He was, accordingly, indignant to be moved sideways to make way for Chatfield in January 1939. Inskip diary, 17 Jan. 1939, Caldecote papers 2.

79. Fisher to Chamberlain, 1 Oct. 1938, Warren Fisher papers.

80. Fisher to Chamberlain, 23 Oct. 1936, ibid;. See also Peden, *British Rearmament*, pp. 127–8.

81. Hore-Belisha to Chamberlain, 3 Dec. 1937, Chamberlain papers, NC 7/11/30/80.

82. H.R.G. Greaves to J.V. Wilson, 26 Jan. 1944, RIIA archives, 9/32a; Grigg to Sir Findlater Stewart (India Office), 2 Jan. 1938, Grigg Papers, PJGG 2/20/33. Hore-Belisha had been Financial Secretary to the Treasury from 1932 to 1934, when he became Minister of Transport.

83. Minutes of the 'Warren Fisher committee' 1938, T162 478/E5479/01; the report is in PREM 1/288. For the debilitating effects on the inter-war army of half pay etc., see Bond, *British Military Policy*, pp. 44–55. He does not mention the Warren Fisher committee, giving all the credit to Hore-Belisha and Liddell Hart.

84. Peden, *British Rearmament*, pp. 144–6; marginal note by Fisher on Fisher to Chamberlain, 23 Oct. 1936, Warren Fisher papers.

85. Minutes of RIIA British security group, 20 Mar. 1944.

86. Sir Folliott Sandford to the author, 11 Oct. 1981; Peden, *British Rearmament*, p. 29; Cross, *Swinton*, p. 176; Clark, *Tizard*, p. 129.

87. Keyes to Chatfield, 7 Feb. 1937, Chatfield papers, CHT 2/7/126–32; Fisher to Simon, 18 Dec. 1937, Warren Fisher papers.

88. Fisher's note on the Inskip report, 15 Feb. 1938, ibid.

89. Fisher to Chamberlain, 2 Apr. 1938, ibid. See PREM 1/252 for the Air Ministry's reply.

90. Taylor, *Munich*, p. 650.

91. Sir Folliott Sandford to the author, 11 Oct. 1981.

92. Fisher to Freeman (RAF), 30 Sept. 1938, T161 923/S40760303/2 (the author owes this reference to Peden, *British Rearmament*).

93. Peden, op. cit., pp. 159–60.

94. The principle was never formally conceded by the Cabinet, but in practice the navy came close.

95. Chatfield's notes on the Fleet Air Arm dispute, Chatfield papers, CHT 3/6/41–8; Chamberlain to Weir, 1 Aug. 1937, NC 7/11/30/139. For the views of Trenchard, another of Fisher's confidants, see his letter to Hoare, 24 July 1937, Templewood papers, x: 2. For Chatfield on Fisher, see Chatfield, *It Might Happen Again* i, 79; see also PREM 1/281, from which it appears that Fisher, without Chamberlain's knowledge, persuaded Chatfield to agree to an extension of his terms as First Sea Lord if required.

96. Peden, *British Rearmament*, pp. 1, 32–4.

97. Fisher to Wilson and Chamberlain, 15 May 1939, Warren Fisher papers.

98. Avon, *Dictators*, p. 319.

99. Templewood, *Nine Troubled Years*, p. 137. Edward Bridges told Templewood (formerly Sir Samuel Hoare) on 6 Jan. 1954 that 'I

greatly welcome' what his book said about Fisher and the Foreign Office, Templewood papers, xix: 12.

100. Watt, *Personalities and Policies*, p. 102.

101. Fisher to Phipps, 21 Jan. 1937, PHPP 3/2.

102. Hankey to Phipps, 21 Jan. 1937, ibid.

103. Snowden to Grigg, 26 Dec. 1935, Grigg papers, PJGG 2/19/5. Interview with R.W. Fisher.

104. Hankey to Phipps, 2 Jan. 1936, PHPP 3/3/69.

105. Cadogan diary, 21 and 23 Sept., 14 Oct. 1936, ACAD 1/5; Stuart, *Reith Diaries*, p. 211, 23 June 1936. The Foreign Office did not give Craigie the new post which Fisher had approved (there had previously been only one post at that level), instead putting in Sir Lancelot Oliphant.

106. Young, *Bruce Lockhart Diaries*, p. 351, 16 Aug. 1936.

107. Fisher to Chamberlain, 15 Sept. 1936, NC 7/11/29/19.

108. Connell, *The Office*, p. 252.

109. Avon, *Dictators*, p. 521, says that he offered Vansittart the Paris embassy in January 1937, but omits to mention that he had done so already four months before. He is wrong also in claiming that Fisher suggested at the end of 1937 that Findlater Stewart of the India Office should take over from Vansittart. In fact Chamberlain mentioned this on 4 May 1937, when Eden firmly rejected it, saying that he wanted Cadogan. Harvey, *Harvey Diaries*, p. 44.

110. Templewood to Bridges, 18 Jan. 1954, Templewood papers, xix: 12. Templewood was referring to Fisher's attitude towards the appointment of Sir Alexander Maxwell to be head of the Home Office in 1938, when he 'could not have been more difficult, and for some reason or other had a prejudice against the Home Office in general and Maxwell in particular'. Maxwell was regarded as a great success as permanent under secretary.

111. Avon, *Dictators*, p. 407.

112. Fisher to Chamberlain, 15 Dec. 1937, NC 7/11/30/49.

113. Dalton diary, 12 June 1938. Over a year earlier Cadogan recorded how Eden had told him he had failed to get Vansittart out, and that no change was likely for eighteen months or so. Cadogan diary, 9 Jan. 1937.

114. e.g. Colvin, *Vansittart*, p. 147, and *The Chamberlain Cabinet*, p. 47. Sir Walford Selby, who hated both Fisher and Vansittart, perversely saw the latter's removal as a promotion and reward for delivering the Foreign Office into Fisher's hands. Selby to Elibank, 5 July 1946, Elibank MS 8809.

115. Vansittart, *Mist Procession*, p. 350.

116. Cadogan diary, 22 Dec. 1937, ACAD 1/6.

117. Cadogan to Fisher, 31 Mar., Rae to Cadogan, 8 June 1938, T162 801/E45276/1.

118. Strang, *The Foreign Office*, p. 76.

119. Papers on this are in T172/1801.

120. Chamberlain diary, 2 and 8 Apr. 1935. Rose, *Study of a Diplomat*, pp. 117–18.

121. Dunbabin, 'The British establishment', p. 183; Peden, *British Rearmament*, p. 115, says it was 'the Admiralty not the Treasury which was keen to sign.' However, the agreement was along all the right lines from Fisher's point of view.

122. Fisher to Chamberlain and Baldwin, 5 July 1935. Two years later Chamberlain found a copy of this while moving to No.10, and returned it to Fisher because of its 'intrinsic interest in the light of subsequent events', 25 Apr. [1937?], Warren Fisher papers.

123. Note by Phillips (Treasury), 26 Aug. 1935, T172/1838. The file contains papers on the sanctions issue, August–December 1935. There are other relevant papers in the T160 series.

124. Minutes of RIIA British security group, 3 July 1944.

125. Fergusson to Chamberlain, 29 Nov. 1935, reporting a conversation with Sir John Cadman of the Anglo-Iranian Oil Company, T172/1838.

126. Quoted in Roskill, *Hankey*, iii, 286.

127. Fisher had brought Dulanty to the Treasury as a principal assistant secretary in 1920. Fisher to Austen Chamberlain, 24 Apr. 1920, TI99/88. He was regarded as a model establishment officer. Interview with Sir Robert Fraser. Dulanty was Irish representative in London from 1930 to 1950. He was the only foreign diplomat to attend Fisher's memorial service in October 1948.

128. Fanning, *Irish Department of Finance*, p. 78. This was not surprising, since the department had been put on its feet by C.J. Gregg, an Irishman loaned to the Dublin Government in 1922. He later returned to Britain, and eventually became Chairman of the Inland Revenue. Sir Edward Playfair has written of the 'extremely close relationship between the ... Treasury and the ...Dept. of Finance'. These 'were most valuable during the war, when the effectiveness of our war-winning exchange control depended on its equally effective application by neutral Ireland. It was so applied; indeed, we sometimes thought' Finance 'were ... more papist than the Pope. For example, we never stopped the RC Church in England remitting money to their missionaries overseas; the Dept. of Finance stopped it completely.' Letter to the author, 9 Aug. 1980; Canning, *British Policy Towards Ireland*, pp. 157–9, 207–9, 315.

129. Notes by Harding and Dulanty of a meeting, 7 Sept. 1936, PREM 1/273.

130. Undated memorandum by Fisher, ibid. Fisher and Dulanty had come to an understanding earlier in the year on some aspects of the economic dispute between Britain and Ireland, but to Fisher's dismay Chamberlain refused to approve the terms already worked out informally.

131. Notes by Fisher, 22 Mar. and 14 Jan. 1938, T160 747/F14026/04. He was invited to the signing ceremony, 'in view of his great and continued interest over a long period of years in the improvement of relations between the two countries', but did not attend. Syers to Chamberlain, 22 Apr. 1938, PREM 1/274. Canning, *British Policy Towards Ireland*, pp. 216–18.

132. Professor Patrick Lynch to the author, 24 Dec. 1987. Professor Lynch heard this from Mr Leydon.

133. Far too much has been made of the loss of the ports. Britain retained Derry, which was the most important one by far on the island. The only one of any consequence ceded in 1938 was Queenstown (or Cobh), which had been quite a large base in the First World War. When the CID approved their return the fall of France was not anticipated. This altered the strategic picture a good deal. See Carroll, *Ireland in the War Years*, for a discussion of Irish neutrality.

134. Minutes of RIIA British security group, 12 Feb. 1945.

135. Grigg, *Prejudice and Judgement*, p. 53.

136. See pp. 63–4 above.

137. Interviews with Sir Thomas and Lady Padmore, Sir John Winnifrith, Sir Edward Playfair, Sir Robert Fraser, and Sir George Dunnett.

138. Watt, *Too Serious a Business*, p. 56.

139. Cadogan diary, 22 Jan. 1934, ACAD 1/2.

140. Interview with Lord Sherfield; Lord Inchyra to the author, 14 June 1981.

9
Final years, 1938–48

I

The Munich negotiations in September 1938 marked the final split between Fisher and the Prime Minister. On 15 September, 'after the Govt. had been sold at Berchtesgaden', Fisher discussed with Horace Wilson the implications of Chamberlain's talks with Hitler. He later put his views in writing.

His note pointed out that 'Germany now demands the disintegration' of Czechoslovakia, 'that is to say a reversal of the policy underlying all our efforts hitherto; and makes it clear that she will use force for the purpose if the claim is not conceded otherwise'. Britain's efforts to maintain peace had 'secured the approval of the world and surely it is vital not to jeopardise that — and to become *particeps criminis* with the Germans — by even appearing to surrender to force'. It was essential 'that our assent shall only be to a *real* plebiscite in contrast to the farcical one engineered in the case of Austria by the Germans after seizing their country'. Such a plebiscite could only take place after the 'demobilisation of the German armed forces now on a war footing', the introduction of neutral police and election officials, and 'an interval of time sufficient for the inhabitants of the areas concerned (which will need the most scientific demarcation) to have cooled off their hysteria'. It would also be necessary 'to rope in the U.S.A. so that they may participate in the plebiscite proceedings.'[1] This advice was not so irrelevant as it might now appear: Halifax and Simon had also dwelt on the importance of an internationally supervised plebiscite.[2] The difficulty was that Chamberlain had no sanction left short of war following his talk with Hitler with which to compel Germany to accept such a solution.

The Munich agreement signed on 29 September was acclaimed in Britain. Support for it was overwhelming, not only from the general public. Most informed people in Whitehall were in favour of it, if only because it bought some time. Hankey, who had retired a few months earlier, wrote to Chamberlain to congratulate him on his achievement. Fisher, however, thought it shameful. On 1 October he suggested 'most earnestly' that Britain and France 'have a definite moral responsibility' to ensure that the inhabitants of ceded territories received compensation for any loss of property, and that if the agreement did not provide for payment by Germany then the two countries 'should undertake to make available out of public monies a very real contribution to their distresses.'[3] On the same day he sent Chamberlain an impassioned memorandum which the Prime Minister 'found ... on his breakfast table ... (& wasn't very pleased with it!).'[4]

The memo began: 'The events of the past few months may well prove for civilization the writing on the wall unless we ... put such time as may still be allowed us to much more effective use than has been done' since 1933. Fisher argued that 'the Germans have from the start recognised the significance of the air' and in consequence possessed an air force more than equal to the combined aerial strength of Britain and France. He then reviewed the efforts made since 1933 to persuade the Air Ministry to face up to the German threat, and said that 'the incompetence and muddle of 1933 have continued their melancholy course right up to the present ... I confine myself to repeating that the only hope is a thorough reform of the Air Staff and ruthless selection to secure the right men.' He further suggested that the DRC be revived, and that it should 'consist of the official heads of the four Crown Services and Sir Horace Wilson and Mr Bridges; but as the alignment and tendencies of the world are quite well known, a Foreign Office representative is unnecessary.'

(He subsequently noted on a copy of this document that he included Wilson as 'I thought this name might induce N[eville] C[hamberlain] to agree.')[5] He called for 'the maximum concentration possible of the resources available for all purposes of an air force' capable of deterring or defeating 'invasion by air', together with the necessary investment in anti-aircraft defences and air raid precautions. He believed there was still time to prepare adequate defences, though this 'will necessitate ... a standard of competence and achievement very different from that of the past five years; and whether we attain it will be determined solely by the quality of the men' put in charge.[6] It was advice which Chamberlain, fresh from his popular triumph, was certainly not going to heed. Fisher, judging by his recriminatory tone, was well aware of this.

The crisis of September 1938 revealed considerable deficiencies in the government's civil defence contingency plans. Fisher spent most of his remaining months at the Treasury trying to set them to rights. During the crisis he had been made 'the Principal Officer to the Minister of Home Security ... with functions akin to those of a Chief of Staff', and as such he laboured until May 1939.[7] He still took a direct interest in the progress of rearmament, although outside the departmental Treasury he no longer carried much weight. As has already been seen, he continued to demand that the RAF build more fighters. He also plunged into fairly deep technical water in making arguments against increased bomber construction.[8] In his last month at the Treasury, he instantly accepted Woolton's plans for clothing the army, a decision which Woolton thought illustrated 'the difference between the peace-time conduct of affairs and war-time conduct'; doubtless this was so, although issuing such decisions *ex cathedra* and without consulting his department was scarcely an efficient way for a head of the Treasury to proceed.[9]

Fisher's final months at the Treasury were not happy. His personal eclipse was made all the more bitter by the government's apparent lack of urgency about preparing the armed services and the people for war. In January 1939 he took the unusual step of proferring advice on the budget to the Chancellor, Sir John Simon, independently of the departmental Treasury. He suggested that Simon should 'introduce a new and more realistic psychology, as well as an adaptation of our "economy" to the grim realities of today' by raising income taxes, taking firm steps against profiteering, increasing duties on tea, sugar, alcohol, and tobacco, and by using 'our protective system to hit luxuries — by which I particularly mean those that lend themselves to flaunting — with great severity'. He prefaced these recommendations with a familiar complaint:

The 1933 reincarnation of Prussianism in the most sinister form that devil's creed has ever assumed during its centuries of existence attracted no attention; and with equal blandness a blind eye was turned to the fact that the emergence of air power, alike from the point of view of speed and destructive capacity, was the devil-sent opportunity of this devilish creed.

If in 1933 or even possibly as late as 1938 we had shaken off our inertia and started to match in the one sphere of air alone the deadly competence of the Prussians ... we might conceivably have been able to amble along in our old and well-tried and (for the small minority) very comfortable economic paths. Which means that business could have gone on profiteering out of the occasion of the country's need, and with this patriotic example before him the workman would have been stimulated to insistence on some improvement of his rather shabby lot in life.

Not surprisingly, Simon chose instead to follow Hopkins's advice, and income tax stayed as it was.[10]

A fortnight later Fisher wrote a curt note to Chamberlain about his intention to retire:

Dear Prime Minister,
Referring to my wish, to which you have already agreed in conversation a year ago, to relinquish in the autumn of 1939 the office I have held from 1919, I propose that my retirement shall take formal effect at the end of this coming October.

Chamberlain's reply was somewhat warmer, although it was hardly effusive:

My dear Warren,
I have received your letter confirming the understanding that you should relinquish formally your office at the end of October next. As you have always made it clear that this is your wish I have felt it better not to try to dissuade you and if I make no such attempt now it is because I think you would prefer that I should not do so.

This is not the moment to record the regret that I and many others will feel at your departure and perhaps we can regard this note as no more than a formal acknowledgement of your note to me.

Yours sincerely,
Neville Chamberlain[11]

By then the question of who was to succeed him had been settled. P.J. Grigg, whose five year stint in India was coming to an end, had expected the job. However, on 4 January Fisher wrote to his ally Hore-Belisha, the Secretary of State for War, confirming that Grigg would be going to the War Office.[12] It is clear from this that the decision on his own successor had already been taken. On 10 February Fisher's impending retirement was announced, and Sir Horace Wilson was named to replace him. *The Times* commented that 'Sir Warren's long course at the Treasury must be accounted, so far as the outside world can judge, to have been eminently smooth and successful.'[13]

His departure nevertheless begot controversy. Grigg, whom Fisher had intended to 'kick ... up the ladder as high as he could & as fast as he could', was disappointed to learn that he would not succeed him at the Treasury, although 'it [is] commonly assumed in the highest circles that ... Fisher's retirement ... would mean a brief interregnum of Horace Wilson ... and then Grigg.'[14] Grigg was not 'well received' at the War Office as there had been 'a man waiting' to take over, and his appointment also embittered John Reith, whom Hore-Belisha had hoped to install.[15] All the disappointed parties seem to have blamed Fisher to a greater or lesser extent, although it seems very unlikely that, after falling out so sharply with the Prime Minister, he had much say in who was to take over at the Treasury.

His final months at the Treasury were spent mainly in preparing himself for his new role in civil defence. He did make one notable intervention before he went, which involved Sir Christopher Bullock. In April he wrote to 'My Dear Sam', the Home Secretary Sir Samuel Hoare:

Horace Wilson tells me that you propose to appoint Sir Christopher Bullock to be Deputy Director General of the Ministry of Information and that you are under the impression that the idea is one which I myself should advocate.

I am on my official death bed — what a relief is a Nunc Dimittis — and therefore I am little more than a death-rattle. But I must make it clear that the suggestion of Bullock has in my opinion *nothing* whatever to commend it . (Of course in common with yourself and others I have been trying to get him employment, naturally outside the State Service and unconnected with Government contracts for rearmament.) If Horace Wilson understood you aright, you propose to select for the Ministry of Information a man who, although in one of the most responsible positions in a Service of the Crown, was so indifferent to the standards of conduct appropriate to 'an Officer and a Gentleman' that he had to be dismissed from the Service.

Incidentally I would add that, with all his cleverness, Bullock is quite unfitted by temperament or aptitude to organise and run a new Ministry such as you have in mind; the place would be a bear-pit, and I cannot imagine any less suitable locale for a Ministry of Information.

Wilson also wrote to Hoare saying that the Prime Minister disliked the idea, 'both on the grounds of Bullock's ability to get on with people', but more especially on account of it being 'much too soon to bring Bullock back into the Public Service in whatever capacity.'[16] Bullock remained in the wilderness.

On 15 May, Fisher composed a 'swan song' for his successor. He did not discuss his views on 'major issues of policy, including foreign affairs and defence', as Wilson was already familiar with them. There were, however,

certain other questions which may be worth a reference.

First, and in a category of importance by itself, is the *selection of men*. Nearly all my efforts to drive this home over the years have been defeated. Indifference to this vital truth and refusal to understand or apply it are the main causes of our present distresses. For instance, had our Foreign Office been efficient we should not have spent most of the post-war period in antagonising important foreign powers. The Germany of 1933 came into being — so soon after her defeat — through previous years of crass folly for which ... we have as much responsibility as any other country. And then we failed to appreciate what this portent might mean. Not content with that, we proceeded by our fatuousness in 1935–6 to throw Italy into the arms of Germany. In the Far East, having mortally affronted Japan's amour-propre in 1923, we subsequently lost no opportunity of driving large-sized hat pins into her, year in and year out.

271

All this was due to the absence of the right men at the centre and overseas. And all my suggestions for Foreign Office reform and the substitution of efficient men (and methods) have been consistently overruled ...

Another illustration is to be found on the military side. Since Hugh Trenchard, we have had no Chief of the Air Staff (except in name) — and the tragic results have been, and still are, there to see and endure. I have done my utmost to induce the Government to have this put right, again without avail. And so with the Army — since George Milne, there has been no Chief of Staff who could think.

It is the same wretched story in almost every direction and as if we gloried in our folly, we refuse to employ such invaluable men as Trenchard, Reith and Fedden.[17]

Fisher had already tried to get Reith, a bad-tempered Scot with an exaggerated view of his own abilities and the deficiencies of everyone else, into the Cabinet, while Trenchard had written: 'for once really help me.'[18] Whatever else had gone, Fisher's fondness for difficult men was undiminished.

Fisher's memorandum went on to complain of the conduct of government business: 'The procedure principally favoured is an indefinite multiplication of Cabinet Committees which start ... without any such matter of fact foundation as previous consultation between the officers of the various Services or Departments ... "Let not the left hand know what the right hand doeth" is the up-to-date rule of business.' He warned Wilson that 'you will find in ... your new Department — alike on its policy, supply, machinery of Government and finance sides — that it is being progressively put out of action', and that it might be better 'to use your men elsewhere than to keep them here largely beating the air'. If Wilson was able to ensure that no major decisions were taken without adequate information and advice, 'chaos might be replaced by some measure of order, inefficiency by some measure of efficiency, and, what is of no little importance, the heart might be restored to the various branches of the Public Service.' He hoped that 'as you are fortunate enough to enjoy the Prime Minister's confidence, you may be more successful in this vital sphere than I have been'. He ended by warning that what is insufficiently understood here is that 'Prussianism' is a creed fully as much as the Sermon on the Mount, though of course diametrically opposed to it. *Mein Kampf* contains nothing new, it is merely a turgid, rather illiterate re-expression of a philosophy (or creed) the classical exponents of which are writers like Clausewitz, Treitschke, and Nietzsche. This devil's creed was not founded or discovered even by Frederick the Great; you can trace it back to the Mark of Brandenburg, the European cradle of this non-European race. As I see the matter, the lists are set — not between nations, e.g. England and Germany — but between incompatible creeds, or, if you prefer, civilisation and barbarism; and the *ultimate* problem is not a war (if that comes) which we shall win in spite of our appalling incompetence especially since 1933, but how to eradicate this doctrine which is wholly independent of individuals.

The memorandum was not a serious attempt to summarize for his successor the main issues to be faced, but an overwrought and reproachful cascade of wild ideas. An element of bathos was added by a list of 'a very few of the many points I have noted over the years and tried — without much success — to bring to some issue' which was enclosed with his memorandum. Under the heading 'Social' he suggested the introduction of sweepstakes, 'all prisons to be in the countryside away from towns', and the amendment of licensing laws 'to replace restriction on hours by requirement that public houses shall be grouped in large premises where food, games like Dominoes, and other amenities shall be provided as well as alcohol (more resembling cafes).' The government should 'make facilities the same for the poor as for the rich and thus reduce the extent to which the former are unconscionably mulcted.' Under other headings he proposed the reorganization of the Colonial Office, the settlement of the American debt, the development of trade routes to China via Burma, and the possible restoration to Spain of Gibraltar in return for an 'equivalent position on the other side of the Straits'. He thought that the Bank of England should be reformed, and that 'one single interchangeable Local Government Service' should be set up. His most pertinent recommendations were on the machinery of government:

1.   Reintroduce Committee of Civil Research and make of it an Economic General Staff.

2.   Include in the Chiefs of Staff Sub-Committee of the CID the official Head of the Civil Service.

3.   Include on the Board of Admiralty, Army Council, and Air Council an officer from each of the other two Defence Services.

4.   Foreign languages to be made compulsory for the whole Civil Service Administrative Examination (not merely as at present for the diplomatic part).

5.   Merge Diplomatic, Commercial, and Consular Branches of the Civil Service.

6.   Re-examine the 'boundaries' of Departments.[19]

Fisher's bizzare miscellany of ideas on social reform had found no expression during his years of power, but what he said about the machinery of government bore at least some relation to his activities from 1919 onwards. Underlying his remarks was his long-held belief that the civil service, including the Foreign Office, should form a single entity, and that its head was not merely an adviser on appointments but the leader of his service just as the chiefs of staff were of theirs. His final point about the boundaries of departments was a genuflection to the shade of Haldane, whose achievements he so much admired.[20]

On 15 May Fisher cleared out his desk and left the Treasury for good. He did not have a formal send-off. It was common knowledge in the Treasury that he had fallen out with the Prime Minister and Sir Horace Wilson over foreign policy, and that he wanted to leave quietly and without ceremony. He declined the offer of a peerage, partly because of his differences with the government, and also because neither he nor his elder son were much interested in being lords.[21] Shortly before he left Admiral Sir Charles Little wrote to ask him to be guest of honour at the King's Birthday Dinner of the Royal Navy Club, to 'give us an opportunity ... to show you how much we appreciate all you have done for the Navy.'[22] That invitation probably meant more to him than a dozen silver salvers from departmental colleagues.

II

There must have been considerable relief in Whitehall at Fisher's departure. He had, like Hankey, been in his job too long. Hankey became a fusspot in office, Fisher a prima donna.

It soon became clear that in his new role as regional commissioner Fisher was going to continue where he left off at the Treasury. Although the civil defence organization had been revised in the wake of Munich to prevent overlapping and to strengthen the position of the regional commissioners, their precise functions remained uncertain. According to the official historian, 'if communications between the Regions and the Home Security headquarters were seriously interrupted they would, at their own discretion, take over full powers of civil government and be held indemnified for everything done in good faith', but what was to happen if such an interruption did not occur?[23] The answer, as far as the commissioners were concerned, was not a great deal. Their activities during 'the twilight war ... can be described ... as planning, authorisation or liaison ... they were peculiarly exposed to the type of outside criticism which regards activities of this kind as the equivalent of doing nothing.'[24]

Fisher did not accept this quietly. In October 1939 it was reported that he 'has taken the law into his own hands' in the 'constant struggle' for jurisdiction between the regional commissioners, the local authorities and the Ministry of Home Security.[25] A few weeks later, he made a vigorous defence of the civil defence organization in a speech reported by *The Times*: 'Just because the Germans had not started bombing, the heroes of peace days were described as "drones". That was monstrous ... If the service did disintegrate as a result of ... unrebutted public criticism, when the balloon went up we should know something about it'.[26] Soon afterwards, he made some pointed remarks about the need to 'set aside self-interest and self-importance, particularly in quarters which had influence. We had to be ready to stand down if more competent people were available, and should be free of prejudice in the selection and treatment of men.' Finding 'the right men ... to take charge ... would help us to shorten the war, because we should not be interfered with by foolish, self-important people, and it would show that we really meant what we professed.'[27] In December he warned that Britain was 'misusing her war resources', and called for unified economic direction under 'a Minister selected for his qualifications and in the War Cabinet.' As it was, 'the industries of this country are interfered with by controllers, sub-controllers, and sub-sub-controllers, appointed all over the place, showering spanners and monkey wrenches into the industrial machine', and obstructing the vital export trade.[28] When at the Treasury, Fisher had demonstrated his passionate resentment of attacks on the civil service; within a few months of leaving, he was making them himself.

He had little but contempt for the Chamberlain War Cabinet, which he described to John Anderson as 'a set of inexperienced mediocrities.'[29] In March 1940 he said that 'the initiative should be wrested from the enemy in every sphere', and that it was 'fatal folly' to allow Germany 'to murder Polish civilians on land and English civilians at sea without hitting back at German civilians.'[30]

Fisher's bellicose utterings may have been the product partly of his having nothing better to do in the absence of the massive air attacks he had expected. This changed in September 1940, when Anderson brought him down to London as special commissioner in charge of the restoration of bomb-damaged roads and public utilities, the demolition of unsafe buildings, and the salvage of 'valuable materials such as timber, metals, bricks and hard core.'[31] He dealt with the logistical side of this well enough, quickly creating an organization to do the work just as thirty years earlier he had devised the machinery of national health insurance; his performance in other respects was less satisfactory.[32] Within a few months he was involved in an acrimonious wrangle with the army about the use of troops on salvage and clearance work. He eventually gave in, assuring the Minister of Home Security that 'my soldier friends and I will continue the cordial relations going back nearly a quarter of a century, unaffected by any difference ... about the significance, psychological and practical, to our war effort of the capital of the Empire', but he had antagonised both the army and the ministry by his obstinacy.[33]

Although some say that he did an excellent job in London — one of his subordinates afterwards planned to write a history of the operation and of Fisher's part in it — there is no doubt that in official civil defence circles he was regarded, rightly or wrongly, as being as much a hindrance as a help.[34] The latter view seems the more realistic: necessary though the efficient restoration of services to bomb-damaged London was, it was only one of thousands of vital tasks performed by thousands of civilians in Britain during the war. In the various rows he got into, Fisher gave the impression that he thought it was of paramount importance. Such an attitude in a young man on the make would not create great difficulty, since if he went too far he could always be brought to heel by superior authority; the trouble was that Fisher would recognize no authority above him save the government. This made him very difficult to deal with, especially as he had little respect for Churchill's Cabinet. When P.J. Grigg was appointed Secretary of State for War in February 1942, Fisher told him 'that's good — an infusion of guts, drive and imagination into a milieu where these commodities are rare.'[35] Shortly afterwards, he defended Chatfield in *The Times* from Randolph Churchill's description of him as a 'man of Munich.'[36] Fisher was soon to be in need of defenders himself.

On 23 March, the *Manchester Guardian* published a letter by Fisher in which he criticized the action taken by the Minister of Home Security, Herbert Morrison, in the case of Colonel Blatherwick of the north-western civil defence region. Blatherwick, a deputy regional commissioner, had allowed the use of official vehicles and petrol for a journey made by a team of firemen to play a football match against the firemen of another region. For this he was severely reprimanded by the minister, whereupon he resigned and demanded a board of inquiry. Fisher posed the question that 'if a single (and far from fatal) mistake of judgement is to be handled with such Prussianism by a Minister ... what should be the fate of ministers for countless and more serious mistakes by them?'[37]

A day later, Morrison wrote to him asking whether 'there can be the degree of confidence between us that is essential to proper working' as the letter 'constitutes a public attack upon the Minister under whom you are serving.' Fisher replied that 'a man who has upheld standards and traditions during 20 years Headship of the Civil Service does not require schooling on such a subject from anyone in political life'; since he was no longer a civil servant, he was unwilling to forego 'the rights and duties of an Englishman', foremost amongst which were 'the prevention or exposure of injustice.'[38] Morrison's biographers detected in this a political slight, but Fisher was simply being sanctimonious.[39] He refused to resign, pointing out that Morrison himself had been offered a regional commissionership in 1939 while an MP, and that 'you know quite well that Civil Defence Commissioners are not "Civil Servants", or debarred from participation in issues of public importance.' He reminded the minister that 'what the country is fighting for is freedom and justice.' Morrison responded by firing him, and by allowing the correspondence to be published.[40]

Fisher got little support for his stand. Barrington-Ward of *The Times* told Geoffrey Dawson that Fisher

> came to see me about his affair before it blew up in public, indeed before he had received the sacking which he demanded. I did not feel able to play him up as the village or metropolitan Hampden ... Fisher had no right to expect that Morrison would not part company with a collaborator who had abused him like a pickpocket in public.[41]

Lord Woolton was somewhat more sympathetic, noting in his diary that

> it's a pity that he insists on tilting at windmills, saying he's a Crusader and couldn't live with himself unless he took up the cudgels on behalf of other people when he felt it necessary, but he doesn't always choose the right thing to be a crusader over.
>
> [Blatherwick] deserved punishment, whether as severe as that imposed or not I cannot judge, but Warren took up the cudgels on his behalf and got himself sacked.
>
> A strong character and a good brain, but he's misguided on occasions.[42]

The matter was raised in the Commons through a parliamentary question, but the affair died a quick death. *The Times* praised Fisher's 'generous motives', said that he left Morrison with no option but to fire him, and regretted the loss of 'an energetic and capable' man to public life.[43] Thus did his official career finally end.

Fisher's intervention in the Blatherwick case was commendable in that he protested against what he saw as injustice. He believed that Blatherwick had been fired essentially for trying to maintain morale and improve team spirit, using sport as a medium just as Fisher had done. But his friend had originally simply been reprimanded for an error of judgement. It was only when Blatherwick refused to accept this meaningless sanction that he was dismissed, which was when Fisher intervened. The episode which culminated in his own dismissal showed him at both his best and his worst. He went quite fearlessly to the defence of someone he believed a victim of injustice; but, both on the facts and in the way he pushed the issue, he completely misjudged the entire affair.

III

Fisher led an active life in retirement. He became a director of Martin's Bank, of the Anglo-Iranian Oil Company, and of Royal Insurance. He was also honorary treasurer of the Royal College of Music, where he was 'a tower of strength and knowledge' through 'all the difficult financial adjustments of the war and its aftermath' and 'was invaluable ... in his approaches to Whitehall.'[44] As will be seen, he said very little publicly about pre-war policies and events. He continued to develop new friendships and to end old ones, while the few scraps of personal correspondence which survive suggest that he remained profoundly interested in spiritual questions, although not in formal religion.

Fisher was very critical of Churchill's government, asking in 1944 whether England was 'at the present time a democracy? He thought conditions were much more like those of Tudor times.'[45] Once, according to Hore-Belisha, he

> had noticed a man with a beard trying to overhear a conversation he was having with a friend in the lounge of an hotel; Warren Fisher had then gone to the management to find out who this man was, and found that he was entered in the register as 'Wing Commander Bloggs'; he then went into the matter and told the department concerned what he thought of their methods, which they made no attempt to deny.[46]

Towards the end of 1943, the council of the Royal Institute of International Affairs agreed to set up a study group to consider Britain's post-war security. Fisher was suggested as a possible chairman by H.R.G. Greaves, a lecturer in Politics at the London School of Economics. After some hesitation because of Fisher's reputation as 'a terrific fighter when he was a civil servant and subsequently', the council agreed to appoint him.[47] Greaves, who had become friendly with Fisher in 1941, was made secretary. Fisher had the major say in the selection of the group: he wanted Hore-Belisha, the radical historian R.H. Tawney, Chatfield and Sir Eric Phipps, but to 'the query of Hankey W.F. says definitely No. Twenty years ago it would have been Yes.'[48]

The group first met in February 1944, and sat fortnightly thereafter until March 1945. Their discussions were extensive, and Greaves as secretary kept very full minutes; these have frequently been drawn on in this book to illustrate Fisher's views. The committee were on the point of producing a final report when disaster struck: Chatfield criticized the pre-war Treasury's attitude to rearmament in a parliamentary speech, whereupon Fisher resigned from the group. There 'is of course nothing personal', he wrote, 'but old-time comrades of the Treasury cannot defend themselves against grossly unfair attacks, & if this episode discourages' further criticism from Chatfield 'it will not have been in vain.'[49] Chatfield pointed out that Fisher 'was not [on] the financial side of the Treasury ... It is absurd of him to give up the Chairmanship ... because he dislikes one of the members.'[50] He told Fisher that

I am sorry you have taken my speech ... as a reflection on yourself. No one in your position could have done more to help the Services than you did ...

You stated to the DRC Committee you did not represent the financial side of the Treasury on that Committee & you subsequently said to me that you had nothing to do with the Service Estimates or with the financial side of affairs in the Treasury, and that that side was ruled by the Lords of the Treasury as the Ad[miral]ty was ruled by the Lords of the Adty. To imply therefore that in attacking the faulty administration of defence by the government, through the Treasury, I was attacking you, is not just and I think on reflection you will realise it .... I am sorry you do not wish to be associated with me any more & I have written to Astor resigning from your Committee. I feel the break up of our friendship deeply.

Fisher was not mollified:

> Your letter ... rests on the fallacy that the Secretary to the Treasury & the First Sea Lord of the Admiralty can be regarded as distinct from their respective institutions ...
>
> The continuous endeavour of the Secretary to the Treasury & the First Sea Lord of the Admiralty in those days [from the first DRC meetings up to 1938] to wake up the Government & to secure re-armament was ... the combined endeavour of the *Treasury* & the *Admiralty*.[51]

Despite Chatfield's resignation, the RIIA council would not have Fisher back as chairman. Greaves then resigned in protest, pointing out that the group had almost finished its work and that Fisher had quit only to support his former Treasury colleagues, not to protect his own name.[52] Fisher's quixotic behaviour wrecked the group, preventing it from making any report after over a year had been spent in serious discussion. Furthermore, it was far-fetched to suppose either that Chatfield could be deterred from criticizing the Treasury by Fisher's resignation, or that anyone in the Treasury would object to the two men sitting side by side on a Chatham House committee. It is doubtful whether his former colleagues even knew of the group's existence, let alone of Fisher's departure from it.[53] The reconstituted group produced a dull report in 1946 which was promptly forgotten.[54]

Fisher made few attempts to answer his critics in the 1940s. This is surprising, given his volatile temperament and his impetuosity in the rows with Morrison and Chatfield. In November 1942 Lord Perth (formerly Sir Eric Drummond, who had been passed over in favour of Vansittart for the headship of the Foreign Office in 1930) initiated a debate in the Lords on the status and functions of the Head of the Civil Service.[55] The strongest attacks on the post came from Hankey and from Addison, though the former was careful to praise Fisher. The status quo was ably defended by the Lord Chancellor, Simon, while Tyrrell stated that during his time as head of the Foreign Office he had received 'nothing but kindness and helpful consideration' from the head of the Treasury and 'never noticed any attempt ... to interfere either in the administration of the Office ... or its policy.'[56]

Despite these authoritative words, Sir Walford Selby and others continued to attack Fisher. When Vansittart asked him had he considered taking an action against Selby, Fisher replied: 'I do not think him worth powder and shot'.[57] Apart from his letter to *The Times* in 1942 defending Chatfield, when he alluded to his own efforts in defence planning, his only public response to the charge that he and the Treasury had obstructed rearmament came in a very poor article on 'the beginnings of civil defence' which he wrote in the last year of his life. In this he complained of the failure of successive inter-war governments to maintain adequate armed services, but he made no detailed effort to explain what his own position had been.[58] He did give copies of what papers he had taken with him when he left the Treasury to his friend H.R.G. Greaves, and he may have hoped that Greaves would some day write his biography. This did not happen, but Professor Greaves later made the papers available to researchers.

Towards the end of his life Fisher wrote a book, extracts of which have been used in the present work. It was more a reflective essay than a memoir, still less an attempt at self-justification. While interesting, the sections that have survived are rather rambling and repetitive. He attempted to put the failure to prepare for the second war in the context of British history. His approach is broadly chronological, but does not get beyond 1919, although he refers in passing to his activities at the Treasury. A number of themes stand out: loathing of the Victorian era for its lack of interest in social conditions; worship of Lloyd George as a social reformer; contempt for politicians generally, except Gladstone and George Wyndham for their efforts to treat the Irish fairly, the 1905 Asquith government for its social policies, and Haldane for the synthesis of intellect and practicality which he brought to his ministerial work; dislike both of Germany and of France; strong sympathy for Irish nationalism; distrust of executive power, the growth of which he blamed on vote-chasing politicians; and a reverential attitude towards women as the wiser, kinder, and better sex. From internal evidence he seems also to have completed other chapters on Parliament, on the civil service, and on the armed services which have not survived.

Fisher said surprisingly little on general civil service questions after his retirement. In December 1942 he wrote an illuminating article on 'problems of the civil service' in which

he said that the idea of 'a single "service" inspired by common
concern for the country's business ... is still far from fruition',
though what had thus far been achieved was 'nevertheless
encouraging.' He deprecated the idea of a civil service staff
college, as 'the trouble with the Civil Service is that it is too
academic and not practical enough', suggested the interchange
of personnel between central government, local government,
and business, and recommended investigation of 'the proper
boundaries between the various departments ... which was one
of the principal interests of the late Lord Haldane.' He opposed
the idea of a junior Treasury minister with responsibility for
the civil service as he 'would find himself merely a fifth wheel
to the coach', and emphasized that 'the most vital of all
problems' was 'the selection of men.'[59]

In 1946 he gave two short radio talks on the British civil
service, evidently intended for Scandinavian listeners. In the
first of these he gave an account of the development of the civil
service, and laid stress on the immense change in its role
brought about by the shift from the 'policy of *laissez-faire* and
of holding the ring' as the 'social conscience of the community'
developed. He emphasized the high standards of conduct required of all public servants, quoting the Francs report
extensively. He said that just as ministers had collective responsibility so departments 'have to recognise to a far greater
degree than hitherto, that they are merely parts of a greater
whole .... this Service sense of being a team includes and must
more and more include the Military Services as well as the Civil
Service.'[60]

A year later he reviewed H.R.G. Greaves's book *The Civil
Service in the Changing State*, a work dedicated to him and in
which his influence is apparent. Fisher's piece was headed: 'The
state and its servants: standards of professional conduct'. He
reiterated his usual themes about the need for the service to
adapt to changes in society, and ended by applauding Greaves's
conclusion that 'the civil servant must remember he is the
servant of our people and not a jack-in-office dressed in a little
brief authority. The give and take and trustingness of our
private relationships must be the guide and touchstone of our
official relations.'[61]

In his final years Fisher continued to display the knack of
making and losing friends. As well as his rift with Chatfield, he
split with Vansittart for no known reason and 'would never see'

him, although he still spoke of him as a 'friend.'[62] However, Chatfield and Vansittart were the first who defended him publicly in relation to rearmament, and Vansittart also refuted Selby's claims about Fisher and the Foreign Office. In his memoirs published in 1948 P.J. Grigg wrote approvingly of Fisher's work on the civil service, but made rather peculiar comments on his 'obsession' with German rearmament after 1934, which Fisher pursued, Grigg said, at the expense of 'his proper Treasury functions'. Grigg then coupled Fisher's name with that of Sir Horace Wilson in a passage which added to instead of sweeping away the confusion about Fisher's views and activities.[63]

On Saturday 25 September 1948, three days after his sixty-ninth birthday, Fisher died at his flat in London, of heart failure following a stroke. His death certificate records that his elder son Norman and a doctor were present. His health had been failing for about a year. A friend who was with him shortly before the end wrote to Norman:

> So our beloved Warren has had his dearest wish fulfilled — he went to sleep without any real pain or suffering or long illness ...
>
> The last two or three weeks Warren had grown terribly tired & exhausted but he was so brave & gallant. Last week he returned from Liverpool & rang me up asking me to go over on Thursday. I spent the greater part of the day with him & Sir Frederick Bain came in. We both agreed that he looked ill — & that night he was very ill & had great difficulty in breathing. He asked me to be with him on the Friday & the Saturday.
>
> What I want to assure you of is in all those three days — he was very happy & at peace, though tired. I think he talked over the whole of his life with me ... When he spoke to you on the telephone I urged him to tell you he was ill but he was indignant & said on no account would he worry you ...
>
> The last time he spoke to me coherently was on Sunday night when he phoned me to ask me to go & see him on Monday. He was his own sweet self — & said he was happy, had complete peace of mind and was not afraid. The rest you know ... Believe me, all was very well with Warren. Everything has worked out just as he would have wished.

Bless him. He was saying to me 'Wouldn't it be lovely to just go to sleep tonight and not wake up!'. He dreaded getting very old and out of action, as you know.[64]

His funeral was 'strictly private, at his own request. No flowers and no letters please.'[65] He was estranged both from his eccentric wife and his younger son Robin; the funeral must have been a lonely affair.[66] In a will drawn up in 1944 Fisher left everything to Norman Fisher, stating that 'no provision is hereby made for my wife ... as she will become entitled to two annuities from the Inland Revenue Benevolent Fund and the Civil Service Widows and Orphans Fund'. The estate came to a little under £10,000.[67] Lady Fisher experienced financial difficulties for the rest of her long life.[68] Although he apparently asked that no memorial service be held, there was one early in October in St Margaret's, Westminster. Lady Fisher did not attend.[69]

His obituary in *The Times* was lengthy but factually inaccurate. His reputation, it said,

> gave only a partly true picture ... He could be ruthless, but he could show endless patience if his sympathies were won. He could work tirelessly, but naturally he was indolent. Highly strung, he was infuriated by minor vexations, but he would confront a serious situation with cynical detachment. His extraordinary handwriting had a touch of the feminine in it, and in that respect it was an index of himself. His preference for the intuitive as opposed to the scientific method, his hatred of professional technique, his inconsistencies, his generosities, even his physical makeup, all had something feminine in them.
>
> Fisher's methods were not above criticism, but that he was endowed with ability of the highest class none can deny; and his career ... is, and will probably remain, unique in the annals of the Civil Service.

The *Manchester Guardian* described him as 'a complex character — of great ability, witty, and unconventional, with a strain of mysticism which sometimes made it difficult for more prosaic spirits to follow him', but devoted most space to the Blatherwick case. Neither newspaper made a single reference to his preoccupation with defence issues in the 1930s, or addressed the claims that he had interfered in foreign policy.[70] Neither did another obituary which appeared in *Red Tape*, the magazine of the Civil Service Clerical Association. Nevertheless, it was probably the one he would have been most proud of: W.J. Brown wrote that Fisher was

> a great Secretary to the Treasury, and a very remarkable human being ... the service never had a finer Chief. He was firm. He had a passion for rectitude in all matters concerning the probity of the Service, and it is a code he wrote which still governs us. But I have seen him go to great lengths to help a man whom he had himself been obliged to dismiss. He distinguished greatly between the sin and the sinner ...
>
> He knew nothing of class, or class-loyalties. He mixed with perfect ease in every kind of social circle, but was happiest among simple folk ... in all personal matters he carried self-effacement and personal humility to the point of passion. It is entirely characteristic of him that he left behind him ... directions that there was to be no public funeral, no memorial service, no letters, no flowers. For him, the dead should 'bury their dead'...[71]

Notes

1. Fisher to Wilson, 17 Sept. 1938, Warren Fisher papers.
2. Harvey, *Harvey Diaries*, p. 176, 11 Sept. 1938; Taylor, *Munich*, pp. 735–7.
3. Interviews with R.W. Fisher, and Sir Thomas and Lady Padmore. Fisher to Simon and Chamberlain, 1 Oct. 1938, Warren Fisher papers.
4. Fisher's marginal note on Fisher to Chamberlain, 1 Oct. 1938, ibid.
5. ibid.
6. Fisher to Chamberlain, 1 Oct. 1938, ibid.
7. Minute by Chamberlain, 26 Sept. 1938, CAB 104/1.
8. See p. 248 above.
9. Woolton, *Memoirs*, p. 152.
10. Fisher to Simon, 3 Jan. 1939, Warren Fisher papers.
11. Fisher to Chamberlain, and Chamberlain to Fisher, both 17 Jan. 1939, Warren Fisher papers.
12. Fisher to Hore-Belisha, 4 Jan. 1939, Hore-Belisha papers, 5/47.
13. *The Times*, 10 Feb. 1939. On 20 Nov. 1948 Leith-Ross told P.J. Grigg that in March 1939 'Van and Warren induced Chamberlain to guarantee Poland and Rumania'. T188/305. This seems highly unlikely, given that both men were by then out in the cold so far as Chamberlain was concerned.
14. Ann Bridge to Strang, 18 Jan. 1931, O'Malley papers, MS 21691(6); Lady Grigg to Tom Jones, 24 July 1938, Grigg papers, PJGG 7/11/5; Geoffrey Dawson to Alexander Inglis, 20 Dec. 1938, Dawson papers.
15. Reith to Liddell Hart, 13 Aug. 1966, Liddell Hart papers, 1/593/1; Liddell Hart's note of a talk with Hore-Belisha, 1 June 1938, Liddell Hart papers, 11/HB1938/138.
16. Fisher to Hoare, 12 Apr.; Wilson to Hoare, 15 Apr. 1939, Templewood papers, x: 4.
17. Fisher to Wilson and Chamberlain, 15 May 1939, Warren Fisher papers. Sir Roy Fedden was an engineer and executive in the aircraft industry.
18. Stuart, *Reith Diaries*, pp. 227–8, 29 Mar. and 21 Apr. 1939; Trenchard to Fisher, 28 Jan. 1939, Trenchard papers, MFC 76/1/184.
19. As in note 17 above.
20. See pp. 129 above.
21. Stuart, *Reith Diaries*, p. 227, 16 Mar. 1939.
22. Little to Fisher, 13 Mar. 1939, Warren Fisher papers.
23. O'Brien, *Civil Defence*, p. 185.
24. ibid., p. 311.
25. John [Hodsoll?] to Ismay, 4 Oct. 1939, CAB 104/1.
26. *The Times*, 28 Oct. 1939.
27. ibid., 8 Nov. 1939.
28. ibid., 7 Dec. 1939.
29. Fisher to Anderson, 29 Sept. 1939, in Wheeler Bennett, *John Anderson*, p. 233.

30. *The Times*, 16 Mar. 1940. Fisher on 14 Dec. 1938 had poured scorn on the policy of dropping leaflets on enemy countries in the first weeks of a war. Minutes of a sub-committee, CAB 16/127. Given the RAF's frequent inability even to hit the right country in the early days of the war, the policy had some unexpected justification. No doubt the Belgians preferred leaflets to bombs.

31. Memorandum by Fisher, 27 Jan. 1941, H.O. 186/1205. See also H.O. 207/75.

32. See pp. 16–18 above.

33. Fisher to Morrison, 18 Feb. 1941, H.O. 186/1205.

34. Lord Allen to the author, 23 Aug.; K.B. Paice to the author, 4 Nov. 1981. Mr Paice was an assistant secretary in the Ministry of Home Security from 1941 onwards. R.W. Fisher and Sir Thomas and Lady Padmore argue that Fisher did exactly what was asked of him very efficiently.

Marwick, *The Home Front*, pp. 63–4, includes very harsh criticism of Fisher's performance in London, and says he proved 'remarkably good at promoting publicity for himself' as 'Chief Cleaner-upper'.

35. Fisher to Grigg, 23 Feb. 1942, Grigg papers, PJGG 9/2/40.

36. *The Times*, 3 Mar. 1942.

37. *Manchester Guardian*, 23 Mar. 1942. Blatherwick had been Fisher's deputy in 1939 and 1940.

38. Correspondence between Fisher and Morrison, 24 and 25 Mar. 1942, in *The Times*, 2 Apr. 1942.

39. Donoghue and Jones, *Herbert Morrison*, p. 300. W.J. Brown commented that 'Morrison can abide great men as ill as Fisher could abide little men.' Text of an obituary of Fisher by W.J. Brown in *Red Tape*, Nov. 1948, Warren Fisher papers.

40. Correspondence between Fisher and Morrison, 27, 28, and 31 Mar. 1942, in *The Times*, 2 Apr. 1942.

41. Barrington-Ward to Dawson, 8 Apr. 1942, Barrington-Ward papers.

42. Woolton diary, 27 Apr. 1942, MS Woolton 8.

43. *The Times*, 14 Apr. 1942.

44. Fisher was an ordinary director of the Anglo-Iranian, not a government nominee. Obituary notice by Sir George Dyson, Director of the college, from the Royal College of Music magazine, 1948; extract from Guy Waverly, 'The Royal College of Music, 1883–1948', p. 370, both with A.D. Beresford (Royal College of Music) to the author, 14 Apr. 1981.

45. Minutes of RIIA British security group, 16 Oct. 1944.

46. Notes of a talk with Hore-Belisha, 24 Sept. 1942, Liddell Hart papers, 11/HB 1942/33.

47. Waldorf Astor to Miss Cleeve, 21 Dec. 1943, RIIA archives, 9/32a.

48. J.V. Wilson to Astor, 31 Jan. 1944, ibid.; Greaves to Wilson 26 Jan. 1944, ibid, 9/32c. Fisher would not have Liddell Hart, whom he thought 'terribly opinionated'. Fisher to Wilson, 7 Feb. 1944, ibid., 9/32a.

49. Fisher to Macadam, 15 Mar. 1945, ibid.

50. Chatfield to Astor, 14 Mar. 1945, ibid.

51. Chatfield to Fisher, and Fisher to Chatfield, 14 and 18 Mar. 1945, Warren Fisher papers.

52. Greaves to Macadam, 5 Apr. 1945, RIIA archives, 9/32A.

53. None of the former Treasury people with whom the author was in touch could recall ever hearing about the group.

54. RIIA, *British Security*.

55. *Parl. Deb.*, *HL*, 5th series, vol. 125, cols 224–326. For the appointment of Vansittart instead of Perth, see p. 184 above.

56. ibid., cols 276–7. For Addison's career, see Morgan and Morgan, *Portrait of a Progressive*.

57. Vansittart to Robert Blake, 15 May 1953, Vansittart papers, VAN 1/50.

58. Fisher, 'Civil defence'. He was clearly failing by this time. The article is rambling and somewhat incoherent.

59. *Manchester Guardian Weekly*, 11 Dec. 1942.

60. Text of a talk, Warren Fisher papers. The talk was broadcast in the series 'London calling Europe' in April 1946. See p. 174, note 88 above.

61. *Manchester Guardian*, 17 Nov. 1947.

62. Vansittart to Harold Nicolson, 30 May 1953, Vansittart papers, VAN 1/50; Fisher memoir, Chapter 14, part 1 (concluded), Warren Fisher papers.

63. Grigg, *Prejudice and Judgement*, p. 53.

64. 'County Cork' [a nickname for Ethel M. Creagh?] to Commander Norman Fisher, 29[?] Sept. 1948, Warren Fisher papers. Sir Frederick Bain was deputy chairman of Imperial Chemicals (ICI).

65. From his death notice in *The Times*, 27 Sept. 1948.

66. Interview with R.W. Fisher.

67. Fisher's will, dated 25 Mar. 1944, and related information obtained in the General Register Office. Fisher's solicitor was Theodore Goddard. During the Abdication crisis in 1936, Goddard had reacted angrily to an attempt by Fisher and Horace Wilson to warn off Mrs Simpson, whose solicitor he also was. Middlemas and Barnes, *Baldwin*, p. 986.

68. Lady Fisher died on 6 Dec. 1970 in London.

69. A report of the memorial service appeared in *The Times*, 9 Oct. 1948.

70. *The Times*, and the *Manchester Guardian*, both 27 Sept. 1948.

71. Text of an obituary by W.J. Brown, as in note 39 above.

10
Conclusion

The course of Fisher's career between 1919 and 1939 was determined largely by the circumstances of his appointment as Permanent Secretary to the Treasury and Head of the Civil Service in 1919. The latter title was devised by his predecessor, who was also responsible for the restructuring of the Treasury along lines which left its head with very little departmental business. Although Fisher disliked the new arrangement he inherited, it worked to his advantage. It allowed him initially to concentrate on his work of reorganizing the civil service. On the other hand, it cut him off from the traditional functions of a Treasury chief of advising the Chancellor on financial questions. For most of the inter-war period Britain experienced severe economic problems; on these Fisher, despite his position as Permanent Secretary to the Treasury, had little to contribute beyond common sense. Whatever arguments he may have advanced to explain this, it was not entirely by choice that it was so. When he came to the Treasury in October 1919, he found the specialists already entrenched. He had no option but to accept this, although he was able to prevent the division of the Treasury into three separate departments as might otherwise have occurred.

In the absence of a decisive role in economic affairs and financial policy, Fisher found it necessary to expand the range of his activities well beyond that envisaged by the ministers who had appointed him. He became not merely an adviser on senior appointments, but a pundit on every sort of question. He developed a quasi-theological explanation of his functions as the principal official adviser to the First Lord of the Treasury; this, however, was a doctrine based entirely on his own experience. He had the confidence of the first three Prime Ministers whom he served, each of whom knew him from their own stints at the Treasury. He so consolidated his position in the first few years after his appointment that the ebb and flow of politics did not affect it: his standing and his influence within Whitehall was not diminished by the election in 1924 and again in 1929 of a Prime Minister, MacDonald, who had no interest in administration and who did not look to him for general advice.

This gave the lie to his theory about the special relationship between the Permanent Secretary and the First Lord — indeed it went into cold storage in 1924, only to be thawed out again once Churchill became Chancellor — but it underlined the personal power in the machinery of government which Fisher had built up. That derived from the strength of his own personality, from his advisory functions on appointments, and from the institutional weight of the Treasury. The permanent head of the Treasury might be disliked by his colleagues; he could not be ignored. Furthermore, his lack of departmental cares left him free to survey the entire field of government activity and to take a hand where he chose — not the least remarkable features of his career were the breadth of his official interests and the amount of time he spent in pursuing them. He augmented his influence by his presence on a large number of committees which generally reached the conclusions he favoured; he was available for these because he could be spared elsewhere. He was able to promote his aim of a corporate spirit in the service by a process of informal consultation with the various heads of departments; this again was a function partly of his having the time to talk. It would be a mistake to see his career entirely in terms of transcendent principles of civil service management: he operated as he did because it was the way in which he could wield most influence, given the organization of the Treasury which he had been obliged to accept.

Fisher played a leading part in the reorganization of the civil service after the First World War, although it must be stressed that a broad degree of acceptance existed within Whitehall of the need for change along the lines adopted. His most vital individual contribution was undoubtedly his enforcement of the principle that the permanent head of a department should ultimately be responsible as its Accounting Officer for all its affairs. The significance of this went far beyond the encouragement of economy in administration, and it remains a cornerstone of civil service organization.

His role as the Prime Minister's adviser on senior appointments, a function which, contrary to general belief, he did not invent for himself, was also crucial. Despite all the controversy, the centralization of appointments was a success from the outset, partly, perhaps, because there were limits to what Fisher could do without the consent of ministers and of his fellow permanent secretaries. He was only *primus inter pares*, not the pope of Whitehall. The task of advising on appointments was continued by his less flamboyant successors, who took care to lessen suspicion of favouritism — or prejudice — by making it a more openly collegiate process.

Fisher was associated too with the strict code of ethics and conduct enforced throughout the civil service between the wars, the Francs affair and the Bullock case being the best known illustrations. He did not achieve everything he set out to with the service, but he set it firmly on the path he favoured, and he handed on the torch to the next generation of Whitehall chiefs. In the long run this was of more significance than the lack of enthusiasm for his aims displayed by some of his colleagues.

Fisher's activities are largely unrecorded, consisting as they did in talking to ministers, in consulting colleagues, and in general manipulation of the policy-making machinery. He and Hankey were at the centre of government for almost two decades; their influence was immense, not only in particular questions of policy but also in the way that government business was conducted. Where economic and financial matters were concerned, Fisher normally fought for whatever his Treasury experts suggested; his influence therefore cannot be distinguished from the general thrust of Treasury advice. The exception to this was the problem of rearmament in the 1930s, when he made it clear to his subordinates that in the last resort the money would have to be found whatever the consequences.

On defence policy his views from the early 1920s were definite and distinctive, and they carried weight: he believed that an independent air force was vital to Britain, and he disputed the navy's assumptions about the country's likely enemies. In 1933 he insisted that war with Germany was probably inevitable, and that war with Japan was avoidable and unwinnable. By the middle 1930s he was preoccupied not simply with rearmament but with broader issues of defence policy. There is no doubt that he had considerable influence on

Neville Chamberlain as Chancellor, and that the line Chamberlain took in the Cabinet owed much to him. Fisher felt that his greatest failure in the years leading up to Munich was that he could not persuade the government to alert the public to the German danger. But it was certainly not for want of trying, although the more insistent and idiosyncratic his memoranda to ministers became, the less importance they seem to have attached to them.

Fisher's views on defence priorities changed as rearmament progressed. In 1933 he accepted that a large bomber force was an essential deterrent against Germany. By 1936 he was convinced that Britain's first priority was to give itself the means of repelling enemy attacks, not of retaliating against Germany, and he pushed this argument very strongly in the face of the RAF's desire to concentrate on building bombers. There is no question that the Treasury's influence, exercised through the hated mechanisms of 'Treasury control', was of vital importance in ensuring that the RAF rather reluctantly did acquire modern fighters in addition to the thousands of obsolescent bomber aircraft demanded by the Air Staff. The Treasury's line was vindicated by the events of August and September 1940, when Britain's aerial defences proved just strong enough to defeat the Luftwaffe's daylight offensive, as well as by the dismal performance of most of the bomber types with which the RAF equipped itself in the years leading up to war.

On foreign policy Fisher's views were clear-cut but, with the exception of the Treasury's farcical initiative in China in 1935–6, they did not count for a great deal. In the 1920s he was pro-German and anti-French on the reparations issue, in common with most of his colleagues; after 1933 he believed a war with Germany to be inevitable and a conflict with Japan to be avoidable, but he made no distinctive contribution except wild denunciations of the Americans as unreliable. Throughout his time at the Treasury he disliked the Foreign Office, a futile prejudice which he probably inherited from Lloyd George, but he was never able to breach its isolation and bring it into the domestic civil service fold. His sporadic attempts to do so resulted only in a string of wild allegations against him, most of which are contradictory and untrue. In general he pursued a much more pragmatic policy than his rhetoric suggested: he was on very good terms with many of the most senior people in the Foreign Office, including at least three of its five permanent under secretaries from 1919 to 1938, and at lower levels co-operation between the Foreign Office and the Treasury was usually good.

Warren Fisher prided himself above all on being an 'average Englishman'. He was nothing of the sort: even his patriotism was expressed with a mawkish intensity quite foreign to his contemporaries, and throughout his life he conceived extraordinarily strong likes and dislikes for people. His volatile personality proved no handicap to him in his career: he was the antithesis of a sycophant, in that he was completely fearless in speaking his mind and would fight anyone for what he felt was right, but he had a knack of getting on with those with whom he had to get on, both politicians and civil servants. In his official life at least, prudence and common sense generally prevailed in his dealings with people, although as time wore on he became less and less able to contain his anxieties and his prejudices. As his composure evaporated, so too did his judgement. He lacked the insulation of self-satisfaction which enveloped the other great civil servants of his era, Hankey and Anderson: they became Cabinet ministers after leaving the service, while he by choice became an outcast, going to Manchester to take up a civil defence post which proved to have few functions and no powers. His final job in London from 1940 to 1942 was at least a real one, but by then his defects outweighed his virtues: he did the work well enough, but he was a difficult colleague and an impossible subordinate. The episode which culminated in his eventual dismissal reflected this. However, it also showed one of his most admirable and distinctive qualities: his absolute fearlessness in confronting what he saw as an injustice. In that respect, while sad it was a fitting end to his public service career.

Appendix A

Treasury circular of 12 March 1920

Control of Expenditure

Sir,

I am directed by the Lords Commissioners of His Majesty's Treasury to acquaint you that His Majesty's Government have had under consideration the question of improving the arrangements now in force in Government Departments for securing effective control over expenditure, and in this connection I enclose a copy of a recent report by the Council of Financial Officers.

It will be seen that this report does not favour the appointment within Departments of a Treasury official as such, but suggests that the appointment (or removal) of the chief Financial Officer in a Department should require the consent of the Prime Minister and the Chancellor of the Exchequer. The report further draws attention to the fact that the Permanent Head of a Department is in no way relieved of responsibility in the sphere of finance and economy by the existence on his staff of a Financial Officer so described; and in the case of the Service Departments it recommends that the Council or Board should be strengthened on its financial side by the inclusion of a permanent Civil Servant (in addition to the Finance Member who is already a member).

The main lines of the report have received the approval of His Majesty's Government, who have reached the following decisions:

(1) *Service Departments* — One of the most important functions of the permanent civilian element is to secure economy in administration, and accordingly the Permanent Civilian Head of the Department must be made directly responsible to the Ministerial Head of the Department for the control of expenditure, and should be given for this purpose the status of a full member of the Council or Board.

(2) *Civil Departments* — For economy in policy and in management the Permanent Head of the Department must be held ultimately responsible (under Ministers), and the inclusion on his staff of a Finance Officer (who is his subordinate) does not relieve him of the responsibility.

(3) In all matters of staff, organisation, and office management, the officer to be held responsible for economy by the Permanent Head of the Department is the Principal Establishment Officer.

(4) The consent of the Prime Minister is required to the appointment (or removal) of Permanent Heads of Departments, their Deputies, Principal Financial Officers, and Principal Establishment Officers.

(5) Arrangements should be made, where they are not already in force, to secure that questions involving finance are referred at an early stage to the Finance Branch of the Department, and that correspondence with the Treasury on proposals involving expenditure is either drafted, or concurred in, by the Finance Branch. In view of the specific responsibility of the Principal Establishment Officer mentioned in paragraph (3) above, this procedure does not apply to questions of staff of office management; but it will be the duty of the Principal Establishment Officer to keep in close touch with the Principal Finance Officer on all such matters where any considerable expenditure is likely to be incurred.

(6) Any case in which an Accounting Officer has, by the written directions of the Head of his Department, made a payment to which he sees objection should be notified by him to the Treasury, and the papers should be communicated to the Comptroller and Auditor General.

I am to request that My Lords may be consulted as to any detailed changes of organisation and procedure which may be proposed with the object of giving effect to the above decisions.

Appendix B

Prime Ministers and Chancellors of the Exchequer under whom Fisher served from 1919 to 1939, with the dates of their appointment:

Prime Ministers

David Lloyd George, 6 Dec. 1916
Andrew Bonar Law, 23 Oct. 1922
Stanley Baldwin, 22 May 1923
Ramsay MacDonald, 22 Jan. 1924
Stanley Baldwin, 4 Nov. 1924
Ramsay MacDonald, 5 June 1929
Stanley Baldwin, 7 June 1935
Neville Chamberlain, 28 May 1937

Chancellors of the Exchequer

Austen Chamberlain, 10 Jan. 1919
Sir Robert Horne, 1 Apr. 1921
Stanley Baldwin, 24 Oct. 1922
Neville Chamberlain, 27 Aug. 1923
Philip Snowden, 22 Jan. 1924
Winston Churchill, 6 Nov. 1924
Philip Snowden, 7 June 1929
Neville Chamberlain, 5 Nov. 1931
Sir John Simon, 28 May 1937

Biographical notes

The people described below are listed with the titles which they held at relevant times in the narrative, rather than those which they may ultimately have attained. Amongst those MPs described as Conservative are some originally elected as Unionists.

Amery, Leo. 1873–1955. MP (Conservative), 1911–45. First Lord of the Admiralty, 1921–2, 1922–4. Secretary of State for the Colonies, 1924–9. Secretary of State for Dominion Affairs, 1925–9. Secretary of State for India and Burma, 1940–5.

Anderson, Sir John (afterwards Viscount Waverley). 1882–1958. Entered Colonial Office, 1905. Secretary to National Health Insurance Commissioners, 1913. Secretary, Ministry of Shipping, 1916–19, and additionally Secretary to the Local Government Board, April 1919. Second Secretary, Ministry of Health, 1919. Chairman of the Board of Inland Revenue, 1919–22, and Joint Under Secretary for Ireland, 1920–2. Permanent Under Secretary, Home Office, 1922–32. Governor of Bengal, 1932–7. MP (National), 1938–50. Lord Privy Seal, 1938–9. Home Secretary and Minister of Home Security, 1939–40. Lord President of the Council, 1940–3. Chancellor of the Exchequer, 1943–5.

Atherton, Ray. 1885–1960. Counsellor, US embassy, London, 1927–37. US minister in Bulgaria, 1937, and in Denmark, 1940. Chief of Division of European Affairs, State Department, 1940–3. US ambassador to Canada, 1943–8.

Baldwin, Stanley (afterwards Earl Baldwin). 1867–1947. MP (Conservative), 1908–37. Financial Secretary to the Treasury, 1917–21. President of the Board of Trade, 1921–2. Chancellor of the Exchequer, 1922–3. Prime Minister, 1923–4, 1924–9, 1935–7. Lord Privy Seal, 1931–4. Lord President of the Council, 1934–5.

Barstow, Sir George. 1874–1966. Entered Local Government Board, 1896. Treasury, 1898. Controller of Supply Services, Treasury, 1919–27.

Bradbury, Sir John (afterwards Lord Bradbury). 1872–1950. Entered Colonial Office, 1896. Treasury, 1898. Joint Permanent Secretary to the Treasury, 1913–19. Principal British Delegate to the Reparations Commission, Paris, 1919–25.

Bridges, Edward (afterwards Lord Bridges). 1892–1966. Entered Treasury, 1919. Secretary to the Cabinet, 1938–46. Permanent Secretary to the Treasury and Head of the Civil Service, 1945–56.

Bullock, Sir Christopher. 1891–1972. Entered Indian Civil Service, 1915. Royal Flying Corps, 1915–18. Air Ministry, 1919–31. Permanent Secretary, Air Ministry, 1931–6. Dismissed, 1936.

Cadogan, Sir Alexander. 1884–1968. Entered Diplomatic Service, 1908. Minister at Peking, 1933–5, and ambassador to China, 1935–6. Deputy Under Secretary, Foreign Office, 1936–7. Permanent Under Secretary, 1938–46.

Chalmers, Sir Robert (afterwards Lord Chalmers). 1858–1938. Entered Treasury, 1882. Chairman, Board of Inland Revenue, 1907–11. Permanent Secretary to the Treasury, 1911–13. Governor of Ceylon, 1913–16. Under Secretary for Ireland, 1916. Joint Permanent Secretary to the Treasury, 1916–19. Master of Peterhouse, Cambridge, 1924–31.

Chamberlain, Austen. 1863–1937. MP (Conservative), 1892–1937. Chancellor of the Exchequer, 1919–21. Lord Privy Seal, 1921–2. Secretary of State for Foreign Affairs, 1924–9.

Chamberlain, Neville. 1869–1940. MP (Conservative), 1918–40. Postmaster General, 1922–3, and Paymaster General, 1923. Minister of Health, 1923, 1924–9, and 1931. Chancellor of the Exchequer, 1923–4 and 1931–7. Prime Minister, 1937–40. Lord President of the Council, 1940.

Chatfield, Sir Ernle (afterwards Lord Chatfield). 1873–1967. Joined Royal Navy, 1886. First Sea Lord and Chief of Naval Staff, 1933–8. Minister for Co-ordination of Defence, 1939–40.

Churchill, Winston. 1874–1965. MP (Conservative, then Liberal, then Conservative), 1900–22, 1924–64. President of the Board of Trade, 1908–10. Home Secretary, 1910–11. First Lord of the Admiralty, 1911–15. Chancellor of the Duchy of Lancaster, 1915. Minister of Munitions, 1917. Secretary of State for War and Air, 1917–21, and for the Colonies, 1921–2. Chancellor of the Exchequer, 1924–9. First Lord of the Admiralty, 1939–40. Prime Minister, 1940–5, 1951–5.

Creedy, Sir Herbert. 1878–1973. Entered War Office, 1901. Joint Permanent Under Secretary, 1920–4, and Permanent Under Secretary, 1924–39. Chairman, Security Executive, 1943–5.

Crowe, Sir Eyre. 1864–1925. Entered Foreign Office, 1885. Permanent Under Secretary, 1920–5.

Eden, Anthony (afterwards Lord Avon). 1897–1977. MP (Conservative), 1923–57. Lord Privy Seal, 1934–5. Secretary of State for Foreign Affairs, 1935–8, 1940–5, and 1951–5, and for Dominion Affairs, 1939–40. Prime Minister, 1955–7.

Fisher, Sir (Norman Fenwick) Warren. 1879–1948. Entered Board of Inland Revenue, 1903. Deputy Chairman, 1914–18, and Chairman, 1918–19. Permanent Secretary to the Treasury and Head of the Civil Service, 1919–39. Regional Commissioner for Civil Defence, North-West Region, 1939–40. Special Commissioner for London Region, 1940–2.

Grigg, P.J. (Sir James). 1890–1964. Entered Treasury, 1913. Army service, 1915–19. Treasury, 1919–30. Chairman, Board of Customs and Excise, 1930. Chairman, Board of Inland Revenue, 1930–4. Financial Member of Council, India, 1934–9. Permanent Under Secretary, War Office, 1939–42. MP (National), 1942–5. Secretary of State for War, 1942–5.

Haldane, Lord Richard Burdon. 1856–1928. MP (Liberal), 1885–1911. Secretary of State for War, 1905–12. Lord Chancellor, 1912–15, and 1924.

Hankey, Sir Maurice (afterwards Lord Hankey). 1877–1963. Joined Royal Marines, 1895. Assistant Secretary, Committee of Imperial Defence, 1908–12. Secretary, 1912–38. Secretary to Cabinet, 1916–38, and Clerk of the Privy Council, 1923–38. Minister without Portfolio, 1939–40. Chancellor of the Duchy of Lancaster, 1940–1. Paymaster General, 1941–2.

Heath, Sir Thomas. 1861–1940. Entered Treasury, 1884. Joint Permanent Secretary to the Treasury, 1913–19. Comptroller General and Secretary to the Commissioners for the Reduction of the National Debt, 1919–26.

Henderson, Arthur. 1863–1935. MP (Labour), 1903–18, 1919–22, 1923–31, 1933–5. Home Secretary, 1924. Foreign Secretary, 1929–31. President of World Disarmament Conference, 1932–4. Awarded Nobel Peace Prize, 1934.

Hoare, Sir Samuel (afterwards Viscount Templewood). 1880–1959. MP (Conservative), 1910–44. Secretary of State for Air, 1922–4, 1924–9, and 1940, and for India, 1931–5. Foreign Secretary, 1935. First Lord of the Admiralty, 1935–7. Home Secretary, 1937–9. Lord Privy Seal, 1939–40. Ambassador to Spain, 1940–4.

Hopkins, Sir Richard. 1880–1955. Entered Board of Inland Revenue, 1902. Chairman, 1922–7. Treasury Controller of Finance and of Supply Services, 1927–32. Second Secretary, 1932–42. Permanent Secretary to the Treasury and Head of the Civil Service, 1942–5.

Hore-Belisha, Leslie (afterwards Lord Hore-Belisha). 1893–1957. MP (National Liberal), 1923–45. Financial Secretary to the Treasury, 1932–4. Minister of Transport, 1934–7. Secretary of State for War, 1937–40. Minister of National Insurance, 1945.

Jones, Thomas. 1870–1955. Secretary, National Health Insurance Commission (Wales), 1912–16. Assistant and later Deputy Secretary to the Cabinet, 1916–30.

Law, Andrew Bonar. 1858–1923. MP (Conservative), 1900–23. Leader of the Conservative and Unionist Party, 1911–23. Chancellor of the Exchequer, 1916–18. Lord Privy Seal, 1919–21. Prime Minister, 1922–3.

Leith–Ross, Sir Frederick. 1887–1968. Entered Treasury, 1909. Deputy Controller of Finance, Treasury, 1925–32. Chief Economic Adviser to HM Government, 1932–46.

Lloyd George, David (afterwards Earl Lloyd-George). 1863–1945. MP (Liberal), 1890–45. President of the Board of Trade, 1905–8. Chancellor of the Exchequer, 1908–15. Minister of Munitions, 1915–16. Secretary of State for War, 1916. Prime Minister, 1916–22.

MacDonald, J.R.M. 1866–1937. MP (Labour and National Labour), 1906–18, 1922–35, 1936. Leader of the Labour Party, 1911–1914, 1918–31. Prime Minister and Foreign Secretary, 1924. Prime Minister, 1929–35. Lord President of the Council, 1935.

Morant, Sir Robert. 1863–1920. Tutor to royal family of Siam. Entered Education Department, Whitehall, 1895. Permanent Secretary, Board of Education, 1903–11. Chairman of National Health Insurance Commission (England), 1912–19. First Secretary, Ministry of Health, 1919–20.

O'Malley, Owen (afterwards Sir Owen). 1887–1974. Entered Foreign Office, 1911. Minister in Mexico, 1937–8. Ambassador to Poland, 1942–5, and to Portugal, 1945–7.

Reith, Sir John (afterwards Lord Reith). 1889–1971. Director General, British Broadcasting Corporation, 1927–38. Chairman, Imperial Airways, 1938–9. Chairman, British Overseas Airways Corporation, 1939–40. MP (National), 1940–5. Minister of Information, and of Transport, 1940. Minister of Works, 1940–2.

Scott, Sir Russell. 1877–1960. Entered Admiralty, 1901. Deputy Controller of Establishments, Treasury, 1920, and Controller, 1922–32. Permanent Under Secretary, Home Office, 1932–8.

Selby, Sir Walford. 1881–1965. Entered foreign service, 1904. Foreign Office, 1908. Principal Private Secretary to Foreign Secretary, 1924–32. Minister in Vienna, 1933–7. Ambassador to Portugal, 1937–40.

Simon, Sir John (afterwards Lord Simon). 1873–1954. MP (Liberal and National Liberal), 1906–18, 1922–40. Solicitor General, 1910. Attorney General, 1913–16. Home Secretary, 1915–16 and 1935–7. Foreign Secretary, 1931–5. Chancellor of the Exchequer, 1937–40. Lord Chancellor, 1940–5.

Swinton, Lord Philip. 1884–1972. MP (Conservative), 1918–35. President of the Board of Trade, 1922–3, 1924–9, and 1931. Colonial Secretary, 1931–5. Secretary of State for Air, 1935–8. Chairman, Security Executive, 1940–2. Cabinet minister resident in West Africa, 1942–4.

Trenchard, Sir Hugh (afterwards Lord Trenchard). 1873–1956. Chief of the Air Staff, 1918–29. Commissioner, Metropolitan Police, 1931–5.

Tyrrell, Sir William (afterwards Lord Tyrrell). 1866–1947. Entered Foreign Office, 1889. Assistant Under Secretary, 1919, and Permanent Under Secretary, 1925–8. Ambassador to France, 1928–34.

Vansittart, Sir Robert (afterwards Lord Vansittart). 1881–1957. Entered Foreign Service, 1905. Foreign Office, 1911. Assistant Under Secretary, 1920. Principal Private Secretary to the Prime Minister, 1928–30. Permanent Under Secretary, Foreign Office, 1930–8. Chief Diplomatic Adviser to HM Government, 1938–41.

Weir, Lord William. 1877–1959. Industrialist. Secretary of State for Air, 1918. Adviser to Secretary of State for Air, 1935–8.

Wilson, Sir Horace. 1882–1972. Entered Board of Trade, 1900. Permanent Secretary, Ministry of Labour, 1921–30. Chief Industrial Adviser to HM Government, 1930–9, seconded to the Treasury for service with the Prime Minister, 1935–9. Permanent Secretary to the Treasury and Head of the Civil Service, 1939–42.

Bibliography

This bibliography contains only material actually cited in the book. It is divided into three sections: original material, which includes manuscript sources, government records, and parliamentary papers; books and articles; and newspapers. Unless otherwise stated, the publishers of all books listed have London offices.

Original material

Abbreviations:

BLPES   British Library of Political and Economic Science, London School of Economics
CCC   Churchill College, Cambridge
HLRO   House of Lords Record Office

Manuscript sources:

Addison papers	Bodleian Library
Amery diaries	in the possession of the Rt Hon Mr Julian Amery MP
Anderson papers	Public Record Office
Attlee papers	Bodleian Library
Baldwin papers	Cambridge University Library
Barrington Ward papers	*The Times* archives
BBC archives	BBC Written Archives Centre, Reading
Beveridge papers	BLPES
Blackett papers	India Office Library
Bonar Law papers	HLRO
Braithwaite papers	BLPES
Cadogan papers	CCC
Caldecote papers	CCC
Chamberlain papers	Birmingham University Library
Chatfield papers	National Maritime Museum
Collier papers	BLPES
Curzon papers	India Office library
Dalton papers	BLPES
Dawson papers (i)	*The Times* archives
Dawson papers (ii)	Bodleian Library
Duggan memoirs	in the possession of the author
Elibank papers	National Library of Scotland
Fisher (I.I.A.L.) papers	Bodleian Library
Fisher papers *	BLPES
Greaves papers	BLPES
Grigg papers	CCC

Gwynne papers	Bodleian Library
Haldane papers	National Library of Scotland
Halifax papers	copies in CCC
E.W. Hamilton papers	British Library
Hankey papers	CCC
Hardinge papers	Cambridge University Library
Harvey papers	British Library
Hore-Belisha papers	CCC
Inverchapel papers	Bodleian Library
Jones papers	National Library of Wales
Knatchbull-Hugessen papers	CCC
Liddell Hart papers	King's College, London
Lloyd George papers	HLRO
Long papers	Wiltshire Record Office
MacDonald papers	Public Record Office
Milne papers	King's College, London
Milner papers	Bodleian Library
Monckton papers	Bodleian Library
O'Malley papers	National Library of Ireland
Passfield papers	BLPES
Pethick-Lawrence papers	Trinity College, Cambridge
Phipps papers	CCC
Rumbold papers	Bodleian Library
St Loe Strachey papers	HLRO
Samuel papers	HLRO
Sankey papers	Bodleian Library
Selby papers	in the possession of Mr Ralph Selby C.M.G.
Simon papers	Bodleian Library
Swinton papers	CCC
Templewood papers	Cambridge University Library
Trenchard papers	RAF Museum, Hendon
Vansittart papers	CCC
Warren Fisher papers*	in the possession of Mrs Annette Pollock
Weir papers	CCC
Woolton papers	Bodleian Library
Zimmern papers	Bodleian Library

---

* The Warren Fisher papers include all the material that is also available at the BLPES, with additional marginal comments by Fisher, as well as other documents that are not. I have, therefore, cited the Warren Fisher papers in the notes although I first read some of the documents involved in the BLPES Fisher collection.

Government records in the Public Record Office

Treasury classes

T1 (pre-1920), T2 (pre-1920 register of correspondence), T160 (finance), T161 (supply), T162 (establishments), T163 (general), T164 (superannuation), T172 (Chancellor's private office), T175 (Hopkins papers), T188 (Leith-Ross papers), T199 (Treasury establishment papers).

Other classes

PREM (Prime minister's office papers) 1, 5; F.O. (Foreign Office papers) 371; H.O. (Home Office papers) 186, 207; I.R. (Inland Revenue papers) 81; PRO 30/59/1–4 (Sturgis diary); PRO 30/69 (Ramsay MacDonald papers).

Cabinet papers

CAB 16; CAB 23; CAB 27; CAB 29; CAB 63; CAB 64; CAB 104.

Parliamentary papers

Committee of public accounts; report, with proceedings, evidence appendices and index, (1920), vi. 1, (1921) vi. 1, (1926), v. 1, (1936–7) vi. 1.

Final report of the committee appointed to enquire into the organisation and staffing of government offices, (1919) xi. 219.

Report of the board of enquiry appointed by the prime minister to investigate certain discussions engaged in by the permanent secretary to the Air Ministry, (1935–6) vii. 461.

Report of the board of enquiry appointed by the prime minister to investigate certain statements affecting civil servants, (1928) vii. 515.

Report of the committee appointed to advise as to the salaries of the principal posts in the civil service, (1921) ix. 331.

Report of the machinery of government committee of the Ministry of Reconstruction, (1918) xii. 1.

Report of the committee on ministers' powers, (1931–2) xii. 353.

Report of the select committee on ministers' remuneration, (1929–30) vi. 308.

Royal commission on the civil service: evidence and appendices, (1912–13) xv. 113.

Royal commission on the civil service: minutes of evidence, (1929–30).
(N.B.: These were published separately, are not in the bound volumes of parliamentary papers, and do not have a command number.)

Royal commission on income tax, minutes of evidence, (1919) xxiii. part 1.

Statement relating to defence, (1934–5) xiii. 803.

The Civil Service, Vol. I, Report of the Committee 1966–1968 (1968).

Books and articles

Agbi, S.O. (1978) 'The Foreign Office and Yoshida's bid for rapprochement with Britain in 1936–1937: a critical reconsideration of the Anglo-Japanese conversations', *Historical Journal* 21 (1): 173–9.
Andrew, C.M. (1979) 'More on the Zinoviev letter', *Historical Journal* 22 (1): 211–14.
    (1985) *Secret Service: The Making of the British Intelligence Community* (Heinemann).
Ashton-Gwatkin, Frank (1950) *The British Foreign Service: a Discussion of the Development and Function of the British Foreign Service* (Syracuse University Press, Syracuse, NY).
    (1955) 'Thoughts on the Foreign Office, 1918–1939', *Contemporary Review* clxxxviii (Dec.): 374–8.
Avon, the Earl of (1962) *Memoirs, Facing the Dictators* (Cassell).
Beloff, Max (1975) 'The role of the higher civil service 1919–1939: the Whitehall factor', in Gillian Peele and Chris Cook, *The Politics of Reappraisal, 1918–1939* (Macmillan).
Berg, M.W. (1971) 'Admiral William H. Standley and the second London naval treaty, 1934–1936', *Historian* xxxiii (2): 215–36.
Boadle, D.G. (1977) 'The formation of the Foreign Office economic relations section, 1930–1937', *Historical Journal* 20 (4): 919–36.
Bond, Brian (1972) (ed.) *Chief of Staff: the Diaries of Lieutenant General Sir Henry Pownall* vol. I *1933–1940* (Leo Cooper).
    (1980) *British Military Policy Between the Two World Wars* (Clarendon Press, Oxford).
Boyd Orr, Lord (1966) *As I Recall* (MacGibbon & Kee).
Boyle, Andrew (1962) *Trenchard* (Collins).
Braithwaite, W.J. (1957) *Lloyd George's Ambulance Waggon* (Methuen).
Bridge, Ann (1971) *Permission to Resign: Goings On in the Corridors of Power* (Sidgwick and Jackson).
Bridges, Lord (1957) 'Haldane and the machinery of government', *Public Administration* xxxv: 254–65.
    (1964) *The Treasury*, New Whitehall series (Allen & Unwin).
Briggs, Asa (1961) *The History of Broadcasting in the United Kingdom* II, *The Golden Age of Wireless* (Oxford University Press).

Brown, W.J. (1943) *So Far* (Allen & Unwin).

Burk, Kathleen (1982) (ed.) *War and the State: the Transformation of British Government, 1914–1919* (Allen & Unwin).

Canning, Paul (1985) *British Policy Towards Ireland, 1921–1941* (Clarendon Press, Oxford).

Carlton, David (1970) *MacDonald versus Henderson: The Foreign Policy of the Second Labour Government* (Macmillan).

Carroll, Joseph (1975) *Ireland in the War Years* (David and Charles, Newton Abbot).

Cassells, Alan (1980) 'Repairing the entente cordiale and the new diplomacy', *Historical Journal* 23(1): 133–53.

'Cato' [Frank Owen, Michael Mackintosh Foot, and Peter Howard] (1940) *Guilty Men* (Gollancz).

Chapman, Richard (1988) *Ethics in the British Civil Service* (Routledge).

Chapman, R.A. and Greenaway, J.R. (1980) *The Dynamics of Administrative Reform* (Croom Helm).

Chatfield, Lord (1947) *It Might Happen Again* (Heinemann).

Chester, Lewis, Fay, Stephen, and Young, Hugo (1967) *The Zinoviev Letter* (Heinemann).

Childs, Sir Wyndham (1930) *Episodes and Reflections: Being Some Records from the Life of Sir Wyndham Childs* (Cassell).

Clarke, Alan (1974) (ed.) *A Good Innings: The Private Papers of Viscount Lee of Farnham* (Murray).

Clarke, R.W. (1965) *Tizard* (Methuen).

Clay, Henry (1957) *Lord Norman* (Macmillan).

Cole, G.D.H. and Margaret (1925) *The Death of a Millionaire* (Collins).

Colvin, Ian (1965) *Vansittart in Office* (Gollancz).

—— (1971) *The Chamberlain Cabinet: How the Meetings in 10 Downing Street 1937–9 Led to the Second World War, Told for the First Time From the Cabinet Papers* (Gollancz).

Connell, John (1958) *The 'Office'* (Allen Wingate).

Cross, Colin (1966) *Philip Snowden* (Barrie & Rockliff).

Cross, J.A. (1982) *Lord Swinton* (Clarendon Press, Oxford).

Dawes, Charles (1970) *Journal as Ambassador to Great Britain* (Greenwood Press, Westport, Conn., originally published in New York, 1939).

Dilks, David (1971) (ed.) *The Diaries of Sir Alexander Cadogan O.M., 1938–1945* (Cassell).

Donoghue, Bernard and Jones, G.W. (1973) *Herbert Morrison: Portrait of a Politician* (Weidenfeld & Nicolson).

Dunbabin, John (1983) 'The British military establishment and the policy of appeasement', in Wolfgang J. Mommsen and Lothar Kettenacker (eds) *The Fascist Challenge and the Policy of Appeasement*, (Allen & Unwin) pp. 174–97.

Endicott, S.L. (1975) *Diplomacy and Enterprise: British China Policy, 1933–37* (Manchester University Press, Manchester).

Fanning, Ronan (1978) *The Irish Department of Finance 1922–58* (Institute of Public Administration, Dublin).

Feiling, Keith (1946) *The Life of Neville Chamberlain* (Macmillan).

Fisher, Sir Warren (1948) 'The beginnings of civil defence', *Public Administration* xxvi (Winter): 211–32.

Fry, G.K. (1969) *Statesmen in Disguise: The Changing Role of the Administrative Class of the British Home Civil Service 1853–1966* (Macmillan).

Furse, Major Sir Ralph (1962) *Aucuparius: Recollections of a Recruiting Officer* (Oxford University Press).

Garner, Joe (1978) *The Commonwealth Office 1925–68* (Heinemann Educational).

Gilbert, Martin (1976) *Winston S. Churchill vol. v 1922–1939* (Heinemann).

(1979) *Winston Spencer Churchill: Companion Volume v, part 1, 1922–1929* (Heinemann).

Gowers, Sir Ernest (1948) *Plain Words. A Guide to the Use of English* (H.M.S.O.).

Greaves, H.R.G. (1947) *The Civil Service in the Changing State. A Survey of Civil Service Reform and the Implications of a Planned Economy on Public Administration in England* (Harrap).

Grigg, P.J. (1948) *Prejudice and Judgement* (Cape).

Haldane, R.B. (1929) *An Autobiography* (Hodder & Stoughton).

Hamilton, Sir Horace (1951) 'Sir Warren Fisher and the public service', *Public Administration* xxix (Spring): 3–38.

Harris, Jose (1977) *William Beveridge: A Biography* (Clarendon Press, Oxford).

Harris, R.W. (1939) *Not So Humdrum: the Autobiography of a Civil Servant* (Lane).

Harvey, John (1970) (ed.) *The Diplomatic Diaries of Oliver Harvey, 1937–1940* (Collins).

Heath, Sir Thomas (1927) *The Treasury*, Whitehall series (Putnam).

Heuston, R.V. (1964) *Lives of the Lord Chancellors 1885–1940* (Oxford University Press).

Hewart, Gordon (1929) *The New Despotism* (Benn).

Hinsley, F.H., et al. (1979) *British Intelligence in the Second World War: Its Influence on Strategy and Operations* vol. 1 (H.M.S.O.).

Howson, Susan and Winch, Donald (1977) *The Economic Advisory Council, 1930–39. A Study in Economic Advice During Depression and Recovery* (Cambridge University Press, Cambridge).

Hyde, H.M. (1976) *British Air Policy between the Wars 1918–1939* (Heinemann).

Ismay, Lord (1960) *The Memoirs of General the Lord Ismay* (Heinemann).

Jackson, Robert (1959) *The Chief: The Biography of Gordon Hewart, Lord Chief Justice of England, 1922–40* (Harrap).

Jeffery, Keith (1984) *The British Army and the Crisis of Empire 1918–22* (Manchester University Press, Manchester).

Jeffery, Keith and Hennessy, Peter (1983) *States of Emergency: British Governments and Strikebreaking since 1919* (Routledge & Kegan Paul).

Jeffries, Charles (1938) *The Colonial Empire and its Civil Service* (Cambridge University Press, Cambridge).

Johnson, Paul Barton (1968) *Land Fit for Heroes: The planning of British reconstruction 1916–19* (University of Chicago Press).

Johnson, Elizabeth (ed.) (1971) *Activities 1914–1919: The Treasury and Versailles* vol. xvi of *The Collected Writings of John Maynard Keynes* (Macmillan)

Johnston, Sir Alexander (1965) *The Inland Revenue*, New Whitehall series (Allen & Unwin)

Jones, G.W. (1976) 'The prime minister's secretaries: politicians or administrators?', in J.A.C. Griffiths (ed.) *From Policy to Administration*, (Allen & Unwin) pp. 13–38.

Jones, Thomas (1954) *A Diary with Letters 1931–1950* (Oxford University Press).

Kent, Sir Harold (1979) *In On the Act: Memoirs of a Lawmaker* (Macmillan).

Larner, Christine (1972) 'The amalgamation of the diplomatic service with the Foreign Office', *Journal of Contemporary History* vii: 107–26.

Lee, Bradford (1973) *Great Britain and the Sino-Japanese War, 1937–1939: A Study in the Dilemmas of British Decline* (Oxford University Press).

Legge-Bourke, Sir (Edward Henry) Alexander (1950) *Master of the Offices. An Essay and Correspondence on the Central Control of His Majesty's Civil Service* (Falcon Press).

Lloyd George, Frances (1967) *The Years that are Past* (Hutchinson).

Lowe, Rodney (1974) 'The Ministry of Labour, 1916–1924: a graveyard of social reform?', *Public Administration* lii: 415–38.

—— (1978) 'The erosion of state intervention in Britain, 1917–24', *Economic History Review*, 2nd series, xxi: 270–86.

—— (1984) 'Bureaucracy triumphant or denied? The expansion of the British civil service 1912–1939', *Public Administration* lxii: 291–310.

—— (1986) *Adjusting to Democracy: The Role of the Ministry of Labour in British Politics, 1918–1939* (Clarendon Press, Oxford).

Lowe, Rodney, and Roberts, Richard (1987) 'Sir Horace Wilson, 1900–1935: the making of a mandarin', *Historical Journal* 30(3): 641–62.

Lyman, R.W. (1957) *The First Labour Government 1924* (Chapman & Hall).

McDermott, Geoffrey (1969) *The Eden Legacy and the Decline of British Diplomacy* (Leslie Frewen).

Macready, General Sir Nevil (1925) *Annals of an Active Life*, vol. II (Hutchinson).

Marquand, David (1977) *Ramsay MacDonald* (Cape).

Marwick, Arthur (1976) *The Home Front: The British and the Second World War* (Thames & Hudson).

Masterman, Lucy (1939) *C.F.G. Masterman, A Biography* (Nicholson & Watson).

Middlemas, Keith (ed.) (1969–71) *Thomas Jones Whitehall Diary*, 3 vols (Oxford University Press).

Middlemas, Keith and Barnes, John (1969) *Baldwin, A Biography* (Weidenfeld & Nicolson).

Moggridge, D.E. (1972) *British Monetary Policy, 1924–1931, the Norman Conquest of $4.86* (Cambridge University Press, Cambridge).

Morgan, K.O. (1979) *Consensus and Disunity: The Lloyd George Coalition Government, 1918–1922* (Clarendon Press, Oxford).

Morgan, K. and J. (1980) *Portrait of a Progressive, the Political Career of Christopher, Viscount Addison* (Clarendon Press, Oxford).

Murray, A.C. (1946) *Reflections on Some Aspects of British Foreign Policy between the Two World Wars* (Oliver & Boyd, Edinburgh).

Murray, Lady Oswyn (1940) *The Making of a Civil Servant: Sir Oswyn Murray G.C.B., Secretary of the Admiralty 1917–1936* (Methuen).

Namier, L.B. (1948) 'Munich survey: a summing up', *The Listener* XL: 835–6.

Naylor, John N. (1984) *A Man and an Institution: Sir Maurice Hankey, the Cabinet Secretariat and the Custody of Cabinet Secrecy* (Cambridge University Press, Cambridge).

O'Brien, T.H. (1955) *Civil Defence, History of the Second World War* (H.M.S.O.).

O'Broin, Leon (1982) *No Man's Man: a Biographical Memoir of Joseph Brennan — Civil Servant and First Governor of the Central Bank* (Institute of Public Administration, Dublin).

O'Halpin, Eunan (1985) 'British government and society in the twentieth century', *Historical Journal* 28(3): 751–62.

(1987) *The Decline of the Union: British Government in Ireland, 1891–1920* (Gill & Macmillan, Dublin).

O'Malley, Sir Owen (1954) *The Phantom Caravan* (Murray).

Parker, R.A.C. (1981) 'British rearmament, 1936–39: Treasury, trade unions and skilled labour', *English Historical Review* xcvi: 306–43.

Parris, Henry (1973) *Staff Relations in the Civil Service: Fifty Years of Whitleyism* (Allen & Unwin).

Peden, G.C. (1979) *British Rearmament and the Treasury, 1932–1939* (Scottish Academic Press, Edinburgh).

(1979) 'Sir Warren Fisher and British rearmament against Germany', *English Historical Review* xciv: 29–45.

Rhodes-James, Robert (ed.) (1969) *Memoirs of a Conservative: J.C.C. Davidson's Memoirs 1910–37* (Weidenfeld & Nicolson).

Robertson, K.G. (ed.) (1987) *British and American Approaches to Intelligence* (Royal United Services Institution/Macmillan).

Rose, Norman (1978) *Vansittart, Portrait of a Diplomat* (Heinemann).

Roskill, S.W. (1970–4) *Hankey: Man of Secrets*, 3 vols (Collins).

(1968–76) *Naval Policy between the Wars*, 2 vols (Collins).

Royal Instutute of International Affairs (1946) *British Security: A report by a Chatham house study group* (RIIA).

Salter, Sir (James) Arthur (1947) *Personality in Politics: Studies of Contemporary Statesmen* (Faber & Faber).

(1961) *Memoirs of a Public Servant* (Faber & Faber).

Seidman, Harold (1970) *Politics, Position and Power: The Dynamics of Federal Organisation* (Oxford University Press).

Shay, R.P.S. (1977) *British Rearmament in the Thirties: Politics and Profits* (Princeton University Press, Guildford).

Skidelsky, Robert (1967) *Politicians and the Slump* (Macmillan).

Steiner, Zara and Dockerill, Michael (1974) 'The Foreign Office reforms, 1919–21', *Historical Journal* 17, (1): 131–56.

Stevenson, John (1984) *British Society, 1914–1945* (Pelican).

Strang, Lord (1955) *The Foreign Office*, New Whitehall series (Allen & Unwin).

Stuart, Charles (1975) (ed.) *The Reith Diaries* (Collins).

Taylor, A.J.P. (ed.) (1971) *Lloyd George: A Diary by Frances Stevenson* (Hutchinson).

(1976) *Essays in English History* (Hamish Hamilton).

Taylor, Telford (1979) *Munich: The Price of Peace* (Hodder & Stoughton).

Templewood, Viscount (1954) *Nine Troubled Years* (Collins).

Thorne, Christopher (1972) *The Limits of Foreign Policy: The West, the League and the Far Eastern Crisis of 1931–1933* (Hamish Hamilton).

Trotter, Ann (1975) *Britain and East Asia 1933–1937* (Cambridge University Press, Cambridge).

Vansittart, Lord (1958) *The Mist Procession* (Hutchinson).

Wade, H.W.R. (1971) *Administrative Law* 3rd ed (Clarendon Press, Oxford).

Waineright, J.B. (ed.) (1907) *Winchester College 1836–1906. A Register* (P. & G. Wells, Winchester)

Waterfield, Gordon (1973) *Professional Diplomat: Sir Percy Lorraine of Kirkhirle Bt. 1880–1961* (Murray).

Waterhouse, Nourah (1942) *Private and Official* (Jonathan Cape).

Watt, D.C. (1965) *Personalities and Policies. Studies in the Formation of British Foreign Policy in the Twentieth Century* (Longmans).

(1975) *Too Serious a Business: European Armed Forces and the Approach to the Second World War* (Temple Smith).

Wellesley, Sir Victor (1944) *Diplomacy in Fetters* (Hutchinson).

Wheeler-Bennett, Sir John (1962) *John Anderson, Viscount Waverley* (Macmillan).

Williams, Francis (1970) *Nothing So Strange* (Cassell).

Wingate, Ronald (1970) *Lord Ismay: A Biography* (Hutchinson).

Winnifrith, Sir John (1970) 'Edward Ettingdean Bridges', *Biographical Memoirs of Fellows of the Royal Society* xvi: 37–56.

Wright, Maurice (1969) *Treasury Control of the Civil Service 1854–1874* (Oxford University Press).

Young, Kenneth (ed.) *The Diaries of Sir Robert Bruce Lockhart 1915–1938* vol. I: *1915–1938* (Macmillan).

Newspapers

Daily Herald

Manchester Guardian

Morning Post

The Times

Index